CLAUSE STRUCTURE and WORD ORDER in HEBREW and ARABIC

An Essay in Comparative Semitic Syntax

UR SHLONSKY

New York   Oxford
Oxford University Press
1997

Oxford University Press

Oxford New York Athens Auckland Bangkok Bogota Bombay Buenos Aires
Calcutta Cape Town Dar es Salaam Dehli Florence Hong Kong
Istanbul Karachi Kuala Lumpur Madras Madrid Melbourne
Mexico City Nairobi Paris Singapore Taipei Tokyo Toronto

and associated companies in
Berlin Ibadan

Copyright © 1997 by Ur Shlonsky

Published by Oxford University Press, Inc.
198 Madison Avenue, New York, New York 10016

Oxford is a registered trademark of Oxford University Press

Library of Congress Cataloging-in-Publication Data
Shlonsky, Ur.
Clause structure and word order in Hebrew and Arabic : an essay in
comparative Semitic syntax / Ur Shlonsky.
p.   cm. — (Oxford studies in comparative syntax)
ISBN 0-19-510866-3; — ISBN 0-19-510867-1 (pbk.)
1. Hebrew language—Clauses.   2. Hebrew language—Word order.
3. Arabic language—Clauses.   4. Arabic language—Word order.
5. Hebrew language—Grammar, Comparative.   6. Arabic language—
Grammar, Comparative.   7. Grammar, Comparative and general—Syntax.
I. Title.   II. Series
PJ4717.S55   1997
492.4'5—dc20   96-30845

1 3 5 7 9 8 6 4 2

Printed in the United States of America
on acid-free paper

Acknowledgments

When I arrived in Geneva in 1991, I discovered that there was insufficient shelf space in the office to store the files and notes that I had been dragging along with me in cardboard boxes across three continents for several years. I therefore decided to reread my notes, load them onto my PC, and then throw away the paper into the recycling bin.

Times have changed, I now have a larger office, shelves, and cabinets along with an unobstructed view of the Jura mountains. I have also brought to a close the process of rearranging my notes, of which this book is the product.

In writing it, I have been assisted and supported by many colleagues. I wish to thank L. Haegeman and L. Rizzi for their encouragement, for discussion, and for their comments on drafts of this work. A. Belletti, G. Cinque, E. Doron, T. Guasti, C. Laenzlinger, T. Siloni, and an anonymous reviewer have read and commented on various parts of this essay. Most of the material covered in this book was presented in my Semitic syntax class over a two-year period, and questions and comments of numerous students have helped me sharpen many points.

Since I have been practically obsessed with this work for quite a while, I doubt whether there is any linguist whom I've spoken to in the last couple of years who hasn't somehow contributed to forging this manuscript. In addition to the people mentioned above, I would like to express my gratitude to J. Ouhalla, I. Roberts, T. A. Cardinaletti, H. Borer, M. Starke, M-A Friedemann, E. Doron, M. Diesing, and R. Kayne.

Parts of this work have been presented at the Second Conference on Afro-Asiatic Linguistics in Sophia Antipolis, in the summer course in linguistics in San Sebastian, at the Generative Linguistics in the Old World colloquium in Vienna, at the Boston meeting of the Linguistic Society of America and at the Incontro di Grammatica Generativa in Milan. I am grateful to participants at these meetings for their questions and comments. I have also presented sections of this work at the School of Oriental and African Languages in London, the University of Wales in Bangor, the University of Venice, the University of Stuttgart, the

Universities of Paris VII and VIII, and Tel Aviv University. I wish to thank my hosts at these schools for providing me with the opportunity to present my work.

An earlier version of Chapter 4 appears in Lecarme, Lowenstamm, & Shlonsky (eds.), (1996), and a draft of Chapter 9 has appeared in the Geneva Generative Papers (see Shlonsky 1994a). The present book supersedes this preliminary work.

The judgments on the Hebrew examples have been double-checked with H. Borer, T. Siloni, I. Hazout, and I. Doron, but responsibility for the facts lies entirely with me. S. Hasan Shlonsky was my primary source for the Palestinian Arabic data, and I also relied on help from O. Awad and M. Rishmawi.

Contents

Note on Transcription and Glosses

American usage is employed throughout. The transcription of Standard Arabic examples follows standard practice. Dialectal Arabic examples are phonetic (wide transcription), with the exception of the final consonant of the definite article—phonetically assimilated to a following coronal—which I have chosen to render in its phonemic form *l*. The Hebrew transcriptions are somewhat arbitrary: Phonetically spirantized stops are transcribed as such, phonemic distinctions between *ʔ*, *ʕ* are maintained in the transcription, while e.g., *x* and *ḥ* are uniformly transcribed as *x*.

In the glosses, verbal stems are morphologically broken down so as to render tense, aspect, and agreement information more transparent. Tense and aspect, being nonconcatenative, are placed in parenthesis following the verbal stem. Agreement morphology appears stem-initially in the Arabic imperfective/Hebrew future tense forms, and stem-finally in the perfect/past and participial forms.

The abbreviations used in the text are the following:

Abbreviation	*Translation*	*Abbreviation*	*Translation*
1,2,3	person of the verb	JUSS	jussive
ACC	accusative	M	masculine
BENONI	Benoni	NEG	negation
CL	clitic	PAST	past tense
DUR	durative	PERF	perfect
F	feminine	PL	plural
FUT	future	PRES	present tense
IMPERF	imperfect	PROG	progressive
INDIC	indicative	S	singular
INF	infinitive	SUBJ	subjunctive

CLAUSE STRUCTURE
and WORD ORDER
in HEBREW and ARABIC

ONE

Introduction

1.1 PROLOGUE

The Principles and Parameters model of Generative Grammar (Chomsky 1981, 1982, 1986a, 1986b, 1991, 1993) provides both a highly articulate model of Universal Grammar (UG) and a relatively explicit theory of language variation. Research within this framework strives to discover and isolate nontrivial linguistic universals, such as the rules comprising the subtheory of Binding, the Empty Category Principle (ECP), the principles of quantification, and so forth.[1] At the same time, it seeks to spell out the extent, and hence the limits, of possible cross-linguistic variation. Within this framework, a study of a particular grammatical system or of several systems can serve to enhance our understanding of the underlying principles of UG as well as of the range of parametric variation which, when taken together, constitute a particular grammar—for example, my Hebrew, your English, her French.[2]

Being a relatively explicit theory of what grammars are, the Principles and Parameters approach allows one to formulate questions, test predictions, and discover facts and patterns—in short, to go beyond the classification of data. Indeed, it is only against the backdrop of a theory of grammar that one can distill and classify facts and patterns in language.

These convictions underlie the present essay, which studies a number of issues in the syntax of Hebrew and the Arabic languages. By the former, I mean my own Hebrew; by the latter, I refer to Standard or literary Arabic and some of the modern spoken dialects (Palestinian Arabic, in particular). Since I speak no Arabic language, I have relied on descriptions and studies of these languages and on work with native speakers.[3] Virtually no mention is made in this book of the Southern Semitic languages (e.g., the Semitic languages of Ethiopia). This is due both to my ignorance and to the near absence of generativist research into the sort of issues taken up here.

This work can be read both as a study of Hebrew syntax and as a comparative exploration of the syntax of Semitic. There are two reasons for which I have chosen to present an analysis of the empirical domain I have carved out in Hebrew, and subsequently to incorporate Arabic into the discussion. First, it is the only Semitic language that I know, and it is a relatively well-studied one. The Arabic languages, and particularly the spoken dialects, have been the subject of relatively little research (in the generative tradition). Second, this choice of content and presentation has a methodological and a heuristic motivation. This way of approaching things will hopefully facilitate the reader's task, since it is rather cumbersome to keep in mind parallel, yet different, sets of facts simultaneously. The development and internal coherence of the argumentation are also better served by this way of approaching things. Moreover, the primary goal of a comparative study—that is, the possibility of showing that a certain pattern manifested in a transparent fashion in one language prevails in a related language, albeit in a more opaque, abstract way—can be more convincingly attained by studying the manifest pattern initially and subsequently extending it to a grammar where the pattern is displayed in a more obscure fashion.

This book presupposes familiarity with the Principles and Parameters Model (for which Haegeman 1994 is a good introduction, and there are others). Since much of this volume is concerned with clause structure, I propose to lay out some of my general assumptions in the following section. Section 1.3 contains a brief introduction to the Semitic languages and some of its subsections introduce material that will not be discussed in detail here and are better exposed as background material.

1.2   CLAUSE STRUCTURE

A clause is fundamentally structured around three layers, a thematic layer (comprising a functor—e.g., a verb and its arguments or θ-marked complements), a functional layer (comprising the domain of functional projections, Asp(ect)P, T(ense)P, etc.—i.e., IP), and an operator layer (i.e., Comp and related projections, or CP). (1-1) diagrams this configuration.

(1-1)

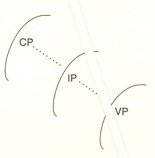

I assume that the VP includes, in addition to the verb, all of its θ-marked arguments. In particular, I take the subject to be base-generated as the specifier of VP (see Huang 1993, Kitagawa 1986, Kuroda 1988; for a somewhat different implementation, see Koopman and Sportiche 1991).

1.2.1   The Functional Layer

One of the major theoretical issues addressed in this book concerns the internal structure of the functional layer. There are two related questions here, and I address them in turn.

First, what is the actual content of this layer, or, in other words, that are the functional projections which make up IP? My starting point is that every clause, by definition contains a TP. I will argue (in particular in chapter 4) that the essential difference between a full clause and a small clause is that only the former contains a TP (and a CP, see ahead).[4] In chapter 3, I will argue that another constituent which forms the backbone of IP is Asp(ect)P, although its presence is not a *sine qua non* for the status of clausehood but depends on the nature of the predicate. For example, AspP is projected in clauses containing verbal predicates because verbs are as-pectual categories, but no AspP is projected in clauses containing nominal predi-cates since nouns are not aspectual categories. I will further assume (essentially following Belletti 1990) that, in a synthetic tense construction, the main predicate is associated with AspP and the auxiliary with TP. In chapter 3, it will be argued that the relationship between TP and AspP is mediated by Move α. NegP is yet another maximal projection that appears in the functional layer (see §1.3.3). TP, AspP, and NegP are explicitly discussed in this essay. Other projections are mentioned in passing, but I neither argue for their existence directly nor use them in any crucial way. The actual size of the functional layer, that is, the number of labeled XPs from which it is constituted is an empirical issue. The research strategy that strives to associate the various modalities of clausal interpretation and mor-phology with a well-defined configurational space has proven to be a very fruitful one, and this work is written with this research orientation in mind.

1.2.1.1   *The Hierarchy of Projections*

The second question to be addressed in an explicit manner and the one I will be mostly concerned with has to do with the dominance relations or hierarchy of functional projections. While it is not a priori inconceivable that the hierarchical position of the major functional projections is subject to cross-linguistic variation, the present study adheres to the assumption that this is not the case. Tampering with this hierarchy, allowing it to vary parametrically, results in a substantial loss of formal power to the theory and a very substantial increase in the options of D-structure and S-structure design.

Moreover, such an approach poses severe learnability problems. In many, if not most languages, the content of functional projections is affixal, and their surface position can be surmised only partially and inconclusively on the basis of phonetic forms. If languages vary with respect to the positions of, say, TP and AgrSP, how is the language learner to determine whether, for example, English TP is higher than or lower than AgrSP, when both options are made available by UG?

There is by now a clear consensus among researchers in the field that clauses have a richer and far more articulate structure than was ever conceived before. We have TPs and NegPs, AspectPs and ParticiplePs, CPs and FocusPs and TopicPs, in between which numerous AgrPs are interwoven. The evidence for these structures is substantial, and the research strategy that has spawned them has proven very successful. Yet there is little in the way of compelling evidence and a great deal of controversy over their hierarchical order. Imagine the enormity of the task facing the learner who must construct a D-structure on the basis of meager morphological evidence and even scantier syntactic clues. Imagine his or her task if clausal hierarchy were not fixed once and for all by UG.

These considerations underlie my reluctance to permit variation in the hierarchy of clausal architecture. My strategy will be as follows: I first *assume* a particular hierarchy, if only in order to have a set of configurational coordinates with which to embark on a detailed discussion. I then *argue* in detail for the particular choice I have made, providing what is, in some cases, novel empirical evidence in favor of that choice and refining it on the way.

My initial starting point is the clausal hierarchy proposed in Belletti (1990) and adopted by Chomsky (1991). I deviate slightly from Belletti's original proposal, to incorporate the modification proposed by Friedemann and Siloni (1993) to the effect that AgrPart(iciple)P should not be confounded with AgrOP. I further assume that the head associated with participial morphology is Asp(P) and that it is projected in both simple and compound tense constructions. The dominance relations of the categories making up IP (in an active sentence) are schematized in (1-2).

(1-2) a. Simple tenses

   AgrSP > (NegP) > TP > AspP > AgrOP > VP

   b. Compound tenses

   AgrSP > (NegP) > TP > VP$_{Aux}$ > AgrPartP > AspP > AgrOP > VP

It should be reiterated that (1-2) constitutes no more and no less than an empirical hypothesis. I would like to argue that not only does this hierarchy, originally proposed for the Romance languages and then extended to English, serve as a useful backdrop or even a coherent model for the discussion of Semitic, but also that the study of Hebrew and Arabic actually supports precisely this hypothesis.

1.2.1.2   The Representation of Agreement

There are two Agr(eement) projections in (1-2a) and three in (1-2b). What is the status of Agr in this system? My initial hypothesis is that whenever a verbal form manifests agreement morphology, an AgrP must be present in the structure. There are two manifestations of agreement in (1-3a)—on the auxiliary and on the past participle—and three manifestations of agreement in (1-3b): on the aspectual auxiliary *have*, on the passive auxiliary *be*, and on the participle.

(1-3) a. les   aubergines ont   été   cuites.
       the *eggplants* *be-AGR* *be(PASS)* *cooked-AGR*
       'The eggplants have been cooked.'

   b. le   melanzane sono   state   cucinate.
      the *eggplants* *be-AGR* *be(PASS)-AGR* *cooked-AGR*
      'The eggplants have been cooked.'

The difference between French, exemplified in (1-3a), and Italian, in (1-3b), is the following: Italian, but not French, has an Agr projection associated with the passive auxiliary. Does this difference call into question the assumption that clause structure is the same cross-linguistically (or cross-Romance)? I believe that the answer is negative and that for the following reasons.

Agreement projections differ from lexical and contentful functional projections in several crucial ways: they do not enter the interpretative component in any meaningful way (there is no difference in meaning between [1-3a] and [1-3b]), they are not selected or subcategorized for, and there can be a number of them in the clause. Assume that *universal core structure* (UCS) includes categories such as VP,TP, and CP and that these are organized hierarchically in a fixed manner, as I have suggested. Agreement projections are not part of UCS. I will argue (in particular in chapters 4 and 9) that agreement projections are associated with categories making up UCS in the following manner: there is a single Agr projection per contentful category, they dominate this category and the choice of whether to project an AgrP or not depends on morphological considerations—that is, we have an AgrP whenever there are Agr features around that need to be licensed.[5] Seen in this way, (1-2) should be restated. In (1-4), the agreement projections of (1-2a) appear in boxes, suggesting that they need not be projected in every clause.

(1-4) $\boxed{\text{AgrSP}}$ > (NegP) > TP > AspP > $\boxed{\text{AgrOP}}$ > VP

The Italian passive auxiliary has Agr features, and hence an AgrP is projected and dominates this auxiliary; the French passive auxiliary lacks Agr features, and hence no AgrP appears.

One slight complication deserves mention at this point: agreement morphology is not necessarily overt. It is thus possible that French does not differ from Italian in the manner discussed here, but only in the phonetic content of the agreement features associated with the passive auxiliary. The question as to whether there is an AgrP associated with this particular auxiliary cannot simply be answered on the basis of overt morphology. Thus, Belletti (1990) argues that Italian infinitives raise to AgrS^0, which is to say that they are associated with AgrS features, albeit covert. Languages like Chinese, which lack overt agreement morphology altogether, may be endowed with no AgrPs at all, or they may project a plethora of them. Both options are a priori consistent with the view of Agr that I wish to defend.

1.2.2 The Operator Layer

Turning finally to the operator or Comp layer, I assume that CP is a cover term for a richer and more articulate structure that includes Topic Phrases, Focus Phrases, and even Agreement Phrases. The reasoning underlying a "split Comp hypothesis" is the same reasoning that motivated the concept of a Split Infl: the X-Bar schemata provide a recursive pattern, allowing the association of clausal modalities and operator and operator-like constituents with a precise position and permitting the resolution of a variety of problems regarding word order, scope, and verb movement. I adopt the Split Comp hypothesis, although I will have virtually nothing to say about the actual internal organization of the Comp layer.

I have assumed that a full clause must contain a TP. TP, however, is dependent upon CP. There is an obvious sense in which T and C (or one of the heads within the CP layer) are related. For example, the choice of complementizer is determined in part by the finiteness of a clause. In Hebrew, the complementizer *še* can only appear as the C^0 of finite clauses; nonfinite ones have a phonetically unrealized C^0:

(1-5) a. Dan xašav   [cp še hu gamar].
          Dan   think(PAST)-3MS   that   he   finish(PAST)-3MS
          'Dan thought that he finished.'

    b. Dan raca   [cpØ PRO li-gmor].
        Dan   want(PAST)-3MS   finish(INF)
        'Dan wanted to finish.'

There are a number of conceivable ways to give substance to the dependency holding between C^0 and T^0. Stowell (1981), for example, argues that T^0 (or I^0) universally moves to C^0 in LF, thus generalizing den Besten's (1983) proposal for V2 languages. While this may be too strong a hypothesis, it is quite generally assumed that C^0 is marked for finiteness (see Enç 1987). I propose that we look at the relationship between C^0 and T^0 in terms of selection: a nonfinite C^0 selects or subcategorizes for a nonfinite T^0 and a finite C^0 takes a finite T^0 complement.[6] I thus assume (1-6).

(1-6)   CP iff TP

The essential difference between full and small (or reduced) clauses is that the former are CPs, and are hence endowed with a TP projection, while the former are clausal chunks that may vary in size—that is, in the number of functional projections they include—but they crucially lack TP and hence CP.

1.2.3 Support Theory and Checking Theory

Before bringing this section to a close, let us very briefly consider the relationship between verb movement and inflectional morphology. Much of the work on this subject has regarded verb movement as being driven, essentially, by the need to support stray affixes (see Lasnik 1981, Marantz 1984, and much other work). A verb moves to T^0, in this approach, because the content of T^0 is an affix in need of lexical support. If the content of T^0 does not require lexical support, there is no drive for verb movement. An alternative view, proposed in Chomsky (1991), is that verb movement is driven by the need to check inflectional features that are base-generated on it. On this view, a verb is inserted under a V node in a morphologically complete form, but it must check its morphological features against identical features that make up the various functional heads. If the features are strong, then movement must take place in the audible syntax, checking the strong features before PF. If the features are weak, checking is postponed to LF.[7] An added component of Checking theory is that argument raising is also driven by the need to check features. Arguments check N (or 'XP') features in a Spec-head configuration with a head bearing the appropriate N features and heads check V (or 'head') features by incorporating into the appropriate functional head. Although Checking theory has received much impetus from Chomsky's recent work, I do not believe that Support theory has been debunked. The choice between the two approaches is of a highly theory-internal nature, and it is extremely difficult to find clear evidence in favor of one and opposed to the other (the decision of what constitutes evidence is, in part, determined by the theoretical choice). In this volume, I take an essentially pragmatic approach and attempt to situate my discussion in both perspectives, whenever possible.

1.3   ELEMENTS OF HEBREW AND ARABIC CLAUSAL SYNTAX

1.3.1   Word Order and Verb Movement

We can begin to inquire into the syntax of Hebrew and Arabic by considering the following three sentences.

(1-7) a. Mona   katva   mixtav.   Hebrew
       b. Mona   katbat   risaale.   Palestinian Arabic
       c. katabat   Mona   risaalatan.   Standard Arabic
       'Mona wrote a letter.'

These sentences manifest the unmarked word order of Hebrew, Palestinian, and Standard Arabic. The pattern in the first two is SVO, while Standard Arabic clauses are unmarkedly VSO. I take VSO word order to essentially involve raising of the verb over the subject. From an underlying structure such as (1-8a), verb-raising to some functional projection (labeled F^0 in [1-8b]) gives rise to a VSO pattern (the dotted lines here and throughout indicate that there may be intervening structure).[8]

(1-8) a. D-structure

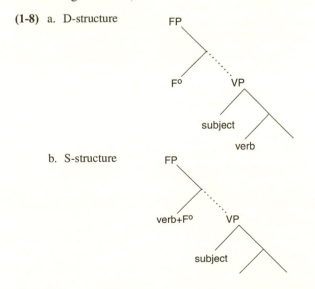

     b. S-structure

Hebrew and Palestinian Arabic differ from Standard Arabic in being SVO languages. Following, in essence, Koopman and Sportiche (1991), I assume that SVO word order is produced by raising the subject over the verb, to the specifier of G^0, yielding (1-9).[9]

(1-9)

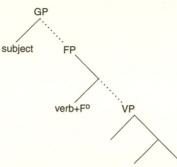

For the sake of completeness, it should be added that Standard Arabic, as well as Hebrew and Palestinian, manifest alternate word order patterns, under a variety of circumstances. SVO is a possible pattern in Standard Arabic root clauses as well as in clauses embedded under the indicative complementizer *ʔinna/ʔanna*. It is a question of some interest as to whether this pattern is produced in the same fashion as in, for example, Hebrew, or whether SVO order is uniquely a form of Topicalization or Focalization. Both proposals have been defended in the literature, but since little in the subsequent discussion hinges on this issue, I will let it rest.[10] VSO patterns are also found in Hebrew and in the colloquial Arabic dialects. Chapter 8 is a detailed study of this alternate "inverted" order, and the reader is referred to that chapter for further discussion.

While verb movement to F^0 in a Standard Arabic VSO pattern is a necessary consequence of the hypothesis that the subject remains in its VP-internal position (for how else does the verb come to appear to the left of the subject?), it is not self-evident that such movement also takes place in Hebrew and in Palestinian. Indeed, the mere manifestation of SVO order does not provide any clue as to whether the verb is in VP at S-structure, or whether it has raised to F^0. Finer diagnostics for movement have been proposed in the recent literature (see, in particular, Pollock 1989). These involve the positioning of adverbs and floating (subject) quantifiers. It is assumed that these categories mark XP boundaries in that their occurrence between two elements, say A and B, shows that an XP boundary occurs between the two.

The sentences in (1-10) show that adverbial adjuncts and floated quantifiers can appear between the verb and the direct object in Hebrew (the facts are the same in Palestinian).

(1-10) a. ha-yladim   katvu ʔetmol   mixtav.
        the children   wrote yesterday   letter
        'The children wrote a letter yesterday.'

     b. ha-yladim   katvu kulam mixtav.
        the children   wrote all   letter
        'The children all wrote a letter.'

It follows that the verb and the direct object in (1-10) are not immediately dominated by the same maximal projection. In other words, these sentences show that the verb has raised out of VP, over the adverb, as illustrated in (1-11).

(1-11)

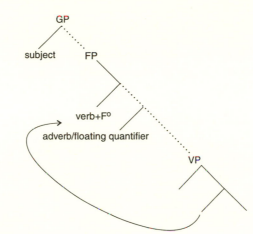

Hebrew and Palestinian can hence be classified as SVO verb-raising languages. In these respects, they are similar to the Romance languages as opposed to English (which is not a verb-raising language) or, say, German, which is not an SVO language, but manifests SOV as its unmarked word order pattern.[11]

1.3.2 The System of Tenses and Agreement

One of my major concerns in this book is to explore issues related to the syntactic representation of the Hebrew present tense (see part I in particular). The verbal form used to express present tense is a curious one: it serves the functions of both an active participle and a tensed verb, as (1-12) shows.

(1-12) a. Dani haya   tofer   smalot.
           Dani be(PAST)-3MS sew-MS dresses
           'Dani was sewing/used to sew dresses.'

   b. Dani tofer   smalot.
      Dani sew-MS dresses
      'Dani sews/is sewing dresses.'

In (1-12a), the form *tofer* follows the past tense auxiliary. In (1-12b), on the other hand, the same verbal form occurs without an auxiliary and the tense specification of the sentence is present.

The case of the Hebrew present tense is rather special when compared with the more familiar Western European languages, where active participles and present tense verbs are morphologically realized by distinct forms, as in the following English example.

(1-13) a. Smith was sewing dresses.

   b. Smith sews dresses.

Hebrew is also rather unique among the Semitic languages in having a three-way tense system in which the present tense and the participle have the same form. In order to place the Hebrew system within the Semitic context, several comments of a comparative nature are in order.

There are two sets of verbal conjugations in Semitic, which can be labeled the *prefixal* and the *suffixal* paradigms (see, e.g., Hetzron 1987, Moscati et al. 1980). Table (1-14) exemplifies this pattern in Hebrew with the triliteral root *tfr* 'sew. (The forms in parentheses are archaic. Modern Hebrew neutralizes gender distinctions in the plural).[12]

(1-14)

	Prefixal Conjugation		Suffixal Conjugation	
	Singular	Plural	Singular	Plural
1	ʔe-tfor	ni-tfor	tafar-ti	tafar-nu
2m	ti-tfor	ti-tfə-u	tafar-ta	tafar-tem
2f	ti-tfər-i	(ti-tfor-na)	tafar-t	(tafar-ten)
3m	yi-tfor	yi-tfər-u	tafar	tafr-u
3f	ti-tfor	(ti-tfor-na)	tafr-a	tafr-u

The prefixal conjugation consists of a stem and a series of agreement affixes, predominantly prefixal. The suffixal conjugation is purely suffixal. Hebrew associates the prefixal pattern with the future tense and the suffixal one with the past tense, as exemplified in (1-15).

(1-15) a. ha-yladim   yi-tfər-u   simla.
      the children 3MPL-sew(FUT) dress
      'The children will sew a dress.'

   b. ha-yladim   tafr-u   simla.
      the children sew(PAST)-3MPL dress
      'The children sewed a dress.'

In Arabic, the two conjugations fundamentally reflect an aspectual, rather than a temporal distinction. The prefixal conjugation is associated with imperfect aspect (or *inaccompli*), and the suffixal pattern with the perfect (*accompli*) (Fleisch 1979). Insofar as this aspectual difference also harbors or entails a temporal one, it is that of past versus non-past and not, as in Hebrew, of past versus future.[13]

While this generalization holds of most varieties of Arabic, dialects differ as to the morphological and syntactic devices used to express the distinction between future tense and present tense (as well as that of anteriority/posteriority distinctions in the past tense). In many cases, though, tense, aspect and occasionally mood, seem to be inextricably connected, giving rise to an extremely rich, and at the same time, notoriously complex system.[14]

In Standard Arabic, the unmarked interpretation of the prefixal conjugation is that of present tense, as in (1-16a). To render (1-16a) in the future tense, the modal particle sa(wfa) is added, (1-16b).

(1-16) a. Mona ta-drusu.
      Mona 3FS-study(IMPERF)
      'Mona studies.'

   b. Mona   sa(wfa) ta-drusu
      Mona   will   3FS-study(IMPERF)
      'Mona will study.'

In Palestinian Arabic, the prefixal or imperfective form is a "dependent" form, so that (1-16a) never occurs as a root indicative sentence, as shown by the ungrammaticality of (1-16).

(1-17)   *Mona tu-drus.
        Mona   3FS-study(IMPERF)
        'Mona studies.'

The prefixal form in this dialect is used where other languages (also Hebrew) would employ the nonfinite form, (1-18a). It also serves as the subjunctive form, as in (1-18b).[15]

(1-18) a. Mona mistʕiddi tu drus.
          M.   ready-FS   3FS-study(IMPERF)
          'Mona is ready to study.'

        b. ṭalab   min-ha   ʔin-ha   t ruuḥ   maʕ-aa.
          ask(PERF)-3MS from-3FS   that-3FS   3FS-go(IMPERF)   with-3MS
          'He asked her to go with him.' Lit: 'He asked her that she goes with him.'

To form the present and the future tense, Palestinian employs a variety of tense/aspect particles and auxiliaries that linearly precede the prefixal (i.e., imperfect) form of the verb. The prefixal particle *b-* converts a dependent form into an independent one, which is interpreted as non-past durative, as shown in (1-19).

(1-19)   Mona b-   tu drus
        Mona DUR 3FS-study(IMPERF)
        'Mona studies.'

Other particles and auxiliaries serve to articulate a future tense interpretation. Thus, we have the auxiliary *raḥ* 'go', (1-20a), *qaʕede* (progressive, lit. 'sit), (1-20b), to cite only two.

(1-20) a. Mona raḥ tu drus   b. Mona qaʕede b tu drus
         Mona go 3FS-study(IMPERF)   *Mona PROG-FS DUR-3FS-study(IMPERF)*
         'Mona is going to study.'   'Mona is going to study.'

As the reader can plainly tell, the temporal/aspectual system of Arabic is highly complex, and we cannot do it justice in this short introduction. What emerges from the foregoing discussion is that one axis of difference between Hebrew and Arabic (as well as among the Arabic dialects themselves) turns on the use of the two morphological paradigms of the Semitic verb to express different tense, modal, and aspectual information. In Arabic, the two verbal conjugations fundamentally encode aspect. Insofar as the Arabic verb encodes tense, it by and large expresses a binary distinction, namely past and non-past.

Modern Hebrew thus differs from Arabic and is rather unique among the Semitic languages in that the two verbal conjugations are clearly and unambiguously associated with tense distinctions. Moreover, the Hebrew tense system is ternary rather than binary, and each tense is associated with a particular morphological form.

Alongside the prefixal and suffixal conjugations (future and past, respectively; see [1-15]), a third verbal form called the *Benoni* 'intermediate', is employed for the expression of the present tense. The Benoni is found across the Semitic languages. In Arabic, its primary role is that of an active participle, and although it does occur as a present tense form with some verbs and in some contexts, it is in Hebrew that this "participial" form serves as the unmarked and productive form of the present tense. Put in different terms, Arabic primarily makes use of the prefixal conjugation (with or without additional particles and auxiliaries) to express the present tense, while Hebrew utilizes this conjugation uniquely for the future tense, the present tense being expressed by the Benoni.[16] These differences are summarized in Table (1-21)

(1-21)	Hebrew	Standard Arabic	Palestinian Arabic
Past	Suffixal pattern	Suffixal pattern	Suffixal pattern
Present	Benoni	Prefixal pattern	Auxiliary/particle + prefixal pattern
Future	Prefixal pattern	Modal particle + prefixal pattern	Auxiliary/particle + prefixal pattern

1.3.3   Clausal Negation

1.3.3.1. *Negation in Hebrew*

Clausal negation is implemented in Hebrew by the particle *lo*, which appears left-adjacent to the verb in a simple tense or to the auxiliary in a compound tense, as shown in (1-22).

(1-22)   a. Dani   lo   ʔafa   ʔugot.
  Dani   neg   bake(PAST)-3MS   cakes
  'Dani did not bake cakes.'

  b. Dani   lo   haya   ʔofe   ʔugot.
  Dani   neg   be(PAST)-3MS   bake(BENONI)-MS   cakes
  'Dani didn't use to bake cakes.'

The adjacency requirement holding of *lo* and the verb is absolute: no adjunct or parenthetical expression can separate them, as shown by the unacceptability of the sentences in (1-23), which should be compared with those in (1-24), where the same intervening elements can occur between the subject and the verb in both affirmative and negative clauses.

(1-23)   a. *Dani   lo   kanirʔe   ʔafa   ʔugot.
  Dani   neg   apparently   bake(PAST)-3MS   cakes
  'Dani apparently didn't bake cakes.'

  b. *Dani   lo   lədaʕati   ʔafa   ʔugot.
  Dani   neg   in opinion-1S   bake(PAST)-3MS   cakes
  'Dani, in my opinion, didn't bake cakes.'

(1-24)   a. Dani   kanirʔe   (lo)   ʔafa   ʔugot.
  Dani   apparently   (neg)   bake(PAST)-3MS   cakes
  'Dani apparently baked (didn't bake) cakes.'

b. Dani,   lədaʕati,   (lo)   ʔafa   ʔugot.
   Dani   in opinion-1S   (neg)   bake(PAST)-3MS   cakes
   'Dani, in my opinion, baked (didn't bake) cakes.'

A straightforward way to characterize the inviolability of the cluster formed by the negative particle and the verb is to treat them as the product of syntactic incorporation of two X^0 elements. This, in turn, entails that *lo* is a head—more precisely, *the* head—of NegP as originally proposed in Hazout (1992). I take the Hebrew NegP to thus consist of an overt head, *lo*, and a silent specifier, as diagrammed in (1-25).

(1-25)

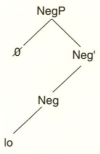

This *lo* is carried along with the verb when the latter raises to Comp, as in the inversion configuration in (1-26); see chapter 7 for discussion of this type of inversion.

(1-26)   meʕolam   lo   taʕam   Dani   xacil   kol kax   bašel.
   never   neg   taste(PAST)-3MS   Dani   eggplant   so   ripe
   'Never has Dani tasted such a ripe eggplant.'

Thus, *lo* looks like a bound morpheme, an affixal head. Such negative heads are far from unfamiliar. The Romance languages—French and Italian, for example—are endowed with exactly this sort of negative head.

Treating *lo* as the head of NegP and admitting a clausal structure in which NegP is situated between AgrSP and TP, as in (1-2), recalls Moritz's (1989) analysis of negative clauses in French, extended to Italian in Belletti (1990). Moritz argues that the Romance affixal negative head cliticizes to $AgrS^0$. This analysis is motivated by the well-known observation that the Romance negative head clusters with pronominal clitics. In order to account for the proclitic nature of negative affixation, Moritz and Belletti argue that T^0, to which the verb is adjoined, raises to $AgrS^0$ and that this is followed by the raising of Neg^0 and its adjunction to the left of the complex in $AgrS^0$. Representationally, the head chain is thus well formed and the Head Movement constraint (HMC) (Baker 1988, Travis 1984) is circumvented.[17]

Can the affixation of *lo* be handled in the same way? At first sight, the answer seems to be positive, given the data surveyed thus far. A problem for such an analysis, presented next, leads me to abandon Moritz's approach for *lo* and to support an alternative (I return to this question in detail in §5.3.1, and modify the analysis once again in several significant respects).

In certain varieties of Hebrew present tense copular sentences, a third person pronoun, agreeing in number and gender with the clausal subject, occurs in lieu of a copula. (In many dialects of Arabic, this "pronoun of separation" fully agrees with the subject in gender, number and person.) Doron (1983) convincingly shows that this pronoun, which she labels *Pron,* is not the present tense form of the copular verb *be,* but rather constitutes the phonetic realization of AgrS^0 in sentences in which a veritable copula is missing.[18] Adopting her basic approach, we have the following structure of a copular sentence.

(1-27)   [$_{AgrSP}$Dani [$_{AgrS^0}$ hu] manhig   dagul]].
        Dani   PRON-MS   leader-MS renowned
        'Dani is a renowned leader.'

Doron notes that negative *lo* cannot precede Pron, but must follow it, as in the contrast in (1-28).

(1-28)   a. *Dani lo   hu   manhig   dagul.
             Dani   neg   PRON-MS leader-MS renowned
             'Dani is not a renowned leader.'

         b. Dani   hu   lo   manhig dagul.
             Dani PRON-MS neg   leader   renowned
             'Dani is not a renowned leader.'

If Moritz's analysis of Romance negative heads carried over to Hebrew, we would be at pain to explain the ungrammaticality of (1-28a), since under his approach Neg^0 invariably moves to cliticize to AgrS^0 and is therefore wrongly predicted to occur to the left of Pron, as in the ungrammatical (1-28a).

Consider the following alternative. Take the affixal nature of *lo* to mean that it is an "incomplete" word and that unlike the Romance negative heads, *lo* morphologically subcategorizes for the category T, in the sense of Rizzi and Roberts (1989). Thus, it is represented as *lo$_{[-+T]}$* and requires T^0 to move into the slot in its subcategorization frame.[19] *lo*-affixation is thus implemented *below* AgrS^0. Further movement of the complex negative head to AgrS^0 (as in [1-22]) or higher (as in [1-26]) is not driven by the affixed nature of *lo.*

The question arises why the complex head [*lo* + T] does not raise to AgrS^0 when this head is filled by Pron. I deal with this matter in detail in §5.3.1. For the time being, let us assume *pace* Doron (1983), that Pron is not itself an affix in need of support (or a strong matrix of features requiring pre-PF checking, in Checking theoretic terms). Consequently, there is no need to raise a lower head to an AgrS^0 filled by Pron. Movement of [*lo* + T] and adjunction to PRON is morphologically redundant and syntactically superfluous.

Although the derivational implementation of Neg-cliticization in Hebrew differs from that of Italian, both give rise to representationally well-formed chains; indeed, the two result in identical representations. In Italian, Neg^0 and T^0 raise to AgrS^0 independently, while in Hebrew, Neg^0 initially hosts T^0 and the two then raise as a unit to AgrS^0. The two derivations are schematized in (1-29).

(1-29)

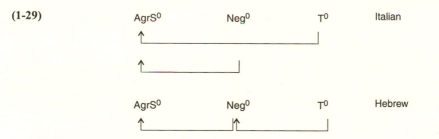

Alongside *lo*, Hebrew has a second negative head, the particle *ʔeyn*, which occurs in a well defined environment: in precedence to present tense (Benoni) verbs and nonverbal predicates, as in the examples in (1-30). (The examples involve embedded sentences to stress the fact that, despite its clause-initial position, *ʔeyn* is not restricted to root contexts.) The syntax of *ʔeyn* is the subject of chapter 4 and the reader is referred there for further discussion.

(1-30) a. (ʔani xošev   še)   *ʔeyn* Ruti yodaʕat   *ʔet*
    I think(BENONI)-MS that neg Ruti know(BENONI)-FS ACC

     ha-tšuva.
     the-answer
   '(I think that) Ruti does not know the answer.'

  b. (ʔani xošev   še)   *ʔeyn* xatulim ba-gan.
    I think(BENONI)-MS that neg cats in-the-garden
   '(I think that) there are no cats in the garden.'

1.3.3.2 Negation in Arabic

Negation in many of the modern colloquial dialects of Arabic is implemented by two discontinuous morphemes. The example in (1-31) is Palestinian (the negative morphemes are underlined.)[20]

(1-31) Zayd <u>ma</u> kan   <u>-(i)š</u> bi l-beet.
   Zayd <u>neg</u> be(PERF)-3MS <u>neg</u> in the-house
   'Zayd was not at home.'

This pattern is highly reminiscent of the French pattern, illustrated in (1-32).

(1-32) Jean <u>ne</u>   fut   <u>pas</u> à la maison.
   Jean neg be-PAST-3S neg in the house
   'Jean was not at home.'

In both languages, the negative morphemes embrace the verb, as it were. In (1-33), the pattern of negation in complex tenses is illustrated: in both languages, negation surrounds the auxiliary verb (the participial properties of the imperfect form in Arabic are discussed in §6.2.1).

(1-33) a. Zayd <u>ma</u> kan   <u>-(i)š</u> yiktib   qiṣaṣ.
    Zayd <u>neg</u> be(PERF)-3MS <u>neg</u> 3MS-write(IMPERF) stories
    'Zayd was not writing stories.'

b. Jean <u>n'</u>   a   pas   écrit   des histoires.
   Jean   neg   be-*PAST-3S   *neg*   write-*PAST PARTICIPLE*   *stories*
   'Jean did not write stories.'

I follow Benmamoun (1992:68) and assume that colloquial Arabic negation is structurally represented as in French, with *ma* being the (clitic) head of NegP and š its specifier. This is diagrammed in (1-34).

(1-34)

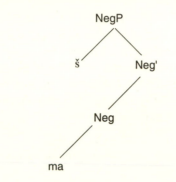

As in French, the negative head raises to AgrS⁰, and since AgrS⁰ is also the landing site of the inflected verb, the order *ma^* verb*^* š is obtained. Although I return to the manner of cliticization of Arabic *š* in §5.3.1, several comments are in order at this point.

Benmamoun (1992) provides important evidence for the X⁰ status of š. He shows that in Moroccan Arabic, which has the same pattern of negation as Palestinian, *š* is in complementary distribution with negative quantifiers.[21] Consider the examples in (1-35) and (1-36); see also the examples in Harrell (1962:154).

(1-35) a. ma   rbeḥt   walu.
             neg   earn(PERF)-1M   nothing
             'I didn't earn anything.' *or* 'I earned nothing.'

            b. *ma rbeḥt   -š   walu.
             neg   earn(PERF)-1M   neg   nothing
             'I didn't earn anything.' *or* 'I earned nothing.'

(1-36) a. ma   šəfna   hədd.   b. *ma šəfna   -š   hədd.
             neg   see(PERF)-1PL   no one   *neg   see(PERF)-1PL   neg   no one*
             'We saw no one.'   We saw no one.'

Precisely the same state of affairs is characteristic of French. Compare (1-35) and (1-36) with (1-37) and (1-38); the French examples are provided with the literary perfect form of the verb in order to highlight the parallelism with Arabic.

(1-37) a. Je ne   gagnai   rien.
             I   neg   earn-PAST   nothing
             'I didn't earn anything.' *or* 'I earned nothing.'

            b. *Je ne   gagnai   pas   rien.
             I   neg   earn-PAST   neg   nothing
             'I didn't earn anything.' *or* 'I earned nothing.'

(1-38)　a. Nous　ne　vîmes　personne.
　　　　　we　*neg*　*see-PAST*　*no one*
　　　　'We saw no one.'

　　　　b. *Nous　ne　vîmes　pas　personne.
　　　　　we　*neg*　*see-PAST*　*neg*　*no one*
　　　　'We saw no one.'

The French pattern has been explained by a number of authors as involving a competition between *pas* and the negative quantifier for the position of Spec/NegP. On the natural assumption that only one element may appear in that position, combined with the view that negative quantifiers must appear in Spec/NegP at the latest by LF, the French pattern receives a coherent explanation (see the discussion in Pollock 1989, Ouhalla 1990, Haegeman 1995, Haegeman and Zanuttini 1991, Rizzi 1991, and Zanuttini 1991, among many others).

We can extend this explanation straightforwardly to Arabic. The incompatibility of *š* and either *walu* or *ḥədd* shows that *š* occupies the specifier position of NegP, just like French *pas*. By extension, *ma* is the head of NegP.

Negation in Standard Arabic is represented by a number of distinct particles, each with its own syntactic properties. They are introduced and discussed in detail in chapter 6.

1.3.4　A Note on *ʔet* and Accusative Case

The particle *ʔet*, which is glossed *ACC* throughout this work, occurs obligatorily to the immediate left of a definite direct object. Some examples are given in (1-39).

(1-39)　a. raʔiti　　ʔet　ha-yeled.
　　　　　saw(PAST)-1S　*ACC*　*the-boy*
　　　　'*I saw the boy.*'

　　　　b. raʔiti　　ʔet　kol ha-yladim.
　　　　　saw(PAST)-1S　*ACC*　*all-the-children*
　　　　'I saw all the children.

　　　　c. raʔiti　　ʔet　Dan.
　　　　　saw(PAST)-1S　*ACC*　*Dan*
　　　　'I saw Dan.'

Before attempting to formulate a hypothesis concerning the role and distribution of *ʔet*, let us clarify a preliminary point. The diagnostic for verb movement on the basis of the distribution of adverbs (see the discussion surrounding [1-10a]), can be extended to show that direct objects preceded by *ʔet* are not moved out of VP at S-structure. Consider the fact that manner adverbs, which I assume mark the upper edge of VP, may occur between a verb and a direct object, as in (1-40).[22]

(1-40)　a. Dani　hika　　　ʔanušot　　ʔet　šlomo.
　　　　　Dani　*hit(PAST)-3MS*　*mortally*　*ACC*　*Shlomo*
　　　　'Dani hit Shlomo mortally.'

b. Dani   patax   bə-ʕadinut ʔet   ha-delet.
   Dani   open(PAST)-3MS   gently   ACC   the-door
   'Dani opened the door gently.'

I take the relevant structure of the sentences in (1-40) to be as in (1-41), where only the verb, but not the direct object, raises to the left of the adverb.

(1-41)

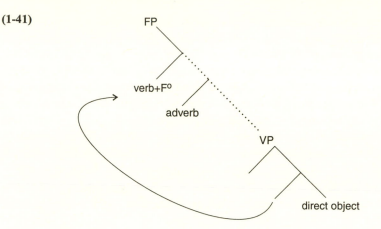

The adverbs *ʔanušot* 'mortally' and *bə-ʕadinut* 'gently' may also follow the direct object, as in (1-42). I interpret such examples as involving an adverb which is base-generated on the right, rather than on the left margin of VP.[23]

(1-42) a. Dani   hika   ʔet   šlomo   ʔanušot.
             Dani   hit(PAST)-3MS   ACC   Shlomo   mortally
             'Dani hit Shlomo mortally.'

          b. Dani   patax   ʔet   ha-delet   bə-ʕadinut.
             Dani   open(PAST)-3MS   ACC   the-door   gently
             'Dani opened the door gently.'

I further assume that the direct object raises to Spec/AgrO in LF in order to check its accusative Case feature. (In chapter 10, we shall see that Hebrew weak pronouns raise to this position in the audible syntax.) As for *ʔet*, I take it to be the morphological realization of accusative Case, in a sense I now render more explicit.

The following empirical consideration sustains the view that *ʔet* is a Case feature. Consider the fact that *ʔet* must also introduce definite subjects of small clauses, as in (1-43).

(1-43) šamaʕnu   ʔet   Dani   menagen   kinor.
            hear(PAST)-1PL   ACC   Dani   play(BENONI)-MS   violin
            'We heard Dani playing violin.'

If *ʔet* were, say, a Case *assigner* to a direct object or a complement small clause subject, then the small clause could be detached or moved away from its (canonical) position. Nevertheless, (1-44a) shows that a small clause cannot be fronted, in contrast to, for example, a full clause, (1-44b) or a bare argument, (1-44c).

(1-44) a. *??et Dani   menagen   kinor   šamaʕnu   ha-boker.
    ACC *Dani play(BENONI)-MS violin hear(PAST)-1PL the-morning*
    'Dani playing violin, we heard this morning.'

   b. še   Dani   menagen   kinor   šamaʕnu   ha-boker.
    that Dani play(BENONI)-MS violin hear(PAST)-1PL the-morning
    'That Dani plays the violin, we heard this morning.'

   c. ʔet Dani   šamaʕnu   ha-boker   menagen   kinor.
    ACC *Dani hear(PAST)-1PL the-morning play(BENONI)-MS violin*
    'Dani, we heard playing violin this morning.'

A Case-theoretic explanation readily suggests itself for this contrast: if accusative Case must be checked in AgrOP, then fronting of the small clause would disable the small clause subject from raising to Spec/AgrO (at S-structure or in LF). When a full clause is fronted, on the other hand, the object can check its Case internally to the fronted clause. Finally, when a bare object is fronted, its trace can check accusative Case by raising in LF to Spec/AgrO. If *ʔet* assigned accusative Case or otherwise rendered it legitimate, then the small clause subject would have Case even in its fronted position and the contrast displayed in (1-44) would be unexplained.

   The view I am thus defending is Chomsky's (1993), namely, that direct objects are marked for Case in some fashion (the mark may, naturally, be nonovert) and that Case is checked rather than assigned in a Spec-head configuration in AgrOP. Suppose further that Case features are represented on the direct object in the form of an X^0 category, K^0. *ʔet Dani* is thus represented as in (1-45).[24]

(1-45)

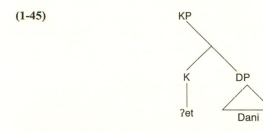

In LF, the KP moves to Spec/AgrO. I assume that indefinite direct objects are also KPs, but that the content of K^0 is phonetically unexpressed.

   Yet the distribution of *ʔet*, in particular, its restriction to definite objects, suggests that more is at stake. It is rather well known that *ʔet* appears in derived nominals in Hebrew, as in (1-46) (cf. Borer 1983, forthcoming, Siloni 1991, 1994, and Hazout 1991).

(1-46) harisat   ha-cava   ʔet ha-ʕir . . .
    destruction the-army ACC the-city
    'The army's destruction of the city . . .'

Structural Case is unavailable internally to DPs, perhaps because these lack an AgrOP projection, as Siloni (1994) argues (see also Borer, forthcoming). Therefore, *ʔet* in (1-46) cannot be a marker of accusative Case, as in the examples in (1-39). Rather, the *ʔet* that occurs in nominals should be taken to be an inherent Case marker, similar to the preposition *of* in, for example, *the destruction of the city* (viz. Chomsky 1981), as Borer (1983) concludes.

Borer (1983) further draws attention to the fact that, in contrast to clausal direct objects, which may be either definite (and hence preceded by *ʔet*) or indefinite, objects in nominals must be definite (but see Hazout 1991 for a different view). Compare (1-46) with (1-47), where the derived nominal's theme is a specific indefinite plural.

(1-47)   ??harisat   ha-cava   ʕarim   ka-ʔelu . . .
destruction   the-army   cities   like-these
'The army's destruction of cities like these . . .'

The contrast between (1-46) and (1-47) should, I think, be interpreted to mean that Hebrew derived nominals have only an *ʔet*-type inherent Case available for assignment to their themes. An inherent Case licensing indefinite themes seems not to be available in the grammar. If we label the latter type of inherent Case "partitive" (viz. Belletti 1988), then we might call the *ʔet*-Case "antipartitive."

To recapitulate, we have seen that *ʔet* marks accusative Case in the verbal system and inherent Case in the nominal system. Can these two functions be related? Let us assume that inherent Case is also assigned in the clausal system, at least to direct objects (as Bellettti's work strongly suggests), so that the incompatibility of indefinite objects with *ʔet* is due to the restriction of antipartitive inherent Case to definite ones.

The structural and inherent Cases marked by *ʔet* cannot easily be teased apart in the clausal system, since both structural and inherent Case are licensed in a clause. Nominals, however, allow us to consider them in isolation, since these only assign an inherent Case, structural Case being entirely unavailable (cf. Chomsky 1981, 1986).[25]

Part I

VERB MOVEMENT
AND CLAUSAL ARCHITECTURE

The following six chapters are essentially concerned with two topics—the structure of IP and the scope of verb movement. The empirical domain studied in chapters 2–5 is drawn primarily from Hebrew, while chapter 6 is almost exclusively concerned with Standard Arabic. Since this essay is a comparative study, however, the discussion often shifts back and forth between Hebrew and the Arabic languages. Moreover, many of the conclusions drawn in Chapters 2–5 for Hebrew are valid for Arabic as well, permitting the formulation of some rather novel generalizations concerning the patterns of negation, verb movement, the nature of participles, and the gamut of positions available to clausal subjects.

Clausal architecture is one of the main issues adressed in part I. In particular, I am concerned with the hierarchical layering of functional projections. While it is not inconceivable that the hierarchical position of the major functional projections is subject to cross-linguistic variation, (see, e.g., Ouhalla 1991), the evidence presented here overwhelmingly supports the particular hierarchy proposed by Belletti for English and the Romance languages (see Belletti 1990) and outlined in chapter 1. I will attempt to show that the hierarchy AgrSP > NegP > TP characterizes not only Hebrew, but Arabic as well. The Arabic languages, comprising the standard language and the colloquial dialects, are closely related to Hebrew from a typological perspective (all are Semitic languages), and they possess a morphological system, both inflectional and derivational, that is extremely similar, indeed, practically identical to that of Hebrew. It would therefore be highly unexpected if the functional categories of Arabic were hierarchically layered differently than in Hebrew. I shall try to show that both languages can be treated uniformly. Insofar as this conclusion is valid, it suggests that the hierarchy of functional projections is perhaps not *accidentally* identical in these languages, but that the skeleton of projections provided by UG is not subject to variation in hierarchy. I will further argue that when the highest projection of IP appears to be

TP or NegP, this is due not to a reversal of the position of these projections with respect to AgrSP, but rather to the nonprojectability of AgrSP, which may, under circumstances discussed here, simply fail to be generated. This has the result that the projection immediately below AgrSP occupies the highest position within IP, under CP.

The analysis of verb movement is intimately tied up with the clausal architecture one assumes. I will try to show that an articulated theory of clausal architecture (in the spirit of Pollock 1989 and much recent work) can be motivated internally to the grammar of Hebrew. Conversely, the adoption of an explicit hypothesis concerning the number and position of functional heads in a clause allows one to draw fine distinctions with respect to the scope of movement of verbs in the different tenses of Hebrew, the position of negation, and the positions available to subjects.

The main focus of the discussion are sentences in the present tense, both affirmative and negative. These constitute a novel empirical domain and are thus in and of themselves worthy of study. Moreover, certain unique features of sentences in the present tense render many facets of Hebrew syntax more transparent than sentences in other tenses, and thus they permit a closer scrutiny of the issues central to my discussion.

The verbal form expressing the present tense, the Benoni, functions both as an (untensed) participle and as a tensed verb (§2.2). Chapter 2 proposes an analysis of the Benoni in both its guises. It is argued that the Benoni is always a participle, but when it is the only audible verb in a clause, it is preceded by a phonetically unrealized auxiliary. Present tense sentences in Hebrew, I argue, are compound tense constructions.

Chapter 3 opens by challenging the conclusion drawn in the preceding one, and in particular, the view that the Benoni is confined to positions below TP. There is ample evidence to the effect that the Benoni is more mobile than what is conventionally assumed for participles—namely, it can raise to TP and to CP. Rather than taking this evidence to show that the Benoni is *not* a participle, I argue that it is the assumption that participles do not raise which is incorrect. I argue that participles (and certain predicative adjectives) raise at least as far as T^0 (and can do so overtly) in the syntax of Hebrew. Participle raising to T can be taken to be a formal expression of the often noted mutual dependence of participles and auxiliaries. A rather unique construction found in Hebrew, wherein a Benoni can incorporate to an auxiliary, provides the overt evidence for participle raising, a process I suggest should be generalized.

While the Benoni arguably raises to T^0, I claim that it does not move to $AgrS^0$. Even if nothing bars such movement, the Benoni cannot license $AgrS^0$ because it lacks $AgrS^0$ features. By a strict interpretation of derivational economy, it follows that the Benoni cannot raise to $AgrS^0$, due to the absence of any motivation for such movement. The Benoni, in other words, is a participle as far as its agreement is concerned—that is to say, its agreement features are realized or checked in the participial agreement head AgrPartP, located below TP (see chapter 1). In the absence of Benoni-raising to $AgrS^0$, the grammar can avail itself of two options for the representation of present tense sentences: either AgrSP is simply not generated, so that the highest layer of IP is TP, or alternatively, AgrSP is generated, but this requires that an auxiliary also be generated, in order to allow the content of $AgrS^0$ to be checked.

Chapter 4 is a study of present tense negation, providing empirical evidence that clauses can lack the AgrSP layer, so that the highest functional projection in the clause is NegP or TP. Negative present tense sentences provide a rather unique view into what might be called the Hebrew "Mittlefeld," that is, the clausal domain lying between VP and TP. It is shown that the Benoni raises to T^0 and that clausal subjects appear in Spec/T at S-structure.

Chapter 5, the more tentative of the 5 chapters constituting part I, attempts to extend the analysis of Benoni to some problematic domains. In particular, I take a brief look at negative sentences that contain nonverbal predicates and indefinite subjects, and I attempt to resolve the problem of why Benoni verbs cannot occur in the company of Pron, the pronominal form filling $AgrS^0$ in certain types of copular constructions (see §1.3.3).

Finally, in Chapter 6, I turn to Standard Arabic and consider the syntax of sentential negation. Although Arabic exhibits a more elaborate system than that of Hebrew, I think it can be shown that both involve the same basic ingredients. The interplay of a small number of cross-linguistically attested morphological differences, such as whether a negative head is a clitic or not and whether it morphologically subcategorizes for another head or not, can fully explain the syntactic properties of different negative structures.

TWO

The Active Participle and the Syntax of the Present Tense

2.1 OVERVIEW

One of the main purposes of this book is to explore the syntactic representation of sentences in the present tense. The verbal form used to express present tense, the Benoni, is a curious one: It serves the functions of both a present participle (active and passive, respectively (2-1a,c)) and a tensed verb, as in (2-1b,d).[1]

(2-1) a. Dani   haya   kotev   sipurim.
          Dani   be(PAST)-3MS   write(BENONI)-MS   stories
          'Dani was writing /used to write stories.

       b. Dani   kotev   sipurim.
          Dani   write(BENONI)-MS   stories
          'Dani writes / is writing stories.'

       c. ha-ʕugot   hay-u   mugašot   ʕal yedei robotim.
          the-cakes   be(PAST)-3PL   serve(PASSIVE BENONI)-FPL   by   robots
          'The cakes were served / used to be served by robots.'

       d. ha-ʕugot   mugašot   ʕal yedei robotim.
          the-cakes   serve(PASSIVE BENONI)-FPL   by   robots
          'The cakes are served by robots.'

In (2-1a), the form *kotev* follows the past tense auxiliary and the sentence is interpreted as past tense. In (2-1b), on the other hand, the same verbal form occurs without an auxiliary and the tense is interpreted as present tense. Sentences (2-1c,d) illustrate the same pattern with the Benoni in the passive voice.

The Benoni can also serve as an (agentive) nominal and as a modifying adjective. This chapter, however, is devoted to a study of the Benoni in its predicative guises (the nonverbal occurrences of the Benoni are briefly discussed in the following subsection and then put aside). After rendering explicit some common assumptions regarding the principal differences between a participle and a tensed verb—assumptions that are challenged in later sections—I proceed to examine a variety of construction types in which the Benoni figures either as a participle or as a tensed verb, or as both.

There is an obvious sense in which the Benoni is ambiguous. What is less obvious is how this ambiguity should be stated and formalized. My initial hypothesis, and perhaps the simplest one, is that the Benoni is *always* a participle. This view denies that the Benoni form is ambiguous in any sense. I account for its occurrence as a tensed verb by appealing to a gap in the paradigm of the auxiliary *be*. Following Berman (1978), I argue that a phonetically null auxiliary appears in (2-1b,d). Seen from this angle, there is no syntactic difference between (2-1a,c) and (2-1b,d): both are periphrastic compound tense constructions, and in both the Benoni appears as a participle.

2.1.1   Benoni Inflection

While encoding the present tense, the Benoni nevertheless differs from the canonical verbal conjugations of the past and future tenses in several respects.

Consider first its morphological pattern. The Benoni is inflectionally impoverished with respect to the past and future forms, in that it encodes only number and gender features. Compare the verbal paradigms in (2-2), which show person, number, and gender inflection, with those in (2-3), where only number and gender are encoded.

(2-2)

	Future Tense		Past Tense	
	Singular	Plural	Singular	Plural
1	ʔe-xtov	nixtov	katav-ti	katav-nu
2m	ti-xtov	ti-xtəv-u	katav-ta	katav-tem
2f	ti-xtəv-i	″	katav-t	″
3m	yi-xtov	yi-xtəv-u	katav	katv-u
3f	ti-xtov	″	katv	″

(2-3)

	Benoni	
	Singular	Plural
Masc	kotev	kotv-im
Fem	kotev-et	kotv-ot

In this respect, the Benoni is like a noun or an adjective. This is revealed by comparing the inflectional paradigm in (2-3) with that of a noun like *šomer* 'guard,' or an adjective such as *mesudar* 'orderly' in (2-4).

(2-4)

	Nominal Declension			Adjectival Declension	
	Singular	Plural		Singular	Plural
Masc	šomer	šomr-im	Masc	mesudar	mesudar-im
Fem	šomer-et	šomr-ot	Fem	mesuder-et	mesudat-ot

Many participles are homophonous with (agentive) nouns. Thus, *šomer* in (2-4) does not only refer to the agentive noun 'guard' but also can mean 'I/you/he guards.' An ambiguity thus arises in the interpretation of sentences such as (2-5).[2]

(2-5) Dani   šomer.
       Dani   guard-MS
       Nominal interpretation: 'Dani is a guard.'
       Verbal interpretation: 'Dani guards/is guarding.'

2.1.2   Categorial Ambiguity of the Benoni

There are a number of ways to tease apart the nominal and verbal occurrences of a Benoni form. For example, the addition of the definite article *ha-* to the Benoni form forces the nominal reading, as does the presence of a complement preceded by the genitive preposition *šel*. These are illustrated in (2-6).

(2-6) a. Dani   haya   ha-šomer.   b. Dani   šomer   šel ha-nasi.
          Dani   be(PAST)-3MS   the-guard   *Dani   guard   of the-president*
          'Dani was the guard.'   'Dani is a President's guard.'

Another difference between nouns and verbs is that they have different types of argument-structures and Case-assigning properties. Verbs invariably have subcategorization frames, while nouns derived from the same root may not. Thus, while (2-5) is ambiguous, (2-7) is not. 'Lead', unlike 'guard', is a strongly transitive verb—that is, one which is obligatorily subcategorized by a DP complement and lacks an intransitive variant.[3] In the absence of a complement, (2-7) cannot have the verbal interpretation and can only be taken to be a noun, as the glosses indicate.

(2-7) Dani   manhig.
       Dani   lead(BENONI)-MS
       'Dani is a leader.'
       *'Dani leads / is leading.'

When 'leader' occurs as a noun with a complement, the latter is either preceded by the genitive marker *šel*, as in (2-8a), or forms a construct with it, as in (2-8b).[4]

(2-8) a. Dani   haya   manhig   šel ha-kvuca.
          Dani   be(PAST)-3MS   lead(BENONI)-MS   of the-group
          'Dani was a leader of the group.'

       b. Dani   haya   manhig   ha-kvuca.
          Dani   be(PAST)-3MS   lead(BENONI)-MS   the-group
          'Dani was the leader of the group.'

As a verb, 'lead' takes an DP complement which, if definite, is preceded by the accusative marker *ʔet*, just as in the past and future forms. Compare (2-9a) with (2-9b,c) (see §1.3.4 for discussion of *ʔet*).

(2-9) a. Dani   manhig   ʔet   ha-kvuca.
          Dani   lead(BENONI)-MS   ACC   the-group
          'Dani leads / is leading the group.'

b. Dani hinhig   ?et   ha-kvuca.
   Dani   lead(PAST)-3MS   ACC   the group
   'Dani led the group.'

c. Dani yanhig   ?et   ha-kvuca.
   Dani   3MS-lead (FUT)   ACC   the-group
   Dani will lead the group.

Finally, when modified by an adjective (itself a Benoni form), *manhig* can only be interpreted as a noun, as in (2-10).[5]

(2-10)   Dani   manhig   dagul.
             Dani   lead(BENONI)-MS   renowned-MS
             'Dani is a renowned leader.'

The question that arises at this point is how the ambiguity of, for example, *manhig* is to be represented. Is the difference between the nominal and verbal usage to be captured by marking the categorial signature in the Lexicon, a lexicalist approach harking back to Chomsky (1970), or is one derived from the other syntactically? Answering this question inevitably leads to a broader discussion of nominalization and adjective formation in Hebrew, topics that lie beyond the scope of this work. I will therefore put these matters aside. My discussion henceforth will be devoted exclusively to the occurrence of the Benoni as a predicate.[6]

2.2   THE VERBAL BENONI

The verbal Benoni thus appears to be a hybrid form: it serves the functions of both a participle and a tensed verb, as demonstrated by the examples in (2-1).

The dual use of the Benoni form, as a participle and as a present tense verb, raises the issue of the syntactic distinction between participles and "full" verbs. That there are questions to be answered here is evident when the Benoni is placed against the background of the more familiar Western European languages, in which participles and present tense verbs are realized by morphologically distinct forms, as in the following English examples:

(2-11)   a. Daniela was writing stories.

             b. Daniela writes stories.

The fundamental question that I shall try to answer is how the duality of the Benoni should be represented. Answering this question presupposes the introduction of some common assumptions and definitions, a task that I take up later in this chapter. I then proceed to discuss the participial use of the Benoni. Having established that the Benoni is a participle, I turn to its present tense usage and attempt to explain how this verbal form can be *both* a participle and a tensed verb.

It suffices to compare the Benoni with the past and future conjugations of Hebrew, which do not have participial occurrences (they cannot, for example, be embedded under an auxiliary), to realize that a distinction needs to be made between participles and full verbs.

(2-12) a. *Daniela hayta   katva   sipurim.
        Daniela   be(PAST)-3FS   write(PAST)-3FS   stories
        'Daniela was writing / used to write stories.'

        b. *Daniela hayta   tixtov   sipurim.
        Daniela   be(PAST)-3FS   3FS-write(FUT)   stories
        'Daniela was writing / used to write stories.'

A widely held view takes a participle to be a verb that is unspecified for tense. Let us state this as follows: a participle is a verb that has all of its morphological and semantic features licensed below TP. Since an independent clause must contain a TP (see §1.2.1), it follows that participles cannot be the unique verb in an independent clause. A "full" verb is a tensed verb—that is, a verb endowed with a tense specification and associated through movement with T^0.

When occurring as the thematic verb in periphrastic constructions, participles are relegated to the lower part of the clause. Take the example of a Romance past participle construction, such as (2-13) (see, in particular, Belletti 1990, Kayne 1989).

(2-13) Marie est   entrée.
        Marie has   entered-FS
        'Marie came in.'

The domain accessible to movement of the past participle *entrée* is delimited by the arc in (2-14), which is the phrase marker assumed in this work (following Friedemann and Siloni 1993; see §1.2.1).

(2-14)

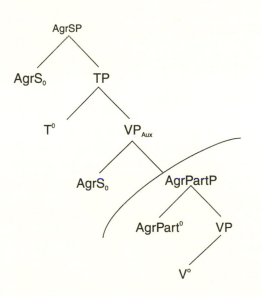

The participle in (2-14) can raise as high as AgrPart^0 (whether in the audible syntax or in LF, depending on the language). The auxiliary or higher verb is active in the upper domain of the clause, raising to T^0 and AgrS^0. Under standard assumptions, then, the observation that participles lack tense is explained by the interaction of morphology and syntax. A participle lacks morphological tense features and thus need not check this feature by moving to T^0. The features of T^0 are checked by the auxiliary, which is a morphologically *tensed* verb.

The inflectional paradigm of the Benoni is impoverished in comparison with the canonical verb forms of the past and future tenses; viz. (2-3). Let us call the agreement borne by the participle *participial agreement* corresponding to the bundle of φ-features which constitute the node AgrPart^0, located below TP in (2-14). Participial agreement is subject agreement: in a compound tense in Hebrew, the subject agrees twice, once with the participle and once with the auxiliary. This state of affairs reflects the presence of two subject agreement projections, AgrSP and AgrPartP.

Being intrinsically unassociated with tense features, participles are also found across languages as predicates in a variety of "small clauses," either as complements to certain verb classes such as perception verbs or as adjuncts on various levels of attachment. Sentence (2-15) draws examples from three relatively well-studied languages.[7]

(2-15)   a. J'ai vu Marie courant dans la rue.   French

b. Conosciuta Maria, Gianni e partito.   Italian

c. John entered the room chewing gum.   English

I take small clause complements to be clausal units of some size, lacking a TP. That is to say, [Marie courant dans la rue] in (2-15a) is minimally a VP and most probably includes some functional projections such as AgrPartP (see Cardinaletti and Guasti 1991). It does not, however, include a TP projection. I assume that a similar structure should be assigned to adjunct small clauses and gerundive clauses of various sorts.

2.3   THE BENONI AS A PARTICIPLE

Three typical occurrences of the Benoni as a participle are illustrated in (2-16). In (2-16a) it occurs embedded under an auxiliary in a periphrastic past tense construction; in (2-16b) it occurs as the main verb in a small clause complement to a perception verb, and in (2-16c) it occurs as an adjunct gerund. I consider each of (2-16) in turn.

(2-16)   a. ha-yladim   hayu   tofrim   smalot.
            the children   be(PAST)-3MPL   sew(BENONI)-MPL   dresses
            'The children were sewing / used to sew dresses.'

b. ra?i-ti   ?et   ha-yladim   tofrim   smalot.
            see(PAST)-1S   ACC   the-children   sew(BENONI)-MPL   dresses
            'I saw the children sewing dresses.'

c. ha-yladim   yašvu   ba-xeder   loʕasim   mastik.
   the children   sit(PAST)-3PL   in-the-room   chew(BENONI)-MPL   gum
   'The children sat in the room chewing gum.'

2.3.1 The Benoni In Complex Tenses

The auxiliary in compound tenses serves to anchor the tense specification of the sentence. Alongside (2-16a), which is specified as past tense, we have (2-17), where the tense is future. The difference between the two lies in the form of the auxiliary: in (2-16a), we have a past, and in (2-17), a future tense form of the verb *be*. The participle has the same form in both.

(2-17) ha-yladim   yhyu   tofrim   smalot.
     the children   3MPL-be(FUT)-be   sew(BENONI)-MPL   dresses
     'The children will be sewing dresses.'

The claim that the participle lacks tense—embodied in the schema in (2-14)—is supported by the distribution of temporal adverbs. When the auxiliary is in the past tense, as in (2-18), only an adverb referring to the past tense is possible.

(2-18) a. ha-yladim   hayu   tofrim   smalot ʔetmol.
       the children   be(PAST)-3MPL   sew(BENONI)-MPL   dresses yesterday
       'The children were sewing dresses yesterday.'

       b. *ha-yladim   hayu   tofrim   smalot maxar/ʕaxšav.
        the children   be(PAST)-3MPL   sew(BENONI)-MPL   dresses tomorrow/now
        'The children were sewing dresses tomorrow/now.'

Let us say that the temporal reference of an adverb must be licensed by an appropriate specification of tense features on T^0 (I put aside the question of how this licensing is accomplished). The participle is dissociated from T^0; hence, it itself cannot license temporal adverbs.

Can one give a more precise characterization of the position of the participle in (2-16a) or (2-17)? Not only can adverbials appear clause-finally in compound tense constructions, as in (2-18), they may also occupy a position between the participle and the direct object, as in (2-19).

(2-19) ha-yladim   hayu   tofrim   b-idey-hem   smalot.
     the-children   be(PAST)-3MPL   sew(BENONI)-MPL   with-hands-3PL   dresses
     'The children were sewing dresses with their hands.'

The appearance of an adverbial element between the verb and the direct object indicates that the verb and the direct object are not sisters at S-structure, because if they were—as in (2-20a)—there would be no position for the adverb. Indeed, (2-19) can be taken as evidence in favor of a structure such as (2-20b), where the verb raises over the adverb to some higher position, yielding the word order verb>adverb>direct object. Following Friedemann and Siloni (1993), I take the landing site of the verb in (2-19) to be AgrPart^0. (This is essentially the line of argumentation used by Emonds (1978) and Pollock (1989) to diagnose verb movement in French.)

(2–20)   a.

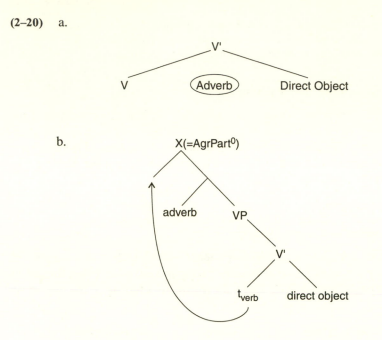

b.

Another standard diagnostic for verb movement uses the distribution of floating subject quantifiers (Sportiche 1988). The occurrence of the floating quantifier *kulam* in (2-21) indicates that the verb raises over the base position of the subject in VP.[8] I shall assume that the Benoni participle incorporates to AgrPart[0] in the overt syntax.[9]

(2-21) ha-yladim   hayu   tofrim   kul-am   smalot.
      the-children   be(PAST)-3MPL   sew(BENONI)-MPL   all-MPL   dresses
      'The children were all sewing dresses.'

2.3.1.1   *Negation in Compound Tenses*

In the clausal design assumed in this work, NegP is situated above TP and below AgrSP, as recapitulated in (2-22).

(2-22)

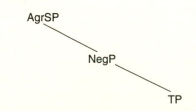

The immediate prediction of this assumption is that only auxiliaries may be negated, but not Benoni participles. This is only partially true, as we shall immediately see.

(2-23) illustrates the normal positioning of *lo*.

(2-23) ha-yladim   lo-   hayu   tofrim   smalot.
       the-children neg- be(PAST)-3MPL sew(BENONI)-MPL   dresses.
       'The children were not sewing dresses.'

The discussion in the preceding section entails the prediction that the negative head *lo* can only appear attached to the auxiliary, as in (2-23), and that it cannot be attached to the Benoni participle. (The auxiliary is contained in T^0. Recall that T^0 incorporates into Neg^0; cf. §1.3.3) The grammaticality of (2-24), where *lo* is attached to the participle, is hence surprising.

(2-24) ha-yladim   hayu   lo-   tofrim   smalot.
       the-children be(PAST)-3MPL neg- sew(BENONI)-MPL   dresses.
       'The children were not sewing dresses.'

We do not expect *lo* to appear lower than TP, yet in (2-24) it is attached to the participle. Does this mean that the participle has raised to $AgrS^0$?

The only licit reading of (2-24) is one in which *lo* is interpreted contrastively. Speakers who find (2-24) bizarre as it stands have no difficulty with (2-25), where the sentence occurs in a contrastive context.

(2-25) ha-yladim   hayu   lo-   tofrim   smalot, ʔela
       the-children be(PAST)-3MPL neg- sew(BENONI)-MPL   dresses, but

       yǝšenim.
       sleep(BENONI)-MPL
       'The children were not sewing dresses, but sleeping.'

I shall take *lo* in (2-24) to be a negative adverb of sorts, attached lower than TP. In (2-24) *lo* should thus be distinguished from the head of NegP, which can only be attached to the auxiliary.[10] As an adverbial, *lo* can also appear immediately to the left of the direct object, imposing here again a contrastive interpretation, as shown by (2-26).

(2-26) ha-yladim   hayu   tofrim   lo-   smalot, ʔela xulcot.
       the-children be(PAST)-3MPL sew(BENONI)-MPL   neg- dresses but   shirts
       'The children were sewing not dresses, but shirts.'

2.3.1.2 Subject-Verb Inversion in Compound Tenses

Under conditions elaborated upon in chapter 8, Hebrew verbs may precede their subjects. Sentence (2-27a) illustrates the unmarked order of the subject and the verb, and (2-27b) shows the "inverted" verb>subject order.

(2-27) a. ʔetmol   ha-yladim   tafru   smalot.
           yesterday   the-children sew(PAST)-3PL dresses
           'Yesterday, the children sewed dresses.'

       b. ʔetmol   tafru   ha-yladim   smalot.
           yesterday   sew(PAST)-3PL the-children   dresses
           'Yesterday, the children sewed dresses.'

Anticipating the discussion in chapter 8 and simplifying somewhat, assume that the inverted sentence—that is, (2-27b)—is derived by fronting the inflected verb into some position in the Comp domain, in a manner reminiscent of I to C movement in the Germanic verb-second languages.

In a sentence incorporating a participle and an auxiliary, only the latter can move to Comp, as shown by the contrast in (2-28). This contrast is expected if participle movement is restricted by the arc in (2-14). Note, moreover, that if the verb is in C^0 in inversion configurations and the participle is in AgrPart^0, then the subject cannot be in VP. I return to this matter later; see, in particular, §8.3.3.[11]

(2-28) a. ʔetmol   haya   Dani   tofer   smalot.
        yesterday be(PAST)-3MS Dani sew(BENONI)-MS dresses
        'Yesterday, Dani was sewing dresses.'

   b. *ʔetmol   haya   tofer   Dani   smalot.
        yesterday be(PAST)-3MS sew(BENONI)-MS Dani dresses
        'Yesterday, Dani was sewing dresses.'

2.3.2   The Benoni in Complement Small Clauses

Turning to the occurrence of the participial Benoni in other constructions, we shall see that the bundle of properties characteristic of the participial Benoni, (2-29), crops up again.

(2-29)   • No anchoring of temporal adverbs.

          • No clausal negation.

          • No subject inversion.

The pair of sentences in (2-30) shows that temporal adverbs are sensitive to the tense specification of the matrix verb. An adverb such as *yesterday* is thus possible when *see* is in the past tense, but not an adverb such as *tomorrow*. The Benoni predicate in (2-30) has no impact on temporal adverb selection.

(2-30) a. raʔiti   ʔet   ha-yladim   tofrim   smalot   ʔetmol.
        see(PAST)-1S ACC the-children sew(BENONI)-MPL dresses yesterday
        'I saw the children sewing dresses yesterday.'

   b. *raʔiti   ʔet   ha-yladim   tofrim   smalot   maxar.
        see(PAST)-1S ACC the-children sew(BENONI)-MPL dresses tomorrow
        'I saw the children sewing dresses tomorrow.'

Following Siloni (1994), let us assume that Benoni-headed small clause complements to perception verbs are embedded AgrPart phrases. Given the fact that an adverbial PP such as *b-idey-hem* 'with their hands' can appear between the verb and the direct object, as in (2-31), I am led to propose that a Benoni-headed small clause complement is derived as in (2-32): the Benoni raises to AgrPart^0 and the subject moves out of VP to Spec/AgrPart.

(2-31) raʔiti   ʔet   ha-yladim   tofrim   b-idey-hem   smalot.
       see(PAST)-1S   ACC   the-children sew(BENONI)-MPL   with-hands-3PL   dresses
       'I saw the children sewing dresses with their hands.'

(2–32)

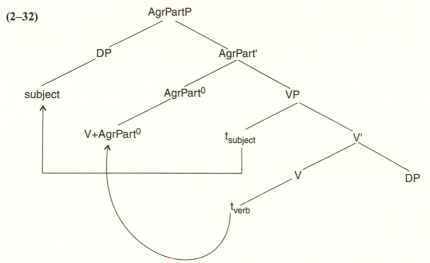

A clear consequence of this derivation is that subject inversion of the sort discussed in §2.3.1 should not be possible in complements to perception verbs. Since the small clause is an AgrPartP, it perforce lacks a CP projection into which the verb can raise over the subject (recall that CP⟺TP). More generally, the subject of a Benoni small clause appears in Spec/AgrPart, and there is simply no AgrPartP-internal position into which the participle may raise over the subject. The ungrammaticality of (2-33) is hence expected under this analysis.[12]

(2-33) *raʔiti   tofrim   ʔet   ha-yladim   smalot.
       see(PAST)-1S sew(BENONI)-MPL   ACC   the-children dresses
       'I saw the children sewing dresses.'

2.3.3   The Benoni in Adjunct Small Clauses

Consider now sentences such as (2-16c), repeated here as (2-34).

(2-34) ha-yladim   yašvu   ba-xeder   loʕasim   mastik.
       the children sit(PAST)-3PL   in-the-room   chew(BENONI)-MPL   gum
       'The children sat in the room chewing gum.'

The gerundive Benoni, like the Benoni complement to a perception verb discussed above, has no intrinsic tense specification. The choice of temporal adverb is determined by the matrix verb, as with the other occurrences of participles that we have seen.

(2-35) ʔetmol   ha-yladim   yašvu   ba-xeder   loʕasim   mastik.
       yesterday the-children   sit(PAST)-3PL   in-the-room   chew(BENONI)-MPL   gum
       'Yesterday, the children sat in the room chewing gum.'

I take (2-35) to indicate the absence of a TP projection and conclude that (2-34) has the same structure as a complement small clause, namely that of a 'bare' AgrPartP (but see note 14 for a possible alternative). Unlike the latter, however, it is not in complement, but in adjunct position.

The subject of a Benoni predicate of a small clause complement, as in (2-16b), is overt and assigned (accusative) Case by the matrix verb. There is no overt subject in the adjunct small clause in (2-34). What is the nature of the empty category in Spec/AgrPart? In chapter 7 we shall see that a referential pro cannot occur as the subject of the Benoni, since its person features cannot be identified by this inflectionally impoverished verbal form. Hence, the null subject in (2-34) is not pro.

Can it be PRO? Under the approach advocated in Chomsky (1981), PRO must occur in a nongoverned position. Suppose that PRO is in Spec/AgrPart in (2-34). Since the adjunct small clause contains neither a TP nor a CP, Spec/AgrPart is not a governed position. Moreover, the subject of the adjunct small clause is not accessible to government by a head external to the adjunct. Suppose, then, that the subject of (2-34) is PRO.

In the absence of a NegP projection inside the adjunct small clause, only adverbial and contrastive *lo* can appear, as in (2-36).

(2-36) ha-yladim   yašvu   ba-xeder   lo   loʕasim   mastik,
        the children sit(PAST)-3PL in-the-room   neg chew(BENONI)-MPL gum

        ʔela   makšivim   lə-morat-am.
        but   listen(BENONI)-MPL to-teacher-their
        'The children sat in the room not chewing gum, but listening to their
        teacher.'

2.3.4   The Benoni in Semirelatives

Semirelatives is the name given by Siloni to relative clauses of the sort illustrated in (2-37), see Siloni 1990, 1994, 1995.

(2-37) hine   ʔiš   ha- xošev   ʕal   kesef.
        here   man   the   think(BENONI)-MS about   money
        'Here is a man who thinks about money.'

This type of relative clause has a number of salient features:

- it can only be used to relativize the subject.
- the relative complementizer is homophonous with the definite determiner.
- the verb inside the relative clause must be a Benoni.

With respect to all three properties, semirelatives differ from the full relatives illustrated by (2-38); in which an object is relativized, the relative complementizer is *še* and the verb is in the past tense.

(2-38) hine   ha-ʔiš   še   Dan   raʔa.
        here   the-man   that Dan   see(PAST)-3MS
        'Here is the man that Dan saw.'

Siloni argues that the relative complementizer *ha-*, like the definite determiner, is a D^0 element and that the relative clause is hence a DP. The sister of D^0 is an

AgrPartP containing a participial Benoni verb. The structure and the analysis she proposes for (2-37) are diagrammed in (2-39).

(2-39)

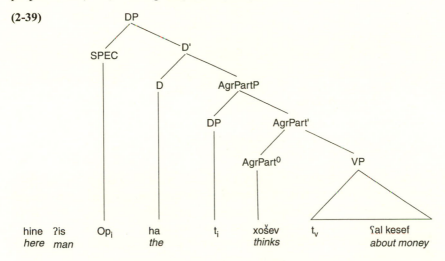

hine   ?is   Op$_i$ ha-   t$_i$ xošev   t$_v$ ʕal kesef
here   man   *the*   *thinks*   *about money*

The relative head is base-generated outside the DP relative clause. Assuming the standard analysis of full relative clauses, let us say that the relative clause is adjoined to it, the two forming a larger DP.

Being DPs, which embed an AgrPart projection, semirelatives lack a TP, and so the Benoni appears in the same reduced structure as in the constructions considered earlier. The absence of temporal adverbial modification, subject inversion, and negation, illustrated in (2-40), (2-41), and (2-42) respectively—in short, the bundle of properties characteristic of the participial Benoni—are predictably found in semirelatives, as Siloni shows.[13]

(2-40) a. ra?i-ti   ?iš   ha- xošev   ʕal   kesef   ?etmol.
       see(PAST)-1S man the think(BENONI)-MS about money yesterday
       'I saw a man who thinks about money yesterday.'

      b. *ra?i-ti   ?iš   ha- xošev   ʕal   kesef   maxar.
       see(PAST)-S man the think(BENONI)-MS about money tomorrow
       'I saw a man who thinks about money tomorrow.'

(2-41) *hine ha- xošev   ?iš   ʕal   kesef.
       here the think(BENONI)-MS man about money
       'Here is a man who thinks about money.'

(2-42) *hine ?iš   ha- lo   xošev   ʕal   kesef.
       here man the neg think(BENONI)-MS about money
       'Here is a man who doesn't think about money.'

2.3.5 The Benoni in Another Type of Negative Structure

For the sake of completeness, I mention another construction in which the Benoni occurs as a participle. Example (2-43) is a negative sentence characterized by the occurrence of the negative head *ʔeyn*, a close study of which is the subject matter of chapter 4. The important thing to note at this point is that only the participial Benoni can occur under *ʔeyn*; tensed verbs may not.

(2-43) a. ʔeyn ha-yladim   tofrim   smalot.
           neg   the-children   sew(BENONI)-MPL   dresses
           'The children do not sew/are not sewing dresses.'

        b. *ʔeyn ha-yladim   tafru   smalot.
           neg   the-children   sew(PAST)-3MPL   dresses
           'The children did not sew dresses.'

        c. *ʔeyn ha-yladim   yitfəru   smalot.
           neg   the-children   3MPL-sews(FUT)   dresses
           'The children will not sew dresses.'

Let us assume for now that the clausal chunk following *ʔeyn* is also an AgrPartP (this assumption will be revised). Tensed verbs must access the higher clausal projections in order to check their morphological features. In the absence of TP in *ʔeyn* negatives, tensed verbs simply cannot be licensed.

To conclude §2.3, we have seen a number of constructions that single out the Benoni as the only possibly occurring verb form. These are participial complements to auxiliaries in compound tenses, complement and adjunct small clauses, semi-relatives, and the *ʔeyn* negative construction.

The Benoni in these constructions is a participle—that is, it is a verbal form endowed with participial agreement features but lacking tense. The Benoni raises to AgrPart^0 in the syntax but can move no higher. Since independent clauses require that a TP be present, participial phrases containing the Benoni must be embedded in a larger structure containing a TP. TP, or more precisely, T^0, is associated with the auxiliary in compound tenses, and with the matrix verb in embedded small clauses and semirelatives. In *ʔeyn* negative sentences, matters are more complex and will be dealt with later, after I introduce some modifications in the analysis of the Benoni.

2.4 THE BENONI AS A PRESENT TENSE VERB

As we noted at the outset, the startling property of the Benoni is that, in addition to its participial use, it can also serve as the main, present tense verb, as in (2-44).

(2-44) Daniela   toferet   smalot.
         Daniela   sew(BENONI)-FS   dresses
         'Daniela sews / is sewing dresses.'

If the Benoni is a participle, it can only raise to the participial Agr head AgrPart^0. Yet (2-44) is a full clause, a CP, and not a small clause or an AgrPartP. Temporal adverbs anchored in the present tense can be accomodated in it and negation is noncontrastive:

(2-45) a. Daniela   toferet   ʕaxšav   smalot.
            Daniela   sew(BENONI)-FS   now   dresses
            'Daniela now sews / is now sewing dresses.'

  b. *Daniela toferet   ʔetmol smalot.
   Daniela sew(BENONI)-FS yesterday dresses
   'Daniela yesterday sews / is yesterday sewing dresses.'

(2-46) Daniela lo toferet   smalot.
   Daniela neg sew(BENONI)-FS dresses
   'Daniela is not sewing dresses.'

The contrast in (2-45) shows that only a present tense adverb is admitted, indicating that there is a TP in the clause, specified for present tense. The possibility of negating a present tense sentence shows that there is a NegP in the structure and therefore, by definition, a TP.

  If present-tense sentences are full clauses, and if the Benoni is a participle, how are the projections located above the arc in example (2-14) licensed? An indication of what is happening here can be gleaned from an observation of the auxiliary system of Hebrew.

2.4.1 The Auxiliary 'Be' and the Benoni

The verb *be* in Hebrew is defective with respect to all other verbs in the language, in that it lacks a present tense form. Consider the distribution of copular *be*, illustrated in (2-47), and note the absence of a present tense form in (2-47c).

(2-47) a. ʔani hayiti   šamen.   hu haya   šamen.
     I be(PAST)-1S fat   *he be(PAST)-3MS fat*
     'I was fat.'   'He was fat.'

    b. ʔani ʔehye   šamen.   hu y-hye   šamen.
     I 1S(FUT)-be fat   *he 3MS(FUT)-be fat*
     'I will be fat.'   33M'He will be fat.'

    c. ʔani šamen.   hu šamen.
     I fat   *he fat*
     'I am fat.'   'He is fat.'

  Following Berman (1978), I shall take *be* in (2-47c) to be defective morphologically, but perfectly regular from a syntactic point of view. Updating her rule of Copula Deletion, suppose that the present tense of the verb *be* is phonetically unexpressed, but syntactically represented. Take this form to be generated with tense, marked present. Example (2-47c) is thus to be represented as in (2-48), where Ø stands for the phonetically unrealized 'be-PRES-1S'; but see Steele et al. 1981:83–97 for arguments against the notion of a null copula in Egyptian Arabic.

(2-48) ʔani Ø   šamen.
   I be-PRES-1S fat
   'I am fat.'

  Recall the examples of compound tense structures formed with *be* and a Benoni verb and discussed at some length in §2.3.1. Now suppose that Benoni present tense sentences are formed in exactly the same way—that is, they contain a participial Benoni and a phonetically unrealized present tense *be*. Example (2-44) can be represented as (2-49).

(2-49) Daniela Ø   toferet   smalot.
         Daniela be-PRES-3FS sew(BENONI)-FS dresses
         'Daniela sews / is sewing dresses.'

I continue to assume that the Benoni form itself lacks a tense morpheme, hence it does not raise to T^0 to check its features. Yet T^0 has features of its own that must be checked, and this is where the auxiliary comes into the picture. *Be*, whether null or overt, is a fully inflected verb endowed with T (and, I assume, AgrS) features; hence, it must raise to T^0 and $AgrS^0$.

The resolution of the paradox of the Benoni consists, therefore, in arguing that present tense sentences should be analyzed on a par with compound tenses. In both, the Benoni verb is a participle and an auxiliary is present in the structure. There are both analytic and synthetic past and future tense structures in Hebrew. The language disposes of both a "simple" and a "complex" or periphrastic structure for these two tenses. The present tense, however, can only be syntactically expressed through the complex construction, there being no "simple" present in Hebrew.

It is useful at this point to return to the various constructions examined in relation to the participial Benoni. It will be demonstrated that all of them possess variants in which a null auxiliary is activated, suggesting that there is a systematic ambiguity as to whether the Benoni is the only verb in the clause, or whether it is preceded by an auxiliary.

Adjunct small clauses and semirelatives have been argued to possess a reduced clausal structure, AgrPartP. The same claim was made with respect to ʔeyn-negatives, though no arguments to that effect were given. We have shown that only a Benoni verb can appear in these constructions, because the Benoni is the only verbal form that does not require access to TP. We now show that the Benoni can also occur in clausal adjuncts, in full relative clauses, and in the company of clausal negation. In these structures, the Benoni is still a participle, but given that these constructions involve the full clausal projection, I argue that a null auxiliary must be posited.

2.4.2 Clausal Adjuncts and Participial (Small Clause) Adjuncts

Example (2-34), repeated here as (2-50a), differs structurally from the almost synonymous (2-50b).

(2-50) a. ha-yladim   yašvu   ba-xeder   loʕasim   mastik.
            the children sit(PAST)-3PL in-the-room chew(BENONI)-MPL gum
            'The children sat in the room chewing gum.'

         b. ha-yladim   yašvu   ba-xeder   k-še   hem   loʕasim
            the children sit(PAST)-PL in-the-room while-that they chew(BENONI)-MPL
              mastik.
              gum
            'The children sat in the room while chewing gum.'

Sentence (2-50b) is characterized by the occurrence of the string *k-še* on the left margin of the adjunct phrase. This item is composed of a prepositional component, *k-*, followed by the finite complementizer *še*.

Most if not all adjunct clauses in Hebrew overtly manifest a complementizer, (2-51).

(2-51) lifney-še   ?axarey-še   mipney-še   biglal-še   lamrot-še
           before-that   *after-that*   *due (to)-that* *because-that* *despite-that*

The occurrence of the complementizer *še* signals the presence of a CP, and the presence of a preposition suggests that CP is embedded under a PP. We can take the structure of the adjunct clause containing *k-še* to be as in (2-52).

(2-52)

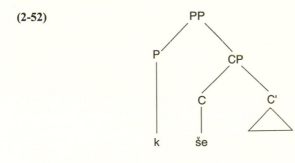

Since C requires T, the clause following the complementizer cannot be a "bare" AgrPartP but must be minimally a TP. The presence of a TP with a Benoni verb implies the generation of an auxiliary, for the reasons discussed earlier.[14]

The subject of the gerund clause in (2-50b) cannot be null, as opposed to the subject of (2-50a) which must be null. Contrast (2-50b) with (2-53).

(2-53) *ha-yladim   yašvu   ba-xeder   k-še   lo\`asim   mastik.
           the children sit(PAST)-3PL in-the-room   while that chew(BENONI)-MPL gum
           'The children sat in the room chewing gum.'

The null subject in the participial or small clause adjunct in (2-50a) is an instance of PRO, licensed, as we have seen, since the adjunct is an AgrPartP and PRO is not governed in Spec/AgrPart. PRO is ruled out in (2-50b) because it would be the subject of a full clause, containing a CP and a TP with the feature [+ present]. Pro, on the other hand, can occur in neither (2-50a) nor the tensed (2-50b). For pro to be licensed, it must be identified by an Agr node explicitly manifesting person features (see chapter 7). While the null auxiliary, which hypothetically occurs in (2-50b), can be taken to bear person features, these features are not morphologically explicit, and hence cannot serve to identify a null subject. For these reasons, (2-53) is ungrammatical; the pronominal subject of an adjunct CP must be overt, as in (2-50b).

2.4.3 Relative Clauses

The Benoni appears in semirelative constructions (§2.3.4) In fact, it is the only verbal form that can appear in this type of relative clause, for, as Siloni (1994, 1995) convincingly shows, these relatives lack a TP projection and the relativizing D^0 selects an AgrPartP complement.

Yet the Benoni can also figure as the main verb in regular relative clauses, patterning like a past or future tense verb. In (2-54), the relative complementizer *še* takes a tensed IP complement.

(2-54) a. ha-xulca še   [IP Dani tafar] ...
            the-shirt that   Dani sew(PAST)-3MS
            'the shirt that Dani sewed ...'

        b. ha-xulca še   [IP Dani yitfor] ...
            the-shirt that   Dani 3MS-sew(FUT)
            'the shirt that Dani will sew ...'

        c. ha-xulca še   [IP Dani tofer] ...
            the-shirt that   Dani sew(BENONI)-MS
            'the shirt that Dani sews / is sewing ...'

Example (2-54c) can be analyzed as a full clause containing a Benoni verb and a null auxiliary. A more precise structural characterization of (2-54c) is thus (2-55).

(2-55) ha-xulca še   [IP Dani Ø   [AgrPartP ... tofer ...]]
        the-shirt that   Dani be(PRES)-3MS   sew(BENONI)-MS
        'the shirt that Dani sews / is sewing ...'

2.4.4   *lo* Negation in Present Tense Sentences

Finally, Benoni present tense sentences can be negated by *lo*, as in (2-56). In other words, they must be taken to contain a NegP projection.

(2-56) Daniela lo   toferet   smalot.
        Daniela neg   sew(BENONI)-FS   dresses
        'Daniela doesn't sew dresses.'

Moreover, *lo* morphologically subcategorizes for T^0, in the manner discussed in §1.3.3 and again in §5.3.1. The slot in its subcategorization frame can be filled by T^0—that is, by the complex containing the null auxiliary and T^0.

2.5 CONCLUSION

The explanation offered in this chapter for the dual behavior of the Benoni is based on two hypotheses: first, the verbal Benoni is a participle; secondly, Hebrew has a null auxiliary. The first hypothesis accounts for the presence of the Benoni in "reduced" structures, where tensed verbs cannot appear. The second hypothesis explains why the Benoni gives the appearance of functioning like a tensed verb in present tense sentences. The basic thrust of the analysis has been reductive: present tense senten-ces, I argued, are to be treated on a par with compound tense constructions.

The next chapter opens with a presentation of some serious difficulties for this analysis. It is shown that the Benoni must be raised higher than what one would expect from a pure participle.

THREE

Participles and Auxiliaries

3.1 THE BENONI RAISES BEYOND AGRPARTP

There is robust evidence that the Benoni in present tense sentences may raise higher than AgrPart[0]. In particular, it can raise to Comp, appearing to the left of the clausal subject.

3.1.1 Subject Inversion in Present Tense Sentences

Consider the pair in (3-1).

(3-1) a. ʕaxšav Daniela toferet   smalot.
        now   Daniela sew(BENONI)-FS dresses
        'Now, Daniela sews / is sewing dresses.'

     b. ʕaxšav toferet   Daniela smalot.
        now   sew(BENONI)-FS Daniela dresses
        'Now, Daniela sews / is sewing dresses.'

Example (3-1a) illustrates the unmarked order of the subject and the verb, and sentence (3-1b) illustrates the inverted order. Recall that we have taken subject inversion to be derived by moving the inflected verb to the Comp domain. Therefore, the Benoni verb in (3-1b) must be in Comp. Yet if the Benoni is a participle, it cannot raise to Comp.

Under the analysis of present tense sentences as involving a phonetically null auxiliary, we expect inversion to be possible, in the sense that the auxiliary can be fronted to Comp over the subject, as in the past tense sentence in (3-2).

(3-2) bə-cʕirut-a   hayta   Daniela yocet ləvalot   lə-ʕitim krovot
      in-youth-3FS be(PAST)-FS Daniela go   out(BENONI)-FS to-have a good time
      'When she was young, Daniela used to go out often.'

43

The order of the Benoni verb and the subject remains, however, unaltered in (3-2). The analysis sketched here cannot account for (3-1b). Indeed, (3-1b) shows that Benoni itself is in Comp.

3.1.2   Inversion in Relative Clauses

The order of the subject and the verb can be optionally permuted in full relative clauses. This type of inversion is also induced by movement of the verb to C. The Benoni patterns with the tensed verbal forms, as shown in (3-3). Again, this shows that the Benoni must be able to raise beyond AgrPartP.

(3-3) a. ha-xulca še   tafar   Dani ...
           the-shirt   that   sew(PAST)-3MS   Dani
           'the shirt that Dani sewed ...'

       b. ha-xulca še   yi-tfor   Dani ...
           the-shirt   that   3MS-sew(FUT)   Dani
           'the shirt that Dani will sew ...'

       c. ha-xulca še   tofer   Dani ...
           the-shirt   that   sew(BENONI)-MS   Dani
           'the shirt that Dani sews / is sewing ...'

3.1.3   Copula Inversion (CI)

We turn finally to what is perhaps the most startling piece of evidence that the Benoni may raise beyond AgrPartP. As Borer (1995) shows, a participle may invert over the auxiliary, appearing to its immediate left. Example (3-4a) shows the canonical order Aux > Participle, and example (3-4b) shows the inverted order.

(3-4) a. Dani   haya   tofer   smalot.
           Dani   be(PAST)-3MS   sew(BENONI)-MS   dresses
           'Dani was sewing dresses.'

       b. Dani   tofer   haya   smalot.
           Dani   sew(BENONI)-MS   be(PAST)-3MS   dresses
           'Dani was sewing dresses.'

Borer argues that the participle incorporates to the auxiliary, forming an inseparable unit with it.[1] That incorporation is indeed involved in (3-4b) is evidenced by (3-5) and (3-6). In (3-5a) an adverb may intervene between the auxiliary and the participle when the order is auxiliary > participle, but as (3-5b) shows, the adverb may not intervene when the order is participle > auxiliary.

(3-5) a. Dan   haya   <u>tamid</u>   tofer   smalot.
           Dan   be(PAST)-3MS   <u>always</u>   sew(BENONI)-MS   dresses
           'Dan was always sewing dresses.'

       b. *Dan   tofer   <u>tamid</u>   haya   smalot.
           Dan   sew(BENONI)-MS   <u>always</u>   be(PAST)-3MS   dresses
           'Dan was always sewing dresses.'

Similarly, a parenthetical expression such as *lə-daʕati* 'in my opinion' can appear between the auxiliary and the participle when they are in that order, but not when the order is reversed.

(3-6) a. Dan   haya   lə-daʕat-i   tofer   smalot.
        Dan   be(PAST)-3MS   in opinion-1S   sew(BENONI)-MS   dresses
        'Dan, in my opinion, was sewing / used to sew dresses.'

     b. *Dan tofer   lə-daʕat-i   haya   smalot.
        Dan   sew(BENONI)-MS   in opinion-1S   be(PAST)-3MS   dresses
        'Dan, in my opinion, was sewing / used to sew dresses.'

When raising to Comp, the cluster formed by CI must raise as a unit. Example (3-7a) illustrates the position of the subject in an inversion configuration in which CI has not applied and the auxiliary raises to Comp on its own; see also the discussion surrounding examples (2-28). Examples (3-7b,c) illustrate CI. Note that the clausal subject must appear to the right of the entire verbal complex, as in (3-7b), suggesting that the complex formed by CI raises over it. Example (3-7c) shows that the participle cannot be raised alone to Comp, stranding the auxiliary in a lower position.

(3-7) a. bə-yaldut-o   haya   Dani   tofer   smalot.
        in-youth-his   be(PAST)-3MS   Dani   sew(BENONI)-MS   dresses
        'In his youth, Dani was sewing / used to sew dresses.'

     b. bə-yaldut-o   tofer   haya   Dani   smalot.
        in-youth-his   sew(BENONI)-MS   be(PAST)-3MS   Dani   dresses
        'In his youth, Dani was sewing / used to sew dresses.'

     c. *bə-yaldut-o   tofer   Dani   haya   smalot.
        in-youth-his   sew(BENONI)-MS   Dani   be(PAST)-3MS   dresses
        'In his youth, Dani was sewing / used to sew dresses.'

The examples in (3-7) show that participle raising indeed constitutes a case of syntactic incorporation. Following the incorporation of the participle to the auxiliary, Move α treats the complex head as a single X^0 category. The ungrammaticality of (3-7c) further demonstrates that excorporation of a head from a complex formed by incorporation is not admissible.

The conclusion that CI involves incorporation raises a host of questions which I attempt to answer next, integrating an analysis of CI into a general theory of the Hebrew Benoni. At this point, however, it is sufficient to simply take CI to constitute robust evidence that the participle can raise beyond AgrPartP.

This section provided evidence that the Benoni can raise beyond AgrPartP, patterning, in this respect, like a tensed verb in the past or future tenses. The Benoni can raise to Comp in a variety of verb-fronting or inversion constructions, and it can be incorporated into the auxiliary. This evidence demonstrates that the analysis of the Benoni as a "pure" participle—that is, as a tenseless verb whose scope of movement is restricted to the lower reaches of the clause is insufficient.

The puzzle posed by the Benoni is that it can also occur as a "pure" participle, raising to AgrPart^0 and no further. Semirelatives, small clause complements and adjuncts, and *ʔeyn* negative clauses all share the property of admitting only Benoni verbs. In chapter 2, I argued that these constructions are characterized by a reduced structure, so that verbs which require access to the functional domain from TP upward simply cannot be morphologically licensed.

The key to the behavior of the verbal Benoni in both its guises is to be found, I believe, in a better understanding of CI. CI provides clear evidence that the Benoni raises, since it places the Benoni linearly to the left of the auxiliary.

Let us therefore make a further move: assume that CI may apply not only when the auxiliary *be* is overt, but also when it is phonetically null. The conclusion this move draws us to is that a Benoni present tense sentence is structurally ambiguous: both (3-8a) with CI and (3-8b) without it are legitimate representations (but see the discussion at the end of the following subsection where this claim is modified).

(3-8) a. Daniela [$_{Aux}$tofer et   +Ø]   smalot.
            Daniela   sew(BENONI)-FS +be-PRES-1S dresses
            'Daniela sews / is sewing dresses.'

       b. Daniela Ø   tofer et   smalot.
          Daniela   be-PRES-1S sew(BENONI)-FS dresses
          'Daniela sews / is sewing dresses.'

If CI may apply in present tense sentences, we have an explanation for why the Benoni, albeit a participle, nevertheless appears in positions which only tensed verbs can access. The Hebrew Benoni is able to raise beyond AgrPartP, by piggybacking, as it were, on the auxiliary.

3.2 WEAK AUXILIARIES AND RAISED PARTICIPLES

What triggers CI? In order to answer this question, we must first expand our empirical base. The first thing to observe is that the auxiliary loses stress when it incorporates the participle. This can be interpreted to mean that the auxiliary loses stress *as a consequence of* CI. It can also be interpreted the other way around, namely, that CI applies *because* the auxiliary is unstressed. Let us pursue the latter path and claim that the unstressed auxiliary is a clitic of sorts, an enclitic on the participle. The lack of stress is characteristic of morphologically dependent or clitic forms. There are then two types of auxiliaries in Hebrew: independent, freestanding formatives or strong forms, and dependent, clitic, or weak forms (see chapter 10 for a refinement of the distinction between *weak* and *clitic* forms).

Clitics, by definition, require hosts. CI is the process by which the participle becomes the host or provides the lexical support for the weak auxiliary. An immediate consequence follows: CI is not an optional process. It obligatorily applies when the weak auxiliary is selected from the Lexicon. What is optional is lexical choice: there are both weak and strong auxiliaries and either one can be chosen.[2]

While we can now suggest a reason that the auxiliary can support an incorporated participle, we still need to explain why the participle itself raises and incorporates to Aux. The idea that a participle is somehow connected to Aux or, more precisely, to the functional domain of the clause, has been expressed by a number of authors in a number of ways.

Gueron and Hoekstra (1988, 1992) argue that participles and (certain) auxiliaries form a tense chain by which they mean that the auxiliaries either "combine with the T morpheme of their complement to form a complex tense morpheme" or "assign a T(ense)-role to their VP complement" (1988: 48).

Grimshaw (1991) argues that functional heads such as T^0 do not *select* their complements, but are licensed as part of an *extended projection* of a lexical head. IP is an extended projection of V, DP an extended projection of N, and so on. A participle in a compound tense construction can be taken to be the root of a projection extending up to I^0. Members of an extended projection, Grimshaw argues, are *transparent* in that they permit the flow of information from the root node all the way up.

Although these proposals are rather different, they share a common core— namely, they attempt to formalize and cast in theoretical terms an observable dependency between participles, auxiliaries, tense, and agreement that standard X-bar theory or theta theory fail to capture.

I would like to tentatively propose a variant of these approaches, incorporating Move α as the basic formal device. Let us first draw the broad strokes of the analysis, refining it in the ensuing paragraphs.

Assume that the Benoni participle is optionally endowed with some feature or features in the Lexicon—call them [F] for now—and that [F] requires head–head checking with T^0. A participle bearing [F] must thus raise and incorporate with T^0. Movement of the participle (or more precisely, movement of the AgrPart complex containing the participle) to T^0 across an auxiliary constitutes a flagrant violation of the ECP, in particular, of the constraint on the locality of head movement (Head Movement constraint or Relativized Minimality). This is shown in (3-9).[3]

(3-9)

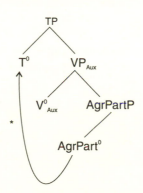

When the participle adjoins to the auxiliary, however, and the two raise to T^0 as a single head, no ECP violation is produced, as shown in (3-10).

(3-10)

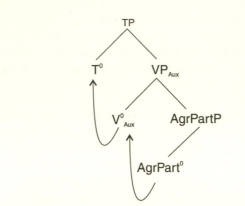

In this way of seeing things, the participle has no intrinsic need to raise to Aux. At the same time, it must raise to check [F] in T^0. The presence of a weak auxiliary requiring a host before PF conspires with the participle's need to raise to T^0, giving rise to the phenomenon of CI.

I have argued that in present tense sentences, the Benoni can incorporate into the null present tense auxiliary and the two raise to T^0 as a single complex head (see the examples in [3-8] and the surrounding discussion). In fact, it is not unreasonable to suppose that the present tense auxiliary invariably triggers CI. As far as overt auxiliaries are concerned, there is a choice between a weak and a strong form. No such choice exists when the auxiliary is null. I shall assume that in such circumstances the default form is always selected, the default form being the weak auxiliary.[4] If this conclusion is valid, it follows that, in present tense sentences, participle-raising always occurs in the overt syntax, and that of the two representations given in (3-8), only (3-8a) is valid.

What is [F]? In order to answer this question, let us momentarily digress and examine more closely the class of categories that undergo CI.

3.3   CI WITH NON-VERBAL PREDICATES AND THE NATURE OF [F]

The facts are as follows: all verbal Benoni forms can, in principle, undergo CI. As (3-11) and (3-12) show, PP predicates and nominal predicates cannot.[5]

(3-11) a. Dani   haya   ʕal   ha-gag.   b. *Dani ʕal ha-gag   haya.
            Dani be(PAST)-3MS on   the-roof   *Dani   on the-roof be(PAST)-3MS*
            'Dani was on the roof.'   'Dani was on the roof.'

(3-12) a. Dani   haya   more.   b. *Dani more   haya.
            Dani be(PAST)-3MS teacher-MS   *Dani   teacher-MS be(PAST)-3MS*
            'Dani was a teacher.'   'Dani was a teacher.'

We can explain this split in one of two ways. First, it can be claimed that the fundamental difference between verbal and nonverbal predicates is that only the former are associated with the agreement head, which we have labeled AgrPartP.

Let us assume that AgrPartP is a verb-related projection. Then, if CI requires a verbal or verb-related host, the ungrammaticality of (3-11b) and (3-12b) follows on basically morphological grounds—namely, the absence of a suitable host for the clitic auxiliary.[6] (How agreement between the nominal predicate and the subject is checked remains an issue, though.)

Taking the angle of the participle, we can claim that only verbal predicates are endowed with [F], that is, only participles and not nominal or prepositional predicates can raise to T^0. The ungrammaticality of examples such as (3-11b) and (3-12b), seen from this perspective, is due to the fact that these predicates have no intrinsic need to raise to T^0 and consequently cannot undergo CI.

Under this latter approach, [F] is a feature of Benoni participles, but not of nouns or prepositions. A possibility that comes to mind is that [F] is a bundle of aspectual features. Stativity or dynamicity are properties of verbs (and also of adjectives, see later in this chapter), but not of nouns or prepositions. The aspectual properties or *event types* proposed in Dowty (1979), such as *stative, accomplishment, protracted, momentaneous*, and so on, are all tense-related. Aspectual distinctions such as *continuous* or *habitual* are always interpreted relative to a particular tense. As Pustejovsky puts it, "While temporal relationships are important for constructing larger level representations of narratives or texts, aspect looks at the finer details of the temporal landscape inside each event" (1988: 20).

Let us suggest that this linkage or interdependence of tense and aspect is expressed grammatically through incorporation. Suppose that aspectual information is coded in morphological features that are represented on a functional head, Asp^0, which I assume lies between AgrPartP and VP (cf., e.g., Belletti 1990 and Ouhalla 1990, among many others). Aspectual features on a verb are then checked through incorporation to Asp^0. Asp^0, however, also has tense features and must enter into a head–head checking configuration with T^0.

AspP is not projected in clauses whose predicate is nonverbal. This assumption rests on the idea that aspect is not a feature of prepositions or nouns. The ungrammaticality of (3-11b) and (3-12b) can thus be explained in the following terms. In the absence of an aspectual projection in these sentences, there is no motivation for predicate raising to T^0 and hence no CI.

It is suggestive to relate the hypothesis that nominal and prepositional predicates are not associated with an AgrPart projection with the idea that these predicates are unassociated with an aspectual one. A rather trivial way of doing this is to simply equate AgrPartP with AspP. While this would achieve the desired result, there is little independent justification for this move. A more principled approach consists in claiming that AgrPartP is the agreement projection associated with AspP. Agreement projections are always layered above either lexical projections or functional projections in which features of lexical heads are checked. This idea is elaborated in chapter 9 and the appendix where it is argued that, for example, AgrSP is the agreement projection associated with TP, AgrOP with VP, and so on. If this generalization is valid, then AgrPartP can be construed as precisely the agreement projection associated with AspP.

Example (3-13) incorporates these assumptions in an illustration of the derivation of CI with a Benoni verb.[7]

(3-13)

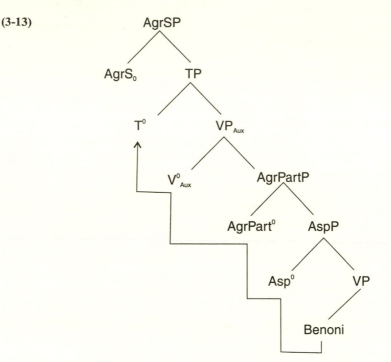

Borer (1995) notes that CI is available not only when the predicate is a Benoni participle, but also when it is an adjective, as in (3-14) (recall note 1).

(3-14)　a. ha-teʕun　　šel-o　　barur　　haya　　　lə-kul-am.
　　　　　the-argument　of-3MS　clear-MS　be(PAST)-3MS　to-all-3PL
　　　　　'His argument was clear to everyone.'

　　　　b. ha-ʕuga　munaxat　hay-ta　　　ʕal　ha-šulxan.
　　　　　the-cake　lying-FS　be(PAST)-FS　on　the-table
　　　　　'The cake was lying on the table.'

Like verbs, adjectives are endowed with aspectual properties; hence, clauses with adjectival predicates harbor an aspectual projection. If AspP requires an agreement projection to be layered above it, then adjectival predicates are also associated with AgrPartP. Incorporation of an adjective to Aux is thus accounted for in the same way as CI with Benoni participles.

　　　The case of adjectives is actually more complex. While certain adjectives, like *barur* 'clear' *ʕayef* 'tired,' *muxan* 'ready', and *ʔafuy* 'baked' readily undergo CI, others such as *cahov* 'yellow,' *gavoha* 'tall', *šamen* 'fat', or *xaxam* 'wise' do not. The adjectives that resist CI are permanent-state or *individual-level* predicates, in Carlson's (1977) terms. They denote temporally invariable properties or states. We might therefore think of such adjectival predicates as lacking tense features. If such adjectives do not raise to T^0, it follows that they do not undergo CI.

While the distinction between stage- and individual-level predicates is discussed at greater length in chapter 5, §5.2, it is worth noting at this point that CI with individual-level adjectives becomes increasingly more acceptable as the interpretation of the adjectives moves away from that of a permanent state and toward an episodic one.[8] The pairs that follow are illustrative of this tendency. In (3-15a) and (3-16a), the adjectives refer to inherent properties and cannot undergo CI. In the (b) examples, they refer to noninherent or stage level properties and CI is acceptable.

(3-15)   a. *ha-ʕec   cahov   haya.
       the-tree   yellow   be(PAST)-3MS
       'The tree was yellow.'

   b. Dani   cahov   haya   mi-kaʕas.
       Dani   yellow   be(PAST)-3MS   from-anger
       'Dani was yellow with anger.' (Tal Siloni, personal communication)

(3-16)   a. *Dani   xaxam   haya.
       Dani   smart   be(PAST)-3MS
       'Dani was smart.'

   b. Dani   xaxam   haya   rak lə-ʔaxar maʕase.
       Dani   smart   be(PAST)-3MS   only after fact
       'Dani was smart only after the fact.'

The adjectives that do not undergo CI cannot raise to Comp in interrogatives, for example, as shown in (3-17)–(3-19). The (a) examples illustrate question formation without inversion. The (b) examples illustrate the inverted counterparts, all of which are ungrammatical. The existence of a correlation between movement to Comp and CI (i.e., $\neg$CI $\Rightarrow\neg$ movement to Comp) further supports the view that Benoni predicates raise to Comp via CI, as argued earlier.

(3-17)   a. matai Dani   ʕal ha-gag?   b. *matai ʕal ha-gag   Dani?
       when Dani   on-the-roof   *when   on the-roof Dani*
       'When is Dani on the roof?'   'When is Dani on the roof?'

(3-18)   a. ʔeifo   Dani   more?   b. *ʔeifo   more   Dani?
       where   Dani   teacher   *where   teacher   Dani*
       'Where is Dani a teacher?'   'Where is Dani a teacher?'

(3-19)   a. lama Dani   xaxam?   b. *lama xaxam Dani?
       why Dani   smart   *why   smart   Dani*
       'Why is Dani smart?'   'Why is Dani smart?'

I have argued that the optionality of CI is rooted in lexical choice. CI only applies when a weak auxiliary is selected from the Lexicon. I have also hypothesized that the participle, or more precisely, Asp^0, is intrinsically attracted to T^0. This implies that participles in compound tense constructions always raise to T^0. Suppose this implication is valid and that participle raising to T^0 is postponed until LF unless it must apply in the overt syntax. It must apply in the overt syntax when the auxiliary selected is a clitic or null.

In the language of Checking theory, matters can be stated in the following terms. The head features of T^0 are strong and must be checked in the overt syntax by a verbal head. When the strong form of the auxiliary appears in the structure, it moves to T^0 in the overt syntax, checking the features of T^0. Asp^0 (which contains the Benoni) then moves to T^0 in LF. In the presence of a clitic auxiliary, two independent conditions must be satisfied: Aux must have a host, and T^0 must be licensed. The Benoni incorporates to the auxiliary to satisfy the first requirement, and the auxiliary moves to T^0 to meet the second. Asp^0 is thus transported to T^0 as part of the Aux^0 complex. Put succinctly, participle raising in LF is the default case; earlier raising applies only as a side effect of CI.[9]

To summarize a bit before proceeding, I have shown that the Benoni can occur both in structures lacking a TP (i.e., small clauses of various sorts) and as the main verb in present tense sentences in which a TP is present. I first argued that in both of its occurrences, the Benoni raises only within a limited domain: it accesses $AgrPart^0$ but moves no higher. When the Benoni occurs as the only verb in present tense sentences, it is preceded by a phonetically null auxiliary, so that, syntactically speaking, present tense sentences are also compound tense constructions.

The claim that the Benoni never raises beyond $AgrPart^0$ was then challenged. I provided a number of empirical arguments, showing that when occurring in both a compound tense structure and in present tense sentences, the Benoni raises into the higher functional domain, and I argued that participle raising is driven by the need to associate or check aspectual features in T^0. I also suggested that AgrPartP is the AspP-associated Agr projection. If the clausal chunks occurring in semirelatives, complement, and adjunct small clauses are AgrPart projections, it follows that they, too, contain an aspectual phrase. Now, if Asp^0 must be associated with T^0, then participle raising also occurs in these structures, contrary to our earlier arguments. There is, however, no overt evidence for such a process. This is not surprising, given the fact that participle raising is overt only when it must be.

I would therefore like to suggest that participle raising occurs not only in auxiliary-participle constructions but also in small clauses. In particular, it should be taken to apply (in LF) even where the Benoni seems to function as a "pure" participle. The consequences of this idea are explored in the following section.[10]

3.4   CI IN A CROSS-LINGUISTIC PERSPECTIVE

Incorporation of the participle to the auxiliary is found in Polish, as Borsley and Rivero (1994) argue. The auxiliary *(e)ś* is a clitic, they claim, and either incorporates the participle, giving rise to the order participle>auxiliary, as in (3-20a), or appears in a variety of positions to its left. In (3-20b), *(e)ś* appears to the immediate right of the subject.

(3-20)   a. Ty   widział   -eś   tę   ksiązkę.
          you   see(PAST) PARTICIPLE AUX-2S   this   book
          'You saw / have seen this book.'

b. Ty -ś widział   tę ksiązkę.
   you AUX-2S see(PAST) PARTICIPLE this book
   'You saw / have seen this book.'

The process of participle incorporation illustrated in (3-20a) is clearly very similar to Hebrew CI. Although Borsley and Rivero do not discuss why the participle incorporates to the auxiliary and why this process is optional, it is not inconceivable that the line of argument which I have used to motivate CI in Hebrew carries over to Polish.

Polish differs from Hebrew, however, in that *(e)ś* is always a clitic form, while the Hebrew auxiliary can be weak or strong. If *(e)ś* is inherently a clitic, we expect CI to be obligatory. This is not the case. Example (3-20b) shows that as an alternative to incorporating the participle, the auxiliary can itself be moved, occurring as a (phonetic) clitic (in a variety of positions; [3-20b] illustrates only one option). This can be explained on the basis of two assumptions. First, participle raising is only effected in the overt syntax when necessary; otherwise it is postponed to LF. Second, the Polish auxiliary has other means to satisfy its need for a host (which, I should add, the Hebrew auxiliary does not). The Polish facts demonstrate, in a rather clear fashion, that CI and participle raising to T^0 are distinct processes, which may, but do not have to conspire together.[11] If the analogy with Polish is valid, we see that CI or, in more precise terms, participle raising to T^0, is not a language-specific process. It is hence not a priori implausible to suppose that it is an endowment of UG. All the language learner has to know is that aspectual categories must incorporate to T^0. Hebrew and Polish provide evidence for overt syntactic movement, since they are endowed with clitic auxiliaries which permit—indeed, require—syntactic CI. In languages that lack an overt indication for participle raising, movement is delayed to LF.

Participle raising to T^0 suggests a strong affinity with a process Rizzi (1982) termed *Restructuring*. Restructuring is a phenomenon in which an embedded infinitival clause is merged with the matrix clause. As a consequence, processes and dependencies that are normally restricted to a single clause can, where the matrix predicate belongs to the class of restructuring verbs, take place across clausal boundaries. Example (3-21) illustrates three consequences of restructuring in Standard Italian.

(3-21) a. Gianni lo vuole fare.
           Gianni it wants to do
           'Gianni wants to do it.'

        b. Pierro è voluto   venire.
           Pierro is want(PAST) PARTICIPLE to come
           'Pierro wanted to come.'

        c. Le nuove case   si cominceranno a   costruire.
           the new   houses SI will-start   to build
           'The new houses will start to be built.'

In (3-21a), we see that the clitic *lo* has climbed or raised to adjoin to the matrix verb. Example (3-21b) shows that the auxiliary associated with the matrix predicate is *essere*, which is the auxiliary selected by the lower verb *venire*, and example (3-21c) illustrates NP movement across a clausal boundary (long passivization).

Only when the matrix predicate belongs to the class of restructuring verbs (essentially modals and aspectuals) are such clause-union effects permitted. Example (3-22) shows that when the matrix verb is, for example, *pensare*, the clitic cannot climb and must remain within the embedded clause. Similar examples can be constructed to show that auxiliary selection and long passivization are only possible if the matrix verb is a restructuring verb.

(3-22) a. Gianni pensa di farlo.   b. *Gianni lo pensa di fare.
          Gianni thinks to do-it   *Gianni it thinks to do*
          'Gianni thinks of doing it.'   'Gianni thinks of doing it.'

Intuitively, the sort of clause union produced by restructuring or more precisely, the relationship between the matrix restructuring predicate and the embedded infinitive is quite similar to the relationship between an auxiliary and a participle (in both, clitics raise to attach to the higher verb, long NP movement occurs from the object of the lower verb to the subject position of the higher verb, and so on). Of course, we do not usually think of compound tense constructions as biclausal.[12]

In a recent study of restructuring, Roberts argues that restructuring verbs trigger the raising of T^0 from the lower clause to the T^0 position in the higher clause: "T-raising makes positions in the higher clause accessible to local operations in the lower clause by making them 'equidistant' in the sense of Chomsky (1993)" (1994: 1-2). Roberts goes further and argues that the crucial property of restructuring predicates is that they fail to assign a role to their complement. He proposes that the complement can be licensed by T-raising. Matters of execution aside, this is quite similar to what arguably occurs in auxiliary-participle constructions. The difference, as Roberts notes, is that auxiliaries never assign a role to their (AgrPartP) complement, while restructuring verbs may choose not to do so.[13]

3.5   BENONI-RAISING: A SECOND LOOK

The analysis of the Benoni developed in the preceding sections engenders a redundancy. Let us see why. I have argued in favor of the hypothesis that present tense sentences contain a null auxiliary. I then showed that the Benoni verb, a participle, moves to the higher reaches of the clause, and I argued that movement of the Benoni in the audible syntax is implemented via CI—that is to say, the participle first adjoins to the null auxiliary, and since the auxiliary itself must raise, both raise as a unit, giving the appearance that the participle has raised independently. A closer look at CI yielded the hypothesis that the participial Benoni is endowed with aspectual features and that raising is driven by the need to associate these features with tense.

Now, if the Benoni must always raise to T^0, why can't it do this directly without first undergoing CI? Put in a more radical fashion, why do we need to posit the null auxiliary at all?

Two facts are hardly contestable. The participial Benoni can occur underneath an (overt) auxiliary, and it may undergo CI. Generalizing CI to present tense sentences and relating the absence of an overt auxiliary to a gap in the morphological paradigm of *be* is both a plausible and an attractive move to make. Yet, I would like to maintain that the redundancy spelled out here reflects a true option in the grammar of Hebrew. In what follows, I shall discuss this option in abstract terms. The empirical evidence supporting this analysis will be discussed in detail in chapter 4, where *ʔeyn* negative sentences are introduced. As we shall see, *ʔeyn* sentences provide two crucial pieces of evidence: namely, that the participial Benoni raises to T^0, and that it does so directly without the intervention of the auxiliary.

3.6   THE "BARE" BENONI PRESENT TENSE

In chapter 1, I set forth my assumptions regarding clause structure and hypothesized that the hierarchy of functional projections, basically CP > AgrSP > (NegP) > TP is invariant cross-linguistically. I also assumed that independent or full clauses must by definition contain a TP projection, and since TP is selected by CP, a full clause must be a CP. Clauses lacking a TP are, to adapt familiar terminology, "small clauses" and cannot occur, for example, as root sentences.

AgrSP, on the other hand, like all Agr projections, is arguably not selected: AgrPs are not part of what one might call *universal core structure*. I have argued that AgrSP is projected to serve the checking of morphological features. Another way to put this is to say that, while AgrPs may be freely generated, they must be licensed by having their head features checked. If their features cannot be checked, clauses containing them cannot be properly interpreted at the phonetic interface level.

In clauses containing a past or future tense verb, AgrSP is projected and its head enters into a checking relationship with the verb and the clausal subject. In this respect, the three auxiliaries in Hebrew—past, future, and the (null) present tense—function like lexical verbs and require the projection of AgrSP. (Recall that the null present tense auxiliary is assumed to possess not only abstract tense features, but also abstract AgrS features.) The Benoni, however, lacks AgrS features; its own agreement features are *participial* in the sense that they are checked in $AgrPart^0$. If an AgrSP is present in the structure, then the Benoni, even if it can raise to T^0, cannot continue up to $AgrS^0$. When a null auxiliary is present in the structure, the auxiliary checks the features of $AgrS^0$.

We can now provide an answer to the problem stated at the outset of this section. The question was whether the presence of a null auxiliary was really necessary in present tense sentences if the Benoni can raise to T^0 on its own. The answer is that the Benoni can indeed raise to T^0, and from this angle the auxiliary is redundant, but because the Benoni lacks AgrS features, the auxiliary must still be generated to check the features of $AgrS^0$.

This, however, is not the last word on the matter. If Agr projections are not part of universal core structure, why must AgrSP appear at all? If AgrSP were simply not projected, the Benoni would be able to check all the relevant features of the functional heads in the clause. In other words, an example conforming to (3-23) would be well-formed.

(3-23)

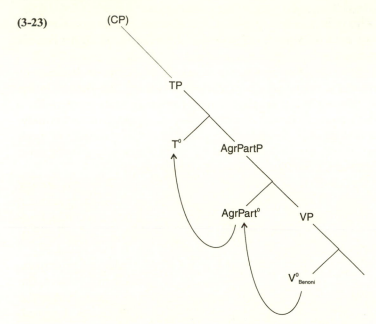

Figure (3-23) contains a CP and a TP and there are no heads with unchecked features. Whether clauses of this type are actually found is an empirical matter to which we attend in the next chapter.

Assuming for now that (3-23) is a viable option, we are led to conclude that Hebrew present tense sentences can be either TPs lacking an AgrSP projection or AgrSPs. If the latter option is taken—that is, if an AgrSP is generated—an auxiliary must also be present in the structure. Once an auxiliary is generated, the only way a participle can raise to T^0 is via CI . If the option of not generating an AgrSP is taken, the auxiliary cannot appear, and the sentence contains only a Benoni. Verbs in the past or future tense do not enjoy this freedom. Being lexically specified for both tense and AgrS features, AgrSP must be projected and they must raise to it. To conclude, we now see that the redundancy that characterizes this system is, in fact, theoretically motivated: it reflects the option or choice of projecting or failing to project AgrSP.

3.7 SUMMARY AND CONCLUSIONS

The subject matter of this and the preceding chapters in part I is the dual function of the Benoni, as a participle and a tensed verb. The final conclusion reached is that the Benoni is, in a sense, a hybrid form, a verb whose agreement features are participial but which raises to T^0.

I took a rather roundabout route to arrive at this conclusion. It was first shown that the Benoni occurs both as a participle in a variety of small clause constructions and as a main verb encoding present tense. The first move I took to relate the two occurrences of the Benoni was to argue that Hebrew makes use of a phonetically null auxiliary. This was a reductive move: present tense sentences, under this analysis, are to be treated as compound tense constructions in which the Benoni figures as a participle.

It was then shown that, while participles in small clauses give no evidence of ever raising beyond the participial agreement head $AgrPart^0$, the Benoni in the present tense can raise to the highest clausal heads patterning, in this respect like a fully tensed verb. I argued that in such cases the Benoni incorporates to the auxiliary, making use of a strategy of participle raising, CI, visible when an overt, but weak auxiliary is used. It was further argued that CI always occurs in present tense sentences because the null auxiliary is an incorporation trigger.

A question was raised as to why CI occurs in the first place, and my answer consisted of two parts. CI applies because the auxiliary is a clitic form requiring a host, and the participle raises because Asp^0—incorporated into the participial form —must raise to T^0. I argued that when CI does not occur, namely when the auxiliary is not a clitic, the participle nevertheless must raise to T^0 and it does so in LF.

This conclusion called for a rather major revision of the theory of participles. If the conclusion is valid not just for Hebrew but can be generalized, it leads to the view that participles are not verbs whose scope of movement is restricted to the "lower part of the clause." All verbs and certain adjectival predicates, I argued, move to T^0. An affinity with Romance restructuring was noted, but a development of a theory of verb movement uniting the two was not seriously undertaken.

There are two differences between a Benoni verb and a past/future tense one. First, a past/future tense verb must raise all the way up in the syntactic component. It must have access to the high functional domain and cannot appear in small clauses. A Benoni verb may raise only up to $AgrPart^0$, accessing T^0 only in LF (unless CI applies). The second difference is that past/future tense verbs must raise to $AgrS^0$, which then means that AgrSP must be projected in the clause. Benoni verbs need only access T^0, and unless an auxiliary is present in the structure, AgrSP is not and cannot be projected. Benoni present tense sentences lacking an auxiliary were argued to contain no AgrSP layer.

Let us finally consider, in abstract terms, the sort of empirical evidence that would support the analysis of clauses containing the Benoni as structurally deficient—that is, as lacking the AgrSP layer. In order to determine empirically whether a verb is in T^0 or in $AgrS^0$, we must find a way of sharply demarcating these two positions. Under familiar circumstances, this is extremely hard to do, since a typical tensed verb that raises to T^0 also raises to $AgrS^0$. What we need is to introduce a wedge, an obstacle preventing a verb in T^0 from moving to $AgrS^0$. Once such an obstacle is found, one could determine with greater precision the position occupied by a verb. The *ʔeyn* negative sentences come equipped with precisely such an obstacle.

FOUR

Negation in the Present Tense

4.1 INTRODUCTION

This chapter serves two purposes at once. First, it constitutes a study of a particular brand of negative sentences, illustrated in (4-1), where the negative particle is IP-initial and the verb is in the Benoni form.

(4-1) ?eyn Ruti yodaʕat ?et ha-tšuva.
      neg Ruti know(BENONI)-FS ACC the-answer
      'Ruti does not know the answer.'

Second, it attempts to extend and enrich the discussion of the Benoni and provide additional evidence for my claim that the Benoni verb raises to T^0 but cannot, unless incorporated into the auxiliary, raise any higher.

We shall see that *?eyn* negative sentences permit a scrutiny of Hebrew clausal syntax in a way that a declarative clause does not. The study of *?eyn* puts us in a position to draw more general consequences regarding the architectural design of the Hebrew clause structure, the hierarchy of functional projections, the scope of verb movement, and the position of subjects.

4.2 PROPERTIES OF *?EYN*

The string following *?eyn* is identical to the affirmative analogue of (4-1), namely, (4-2): familiar by now, it is a present tense sentence with a Benoni verb. Pre-theoretically, (4-1) simply looks like (4-2) to which a negative particle is appended.

(4-2) Ruti yodaʕat ?et ha-tšuva.
      Ruti know(BENONI)-FS ACC the-answer
      'Ruti knows the answer.'

There are several other facts that an account of *?eyn* sentences must grapple with. I present them below.

Clausal negation by means of *?eyn* is restricted to clauses whose main predicate is either a Benoni verb, as in (4-1), or nonverbal, as in (4-3). Since the syntax of *?eyn* sentences bears on the syntax of sentences with a Benoni verb, I shall concentrate on examples such as (4-1), postponing discussion of *?eyn* in clauses with nonverbal predicates to §5.2.[1]

(4-3) ?eyn   xatulim   ba-gina.
      neg   *cats*   *in-the-garden*
      'There are no cats in the garden.'

Under no circumstances can past tense and future tense verbs occur in the company of *?eyn*, as shown in (4-4).

(4-4) a. *?eyn   Ruti   tafra   smalot.
         neg   *Ruti*   *sew(PAST)-3FS*   *dresses*
         'Ruti did not sew dresses.'

      b. *?eyn   Ruti   titfor   smalot.
         neg   *Ruti*   *3FS-sew(FUT)*   *dresses.*
         'Ruti will not sew dresses.'

Example (4-5) is a variant of (4-1). The clausal subject appears to the left of *?eyn*, and *?eyn* agrees with it.

(4-5) Ruti   ?eyn-a   yodaʕat   ?et   ha-tšuva.
      Ruti   *neg-3FS*   *know(BENONI)-FS*   *ACC*   *the-answer*
      'Ruti does not know the answer.'

The agreement paradigm of *?eyn*, consisting purely of suffixes, is tabulated in (4-6).

(4-6) Agreement Paradigm of *?eyn*

	Singular	Plural
1	-(ən)i	-enu
2m	-xa	-xem
2f	-ex	-xen
3m	-o	-am
3f	-a	-an

Thus, *?eyn* can be lacking in any manifestation of agreement, in which case the subject follows it, as in (4-1). Alternatively, *?eyn* can bear agreement and the subject precedes it, as in (4-5). The two other conceivable options—agreement in an *?eyn*-initial clause and a bare, agreementless *?eyn* in a subject-initial one—are both excluded.[2]

(4-7) a. *?eyn-a   Ruti   yodaʕat   ?et   ha-tšuva.
         neg-3FS   *Ruti*   *know(BENONI)-FS*   *ACC*   *the-answer*
         'Ruti does not know the answer.'

b. *Ruti ʔeyn yodaʕat   ʔet   ha-tšuva.
   Ruti   neg   know(BENONI)-FS   ACC   the-answer
   'Ruti does not know the answer.'

4.3   *ʔEYN AS A NEG⁰*

The accumulated research into the syntax of negation is by now rather substantial. Much of this research has converged on the view that negation is represented on the sentence level by means of a labeled XP, NegP, containing a head Neg^0 and a specifier, as discussed in §1.3.3 and diagrammed in (4-8). Neg^0 dominates lexical items such as French *ne* and Italian *non*, while Spec/Neg contains such elements as English *not*, French *pas*, and negative operators and adverbs such as English *never*.

(4-8)

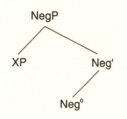

The are firm grounds to believe that *ʔeyn* is a negative head, that is, a Neg^0 element, and not the (XP) specifier of NegP. The sentence in (4-5) demonstrates that *ʔeyn* can manifest an agreement affix, patterning in this respect like an X^0 and not like an XP, since the capacity to bear agreement affixes is a property of heads and not of maximal projections. (The pattern in Semitic is that nouns, verbs, prepositions, certain adverbs, and complementizers can manifest agreement. This matter is attended to in chapter 9.)

In chapter 1, I discussed another diagnostic for the X-bar status of a negative morpheme, namely, whether or not it can cooccur with a negative adverb. I argued that, in a language in which negative concord is manifested, the presence of such cooccurence restrictions means that the negative marker is an XP, a specifier of NegP. The restriction on its cooccurrence with negative adverbs follows from the fact that NegP has a single Spec position. I showed that Hebrew *lo* is, under these assumptions, an X^0 and not an XP.[3]

This diagnostic places Hebrew *ʔeyn* firmly in the family of negative heads, since its cooccurrence with a negative adverb yields a perfectly grammatical output, as in (4-9).

(4-9) *ʔaf paʕam ʔeyn Ruti yodaʕat   ʔet   ha-tšuva.*
          never   neg   Ruti   know(BENONI)-FS   ACC   the-answer.
          'Ruti never knows the answer.'

A negative head and a negative adverb can cooccur in the same clause, because both occupy distinct positions. Two negative heads, however, cannot occur in the same clause because they would compete for the same position.

While both *?eyn* and *lo* can be used to negate present tense sentences, they cannot appear together in the same sentence. Example (4-10) is acceptable with either *lo* or *?eyn*, but is unaccepatble when both appear (I illustrate this point with the agreeing *?eyn* so that both negative formatives appear between the subject and the verb.)[4]

(4-10) *Ruti lo   ?eyn-a   yodaʕat   ?et   ha-tšuva.
        Ruti   neg   neg-3FS   know(BENONI)-FS   ACC   the-answer

I argued that *lo* is a clitic head, much like French *ne* or Italian *non*. Its mode of cliticization is somewhat different than that of, say, Italian *non*, but as I showed in §1.3.3, the two are incorporated into the verbal chain so that, representationally, the cliticization of *lo* and *non* is identical.[5]

4.4 THE POSITION OF NEGP IN THE CLAUSAL HIERARCHY

The comparison of (4-1) and (4-5) leads to a characterization of the relative position of NegP in the clausal hierarchy. In particular, it shows that NegP is situated below AgrSP and above TP.

4.4.1 *?eyn* and AgrsP

Notice that in a sentence such as (4-5), the subject agrees twice: once with the verb, and once with *?eyn*. I have argued that agreement with the Benoni is realized or checked in a Spec-head configuration in AgrPartP. The double agreement mainfested in (4-5) should be viewed on analogy with the pattern of agreement in periphrastic constructions containing an auxiliary and a participle. Thus, compare (4-5) with (4-11).

(4-11) Ruti   hayta   toferet   smalot.
        Ruti   be(PAST)-3FS   sew(BENONI)-FS   dresses
        'Ruti was sewing / used to sew dresses.'

I have argued that subject agreement between the subject and the auxiliary is a manifestation of a Spec-head relation established in AgrSP, while agreement with the Benoni is effected in AgrPartP. Let us conjecture that (4-5) is similarly analyzed. Suppose that *?eyn*, i.e., Neg^0 undergoes head movement to AgrS^0 and adjoins to its left, thus giving rise to the pattern of enclisis observed in *?eyn* agreement.

The subject, under this view, is in Spec/AgrS in (4-5). (Spec/Neg is not a subject position, since it is the position where negative adverbs and operators appear (see Rizzi 1991 and Haegeman and Zanuttini 1991.) I take the relevant structure of (4-5) to be as in (4-12): *?eyn* moves from Neg^0 to AgrS^0, and the clausal subject raises to Spec/AgrS.

(4-12)

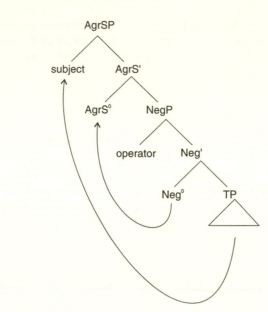

Let us now consider the ungrammaticality of (4-7). Example (4-7a) is ruled out because the subject must raise to Spec/AgrS. There are various ways to express this requirement. For now, assume that it follows from the stipulation that the nominal features of $AgrS^0$ are strong, and thus in need of early checking in Chomsky's (1993) sense.[6] The unacceptability of (4-7b) could presumably follow from a strict interpretation of the principles of derivational economy. If there is no reason for the subject to raise to Spec/AgrS when *ʔeyn* contains no agreement features (or raise in the overt syntax if *ʔeyn* contains weak features), then it is barred from doing so. I would like to maintain, however, that when *ʔeyn* does not manifest an agreement affix, it literally lacks it, as opposed to having abstract or weak features. The interpretation of the facts in this manner yields a number of what I think are interesting consequences.

One consequence is that when *ʔeyn* is bare, that is, when it does not agree with the subject, Neg^0 does not raise to $AgrS^0$ because AgrS is simply not present. A stronger consequence, however, can be derived. If the order of constituents manifested by (4-5)—namely, subject > *ʔeyn* + agreement > Benoni—indicates that IP = AgrSP, then word order in (4-1) shows that IP ≠ AgrSP. I suggest that, in the absence of agreement morphology on *ʔeyn*, the AgrSP layer is simply unprojected, and therefore IP = NegP. The ungrammaticality of (4-7b) follows from this suggestion since, in the absence of the AgrSP layer, there is no subject position to the left of *ʔeyn*.

A subject can occur to the left of *ʔeyn* only when it is left-dislocated, that is, base-generated in a left-peripheral position, and resumed by a pronoun. Example (4-13) should be contrasted with (4-7b).

(4-13)   Ruti   ʔeyn   hi   yodaʕat   ʔet   ha-tšuva.
        Ruti   neg   she   know(BENONI)-FS   ACC   the-answer
        'Ruti, she does not know the answer.'

To reiterate, the structure of (4-1) (and [4-7b]) should be thought of as containing a NegP immediately dominated by CP, as in (4-14). AgrSP is unprojected in such sentences.

(4-14)

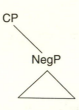

Chapter 2 argues that present tense sentences with a Benoni verb as in (4-2) are ambiguous between two structures. The first, diagrammed in (4-15a), contains a null auxiliary to which the Benoni is incorporated, and the two move up together to AgrS^0; for ease of exposition, I leave out AgrPartP and AspP (see §3.2). The second is what might be called the "bare" Benoni construction: AgrSP is not generated, there is no auxiliary in the structure, and the Benoni verb raises to T^0. This alternative is diagrammed in (4-15b).

(4-15) a.

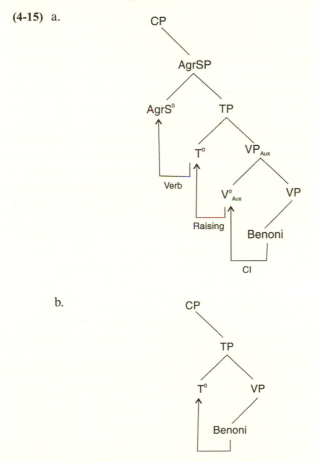

b.

ʔeyn sentences provide evidence that AgrSP need not be projected since they give rise to a word order alternation expressible in terms of the presence or absence of this clausal layer. Our discussion of *ʔeyn* allows us to draw the following conclusion:

(4-16)   The sequence subject > Benoni can occur in a clause lacking the AgrSP layer.

4.4.2   *ʔeyn* and TP

The clausal material embedded under *ʔeyn* is endowed with a (present) tense interpretation. Only adverbs rooted in the present tense may occur in an *ʔeyn* clause, as shown in (4-17). In this repsect, *ʔeyn* sentences are like present tense sentences that contain a TP.

(4-17)   a. ʔeyn   Daniela   toferet   ʕaxšav   smalot.
                      neg   Daniela   sew(BENONI)-FS   now   dresses
                      'Daniela doesn't sew / isn't sewing dresses now.'

   b. *ʔeyn   Daniela   toferet   ʔetmol   smalot.
                      neg   Daniela   sew(BENONI)-FS   yesterday   dresses
                      'Daniela didn't sew / wasn't sewing dresses yesterday.'

   I have argued that the Benoni raises to T^0. Word order considerations can allow us to confidently draw the conclusion that TP is lower than NegP, so that the hierarchy of projections in an *ʔeyn* sentence is as in (4-18).

(4-18)

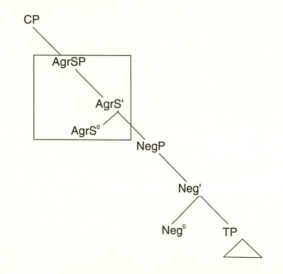

   The statement in (4-16) expresses the view that (4-15b) is a licit structure. In *ʔeyn* sentences, the Benoni is trapped, so to speak, under *ʔeyn* and can only move as high as T^0. Verb movement in agreement less *ʔeyn* sentences such as (4-1) is diagrammed in (4-19).

(4-19)

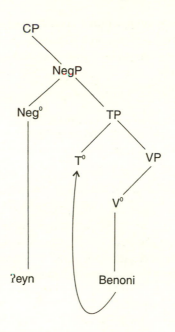

In an affirmative Benoni sentence, which conforms to (4-15b), CP immediately dominates TP. I have argued that topicalized and focalized constituents are positioned in the CP domain. In (4-20), the direct object is topicalized or focalized and moved to CP.[7]

(4-20) ?et ha-tšuva   Ruti yodaʕat.
ACC *the-answer   Ruti   know(BENONI)-FS*
'The answer, Rina knows.'

In *?eyn* sentences, NegP intervenes between CP and TP. Predictably, Topicalization/Focalization is not possible under *?eyn*, but only above it, as shown in (4-21).

(4-21) a. *?eyn ?et   ha-tšuva   Ruti yodaʕat.
   neg   ACC the-answer   Ruti   know(BENONI)-FS
   'The answer, Rina doesn't know.'

 b. ?et   ha-tšuva   ?eyn Ruti yodaʕat.
   ACC the-answer   neg   Ruti   know(BENONI)-FS
   'The answer, Rina doesn't know.'

4.5 *?EYN* AND VERB MOVEMENT

I have argued that AgrSP is not projected in "bare" *?eyn* sentences such as (4-1), and I suggested earlier that the generation of Agr projections is a function of morphology: they are projected only to serve as loci for feature checking. Let us consider some consequences.

First, note that *?eyn* is not a clitic. It does not appear attached to some other element in the surface string, but occurs as an independent freestanding morpheme, and need not be adjacent to the verb. In (4-1), the subject appears between *?eyn* and the verb, and (4-22) shows that a parenthetical expression can appear between the agreeing form of *?eyn* and the verb.

(4-22)   Ruti   ?eyn-a   lə-daʕat-i   yodaʕat   ?et   ha-tšuva.
          Ruti   neg-3FS   in-opinion-1S   know(BENONI)-FS   ACC   the-answer
          'Ruti doesn't, in my opinion, know the answer.'

Let us now bring the sentences in (4-4) back into the picture. Why is *?eyn* incompatible with the past and future tense verbal forms? A partial answer is the following. These verbal forms differ from the Benoni in that they are endowed with AgrS features. That is to say, they must access AgrS^0. If AgrSP is not projected, these features cannot be checked. The sentences in (4-4) are thus ruled out for the same reason as (4-7b): all require that AgrSP be present in the structure. In (4-7b) the IP-initial subject must be in a clause-initial argumental specifier position, absent when AgrSP is unprojected; in (4-4), the verbs must be in AgrS^0, which again is absent if AgrSP is not generated.

I have conjectured that when *?eyn* manifests no agreement suffix, there is no AgrS affix and AgrSP is not projected. Conversely, when *?eyn* does manifest agreement, AgrSP must be present in the structure and *?eyn* moves to AgrS^0. The ungrammaticality of the sentences in (4-23), which are simply the variants of (4-4), but with an agreeing *?eyn*, is due to the fact that when *?eyn* is in AgrS^0, the verb cannot raise there.

(4-23)   a. *Ruti   ?eyn-a   tafra   smalot.
              Ruti   neg-3FS   sew(PAST)-3FS   dresses
              'Ruti did not sew dresses.'

          b. *Ruti   ?eyn-a   titfor   smalot.
              Ruti   neg-3FS   3FS-sew(FUT)   dresses.
              'Ruti will not sew dresses.'

Example (4-24) shows that a past or future tense verb cannot move to AgrS^0 crossing over *?eyn*.

(4-24)   a. *Ruti   tafra   ?eyn   smalot.
              Ruti   sew(PAST)-3FS   neg   dresses
              'Ruti did not sew dresses.'

          b. *Ruti   titfor   ?eyn   smalot.
              Ruti   3FS-sew(FUT)   neg   dresses
              'Ruti will not sew dresses.'

The ungrammaticality of (4-24), taken together with that of the sentences in (4-4), shows that movement of the verb to AgrS^0, crossing over *?eyn*, is prohibited both at S-structure and in LF. Put differently, (4-4) and (4-24) show that a derivation such as the one diagrammed in (4-25) is illicit.

(4-25)

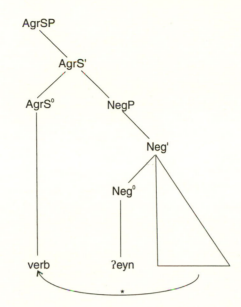

I would like to suggest that the ungrammaticality of the sentences in (4-4) and (4-24) is a direct consequence of the nonclitic status of *ʔeyn*, which creates an intervention effect for head movement to $AgrS^0$. Head movement over a Neg^0 filled by *ʔeyn* is ruled out by the ECP, under Relativized Minimality stated in (4-26), where α, in this case, is X^0.

(4-26)   Relativized Minimality
　　　　X α governs Y only if there is no Z such that
　　　　(i)　Z is a typical potential α-governor for Y,
　　　　(ii)　Z c-commands Y and does not c-command X.
　　　　　　　　　　　　　　　　　　(Rizzi 1990a:7)

Sentences in which the main predicate is a verb in the past or future tense contain AgrS features and must move to $AgrS^0$. *ʔeyn* blocks head movement to $AgrS^0$. The only head capable of moving to $AgrS^0$ without incurring a violation of the ECP is Neg^0—that is, *ʔeyn* itself. When the contents of $AgrS^0$ appear suffixed on *ʔeyn*, *ʔeyn* and only *ʔeyn* raises to $AgrS^0$. The sentences in (4-24) are unacceptable because the verbs cannot reach $AgrS^0$ without violating the ECP.

Another situation in which *ʔeyn* gives rise to a minimality effect for head movement is in interrogative clauses, where subject-verb inversion occurs. Examples (4-27a,b) are both acceptable variants. Assume, as before, that the verb is moved to C in (4-27b); the nature of this inversion process and questions related to the satisfaction of Rizzi's (1991) Wh-Criterion are discussed in chapter 8.

(4-27)　a.　ʔeize　tšuva　Ruti　yodaʕat?
　　　　　　which　answer　Ruti　know(BENONI)-FS
　　　　　　'Which answer does Ruti know?'

　　　　　b.　ʔeize　tšuva　yodaʕat　　　　Ruti?
　　　　　　which　answer　know(BENONI)-FS　Ruti
　　　　　　'Which answer does Ruti know?'

Recall that sentences such as (4-27b) are structurally ambiguous and may be analyzed either as involving a null auxiliary, to which the participle is incorporated, or as involving direct movement of the Benoni to T^0 and subsequently to C^0. When *ʔeyn* is present in the structure, however, inversion may not take place, since *ʔeyn* blocks head movement from T^0 to C^0, whether of the auxiliary complex or of the bare Benoni. Like the sentences in (4-4) and (4-24), sentence (4-28b) illustrates the workings of the head movement constraint. Only (4-28a) is acceptable, it being the uninverted variant where raising of the verb beyond T^0 does not take place.

(4-28) a. ʔeize   tšuva   ʔeyn   Ruti   yodaʕat?
        which   *answer*   *neg*   *Ruti*   *know(BENONI)-FS*
        'Which answer doesn't Ruti know?'

    b. *ʔeize   tšuva   yodaʕat   ʔeyn   Ruti?
        which   *answer*   *know(BENONI)-FS*   *neg*   *Ruti*
        'Which answer doesn't Ruti know?'

We have seen that *ʔeyn* in (4-1) demarcates the upper boundary of IP and is immediately dominated by CP (recall that AgrPs and AgrSP in the case at hand are not part of Universal Core Structure and need not be projected). Specifically, *ʔeyn* blocks verb movement to and above Neg^0 and the nonoccurrence of *ʔeyn* with verbs in the past or future tenses is explained. If the null auxiliary of the present tense must also access $AgrS^0$, it follows that *ʔeyn* sentences cannot contain an auxiliary. Putting this consequence together with (4-16), we can state (4-29):

(4-29)   The sequence subject > Benoni
     (i)   can occur in a clause lacking the AgrSP layer; and
     (ii) can occur in a clause without an auxiliary.

Given the demarcating or wedgelike property of *ʔeyn* and the fact that the order of constituents in an (agreementless) *ʔeyn* sentence is *ʔeyn* > subject > verb, we can utilize this construction to test the hypothesis that the Benoni is in T^0. If that hypothesis is valid, we are inevitably drawn to yet another consequence—namely, that the subject of an *ʔeyn* sentence is in Spec/T. I attend to these matters in the following sections after a brief note comparing *ʔeyn* and *lo*.

Alongside *ʔeyn*, which is not a clitic and hence a barrier for verb movement, Hebrew possesses a clitic negative head, the particle *lo*. Being a clitic, *lo* does not block head movement of the verb, and is hence compatible not only with Benoni verbs, but with verbs of all tenses, as well as with nonfinite ones. Although *lo* was discussed earlier, I repeat the relevant data so as to highlight the difference with *ʔeyn*. Consider (4-30).

(4-30) a. Dani   lo   yodeʕa   ʔet   ha-tšuva.
        Dani   *neg*   *know(BENONI)-MS*   *ACC*   *the-answer*
        'Dani doesn't know the answer.'

    b. Dani   lo   yadaʕ   ʔet   ha-tšuva.
        Dani   *neg*   *know(PAST)-3MS*   *ACC*   *the-answer*
        'Dani did not know the answer.'

    c. Dani   lo   yedaʕ   ʔet   ha-tšuva.
        Dani   *neg*   *3MS-know(FUT)*   *ACC*   *the-answer*
        'Dani will not know the answer.'

Unlike *ʔeyn*, *lo* is carried along with the verb when the latter raises over the subject to Comp. This is shown in (4-31).

(4-31) a. ʔeize tšuva Ruti lo yadʕa?
  which answer Ruti neg know(PAST)-3FS
  'Which answer didn't Ruti know?'

  b. Meʕolam lo taʕam Dani xacil kol kax bašel.[8]
  never neg taste(PAST)-3MS Dani eggplant so ripe
  'Never has Dani tasted such a ripe eggplant.'

4.6 THE SCOPE OF VERB MOVEMENT IN HEBREW

4.6.1 Benoni Movement

The claim to the effect that the Benoni is in T^0 at S-structure has been by and large rooted in theoretical considerations. In this section, I discuss certain adverb placement facts that provide independent empirical evidence for that claim.

The following contrast is quite robust: adverbs of the appropriate semantic classes may occur quite freely in a position between the subject and the verb in affirmative clauses in Hebrew, yet no adverb may intervene between a subject and a Benoni verb embedded under *ʔeyn*. This is strikingly evident in the contrast displayed in (4-32), where the morphological form of the verb is kept constant and the only difference is the presence or absence of *ʔeyn* (adverbs underlined).

(4-32) a. Ruti bə-derex klal yodaʕat ʔet ha-tšuva.
  Ruti usually know(BENONI)-FS ACC the-answer
  'Ruti usually knows the answer.'

  b. *ʔeyn Ruti bə-derex klal yodaʕat ʔet ha-tšuva.
  neg Ruti usually know(BENONI)-FS ACC the-answer
  'Ruti usually doesn't know the answer.'

There is, of course, no semantic reason for the contrast in (4-32), since the same adverb may appear in other positions in an *ʔeyn* sentence, for example, clause-initially, (4-33a), or clause-finally, (4-33b), as well as between the verb and the direct object, (4-33c).

(4-33) a. bə-derex klal ʔeyn Ruti yodaʕat ʔet ha-tšuva.
  usually neg Ruti know(BENONI)-FS ACC the-answer
  'Ruti usually does not know the answer.'

  b. ʔeyn Ruti yodaʕat ʔet ha-tšuva bə-derex klal.
  neg Ruti know(BENONI)-FS ACC the-answer usually
  'Ruti does not know the answer usually.'

  c. ʔeyn Ruti yodaʕat bə-derex klal ʔet ha-tšuva.
  neg Ruti know(BENONI)-FS usually ACC the-answer
  'Ruti does not usually know the answer.'

The contrast in (4-32) can be explained by making the rather plausible assumption that adverbs may not attach to X'. If the participle in an *ʔeyn* construction is in T^0 at S-structure and the subject occupies Spec/T, there is simply no room to position an adverb. This is diagrammed in (4-34).

(4-34)

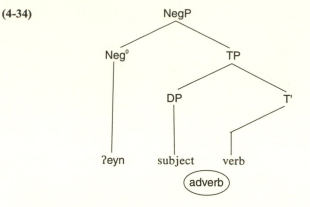

There remains, of course, the question of where adverbs are attached in affirmative sentences, for example, in (4-32a). This is a familiar problem in comparative syntax, since languages differ in the degree to which the order subject > adverb > verb is admissible. Whether one holds that adverbs are adjoined to maximal projections, or believes that adverbs project independent projections (see Cinque 1995 and Kayne 1994), some mechanism is needed to allow a maximal projection boundary to occur between the surface positions of the subject and the verb in some grammatical systems, but not in others. There are fundamentally two ways of achieving this: allowing the subject to raise above the adverb by a process of or akin to Topicalization (as proposed in Belletti 1990) or allowing the verb to remain lower than the head of the projection, the Spec of which is occupied by the subject. Both options yield a representation such as (4-35) where a maximal projection boundary intervenes between the subject and the verb.

(4-35)

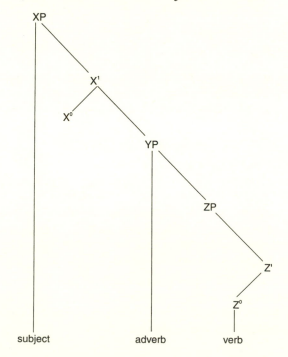

Raising the subject to a position higher than Spec/AgrS cannot be a priori ruled out. There are several options here: Topicalization of the subject is one, as is raising the subject to the Spec of a Mood Phrase containing a phonetically null mood marker (see Fassi-Fehri 1993 and Pollock 1993).

The contrast in (4-32) should be therefore interpreted to mean that, under *Peyn*, the subject and the verb are in the same maximal projection. I have argued that Topicalization requires the presence of a CP domain, unavailable under *Peyn*. A putative MoodP is arguably positioned above NegP so that it is not a candidate for hosting the subject (see Pollock 1993). Thus, the contrast in (4-32) argues strongly in favor of the idea that the verb occupies the head position of TP and the subject is in its specifier position.

4.6.2 Verb Movement in Hebrew: A Synoptic View

Finite verbs in Hebrew raise to $AgrS^0$ in the overt syntax, as the accumulated evidence seems to strongly suggest. That they raise out of VP is signaled by the fact that VP-adverbials can occur between the verb and the direct object (see §1.3.1). The claim that they raise beyond T^0 is evidenced by the incompatibility of *Peyn* with finite verbs.

Note, now, that *Peyn* cannot occur in the presence of a nonfinite verb, as shown in (4-36).

(4-36) *Dani metaxnen   Peyn la-ʕanot   la-telefon.
   Dani plan(BENONI)-MS neg to-answer to-the-telephone
   'Dani plans not to answer the telephone.'

I interpret the ungrammaticality of (4-36) to mean that nonfinite verbs pattern with finite ones in that they are endowed with AgrS features, forcing them to raise to $AgrS^0$. Belletti (1990) argues that Italian infinitives raise to $AgrS^0$ in the overt syntax, since they are invariably followed by negative adverbs, occupying Spec/Neg. She shows that in this respect Italian differs from French, where nonfinite verbs (with the exception of *être* and *avoir*) must follow negative adverbs (Pollock 1989). The relevant contrasts are illustrated in (4-37).

(4-37) a. Non parlare più arabe . . .   Italian

   b. *Ne parler plus l'arabe . . . French
    neg speak anymore Arabic . . .
    'To not speak Arabic anymore . . .

   c. *Non più parlare arabe . . .   Italian

   d. Ne plus parler l'arabe . . . French
    neg anymore speak Arabic . . .
    'To not speak Arabic anymore . . .

Even though neither Italian nor French infinitives are endowed with overt subject agreement features, the indication that they occupy different positions in the clause is provided by their position relative to NegP. A similar diagnostic is provided by *Peyn*. The absence of *Peyn* negation with infinitives in Hebrew shows that they are like Italian in raising all the way up to $AgrS^0$.[9]

We have seen that all Hebrew verbs raise into the inflectional domain in the syntax. Their scope of movement, however, is not uniform: past and future verbs raise to $AgrS^0$, but Benoni verbs raise only as high as T^0. The targets of verb movement in Hebrew are diagrammed in (4-38), summarizing the discussion of verb movement.

(4–38)	Target	Past and Future	Benoni	Nonfinite
	T^0	yes	yes	yes
	$AgrS^0$	yes	no	yes

4.7 SUBJECT POSITIONS

An issue I have not directly addressed until now concerns the position or positions of subjects in the Hebrew clause. It is useful to take up this discussion in the context of an analysis of *?eyn* sentences, because, as we have seen, *?eyn* serves as a wedge between AgrSP and TP, allowing a more precise examination of the positional options within the clause. Moreover, we shall see that the results of this section provide independent evidence that the Benoni occupies, at S-structure, the X^0 position immediately below Neg^0—that is, T^0.

Consider first an affirmative sentence with a Benoni verb, (4-39).

(4-39)	ha-yladim	tofrim	smalot.
	the-children	*sew(BENONI)-MPL*	*dresses*

'The children sew/are sewing dresses.'

If the subject in (4-39) is in Spec/AgrS, then it follows that (4-39) contains an AgrSP and by extension, a (phonetically null) auxiliary. If, on the other hand, (4-39) lacks an AgrSP projection, it follows that the subject is not in Spec/AgrS, and the question arises as to what position it actually occupies.

There are numerous arguments in the contemporary literature to the effect that Spec/AgrS is a *derived* subject position. Most researchers are in concord that subjects are base-generated internal to the VP in what I have called the *thematic domain* of the clause (cf. §1.2). Under what has come to be known as the *VP-Internal Subject Hypothesis*, the subject moves from its position in VP to Spec/AgrS to be assigned nominative Case.

Raising of the subject takes place overtly in languages in which a phonetically null expletive is not licensed (e.g., English, French) and covertly in Null-Subject languages such as Italian or Standard Arabic.

The VP-Internal Subject Hypothesis can be used to analyze the order verb > subject, exemplified in (4-40), as involving no actual movement of the subject. Rather, the subject remains in VP and the verb is raised to some inflectional head.[10]

(4-40)	Mangiava	Zayd.	Italian
	?akala	Zayd.	Standard Arabic
	ate	*Zayd*	

'Zayd ate.'

Reconsidering (4-39), we see that it is highly unlikely that the subject is in VP in that example, since it *precedes* the verb, and the verb, we know, has raised out of VP.

Some further evidence that the subject is not in VP is provided in (4-40), where a floating quantifier occurs between the verb and the direct object. Floating quantifiers mark subject traces and can thus be taken to designate positions from or through which the subject has moved.

(4-41)   ha-yladim   yodʕim   kul-am   ʔet   ha-tšuva.
         the-children   know(BENONI)-MPL   all-3MPL   ACC   the-answer
         'The children all know the answer.' Lit.: 'The children know all the answer.'

If the subject in (4-39) is neither in VP nor in AgrSP—when the latter is not projected—it follows that there must be an additional subject position in the clause. I have argued that the subject moves through Spec/AgrPart (where agreement with the Benoni is effected). However, since the Benoni verb itself is in T^0, it follows that when (4-39) does not include an auxiliary, the subject must be in Spec/T.[11] Subject-raising in, for example, (4-39) is diagrammed in (4-42).

(4-42)

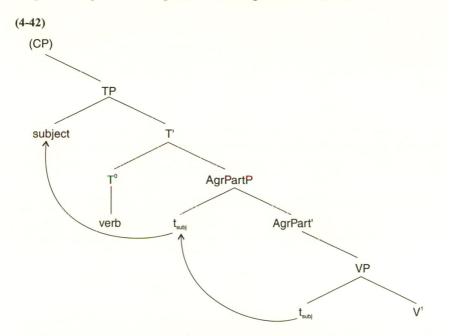

Confirming evidence to the effect that Spec/T is a licit subject position is provided by *ʔeyn* sentences such as (4-1), repeated here as (4-43).

(4-43)   ʔeyn Ruti   yodaʕat   ʔet   ha-tšuva.
         neg   Ruti   know(BENONI)-FS   ACC   the-answer
         'Ruti does not know the answer.'

To recall, (4-43) lacks an AgrSP layer: the verb in (4-43) is in T^0. The only possible position for a subject in (4-43) is therefore Spec/T, since it lies between *ʔeyn* and the verb. A plausible structure for (4-43) is (4-44).

(4-44)

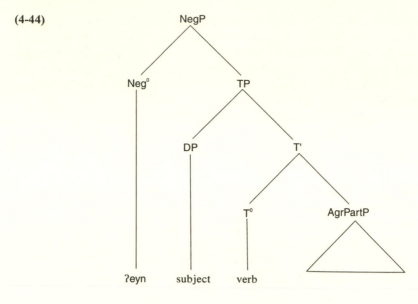

The subject checks the agreement features of the Benoni verb in Spec/AgrPart and nominative Case in Spec/T. The nominal feature checking configurations of (4-43) are more explicitly schematized in (4-45).

(4-45)

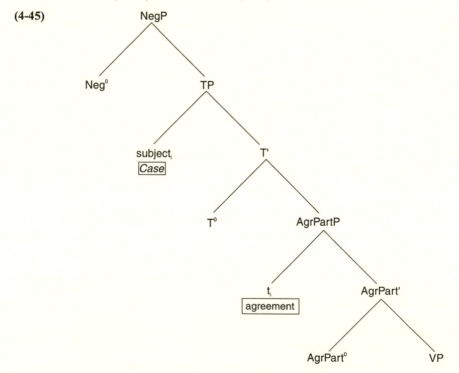

While the subject is in Spec/T in (4-43), I am led to conclude that it is in Spec/AgrS when *ʔeyn* bears agreement—that is, when AgrSP is projected. After all, this is what is shown by the contrast between (4-5) and (4-7a). Moreover, I would like to argue that in such sentences, the subject must move through Spec/T, as diagrammed in (4-46).

(4-46)

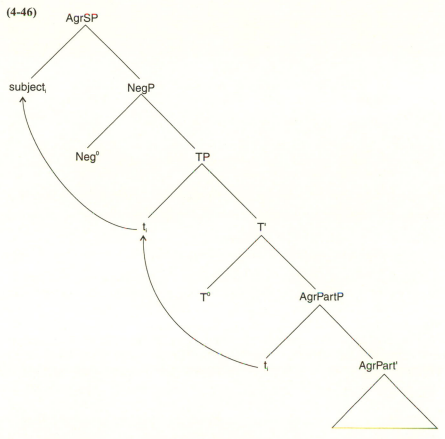

Chomsky (1993) argues that T^0 is incorporated into $AgrS^0$ (at least in English), so that nominative Case features and agreement features are both checked in a Spec-head configuration in AgrSP.[12] While this theoretical possibility cannot be ruled out for affirmative sentences, the barrier status of *ʔeyn* would prohibit T^0 raising to $AgrS^0$ (over Neg^0) in negative ones. In order for the subject to check both sets of features, it must move first to Spec/T to check Case and then to Spec/AgrS, where the nominal features of AgrS are checked.

To summarize: I have tried to show that subjects in Hebrew may occur in Spec/T, a Case position. Hebrew makes available two S-structure positions for the subject, namely Spec/T and Spec/AgrS. The latter is obligatorily targeted when AgrSP is projected. Hebrew subjects move to the highest available subject position in the clause. When AgrSP is not projected, the subject nevertheless raises out of VP and is licensed in Spec/T. The question of why Hebrew subjects cannot appear in VP is taken up in chapter 8. Further evidence that the subject in a sentence such as (4-1) is in Spec/T comes from a consideration of subject extraction in *ʔeyn* clauses, to which I now turn.

4.8   SUBJECTS UNDER *ʔEYN, THEIR TRACES AND THE COMPLEMENTIZER-TRACE EFFECT*

4.8.1   Overt Wh-movement under *ʔeyn*

Subjects embedded under *ʔeyn* cannot be wh-moved, as (4-47) clearly shows.

(4-47)   *mi   /ʔeize   student   ʔeyn   yodeʕa   ʔet   ha-tšuva?*
  who   /which   student   neg   know(BENONI)-MS   ACC   the-answer
  'Who/which student doesn't know the answer?'

In contrast, objects can be freely extracted over *ʔeyn*, as in (4-48).

(4-48)   ma   /ʔeize   tšuva   ʔeyn   Dani   yodeʕa?
  what   /which   answer   neg   Dani   know(BENONI)-MS
  'What/which answer doesn't Dani know?'

This asymmetry between subjects and objects is highly reminiscent of extraction over a filled complementizer in languages such as English.

(4-49)   a. *Who do you think that knows the answer?

        b. What/which answer do you think that John knows?

Rizzi (1990a) argues that (4-49a) is ruled out since the complementizer *that* is not a proper head governor for the subject trace. In this theory, certain heads are intrinsically capable of serving as head governors. These include all the lexical heads and the functional heads, Agr^0 and T^0. C^0 and, as we shall momentarily see, Neg^0 are not head governors. However, even a nonintrinsic head governor like C^0 can become one if associated with Agr. The Ø head of Comp in (4-50) is taken by Rizzi to be a C^0 marked [+Agr], and subject extraction leaves a properly governed trace.

(4-50)   Who do you think Ø knows the answer?

In some languages, a C^0 containing Agr is marked morphologically. This is arguably the case of the French complementizer *qui*, which cooccurs only with subject variables, as shown in the contrast in (4-51).

(4-51)   a. Quelle étudiante   penses-   tu   qui   /*que   ne   connaît   pas   la
  which   student   think-   you   qui   /que   neg   knows   neg   the
       réponse?
       answer
       'Which student do you think doesn't know the answer?'

        b. Quelle   réponse   penses-   tu   *qui   /que   cette   étudiante   ne   connaît
  which   answer   think-   you   qui   /que   this   student   neg   knows
       pas?
       neg
       'Which answer do you think that this student doesn't know?'

If we now assume, as seems reasonable, that Neg^0 is also not an intrinsic head governor, we predict that if Neg^0 contained Agr features, it would be transformed into a proper head governor. Rizzi's approach is supported to a substantial degree by the contrast between (4-47) and (4-52).[13]

(4-52) mi   /ʔeize   student   ʔeyn-o   yodeʕa   ʔet   ha-tšuva?
who   /which   student   neg-3MS   know(BENONI)-MS   ACC   the-answer
'Who/which student doesn't know the answer?'

Subject extraction is rendered acceptable in (4-52) due to the occurrence of an agreement suffix on the negative head. By the same token, (4-47) is ruled out as an ECP violation, since a bare—that is, Agr-less—*ʔeyn* is not a proper head governor for the subject trace.

To recall, *ʔeyn* clauses appear in two varieties, illustrated in (4-1) and (4-5). In the first variety, *ʔeyn* is IP-initial and does not manifest an agreement affix. In the second variety, the subject is initial, in which case *ʔeyn* must agree with it. The two *ʔeyn*s should thus be seen as formally equivalent to French *que* and *qui*, in that one bears no agreement and is therefore not a proper head governor, while the other is a proper head governor by virtue of bearing Agr.

Note now that if *ʔeyn* is the closest potential head governor for the subject, then the latter must be in the specifier position of the XP immediately c-commanded by *ʔeyn*. This follows from the definitions of head government proposed by Rizzi. In particular, for X^0 to govern YP, it must c-command it, where c-command is defined in terms of branching nodes (in the sense of Reinhart 1976; see Rizzi 1990a:32 ff.). This consideration underpins my conjecture to the effect that the subject of an agreementless *ʔeyn* construction is in Spec/T. If the subject were in the specifier position of a projection lower than Spec/T—say Spec/AgrPart or Spec/V—then its closest head governor would not be Neg^0 but another head, and the contrast between (4-47) and (4-52) could not be assimilated to the "complementizer-trace effect.[14,15]

The extraction of the subject in (4-52), for example, thus incorporates an intermediate step of movement from Spec/T to Spec/AgrS. The head of NegP, which bears an agreement affix, is raised to $AgrS^0$. The chains thus formed are schematized in (4-53), where t_i is properly head governed by the trace of the Agr-bearing Neg^0, namely t_k.[16]

(4-53)

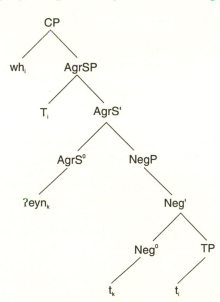

In the following sections, I show that not only overt movement of a subject over *ʔeyn* is blocked by the ECP, but that covert movement is subject to the same constraint. Three such cases are discussed, in turn.

4.8.2   Wh in-situ under *ʔeyn*

In (4-54a), a wh-subject appears in situ. Following a long tradition, let us assume that a wh-element in situ undergoes LF wh-movement leaving, perforce, a trace. The sharp ungrammaticality of this sentence, in contrast to the full acceptability of (4-54b), can thus be attributed to a violation of head government, just as in the cases of overt wh-movement previously discussed.[17]

(4-54)   a. *mi   xašav   še   ʔeyn mi   yodeʕa   ʔet   ha-tšuva?
            who   think(PAST)-3MS   that neg   who   know(BENONI)-MS   ACC   the-answer
            'Who thought that who doesn't know the answer?'

      b. mi   xašav   še   ʔeyn Ruti   yodaʕat   ma?
            who   think(PAST)-3MS   that neg   Ruti   know(BENONI)-FS   what
            'Who thought that Ruti doesn't know what?'

4.8.3   Quantifier-Raising Under *ʔeyn*

An additional subcase of covert movement is that of subject quantifiers. While subjects of declarative sentences may be quantificational, as in (4-55), subjects embedded under *ʔeyn* may not, as in (4-56).[18]

(4-55)   a. kol   student   yodeʕa   ʔet   ha-tšuva.
            every   student   know(BENONI)-MS   ACC   the-answer
            'Every student knows the answer.'

      b. harbe   studentim   yodʕim   ʔet   ha-tšuva.
            many   students   know(BENONI)-MPL   ACC   the-answer
            'Many students know the answer.'

(4-56)   a. *ʔeyn   kol   student   yodeʕa   ʔet   ha-tšuva.
            neg   every   student   know(BENONI)-MS   ACC   the-answer
            'It is not the case that every student knows the answer.'

      b. *ʔeyn   harbe   studentim   yodʕim   ʔet   ha-tšuva.
            neg   many   students   know(BENONI)-MPL   ACC   the-answer
            'It is not the case that many students know the answer.'

An idea that immediately comes to mind is to relate the ungrammticality of (4-56) to that of (4-54a) and claim that the ECP is responsible. The conclusion to be drawn from the status of (4-56) is that quantifiers are raised in LF, leaving a variable (Quantifier Raising [QR]:May [1985]). This variable must be properly head-governed, and the closest potential head governor is Neg^0, which, as we have seen, is not a proper head governor.[19]

In clauses with an agreeing *ʔeyn*, quantifiers are moved from Spec/AgrS and yield a perfectly grammatical output.

(4-57) a. kol   student   ʔeyn-o   yodeʕa   ʔet   ha-tšuva.
           every student   neg-3MS   know(BENONI)-MS   ACC   the-answer
           'Every student doesn't know the answer.'

       b. harbe studentim ʔeyn-am   yodʕim   ʔet   ha-tšuva.
           many students   neg-3MPL know(BENONI)-MPL ACC   the-answer
           'Many students don't know the answer.'

Concluding that Quantifier-Raising must indeed take place in (4-56), the question arises as to the position to which the quantifier is moved in LF. There are two alternatives: the quantifier phrase adjoins to TP, or the quantifier adjoins to NegP (or to some higher projection). The two options are diagrammed in (4-58).

(4-58) a.

b.

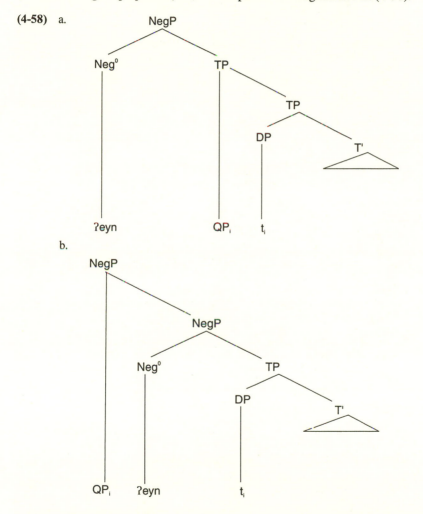

To the degree that quantifiers under *ʔeyn* can be felicitously interpreted, they must have lower scope with respect to negation, as indicated in the English translation of (4-56). This suggests that only the first alternative is valid, and that the quantifier is not raised above NegP.[20]

4.8.4   Focus-Movement under *ʔeyn*

To conclude the discussion of subject extraction under *ʔeyn*, let us consider yet another case of covert movement, namely focalization. Clause-initial subjects can be focalized by being contrastively stressed or by the focalizing particle rak 'only'.

(4-59) a. Dani   yodeʕa   ʔet   ha-tšuva.   (lo   Ruti).
      Dani   know(BENONI)-MS   ACC   the-answer   (neg   Ruti)
      'DANI knows the answer (not Ruti).'

   b. rak   Dani   yodeʕa   ʔet   ha-tšuva.
      only   Dani   know(BENONI)-MS   ACC   the-answer
      'Only Dani knows the answer.'

Under *ʔeyn*, however, the subject may not be focalized.

(4-60) a. *ʔeyn   Dani   yodeʕa   ʔet   ha-tšuva.
      neg   Dani   know(BENONI)-MS   ACC   the-answer
      'DANI doesn't know the answer.'

   b. *ʔeyn   rak   Dani   yodeʕa   ʔet   ha-tšuva.
      neg   only   Dani   know(BENONI)-MS   ACC   the-answer
      'Only Dani doesn't know the answer.'

The fact that a subject under *ʔeyn* cannot be focalized receives a natural explanation if focalization involves covert movement, analogous to wh-movement. In languages such as Hungarian, Focus movement takes place in the overt component, raising the focalized constituent to a Comp-like position and leaving an ECP-sensitive trace (see Brody 1990; Horvath 1976, 1986; Kiss 1987; and Puskas 1992).

   The analysis predicts that focalization of a subject preceding an agreeing *ʔeyn* should pose no problems for the ECP. Indeed, both (4-61a,b) are fully acceptable.

(4-61) a. Ruti   ʔeyn-a   yodaʕat   ʔet   ha-tšuva.
      Ruti   neg-3MF   know(BENONI)-FS   ACC   the-answer
      'RUTI doesn't know the answer.'

   b. rak   Ruti   ʔeyn-a   yodaʕat   ʔet   ha-tšuva.
      only   Ruti   neg-3MF   know(BENONI)-FS   ACC   the-answer
      'Only Ruti doesn't know the answer.'

Finally, direct objects may be focalized in an *ʔeyn* clause, since their trace is properly head-governed, presumably by the verb.

(4-62) ʔeyn   Dani   yodeʕa   ʔet   ha-tšuva   /rak   ʔet   ha-tšuva.
      neg   Dani   know(BENONI)-MS   ACC   the-answer   /only   ACC   the-answer
      'Dani doesn't know THE ANSWER / only the answer.'

4.9   CONCLUSION

In this chapter, I showed that *ʔeyn* is the nonclitic head of NegP. It is precisely this property of *ʔeyn* that affords insight into Hebrew clause structure. This is so because *ʔeyn* is a barrier for head movement. Various positions of verbs and subjects which, in the absence on an IP-internal head barrier, serve only as intermediate or transit positions, become landing sites when *ʔeyn* is used. The Hebrew 'Mittlefeld' (a term used in Germanic syntax to refer to what I have called the inflectional domain of the clause—that is, the clausal chunk lying between VP and CP) is thus more open to examination in an *ʔeyn* sentence than in constructions where the verb and the subject are attracted to the top of the clause.

I provided evidence that the Benoni in an *ʔeyn* sentence is in T^0 at S-structure and that the subject is in Spec/T. Starting from the latter, I showed that subject extraction over *ʔeyn* patterns with subject extraction over a filled C^0. This parallelism, when rendered explicit within the framework of Rizzi's work, implies that the subject occupies the specifier position immediately c-commanded by Neg^0. I then showed that adverbs which may occur under the scope of negation cannot occur between the subject and the verb under *ʔeyn*. These facts argue that the verb and the subject are in a Spec-head configuration. Finally, if *ʔeyn* sentences contain a TP, and if TP is located higher than the participial agreement phrase AgrPart, it follows that the subject under *ʔeyn* is in Spec/T and the Benoni verb is in T^0.

In the latter part of chapter 3, I argued that Benoni sentences may lack an auxiliary and that the Benoni can raise to T^0 independently of CI. Chapter 4 has shown that when *ʔeyn* is inserted, such a derivation becomes the only grammatical option.

It was shown that *ʔeyn* has two variants. When it occurs with an agreement suffix, AgrSP is projected, *ʔeyn* raises to $AgrS^0$, and the subject is moved to Spec/AgrS. The alternation between the two variants of *ʔeyn* demonstrates, I believe, that agreement must be associated with an independent projection (contra, e.g., Chomsky 1995, chapter 4, and Iatridou 1990). Otherwise, the alternation in the position of the subject cannot be expressed.

Once again, chapter 4 enriches and substantiates a point that was a mere conjecture in chapter 3: AgrSP and, by implication, all Agr projections, have a different status from other, semantically pertinent functional projections. In particular, I hope to have convincingly shown that AgrSP is not obligatory in every IP.

At this point, it is rather tempting to propose that, when projected, AgrSP is always higher in the clause than TP (and NegP). The hypothesis which suggests itself is the following. To the degree that a language manifests a "TP-initial" or a "NegP-initial" phrase marker, this is due *not* to parametric variation in the hierarchy of functional projections, but to the optional character of AgrSP.

In chapter 6, I attempt to validate this hypothesis with respect to Standard Arabic, a language that has been explicitly argued to differ from, e.g., Italian, in the positioning of AgrSP and TP (Ouhalla (1991). Insofar as the invariance of hierarchical ordering can be validated beyond the circumscribed data discussed in this work, it would plausibly count as a universal constraint on clause structure, limiting in a sharp fashion the range of a priori available options of clausal design.

FIVE

Some Remaining Issues

5.1 INTRODUCTION

My discussion of present tense sentences, both affirmative and negative, has been almost entirely focused on those that contain a verbal Benoni predicate. In the following sections, I discuss, albeit in a limited and tentative manner, two issues pertaining to present tense sentences with nonverbal predicates. I first consider the occurrence of *ʔeyn* in locative/existential sentences, and show that the subject of such sentences must be taken to occupy a position lower than Spec/T. Second, I attempt to resolve a potential problem with the analysis of the Benoni, namely, its incompatiblility with copular Pron.

5.2 EXISTENTIAL/LOCATIVE PREDICATES UNDER *ʔeyn*

I am essentially concerned with the two sentence types illustrated in (5-1). Example (5-1a) is marginal and belongs to a very elevated register of Hebrew, while example (5-1b) is colloquial. Nevertheless, their syntactic properties can be compared.

(5-1) a. ??eyn ha-yladim ba-gina.
     neg   *the-children* *in-the-garden*
     'The children are not in the garden.'

   b. ʔeyn yladim ba-gina.
     neg   *children* *in-the-garden*
     'There are no children in the garden.'

   The first and crucial difference between the two examples in (5-1) is that the subject of (5-1a) is a definite description, while the subject of (5-1b) is an indefinite DP, a bare plural. Indefinite (bare) plurals admit of two interpretations, generic and existential (Carlson [1977]). Thus, (5-2) may mean either (i) or (ii).

(5-2) Firemen are available

    i. In general, firemen are available   (Generic)

    ii. There are firemen who are available   (Existential)

Various factors can influence or force one of the two interpretations. One of these, discussed in Diesing's work (see, e.g., Diesing 1992a,b), concerns the position occupied by the subject. Diesing argues that the generic interpretation is associated with the highest or "outer" subject position, namely Spec/I, while the existential reading is associated with the lower, VP-internal or "inner" subject position. Diesing handles the ambiguity in (5-2) by arguing that the interpretation in (5-2i) is to be had by base-generating the subject in Spec/I, where it is interpreted in the restrictive clause of an abstract generic operator, while in (5-2ii), the subject is interpretatively associated with the lower position, where it is bound by existential closure.

In English, the two interpretations are disambiguated in There-sentences, as noted, originally, in Milsark (1974). In (5-3a), with the subject in the lower position, only the existential reading is available; (5-3b) is ambiguous, since the subject can be associated in LF with either Spec/I (its surface position) or, via a trace in a Raising chain, with the lower subject position.

(5-3) a. There are firemen available   Existential

       b. Fireman are available   Generic and Existential

As indicated by its gloss, the subject of (5-1b) is, and can only be interpreted existentially. The correlation thus observed between (5-1b) and the There-sentence in (5-3a) lends independent support to the claim put forth earlier that subjects occurring to the right of *ʔeyn* are not in Spec/AgrS, but in a lower subject position. (Spec/AgrS is filled with the expletive *there* in [5-3a]. There is no AgrSP in [5-1b]).

Drawing a parallel between (5-1b) and (5-3) engenders two predictions. We have already noted the first: a bare plural subject occurring to the right of *ʔeyn* admits only the existential reading. The second prediction is that the clausal subject is ambiguous when occurring to the left of *ʔeyn*—cf. (5-3b)—for it occupies Spec/AgrS, Diesing's "outer" subject position.

Consider then the variant of (5-1b) with an agreeing *ʔeyn*, where the subject occurs in Spec/AgrS.

(5-4) *yladim   ʔeyn-am ba-gina.
      children   neg-MPL in-the-garden
      'Children are not in the garden.'

Example (5-4) is ungrammatical. To the degree that it is interpretable, it gives rise only to the generic interpretation of the bare plural, the existential interpretation being entirely unavailable. Although the second prediction of the previous paragraph is partially validated (in that the generic interpretation becomes available once the subject occurs to the left of *ʔeyn*), it is undesirable to draw conclusions on the basis of (5-4), given the fact that *being in the garden* is typically interpreted as a stage-level predicate—that is, that attributes an episodic state and not a permanent property to its subject, and hence conflicts with the assignment of a generic interpretation to the latter.

Matters are clearer when one selects a predicate that imposes a generic reading on a bare plural subject—that is, that unambiguously attributes to it a permanent property. The prediction is that a bare plural subject will only be acceptable to the left of *ʔeyn*. Consider an alternation involving the individual-level predicate *intelligent*.

(5-5) a. *ʔeyn balšanim ʔintiligentim.   b. balšanim ʔeyn-am ʔintiligentim.
       neg   linguists   intelligent   *linguists neg-MPL   telligent*
       'There are no linguists intelligent.'   'Linguists are not intelligent.'

Due to the nature of the predicate, example (5-5a) cannot be interpreted existentially, but only generically. Yet the generic interpretation requires that the subject be positioned in the restrictive clause of a generic operator—that is, in Spec/AgrS. The interplay of a semantic condition on possible interpretation and the syntactic configuration (5-5a) serve to rule it out as a sentence in which *intiligentim* 'intelligent' is a predicate. The only grammatical output of (5-5a) consists of denying *intiligentim* ('intelligent') the status of a predicate and treating it as a modifier of the NP *balšanim* 'linguists', as in 'there are no intelligent linguists.'

Example (5-5b) is well formed since the subject occurs in Spec/AgrS, within the restrictive clause of a generic operator.

I have established that the positioning of a bare plural subject to the left or to the right of *ʔeyn* correlates with two distinct interpretations, a fact which agrees well with Diesing's approach to subject positions. We now need to identify more precisely these positions in the clausal structure. There being no reason to suppose otherwise, I take the subject position preceding the agreeing variant of *ʔeyn* to be the same position occupied by pre-*ʔeyn* subjects of the sort discussed in the previous chapter, namely Spec/AgrS. As for the lower, post-*ʔeyn* position, there are strong empirical grounds to believe that it is not Spec/T, the subject position under *ʔeyn* identified in the preceding chapters. Rather, I argue that the subject in (5-1b) occupies yet a lower position.[1]

We can best approach this issue by concentrating on the two sentences in (5-1). While giving no immediate indication that two distinct subject positions are involved, some manipulation of the data yields rather dramatic differences between the two.

In §4.8, various trace-creating transformations were applied to subjects under *ʔeyn*. We saw that overt and covert wh-movement, quantifier-raising, and covert focus movement were all uniformly excluded from the subject position to the right of *ʔeyn*. This led to the conclusion that this position is not properly governed. We get identical results when we apply these transformations to (5-1a).

(5-6) a. *mi   ʔeyn ba-gina?
          who neg   in-the-garden
          'Who isn't in the garden?'

       b. *mi   xašav   še-   ʔeyn mi   ba-gina?
          who thought that neg   who   in-the-garden
          'Who thought that who isn't in the garden?'

c. *ʔeyn kol   yeled ba-gina.
   neg   every   child   in-the-garden
   'Every child is not in the garden.'

d. *ʔeyn rak   ha-yladim   ba-gina.
   neg   only   the-children   in the garden
   'Only the children are not in the garden.'

e. *ʔeyn <u>ha-yladim</u>   ba-gina.
   neg   <u>the children</u> in-the-garden
   '<u>THE CHILDREN</u> are not in the-garden.'

Sharply contrasting with (5-6) are the sentences in (5-7), which result from the application of the same gamut of operations to (5-1b).

(5-7) a. ma   ʔeyn ba-gina?
     what   neg   in-the-garden
     'What isn't there in the garden?'

b. mi   xašav   še-   ʔeyn ma   ba-gina?
   who thought that neg what in-the-garden
   'Who thought that there isn't what in the garden?'

c. ʔeyn harbe yladim   ba-gina
   neg   many   children in-the-garden
   'There aren't many children in the garden.'

d. ʔeyn rak   yladim   ba-gina?
   neg   only   children in-the-garden
   'There aren't only children in the garden.'

e. ʔeyn <u>yladim</u>   ba-gina?
   neg   <u>children</u> in-the-garden
   'There aren't <u>CHILDREN</u> in the garden.'

Let us comment on these sentences one by one. The difference between (5-6a) and (5-7a) lies in the type of wh-word extracted. In the former, it is *who*, while in the latter it is *what*. Why should the choice of wh-element give rise to a different grammaticality judgment? Hebrew *ma* 'what', when ranging over DPs, calls for an answer in the form of either an indefinite or a definite DP, while *mi* 'who' requires a definite one.

This is patently clear when direct objects are extracted. Direct objects, to recall, are preceded by the accusative marker *ʔet* when definite. The paradigm in example (5-8) shows that extraction of object *mi* requires that *ʔet* be carried along. Put a different way, the object wh-operator must be taken to range over definite descriptions. Extraction of *ma*, however, can proceed either with or without *ʔet*. The former elicits an answer in the form of a definite description, while the latter calls for an indefinite one. Example (5-7a) can be felicitously answered only by an indefinite DP, as in (5-9a).

(5-8) a. ??mi raʔita   ʔetmol?
      who see(PAST)-2MS yesterday
      'Whom did you see yesterday?'

     b. ʔet mi   raʔita   ʔetmol?
      ACC who see(PAST)-2MS yesterday
      'Whom did you see yesterday?'

(5-9) a. ma   raʔita   ʔetmol?
      what see(PAST)-2MS yesterday
      'What did you see yesterday?'

     b. ʔet ma   raʔita   ʔetmol?
      ACC what see(PAST)-2MS yesterday
      'What did you see yesterday?'

Answer: seret
         movie

      'a movie.'

Answer: ʔet ha-woodiyalen
         ACC the-Woody Allen
         ha-xadaš
      'The new Woody Allen.'

The contrast between examples (5-6b) and (5-7b) illustrates the same observation with a wh-element in situ. In (5-7c), the subject is preceded by a weak quantifier of the sort that patterns with indefinites in being able to occur under *there* in There-sentences (Milsark 1974). Borer (1983) notes that the quantifier in such examples has lower scope than negation, entailing the availability of a scope position under *ʔeyn*. Finally, examples (5-7d,e) show that focalization of an indefinite DP under *ʔeyn* yields perfectly grammatical results.

The glosses provided for the sentences in (5-7) suggest an affinity with English There-sentences. The nature of this affinity needs to be spelled out more precisely. If a full analogy could be drawn between *ʔeyn* sentences containing a locative PP and There-sentences, the ungrammaticality of the sentences in (5-6) could be reduced to the familiar constraint banning strong DPs from the subject position following there, however that constraint is to be stated (see, e.g., Safir 1985 and the papers in Reuland and ter Meulen 1989). Yet such an analogy is called into question by (5-1a), in which a definite DP licitly occurs under *ʔeyn*, where one cannot occur under *there*.

Continuing to assume that *ʔeyn* is the head of Neg^0, I would like to argue that the fundamental difference between (5-1a) and (5-1b) has to do with the position of the subject under *ʔeyn*. The account given in the previous chapter for the ungrammaticality of the sentences in (5-6) appealed to the absence of head government by *ʔeyn* (see §4.8). By the same line of reasoning, the sentences in (5-7) can be taken to demonstrate that *ʔeyn* is *not* the closest governor for the subject trace. Rather, the trace formed by moving the subject, at S-structure or in LF, is governed by some other head, capable of functioning as a head governor. This reasoning leads to an immediate structural consequence: the subject in (5-1b) is not in Spec/T, but in a lower position, one which is properly head-governed. Thus, the facts discussed in this section lead to the positing of an additional subject position, distinguishable from the other two we have identified.

As for the identity of the head governor of this "lower" subject trace, consider the idea that the sentences in (5-1) incorporate a phonetically null verb. The most likely candidate for such a role is existential *be* or *be$_3$* (which should not be confounded with the null copular or auxiliary be occuring in present tense sentences with Benoni verbs; chapters 2 and 3). I assume, further, that *be$_3$* is like the Benoni verbs discussed in previous chapters, so that it can licitly occur under *ʔeyn*.[2]

In order to capture the fact that only when a subject is indefinite may it appear in the "lower" subject position, head-governed by be_3, as the extraction data lead one to believe, we must assume that this verb has the capacity to license a postverbal subject only when the subject is indefinite. Take be_3 then, to be an ergative verb—that is, a verb that assigns no external θ role and licenses a postverbal "subject" by assigning it partitive Case (viz. Belletti 1988).[3]

Subjects of ergative verbs other than be_3 and subjects of passive verbs must be taken to be in Spec/T, given the fact that they are inextractable over *?eyn*, as shown in (5-10).

(5-10) a. *ma ?eyn mitxolelet   ba-xuc?
           what neg   rage(BENONI)-FS outside
           'What isn't raging outside?'

       b. *ma ?eyn mitnahelet   ba-kikar?
           what neg   take place(BENONI)-FS in the square
           'What isn't going on in the square?'

By way of contrast, (5-11) shows that extraction of the subject is possible in both affirmative sentences as well as in negative ones with an agreeing form of *?eyn*.[2]

(5-11) a. ?ma (?eyn-a)   mitxolelet   ba-xuc?
           what (neg-3FS) rage(BENONI)-FPL outside
           'What is(n't) raging outside?'

       b. ?ma (?eyn-a)   mitnahelet   ba-kikar?
           what (neg-3FS) take place(BENONI)-FS in-the-square
           'What is(n't) going on in the square?'

The fact that extraction is possible over be_3 but not over other ergative verbs is reminiscent of a well-known contrast in English There-sentences. Postverbal subjects of existential/locative *be* can be extracted, while postverbal subjects of other ergative verbs cannot. This contrast is illustrated in (5-12).

(5-12) a. Who was there in the garden?

       b. *Who did there arrive?

The question why this is so, like some of the other queries raised in this section, await further investigation.

5.3 COPULAR SENTENCES AND BENONI VERBS

This section is concerned with the interaction of Pron, or the pronominal realization of $AgrS^0$ introduced in §1.3.3 (see in particular chapter 1, note 18) with affirmative and negative Benoni sentences. Berman (1978) and

Doron (1983) point out that Pron cannot occur in the company of Benoni predicates. *Manhiga(t)* in (5-13a) below means 'the leader', while in (5-13b) it occurs in a verbal guise, that of a present tense Benoni verb. Pron can only appear in the sentence containing the nominal *manhiga(t)*. (Recall that the Benoni is morphologically ambiguous between a verb and an agentive nominal; see §2.1.1.)

(5-13)   a. Daniela   (hi)   manhigat ha-kita.
             Daniela   (pron-3FS)   leader   the-class
             'Daniela is the leader of the class.'

         b. Daniela   (*hi)   manhiga ʔet   ha-kita.
             Daniela   pron-3FS   leader   ACC   the-class
             'Daniela leads / is leading the class.'

Doron explains the ungrammaticality of (5-13b) by arguing that the verb and Pron compete, as it were, for the position of I0. The analysis of the Benoni in the preceding chapters, however, renders this explanation untenable as formulated. This is so because Pron is in AgrS^0, while the Benoni is a participle that can raise independently only as high as T^0. No competition then arises between Pron and a Benoni predicate.

I would like, however, to maintain a modified version of Doron's proposal and argue for the following two points:

   a. AgrS^0 is a functional head, the contents of which must be checked by raising and incorporating to it a head with appropriate (AgrS) features.
   b. Pron, being a freestanding, lexical formative, cannot serve as an incorporation host for lexical items in a derivation that feeds PF.

These two conditions of wellformedness are rather familiar constraints on PF output. The first simply restates Chomsky's (1993) idea that only checked features are legitimate objects at Spell Out. The second condition encapsulates the idea that lexical items—with the exception of compounds—are integral words and cannot be freely adjoined to other words.[5]

Taken in tandem, these two claims explain the ungrammaticality of (5-13b). Let us consider the technical details of the proposal. To start with, recall that sentences containing a Benoni predicate are structurally ambiguous (see §3.5). Under one structural description, such sentences have the rough D-structure of (5-14). AgrSP is generated, as is willy nilly a phonetically unexpressed auxiliary. CI then applies, and the Benoni is raised to AgrS^0 as a segment of the auxiliary complex.

(5-14)

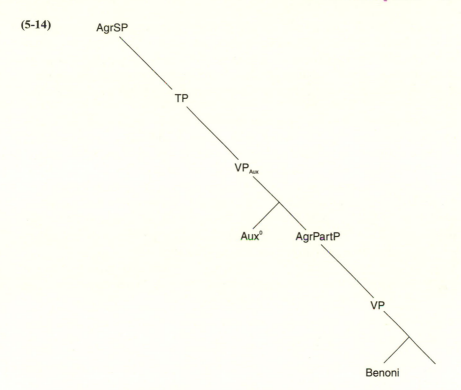

But Benoni present tense sentences can also be structured as in (5-15), where AgrSP is not projected and there is no auxiliary. Under such an analysis, the Benoni predicate raises to T^0.

(5-15)

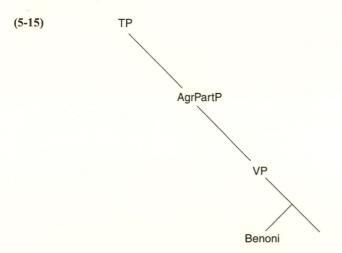

If (5-15) is chosen, then $AgrS^0$ cannot be checked, neither at S-structure nor in LF, since there is no verb in the clause with AgrS features. Representing a Benoni sentence as in (5-14) allows AgrS to be checked since the auxiliary, albeit phonetically unexpressed, is endowed with AgrS features. However, Pron is not only the head of AgrP, it is a lexical item, a pronoun, and not an affixal head, and cannot serve as a host for syntactic incorporation. CI and subsequent auxiliary raising to AgrS^0 must occur in the audible syntax. Yet the auxiliary does not raise alone to AgrS^0, it carries along the incorporated Benoni and, by adjoining to Pron, it violates its lexical integrity, as it were.[6]

It transpires, then, that Pron can either be licit in structures in which its checking is effected in LF—which does interface with the morphological or phonetic modules—or be checked by a phonetically null auxiliary, the incorporation of which to Pron has no overt morphological correlate.

Take nominal sentences such as (5-13a) to contain a null auxiliary. Now, I have shown that nominal predicates do not undergo CI, presumably because in the absence of an AspP in such sentences, there is no predicate raising to T^0 (see the discussion in §3.3). How is the null auxiliary lexically supported in the absence of CI? I would like to suggest that raising and incorporation to Pron, a lexical item, is precisely what provides the auxiliary with the necessary support and renders it legitimate. Since CI does not apply, the auxiliary raises to AgrS^0 alone, checking its features. I have in mind a derivation such as (5-16).[7]

(5-16)

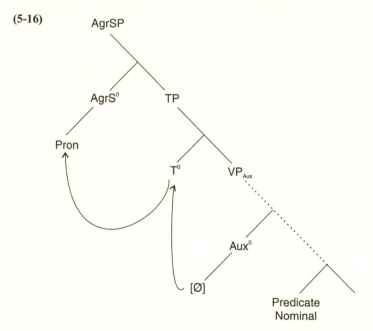

The preceding discussion can also shed light on the interaction of *ʔeyn* and Pron. It was shown that the variant of *ʔeyn* manifesting agreement raises to AgrS^0 in the audible syntax. Thus, it is predicted that sentences containing an agreeing form of *ʔeyn* can not cooccur with Pron. Example (5-17) shows that this prediction is fulfilled. Indeed, the ungrammaticality of (5-17) shows that the occurrence of Pron is not directly linked to the type of predicate involved, since in both the illicit (5-17) and the acceptable (5-13a), the predicate is a DP, but is rather tied up with whether AgrS^0 is accessed by a phonetically realized or by an invisible head. Neg^0 is a phonetically realized head and (5-17) is thus excluded.[8]

(5-17) *Daniela hi   ?eyn-a   manhigat ha-kita.*
Daniela pron-3FS neg-3FS leader   the-class
'Daniela is not the leader of the class.'

5.3.1   Negation in Copular Sentences

5.3.1.1   *Negation in Hebrew Copular Constructions*

A question now arises with respect to the derivation of the grammatical sentence in (5-18).

(5-18) Daniela   hi   lo   manhigat ha-kita.
Daniela   pron-3FS   neg   leader   the-class
'Daniela is not the leader of the class.'

In §1.3.3, I used data such as (5-18) to motivate the claim that *lo* does not raise independently to AgrS^0, but rather incorporates T^0 and the two raise to AgrS^0 together. The relevant contrast, to recall, was between (5-18), where *lo* follows Pron, and (5-19), for example, where it *precedes* the verb in AgrS^0.

(5-19) Daniela   lo   hinhiga   ?et   ha-kita.
Daniela   neg   lead(PAST)-3FS   ACC   the-class
'Daniela did not lead the class.'

Figure (5-20) diagrams a typical derivation of a negative sentence such as (5-19).

(5-20)

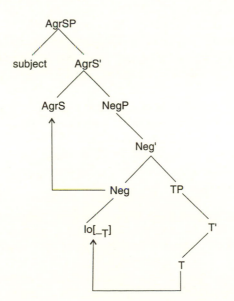

I would like to argue that the impossibility of representing negation to the left of Pron, as indicated by the ungrammaticality of (5-21), is due to the condition barring the incorporation of lexical material into Pron. By raising *lo* to AgrS^0 in the audible syntax, this condition is violated.

(5-21)   *Daniela lo   hi   manhigat   ha-kita.
          Daniela   neg   pron-3FS   leader   the-class
          'Daniela is not the leader of the class.'

The only legitimate derivation of a negative Pron sentence would then consist of postponing the raising of Neg^0 to AgrS^0 to LF. Let us consider the details of this more closely. Example (5-18) contains a null auxiliary requiring lexical support. In the absence of *lo*, the auxiliary moves all the way up to Pron. When *lo* is present, however, the auxiliary can meet the condition of lexical support by incorporating to Neg^0. In LF, the entire Neg complex, containing the null auxiliary, moves to Pron to check the features of AgrS.[9]

5.3.1.2 *Negation in Colloquial Arabic Copular Construction*

Now I turn to a comparative discussion of negation in Arabic dialects in the context of Pron. As discussed in §1.3.3, negation in many spoken dialects of Arabic is bimorphemic, resembling in this respect the pattern found in written French, where the verb is surrounded by the two components of negation. A typical example, drawn from Palestinian Arabic, is provided in (5-22).

(5-22)   Zayd   ma   katab   -(i)š   l-qiṣṣa.
          Zayd   neg   write(PERF)-3MS   neg   the-story
          'Zayd did not write the story.'

Following Benmamoun (1992), I argued that *ma* is the head of NegP, while *(i)š* is a negative operator in Spec/Neg. I would like to now examine the pattern of Arabic negation, comparing it with the Hebrew one, in particular in constructions involving Pron.

Two patterns of negation can be discerned in Arabic copular sentences. In one, illustrated in (5-23a), *ma* and *(i)š* are fused together into a single morpheme and occur to the right of Pron. In the other, (5-23b), the two negative morphemes surround the copular pronominal, just as if it were a regular verb. In many dialects of Arabic, notably Southern Palestinian and Egyptian (see Eid 1983), both patterns can be found side by side.

(5-23)   a. Zayd   hu   miš   mʕallem.

              Zayd   pron   neg   teacher
              'Zayd is not a teacher.'

          b. Zayd   ma-   hu   -š   mʕallem.
             Zayd   neg   pron   neg   teacher
             'Zayd is not a teacher.'

Excluded in all dialects are sentences such as (5-24) where the fused form *mɨ̌š* appears to left of Pron.

(5-24) *Zayd <u>miš</u> hu mʕallem.
     Zayd <u>neg</u> Pron teacher

I shall take the form *mɨ̌š* to be parallel in relevant respects to Hebrew lo in copular sentences. The ungrammaticality of (5-24) is then to be treated on par with that of (5-21).

The pattern exemplified in (5-23b) is more intriguing, since it contrasts sharply with the situation in Hebrew. An anonymous reviewer has brought to my attention that the pronominal form appearing between *ma* and *(ɨ)š* differs from that which precedes *mɨ̌š*, and from Hebrew Pron, in that it is not uniquely a third person pronoun, but a pronoun that agrees in all features with the subject. Consider the following sample of what descriptive grammars frequently refer to as the *negative copula* (see e.g., Cowell 1964:388).

(5-25)

a.	ma	hu	š		c.	ma	nt	ɨš
	neg	*3MS*	*neg*			*neg*	*2S*	*neg*
b.	ma	hi	š		d.	ma	ḥnaa	š
	neg	*3FS*	*neg*			*neg*	*1PL*	*neg*

I would like to put forward the tentative proposal that the pronominal forms that appear in (5-25) are indeed present tense copular verbs. In other words, these are the phonetically realized versions of the Hebrew null copula. This proposal is motivated by the observation that these pronominal forms are embraced by the negative morphemes and, in this respect, behave like tensed verbs in raising upward *through* Neg^0. The upshot of this proposal is that there is no Pron in AgrS^0 in (5-23b).

5.3.2 Conclusion

The basic problem dealt with in §5.3 is the incompatibility of Pron with Benoni verbs. I have argued that if no auxiliary is generated in a present tense sentence, the contents of Pron cannot be checked (or supported) by an appropriate head. When an auxiliary does appear, Pron may be checked, but raising of the auxiliary + Benoni complex into AgrS^0 yields an ill-formed morphological object. The ungrammaticality of (5-13b) is thus explained. Pron can coexist with nonverbal predicates, as in (5-13a), precisely because these do not incorporate into Aux and the latter can raise to AgrS^0 and check its features against those of Pron.

I also returned to a discussion of Negation in both Hebrew and dialectal Arabic, pointing out their similarities and differences in copular sentences.

SIX

Arabic Negation and
Arabic Clause Structure

6.1 INTRODUCTION

The study of Hebrew negation and the consequences that it entails for the structure of the Hebrew clause can serve as a set of coordinates to guide us through similar issues in typologically related languages. Therefore, I now proceed to discuss some related issues in the syntax of Standard Arabic. Through the lens of Hebrew negation, we have been able to gain insight into some of the characteristic features of Hebrew syntax. We employ the same strategy with respect to Arabic. I first consider negation with the particle *laa*, using the syntax of negative clauses to pose and answer some questions regarding word order and the hierarchy of functional projections. I then discuss negation by means of the particles *laysa* and *maa*. Drawing together our analysis of Hebrew and Arabic, I conclude this chapter by providing an analytic typology of negative particles.

6.2 *Laa* NEGATION AND CLAUSAL HIERARCHY

The typical format of a negative sentence in Arabic is as follows: the negative particle, which I will assume is a Neg^0 element, appears clause-initially and is immediately followed by the verb in the imperfect form. The verb is inflected for φ features and mood. The form of the Arabic imperfect corresponds to the form of the Hebrew future, though Hebrew does not overtly mark mood (see §1.3.2 for a discussion of the verbal paradigms of Semitic).[1]

(6-1) laa y uḥibb u   Zayd ʔal-qiraaʔa.
      neg 3MS-like(IMPERF)-INDIC Zayd the-reading
      'Zayd does not like reading.'

The verb under *laa* must occur in the imperfect form. Example (6-2) shows that a perfect form cannot appear under *laa*.

(6-2) **laa   ?aḥabb a   Zayd   ?al-qiraa?a.*
        neg   like(PERF)-3MS   Zayd   the-reading
        'Zayd did not like reading.'

The restriction to a particular form is reminiscent of Hebrew *?eyn* sentences. However, while in Hebrew the verbal form must be the Benoni, in Arabic it must be the imperfect.

There is, however, a more spectacular difference between Hebrew and Arabic. While *?eyn* sentences can only be interpreted as present tense, Arabic *laa* sentences have variants expressing past, future, and present tenses. The tense value of a negative clause in Arabic is signaled by a morphological alternation in the form of the negative head. The three alternants are illustrated in (6-3). Here *laa* is associated with the present tense, *lan* with the future and *lam* with the past.[2]

(6-3) a. *laa   y uḥibb u   Zayd   ?al-   qiraa?a.*
           neg   3MS-like(IMPERF)-INDIC   Zayd   the-   reading
           'Zayd does not like reading.'

       b. *lan   y uḥibb a   Zayd   ?al-   qiraa?a.*
           neg   3MS-like(IMPERF)-SUBJ   Zayd   the-   reading
           'Zayd will not like reading.'

       c. *lam   y uḥibb   Zayd   ?al-   qiraa?a.*
           neg   3MS-like(IMPERF)-JUSS   Zayd   the-   reading
           'Zayd did not like reading.'

The last fact to note at this point is that the clausal subject appears in one of two positions in a negative sentence. In all of the preceding examples, it follows the verb so that the order of constituents is Neg > V > S > O, while in (6-4) it precedes the negative particle.

(6-4) *Zayd   laa   y uḥibb u   ?al-qiraa?a.*
        Zayd   neg   3MS-like(IMPERF)   the-reading
        'Zayd does not like reading.'

The paradigm in (6-3) is utilized by Benmamoun (1991, 1992) and Ouhalla (1988, 1991, 1993a) to argue that the clausal structure of Arabic, and perhaps that of other VSO languages, observes a different hierarchy of projections than the one argued for in Belletti (1990) and which also characterizes Hebrew, as demonstrated in earlier chapters. The hierarchy they propose is (6-5), where, crucially, TP is higher than AgrSP and NegP is lower than TP.

(6-5) TP (> NegP) > AgrSP . . .

These authors argue that, in (6-3), Neg^0 raises and incorporates to T^0, and the morphological alternation in the form of the negative head reflects this incorporation. Ouhalla, in particular, argues that the relative positioning of TP and AgrSP is subject to parametric variation. He proposes that Arabic is endowed with a structure such as (6-6a), while the Romance languages are characterized by a hierarchy such as (6-6b).

(6-6)

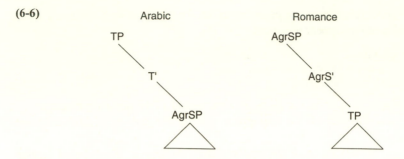

Since the nonexistence of a parameter governing clausal hierarchy is one of the theses defended in this work, it is incumbent upon me to provide an alternative analysis of Arabic negation, consistent with the view that Hebrew and Arabic do not vary in the hierarchical positioning of functional projections, in particular, those of TP, AgrSP, and NegP.

6.2.1   The Arabic Imperfect

Let us first discuss the imperfect form and its interaction with tense and agreement in affirmative sentences. Many descriptions characterize the Arabic imperfect as a purely aspectual category, lacking in any inherent tense specification (Ouhalla 1993, but see Fassi-Fehri 1993 for a different view). I interpret this to mean that, minimally, the imperfect is associated with Asp^0.

Nonetheless, sentences with a "bare" imperfective verb, as in (6-7a), have a tense component: they are most saliently interpreted as present tense. To obtain a future reading, a particle appears preceding the imperfect form, as in (6-7b).

(6-7)   a. y uḥibbu   Zayd ʔal- qiraaʔa.
    3MS-like(IMPERF) *Zayd the-reading*
    'Zayd likes reading.'

  b. sa(wfa)   y uḥibbu Zayd ʔal-qiraaʔa.
    will 3MS-like(IMPERF) Zayd the-reading
    'Zayd will like reading.'

While it may appear that *sa(wfa)* is the future tense marker, namely T^0, traditional descriptions consider this particle to be a modal element (a "particle of amplification," to quote Wright 1896, part II, §361[b], expressing "real futurity"; this view is defended in contemporary research, e.g., by Fassi-Fehri 1993:82, 150, 160). Conceivably, then, *sa(wfa)* occupies a position independent of T and serves to situate tense coordinates, much like a temporal adverb.

As for T itself, suppose that sentences such as (6-7a), which contain a "bare" imperfect, harbor a phonetically unexpressed TP, the head of which is specified [–PAST]. Suppose, further, that in the absence of any modal anchor such as *sa(wfa)*, [–PAST] is interpreted as present rather than future. The claim, then, is that the imperfect is not itself associated with a tense specification—that is, it is not intrinsically a tensed verb.

This claim seems to be necessary to account for the fact that the imperfect occurs in a variety of constructions where Romance and English employ genuine participial, or tenseless, forms. Example (6-8a) below illustrates an adjunct clause, (6-8b) a (small clause) complement to a perception verb, and (6-8c) a periphrastic past tense incorporating an auxiliary.[3]

(6-8) a. žalas a   y ašrabu   ?al xamra.
           sit(PERF)-MS   3MS-drink(IMPERF)   the wine
           'He sat, drinking wine.'

       b. ra?ai tu   Zayd   y ašrabu   ?al xamra.
           see(PERF)-1MS   Zayd   3MS-drink(IMPERF)   the wine
           'I saw Zayd drinking wine.'

       c. kaan a   ?al-walad   y al?abu.
           be(PERF)-3MS   the boy   3MS-play(IMPERF)
           'The boy was playing.'

Fassi-Fehri (1993:147) makes it clear that the constituents containing the imperfective verb have no tense marking of their own and are dependent on the tense of the matrix. It is thus quite suggestive to think of the imperfect as the equivalent of the Hebrew Benoni; that is to say, both are verbal forms associated with aspectual features but not with tense.

The Arabic imperfect poses the same sort of puzzle as the Hebrew Benoni: it appears to be both a participle in (6-8) and a tensed verb in (6-7a). I will attempt to extend the analysis proposed for the Benoni in chapters 2–4 to the Arabic imperfect, claiming that it is an aspectually marked, but not a tensed, verb and that since Aspect^0 must incorporate to T^0, the imperfect raises to T^0. Before proceeding, however, let us consider an alternative.

Under the view that TP dominates NegP, it seems rather natural that the negative head *laa* can occur with imperfective verbs and not with, say, the perfect form. This latter form, like its Hebrew counterpart, the past tense, encodes both aspectual and (past) tense information. Take it, then, to contain tense features that require checking through incorporation with T^0. Admitting (6-5), the Neg^0 *laa* simply blocks movement of the perfective verb to T^0. Since the imperfect form does not encode tense information, it need not raise to T^0. In Benmamoun's and in Ouhalla's analyses, then, the imperfect raises no higher than AgrS^0 and T^0 is accessed by Neg^0, as in the derivation schematized in (6-9).

(6-9)

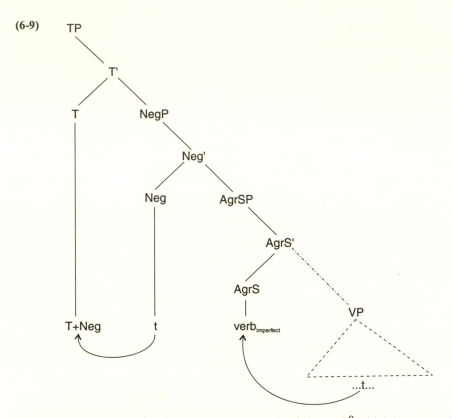

In the discussion of Hebrew *ʔeyn*, I argued that it is not T^0 which is rendered inaccessible to verb movement by the occurrence of the nonclitic negative head, but rather $AgrS^0$. The split between past/future tense verbs, on the one hand, and the Benoni, on the other, was drawn, to recall, on the basis of the presence or absence of AgrS features: the former possess them and therefore must move to $AgrS^0$ to check them, while the latter only manifest participial agreement which is checked in a participial agreement head, positioned below NegP (and below TP).

In Benmamoun's and Ouhalla's view, AgrSP is lower than TP, so that both imperfective and perfective verbs check their AgrS features in AgrSP. The latter, but not the former, require further access to TP, which is blocked by the occurrence of *laa*.

The question we must now tackle concerns, therefore, the correct positioning of AgrSP in the clausal hierarchy. The gist of my argument is that Benmamoun and Ouhalla erroneously identify the agreement features on the imperfect with AgrS features. I shall attempt to show that they should be viewed as AgrPart features, associated with the participial agreement position, as in the case of the Hebrew Benoni.

Consider first the clearly "participial" occurrence of the imperfective in the auxiliary construction illustrated in (6-8c). If AgrSP is below TP, and the imperfect is in $AgrS^0$, then the only way to make sense of the seemingly multiple occurrence of agreement in the clause is to argue that it contains two AgrPs. A reasonable phrase marker for (6-8c), putting aside the subject, is then (6-10).

(6-10)

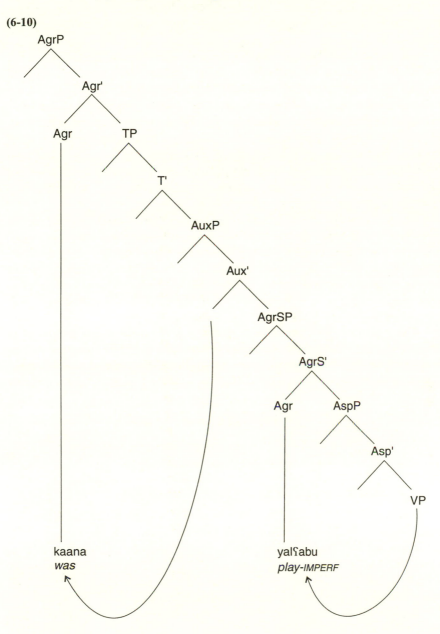

The imperfect raises no higher than AgrSP, and it is the auxiliary that raises to T^0 and then to its Agr^0. While (6-10) is consistent with the view that TP is higher than

AgrSP, it raises the question of the nature of the higher AgrP. At the same time, (6-10) looks remarkably familiar: with a mere adjustment of the labels of the two AgrPs in question, (6-10) is precisely the structure I proposed for Hebrew complex tenses. AgrSP in (6-10) is my AgrPartP, and the AgrP associated with the auxiliary is my AgrSP.

Benmamoun and Ouhalla identify the agreement features borne by the imperfect form as AgrS features. One wonders whether there are morphological indications that imperfect agreement is not AgrS, but participial. At first sight, the morphological evidence seems to suggest the contrary. Imperfective agreement instantiates person, number, and gender distinctions, while the participial agreement of Hebrew and the more familiar Romance or even Indo-European variety manifests only number and gender distinctions. The question becomes all the more interesting, since, beside the imperfect participle, Arabic also has a Benoni-like participle, although its distribution is more restricted (see §1.3.2). I will briefly return to this variety of participles later in this chapter.

Let us tackle this problem by first noting that there is no principled reason why Romance and Hebrew participles should not manifest person distinctions. That is to say, there are no theoretically motivated considerations why AgrPart^0 should only contain a subset of the features manifested by AgrS^0. Indeed, there may be grounds to believe that such a feature is in fact covertly manifested even in Romance and that its dialects differ with respect to whether this feature is inert or active.[4]

Thus, Bianchi and Figuereido (1993) argue that the participial agreement head in Brazilian Portuguese is endowed with phonetically unrealized Person features, serving to identify a null referential object, (6-11a), and hosting object clitics, as in (6-11b).

(6-11) a. O   José   tinha comprado   ontem.
       the   José   has   bought   yesterday
       'José bought it/them yesterday.'

    b. O   José   tinha realmente me   decepcionado.
       the   José   has   really   me   deceived
       'José has really deceived me.'

Kayne (1993) shows that auxiliary selection in some Romance dialects is sensitive to the person specification of the clausal subject. He proposes that participles in these languages have an active AgrS, inert in, say, Standard Italian. Modifying Kayne's proposal, we might say that it is not the presence of an active AgrSP that characterizes these dialects, but rather the presence of a syntactically active person feature on the participial agreement head.

Further, the inflectional paradigm of the imperfect has a different format than that of the perfect and is morphologically distinct both in the form of the inflectional affixes and in their positioning. The paradigms, introduced in §1.3.2, are displayed in (6-12) for a regular verb in the first pattern (or *Binyan*), active voice.

(6–12)   Imperfect Conjugation

	Singular	Plural	Dual
1	?a-ktub-u	na-ktub-u	
2m	ta-ktub-u	ta-ktub-uuna	ta-ktub-aani
2f	ta-ktub-iina	ta-ktub-na	"
3m	ya-ktub-u	ya-ktub-uuna	ya-ktub-aani
3f	ta-ktub-u	ta-ktub-na	ta-ktub-aani

                                       Perfect Conjugation

	Singular	Plural	Dual
1	katab-tu	katab-naa	
2m	katab-ta	katab-tum	katab-tumaa
2f	katab-ti	katab-tunna	"
3m	katab-a	katab-uu	katab-aa
3f	katab-at	katab-na	katab-ataa

While Agreement on the perfect verb is uniquely suffixal, that on the imperfect is both suffixal and prefixal (the former fusing mood with φ features). Moreover, most of the inflectional affixes have different forms in the perfect and in the imperfect. In the context of the present discussion, these differences can be taken to indicate that two types of features complexes are involved, AgrS features on the perfect verb, but AgrPart features on the imperfect.

The correlation between morphological pattern and syntactic function in Arabic is lost in Modern Hebrew, where the imperfect is redefined as a tensed verb and its agreement features are reanalyzed as AgrS features. The fundamental tense/aspect distinction in Arabic is binary—past versus non-past (perfect versus imperfect)—and it correlates with the existence of two verbal paradigms in Semitic, the suffixal and the prefixal. Modern (more precisely post-biblical) Hebrew is characterized by a three-way tense system. There arises, then, a lack of correspondence between the number of morphological forms for the tensed verb and the number of tenses. The Benoni, which is primarily used as a nominal category in Arabic and, morphologically speaking, does not belong to the verbal system, is integrated into the system of tensed verbs to fill a paradigmatic gap, and the Semitic *prefixal* verbal paradigm is redefined as the future tense.[5] The existence of a stricter correspondence in Arabic than in Hebrew between morphological pattern and syntactic function attests to the conservative nature of Arabic grammar, as opposed to the more innovative system of Hebrew.[6]

The considerations discussed here lead me to conclude that the Arabic imperfect is an aspectually marked, but not a tensed verbal form. This explains why it can occur as the predicate in a variety of small clauses. Where in English and Romance a participle is used, and in Hebrew the Benoni appears, in Arabic it is the imperfect.

Consider, now, the occurrence of the imperfect in root clauses such as (6-7a). We have seen that Hebrew present tense sentences can be analyzed either as involving a null auxiliary or as implicating direct movement of the Benoni to T^0. Under the latter analysis, present tense sentences lack the AgrSP layer.

The presence of a syntactically represented, yet phonetically unrealized, present tense form of *be* in Hebrew is a natural consequence of *paradigm regularization*. Since Hebrew has three tenses, the morphological gap in the paradigm of *be* is regularized in the syntactic representation. While *be* is morphologically defective in Arabic, as in Hebrew, it is harder to make a case for paradigm regularization in the case of Arabic, since the language has a binary tense system in which the present tense is expressed, in the unmarked case, by the imperfect form of *be*, which is morphologically regular (i.e., phonetically realized). It is thus difficult to maintain that (6-7a) is a complex tense construction containing a null auxiliary.

Rather, I believe that the most appropriate analysis of (6-7a) is one where the verb (or Asp^0) raises to T^0 in the overt syntax. Under this view (6-7a) is a "bare" TP, as in (6-13).

(6-13)   [CP[TP   yu ḥibbu   Zayd   ʔal-qiraaʔa.]]
         3MS-like(IMPERF)   Zayd   the-reading
         'Zayd likes reading.'

Note that this analysis of (6-7a) captures the essence of Ouhalla's claim that TP is the highest projection within IP without positing a parameter inverting the position of AgrSP and TP. As in Hebrew Benoni sentences, the AgrSP layer is simply unprojected in such sentences.

Consider the paradigm in (6-14).

(6-14)   a. kuntu   ʔalʕabu.
           be(PERF)-1S-   play(IMPERF)
           'I was playing.'

         b. ʔakuunu   ʔalʕabu.
           1S-be(IMPERF)   1S-play(IMPERF)
           'I will be playing.'

         c. ʔalʕabu.
           1S-play(IMPERF)
           'I am playing.'

In (6-14a,b), the auxiliary raises to T^0 and then to $AgrS^0$. The imperfect remains at S-structure in $AgrPart^0$. Arabic lacks clitic auxiliaries, and hence CI does not take place. The participle (the imperfect) raises to T^0 only in LF, just as when a nonclitic auxiliary is selected in Hebrew (cf. §3.2). In (6-14c), on the other hand, no auxiliary is present in the structure. The imperfect must now raise to T^0 in the overt syntax (recall that T^0 has strong features and must be checked by incorporating a verbal head). We have seen precisely the same pattern in Hebrew sentences under *ʔeyn*: when an auxiliary is not generated, the Benoni must raise to T^0 in the overt syntax.

Returning to the negative sentences in (6-3), we can now explain why *laa* is restricted to occur with imperfect verbs. Like *ʔeyn*, it is a barrier to head movement. The only type of verb that can occur under *laa* is therefore one that does not need to acces $AgrS^0$. The Arabic imperfect is precisely that kind of verb. The *laa* sentences in (6-3) should be analyzed as "bare" NegP structures. Neither the imperfect nor Neg^0 has AgrS features, and, hence, an AgrSP is not projected in Arabic negative clauses.

6.2.2 *laa* and Its Tense Variants

The sentences in (6-3) show that Arabic differs from Hebrew in that *laa* sentences are not restricted to a particular tense, but can be associated with past, future, or present. Let us attempt to characterize this difference more precisely.

As a first step, consider the fact that, while lexical material may appear between *ʔeyn* and a Benoni verb in Hebrew, no material can intervene between *laa* and the imperfect in Arabic.[7] A particularly telling case of this is illustrated in (6-15). A subject may occur between *ʔeyn* and the verb, but not between *laa* and the verb.

(6-15) a. ʔeyn   Dani   ʔohev   li-qro.   Hebrew
            neg   Dani   like(BENONI)-MS to-read
            'Dani doesn't like to read.'

       b. *laa   Zayd   y uhibbu   ʔal-qiraaʔa.   Arabic
            neg   Zayd   3MS-like(IMPERF) the-reading
            'Zayd doesn't like reading.'

Similarly, an adverb such as *ʔal-yawm* 'today' can either follow the verb, precede *laa*, or follow the direct object; it cannot occur in between the two.

(6-16) a. Zayd   laa   y aktubu   ʔal-yawm   ʔal-risaala.
            Zayd   neg   3MS-write(IMPERF)   today   the-letter
            'Zayd is not writing the letter today.'

       b. ʔal-yawm   laa   y aktubu   Zayd   ʔal-risaala.
            today   neg   3MS-write(IMPERF)   Zayd   the-letter
            'Today, Zayd is not writing the letter.'

       c. laa   y aktubu   Zayd   ʔal-risaala   ʔal-yawm.
            neg   3MS-write(IMPERF)   Zayd   the-letter   today
            'Zayd is not writing the letter today.'

       d. *laa   ʔal-yawm   y aktubu   Zayd   ʔal-risaala.
            neg   today   3MS-write(IMPERF)   Zayd   the-letter
            'Zayd is not writing the letter today.'

I have argued that in (6-15a) the subject is in Spec/T and the Benoni occupies T^0. I now hypothesize that the basic difference between *laa* and *ʔeyn* is that *laa* incorporates T^0 in the audible syntax, leading to its movement across the subject. Since the imperfect verb is in T^0, the incorporation of T^0 into Neg^0 leads perforce to the formation of a complex head, $[_{Neg}T[\ldots V_{Imperf} \ldots]]$. Subjects and adverbs can therefore either precede the entire complex or follow it.

We can view this incorporation process as being the consequence of generating negative features on T^0 and then raising T^0 to Neg^0 in order to establish a Spec-head configuration in NegP and thereby to satisfy the Negative Criterion. The existence of the three variants of *laa* should then be taken to be the different morphological realizations of $Neg^0_{[+T]}$, the product of syntactic incorporation.[8]

I further assume that the incorporation of T^0 to *laa* is a case of selected substitution, in the sense of Rizzi and Roberts (1989). Example (6-17) illustrates the derivation of, for example, (6-3a).[9]

(6-17)

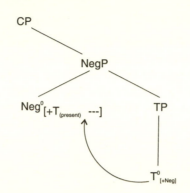

Hebrew *ʔeyn* differs from Arabic *laa* in that [neg] features are generated uniquely on the negative head and not on T^0. Therefore, T^0 does not incorporate to Neg^0 in Hebrew *ʔeyn* sentences. In more general terms, *laa* should be viewed as a cross between the two negative heads of Hebrew *ʔeyn* and *lo*. Like the former, it is a nonclitic head, but like the latter, it contains a morphological subcategorization slot for T^0, requiring movement of T^0 into this slot in the overt syntax.

We have seen that the clausal subject cannot appear between *laa* and the verb. There are two licit subject positions in a *laa* clause. The subject can either follow the verb, as in (6-18a) or precede *laa*, as in (6-18b).

(6-18) a. laa   y uḥibbu   Zayd   ʔal-qiraaʔa.
  neg   3MS-like(IMPERF)   Zayd   the-reading
  'Zayd doesn't like reading.'

  b. Zayd   laa   y uḥibbu   ʔal-qiraaʔa.
  Zayd   neg   3MS-like(IMPERF)   the-reading
  'Zayd doesn't like reading.'

Without pursuing the matter further at this point, I assume that the subject is in Spec/T in (6-18a), as in the Hebrew (6-15a), which I take to be the nominative Case position. I will return to a discussion of subject positions in chapter 8, §8.3.3 and §8.4 and slightly modify this assumption.

As for the clause-initial subject position illustrated in (6-18b), I would like to argue that it should be identified with Spec/AgrS. I conjecture that in (6-18b), AgrSP is projected and the subject moves into its Spec. Yet in order for AgrSP to be licit, there must be a head present, capable of raising to $AgrS^0$. Given the barrier status of *laa*, a verb occurring below it could not raise (over it) to $AgrS^0$ to check its features. We must retain this result to exclude the occurrence of the perfect form of the verb in *laa* sentences. The only option, then, is that *laa* itself (may) contain AgrS features. Although there is no morphological evidence to this effect, it is quite plausible that AgrS features may be abstractly represented on *laa*, since this option is clearly available in Hebrew, and it is frequently the case that features which are morphologically realized in one language lack a phonetic matrix in a closely related one, as work on comparative Romance syntax seems to strongly suggest (see, in particular, Kayne 1989).

Recall that *ʔeyn* comes in two varieties, with or without AgrS features. When those do appear on *ʔeyn*, an AgrSP is generated and the subject raises to its specifier. On comparative grounds, then, take *laa* to be optionally generated with Agr features. Example (6-18a) should thus be seen as equivalent to the Hebrew (6-19).[10]

(6-19) Ruti ʔeyn-a   yodaʕat   ʔet   ha-tšuva.
        Ruti neg-3FS   know(BENONI)-FS   ACC   the-answer
        'Ruti does not know the answer.'

6.3 TWO OTHER NEGATIVE STRUCTURES

In the following two sections, I briefly discuss two other negative structures in Standard Arabic. In the first, the negative head is the formative *laysa*, and in the second, it is *maa*.

6.3.1 Participial Negation

The negative head *laysa* occurs with nonverbal predicates, Benoni forms, and imperfective verbs, as shown in (6-20).

(6-20) a. lays-at   Mona   ʔuxt   ʔal-ustaað.
           neg-3FS   Mona   sister   the-teacher
           'Mona is not the teacher's sister.'

        b. lays-at   Mona   fi-l-bayt.
           neg-3FS   Mona   in-the-house
           'Mona is not at home.'

        c. lays-at   Mona   ḍaaribatan   Zayd.
           neg- FS   Mona   hit(BENONI)-FS   Zayd
           'Mona is not hitting Zayd.'

        d. lays-at   Mona   ta ḍribu   Zayd.
           neg-3FS   Mona   3FS-hit(IMPERF)   Zayd
           'Mona does not hit Zayd.'

Like Hebrew *ʔeyn* and Arabic *laa*, *laysa* is a nonclitic head blocking raising of the clausal predicate to AgrS⁰. The paradigm in (6-20) indeed recalls the paradigm of *ʔeyn* negation discussed in chapter 4. There are, however, three major differences between *laysa* and *ʔeyn*. First, among the predicate types occurring under *laysa*, we find the imperfect form, while the morphologically parallel form in Hebrew, that of the future tense, is impossible under *ʔeyn*. Second, *laysa* always manifests subject agreement, while *ʔeyn* can agree or not. Third, subjects of *laysa* appear to its right, while subjects of agreeing *ʔeyn* must occur to its left.

This is not the only subject position in a *laysa* clause: the subject may also occur to the left of the negative particle, as in (6-21).

(6-21) a. Mona lays-at ʔuxt ʔal-ustaaḍ.
            Mona neg-3FS sister the-teacher
            'Mona is not the teacher's sister.'

      b. Mona lays-at fi-l-bayt.
            Mona neg-3FS in-the-house
            'Mona is not at home.'

      c. Mona lays-at ḍaaribatan Zayd.
            Mona neg-3FS hit(BENONI)-FS Zayd
            'Mona is not hitting Zayd.'

      d. Mona lays-at ta ḍribu Zayd.
            Mona neg-3FS 3FS-hit(IMPERF) Zayd
            'Mona does not hit Zayd.'

The occurrence of an imperfect verb in the company of *laysa* argues that the imperfect form is a participle. Otherwise, it would be hard to characterize the natural class of predicates occurring in this construction. Once it is admitted that the imperfect is a participle, then the distinctive feature of this class is clearly the absence of tense marking.

Let us say, then (following, in essence, a suggestion by E. Doron [personal communication]) that Arabic has two participles, one verbal—the imperfect—and the other nominal. Hebrew, on the other hand, has a single participle endowed with both verbal and nominal characteristics.

Note the difference in the gloss between (6-21c) and (6-21d): the former is translated by the present continuous, the latter by the simple present. This suggests that the two participles of Arabic also differ aspectually—that is, in the feature bundle comprising Asp^0.[11]

As for the fact that *laysa* must agree with its subject, that should be taken to be a fact about the Arabic lexicon: there is simply no form of *laysa* without subject agreement. In this respect, *laysa* differs from *ʔeyn*, which has both an agreeing and a nonagreeing variant. The manifestation of AgrS features on *laysa* implies, exactly as in the case of *ʔeyn*, that AgrSP is triggered, and that Neg^0 is raised to AgrS^0 for feature checking.

Consider finally the position of the subject. The clause-initial position—illustrated in (6-21)—can be taken to be Spec/AgrS, just as in Hebrew. Hebrew, however, does not permit a subject to the right of an agreeing *ʔeyn*. Compare examples (6-20c) and (6-22). Why should this be so?

(6-22) *ʔeyn-na Ruti maka ʔet Dani.
      neg-3FS Ruti hit(BENONI)-FS ACC Dani
      'Ruti does not hit / is not hitting Dani.'

In §4.4.1, I showed that when AgrSP is projected in an *ʔeyn* sentence, the subject must move to its specifier position. Evidently this is not true in Arabic. I believe that the reason for this has to do with the different conditions under which a null subject expletive is licensed in the two languages. In the examples in (6-20), Spec/AgrS is filled by an expletive pro and the subject remains in some position lower than negation, perhaps its base position. The ungrammaticality of (6-22) is due to the fact that expletives are not licensed in Spec/AgrS in Hebrew *ʔeyn* sentences, a matter I discuss at length in §7.5. In the absence of an expletive, the subject must raise to the highest available subject position, namely to Spec/AgrS in sentences with an agreeing *ʔeyn*.[12]

6.3.2 Neutral *Neg*

In the terminology introduced by Fassi-Fehri (1993), *maa* is classed as a "neutral" negative particle. It is neutral in the sense that it can cooccur with all predicate types, as shown in (6-23).[13]

(6-23) a. maa Zaynab   katab at   ʔal-risaala.
           neg Zaynab   write(PERF)-3FS   the-letter
           'Zaynab did not write the letter.' *or* 'It is not the case that Zaynab wrote the letter.'

     b. maa Zaynab   ta ktubu   ʔal-risaala.
         neg Zaynab   3FS-write(IMPERF)   the-letter
         'Zaynab does not write the letter.' *or* 'It is not the case that Zaynab writes the letter.'

     c. maa Zaynab   daariba tan   Zayd.
         neg Zaynab   hit(BENONI)-FS   Zayd
         'Zaynab is not hitting Layla.' *or* 'It is not the case that Zaynab is hitting Layla.'

     d. maa Zaynab   fii-ʔal-daar.
         neg Zaynab   at-the-house
         'Zaynab is not at home.' *or* 'It is not the case that Zaynab is at home.'

The absence of restrictions on the cooccurrence of *maa* and a predicate suggest a similarity between *maa* and Hebrew *lo*. I therefore suggest that *maa*, like *lo*, is a clitic negative head, and thus not a barrier to movement to AgrS^0. Pursuing the parallelism with *lo*, take *maa* to morphologically subcategorize for T^0.

Like its Hebrew counterpart *lo*, *maa* does not have any AgrS features. Thus, when *maa* occurs on the left edge of a clause containing, as a main predicate, an AgrS-less verb, an imperfect or active participle, as in (6-23b,d), the subject cannot precede it, because no AgrSP is generated in the clause. This is illustrated by the ungrammaticality of (6-24a). However, when the main predicate of a *maa* sentence is a perfect verb that differs from the imperfect participial form in being intrinsically endowed with AgrS features, then AgrSP must be projected. The verb then moves to AgrS^0 (by first substituting into the slot on *maa*), a subject position becomes available in Spec/ArgS, and as a consequence, the subject can occur clause-initially. This is indicated by the grammaticality of (6-24b).

(6-24) a. *Zaynab maa ta dribu   /daariba tan   Zayd.
           Zaynab neg 3FS-hit(IMPERF)   /hit(BENONI)-FS Zayd
           'Zaynab does not hit / is not hitting Zayd.'

     b. Zaynab   maa katab at   ʔal-risaala.
         Zaynab   neg write(PERF)-3FS   the-letter
         'Zaynab did not write the letter.'

6.4   A TYPOLOGY OF NEGATIVE HEADS

Hebrew has two negative particles: *?eyn* is a nonclitic head which occurs either in an agreeing form or a nonagreeing form; *lo* is a clitic negative head, similar to the Romance variety, but having its clitic properties satisfied, not by adjunction to $AgrS^0$, as in French or Italian, but by morphologically subcategorizing for T^0.

The discontinuous form in Colloquial Arabic, namely, *ma...š*, has a head, *ma*, which is a clitic like *lo*, and can be taken to morphologically subcategorize T^0.

Finally, the three Standard Arabic negative heads—*laa*, *laysa*, and *maa*—instantiate combinations of these properties. Table (6-25) summarizes the characteristic features of the negative heads discussed in this work. The three variable properties that allow for a full classification of negative heads are clitic, subcategorization for T^0, and AgrS features.

(6–25)   Arabic and Hebrew Negative Heads

	Neg^0	Clitic	Morphological Subcategorization for T^0	AgrS Features
Hebrew	?eyn	−	−	±
Hebrew	lo	+	+	−
Coll. Arabic	ma	+	+	−
Stand. Arabic	laa	−	+	±
Stand. Arabic	laysa	−	−	+
Stand. Arabic	maa	+	+	−

PART II

NULL SUBJECTS AND INVERSION

Rizzi (1982) drew a connection between three seemingly unrelated facts in Italian, namely, the sanctioning of phonetically unexpressed pronominal subjects, the possibility of inverting the order of the verb and the subject, and the legitimacy of subject extraction over a filled complementizer—that is, the absence of Complementizer-Trace effects. These three facts are illustrated in (1).

(1) a. Verrà.
       come-FUT
       'He will come.'

     b. Verrà   Gianni.
        come-FUT   Gianni
        'Gianni will come.'

     c. Qui   credi   que   verrà?
        who   think-PRES-2S   that   come-FUT
        'Who do you think will come?'

Rizzi's analysis, transposed into contemporary terms (and refined; see, in particular, Rizzi 1986), contends that if the null subject is licensed in a given language, that is, if a language has sentences like (1a), then the null subject may serve not only as an argument but also as an expletive, associated via a chain with a subject remaining unmoved in its base, VP-internal position, whence (1b). Futhermore, if subjects are licensed in VP, then subject extraction can proceed directly from that position to Comp, and no trace is left in Spec/IP. The base position of the subject is a governed one, while Spec/IP is not. The option of effecting wh-movement directly from VP allows the grammar to circumvent the Complementizer-Trace effect and explains the grammaticality of (1c); see, in this context, the appendix to Rizzi (1991).

It is against this background that I have chosen to present studies of pro-drop and of inversion in two consecutive chapters. I hope to show, however, that the theoretical results obtained on the basis of Italian (and other Romance null subject languages) and, in particular, the unified analysis of the sentences in (1) requires some refinement if they are to hold more generally.

Hebrew differs from Italian in two fundamental respects. First, referential null subjects are only licensed in part of the verbal paradigm. I will show that this is due to constraints operative on the syntax internal to pronominal DPs, and not on what one might call the "external licensing conditions" of pro. These matters are treated in detail in chapter 7. Chapter 8 argues that the grammaticality of an inversion structure such as (1b) depends on the satisfaction of two conditions. Pro must be licensed in Spec/I and, in addition, the subject must be licensed in VP. In Italian, both conditions are satisfied, while in Hebrew the latter condition is not. I show that Hebrew subjects are, in general, not licensed at S-structure in their VP-internal position and must raise at least to their Case-position, which I have identified with Spec/T on the basis of the discussion in §4.7 ff. (Hebrew differs in this respect from Standard Arabic, cf. §6.2.2.) It then follows that the VS word order found in Hebrew does not involve moving the verb to I over an unmoved subject. I argue that, with the exception of the restricted phenomenon of Free Inversion, VS order is derived by raising the verb to Comp over a subject itself raised to Spec/I. I thus hope to show that it is not the case that, if a language has sentences such as (1a), it willy nilly has sentences such as (1b).[1]

SEVEN

Null Subjects

7.1 INTRODUCTION

Hebrew is often classified as a "semi" pro drop or null subject language. This is due to the fact that the distribution of referential null subjects cuts across the verbal paradigm in a rather unique fashion: Null subjects are admitted in conjunction with first and second person, but not with third person inflection.

This chapter aims at explicating this and related phenomena. I begin by introducing the basic conceptual framework that has been elaborated in recent years and which serves as a convenient starting point for the discussion of the Hebrew facts. The notion of morphological richness of an inflectional paradigm is brought under particular scrutiny, leading to some modifications in what might be called the subtheory of pro.

One of the conclusions reached in this chapter is that a large part of the mystery of the distributional pattern of Hebrew pro can be resolved through a better understanding of the internal structure of pronominal DPs and of the well-formedness conditions that apply to it. Elaborating on recent work of E. Ritter's (see, in particular, Ritter 1995), I propose a characterization of pronouns, relating their form to their referential attributes.

A recurring theme of this chapter revolves around the positional options of clausal subjects. In this context, a question arises as to the position of null subjects in the clause. We have seen that overt subjects can occur in a number of different positions. Can one conclude the same for pro? Since pro is an empty category, it is often difficult—indeed, impossible—to determine precisely its position with respect to the verb (does it precede it or follow it, for example).[1] The study of pro in negative clauses formed with *ʔeyn* allows one to answer this question with greater precision, since *ʔeyn* sharply demarcates the boundary of verb movement and restricts the number of possible subject positions.

7.2 THE DISTRIBUTION OF NULL SUBJECTS

7.2.1 Null Subjects and Pro

I take *null subjects* to be the phonetically unrealized or unpronounced subject pronouns in examples such as (7-1).[2]

(7-1) dibar tem   ʃal-av.
　　　talk(PAST)-2PL   about-3MS
　　　'You (*pl.*) talked about him.'

There is ample syntactic evidence that (7-1) contains a subject, which is not only understood, but syntactically represented, that is, (7-1) contains a DP which occupies a particular position in the clause, just like (7-2).

(7-2) ʔatem   dibar tem   ʃal-av.
　　　you-3PL   talk(PAST)-2PL   about-3MS
　　　'You (*pl.*) talked about him.'

　A familiar diagnostic for the syntactic presence of a nominal expression is whether it can serve as an antecedent for an anaphoric pronoun. In (7-3a,b), the anaphoric pronoun *self* is bound by the overt subject. As the English translation indicates, (7-3c) has exactly the same interpretation as (7-3a), demonstrating that (7-3c) contains a second person plural pronoun, albeit a phonetically unrealized one.

(7-3) a. ʔatem   dibar tem   ʃal ʃacmə-xem.
　　　　　you-PL   talk(PAST)-2PL   about self-2PL
　　　　　'You (*pl.*) talked about yourselves.'

　　　b. ʔata ve-Rina   dibar tem   ʃal ʃacmə-xem.
　　　　　you-PL and Rina   talk(PAST)-2PL   about self-2PL
　　　　　'You (*sing.*) and Rina talked about yourselves.'

　　　c. dibar tem   ʃal ʃacmə-xem.
　　　　　talk(PAST)-2PL   about self-2PL
　　　　　'You (*pl.*) talked about yourselves.'

I will henceforth assume that (7-1) contains a null pronominal subject, bearing—in that particular example—the features 2PL. I shall take the null subject to be an empty category of the type *pro*. The reader is referred to Chomsky (1982) and much subsequent work for justification of this point.

7.2.2 Personal and Impersonal Pronouns

Null subjects, like phonetically realized ones, can be personal or impersonal, to employ traditional terminology, and appear in a variety of constructions. In the French examples that follow, the pronoun *il* appears as a personal pronoun in (4a), and in an impersonal guise in (7-4b-d).

(7-4) a. Il   a   mangé.
  He has eaten
  'He has eaten.'

  b. Il est   arrivé   trois   filles.
  it has arrived three girls
  'Three girls have arrived.'

  c. Il est clair   que   Jean   a   terminé.
  it is clear that Jean has finished
  'It is clear that Jean has finished.'

  d. Il fait   froid.
  it makes cold
  'It is cold.'

The following examples from Spanish show that null subject pronouns have the same range of reference.

(7-5) a. Ha   comido.   c. Es evidente que Juan ha   terminado
  has eaten   *is clear   that Juan has finished*
  'S/he has eaten.'   'It is clear that Juan has finished.'

  b. Han   llegado tres   chicas.   d. Hace   frio.
  have arrived three girls   *makes cold*
  'Three girls have arrived.'   'It is cold.'

In (7-4a) and (7-5a), the null pronoun is referential, in (7-4b,c) and in (7-5b,c) it is a pleonastic (also known as expletive or a dummy) pronoun and has no referential value, serving as a placeholder, as it were, for a postposed subject, a DP in (7-4b), (7-5b) and a CP in (7-4c) and (7-5c). In (7-4d) and (7-5d), the pronoun is not, strictly speaking, referential, in that it does not single out a referent in the universe of discourse. It is, nonetheless, a syntactic argument (it has properties of arguments such as the ability to control a c-commanded PRO subject in an embedded clause). Following Chomsky (1982), I shall refer to such pronouns as quasi-referential arguments—that is, as having a nonspecific and grammatically determined reference to the climate, the atmosphere, the situation, and so forth.[3] Many languages also possess an impersonal pronoun referring to an unspecified, arbitrary group of people. Such pronouns often occur in sentences with generic time reference. In French, this is the pronoun *on*. In Hebrew, it is a null pronoun. I include arbitrary pronouns among the quasi-referential ones.

(7-6) a. On   distribue   le   courrier ici   trois   fois   par semaine.
  one distributes the mail   here three times a   week
  'The mail is distrtibuted here three times a week.'

  b. mexalkim   kan   do?ar šaloš pəʕamim bə-šavuʕa.
  distribute(BENONI)-MPL here mail three times   in-week
  'Mail is distributed here three times a week.'

Table (7-7) summarizes the referential and argumental attributes of pronouns null and overt, and (7-8) is a more explicit representation of (7-5), where the class to which pro belongs is labeled.

(7-7)   Pronoun Types

	Argumental	Referential
Argumental pro	+	+
Quasi-referential pro	+	−
Expletive pro	−	−

(7-8) a. pro_{ref} ha comido.

     b. pro_{exp} han llegado tres chicas.

     c. pro_{exp} es evidente que Juan ha terminado.

     d. $pro_{quasiref}$ ha llovido.

7.2.3   The Theory of Pro

Null pronouns typically have the same range of referential possibilities as overt ones. Their hallmark is that they are phonetically unexpressed. Not all languages have phonetically unrealized pronouns. Spanish and Italian do, but English and French do not.

There is an intuitive sense in which languages like English or French lack null subject pronouns because the paradigm of inflection in these languages is too impoverished to assign or recover the content of pro. Conversely, both Spanish and Italian are endowed with an inflectional system robust enough to identify discretely each and every combination of number and person features—that is, the core φ features of which the pronoun is constituted.

Much of the research on null subjects in inflecting languages has revolved around attempts to state explicitly the property of the morphological system that allows for their occurrence. A common thread running through work on this topic has been to associate formally the availability of null subjects and the degree of richness exhibited by the morphological system (see Taraldsen 1978 and much subsequent work).

That there is a clear link between the two (in inflecting languages, that is, putting aside the East Asian languages, on which see Huang 1984 and other work) is rather hard to deny. The correlation between rich agreement and null subjects is found not only in the Romance family (e.g., Spanish and French) but in other language groups as well. For example, while verbs in the (Germanic) Mainland Scandinavian languages Danish, Swedish, and Norwegian do not inflect for agreement and null subjects are not admitted, the insular Scandinavian languages Icelandic and Faroese manifest both a fairly rich system of verbal agreement and allow for null subjects (Platzack 1987). Irish and other Celtic languages are typically endowed with two agreement paradigms, a rich or "synthetic" one, and a poor or "analytic" one. Null subjects are found in the synthetic paradigm and overt pronouns in the analytic one (see McCloskey and Hale 1984).

Evidence from language change also points in the direction of a robust connection between inflectional richness and null subjects. Platzack and Holmberg (1989) demonstrate that Swedish lost null subjects at roughly the same period that verbal agreement disappeared, and Adams (1987) shows that Old French had both null subjects and a richer paradigm of subject agreement than Modern French.

Yet it is not obvious how this intuition can be cast into a coherent conceptual framework. Consider the inflectional paradigm of the English verb *smoke*.

(7-9) I/you (*SING*)/we/you (*PL*)/they   smoke
       he/she   smokes

The ungrammaticality of an English sentence such as *smoke* is surely related to the fact that the inflectional morphology of English provides no clues as to whether the subject is *I*, *you-SING*, *we*, *you-PL*, or *they*. While it is intuitively clear why *smoke* is an ungrammatical sentence, it is far from clear why, on the same intuitive grounds, *smokes* is as ungrammatical, since the suffix *-s* unambiguously identifies the subject as one of the two third person singular pronouns *he* or *she*.

Rizzi (1986) proposes a more articulate theory of pro capable of resolving this and similar problems (see also Adams 1987). His basic idea is that the Pro Module of UG is comprised of two distinct components, a system of *formal licensing*, and a convention for content *assignment* or *recoverability*.

(7-10)   The Pro Module (Rizzi, 1986)
       a. Formal Licensing
          pro is Case-marked by X^0.

       b. Feature Assignment/Recoverability
          Let X be the licensing head of an occurrence of pro; then pro has the grammatical specification of the features on X coindexed with it.

Formal licensing is the parameter that determines for each head in a given grammar whether it is or whether it is not a licit licenser. Subject pro is formally licensed in this system through Case assignment by Infl. Null pronouns occurring in other positions need to be licensed by their respective Case assigning head. In French, only V^0 and P^0 are formal licensers; in Italian $Infl^0$ and V^0; and so on.[4] In English, no head is a licit licenser for pro, hence *smokes* is ungrammatical on purely formal grounds, independently of any other factor.

If a head is specified positively for the licensing parameter, pro is formally licensed by it whenever it is Case marked by it. Rizzi shows, however, that different types of pro have different patterns of distribution which cannot be perspicuously explained on the basis of this parameter setting alone.

The distribution of different types of pro depends on two factors: the type of pro in question (e.g., argumental, nonreferential) and the specific φ-features available on the licensing head. Referential pro requires coindexation with person features; argumental pro (quasi-arguments and arbitrary pro) requires coindexation with number features; expletive pro requires no identification at all, being in some sense featureless; see Table (7-11). In this system, the features of subject pro are assigned or recovered through coindexation with the relevant features of $Infl^0$.

(7-11)   φ-features Required for
          the Identification of Pro

	Person	Number
pro$_{ref}$	+	+
pro$_{quasiref}$		+
pro$_{exp}$		

A slight updating of the formulation of (7-10), in line with the more articulate structure of the system of functional heads assumed in this work, will facilitate the unfolding discussion. I have argued that nominative Case is assigned or checked in a Spec-head relationship with T^0. I thus take T^0 to be the licensing head for subject pro. As for the source of features, I take that to be an Agr head. Pro must be in the Spec position of the relevant Agr head in order for its features to be identified.

In Rizzi's schema, the licensing head is itself the source of features. Clearly, this cannot be maintained in its strict formulation if the above assumptions regarding clause structure and nominative case assignment are adopted, since nominative Case and agreement features are located on two distinct heads, T^0 and $AgrS^0$.

7.2.4   Referential Pro in Hebrew

Let us now consider the distribution of null subjects in Hebrew, starting with the referential variety.[5] In (7-12), I repeat the two basic inflectional paradigms of Hebrew—that of the past and future tenses. Null subjects are only admitted in conjunction with verbs in the boxed area of the table. What (7-12) shows is that only when the verb is inflected for first and second person is a null referential subject possible.

(7-12)   Hebrew Inflectional Paradigms: √ktb 'write'

	Future Tense		Past Tense	
	Singular	Plural	Singular	Plural
1	?e-xtov	ni-xtov	katav-ti	katav-nu
2m	ti-xtov	ti-xtəv-u	katav-ta	katav-tem
2f	ti-xtəv-i	"	katav-t	"
3m	yi-xtov	yi-xtəv-u	katav	katv-u
3f	ti-xtov	"	katv-a	"

Of the two examples in (7-13), only the first, (7-13a), is grammatical. The same sentence but with a null subject is excluded, as in (7-13b). The contrast between (7-13b) and (7-14) shows that an overt pronoun is obligatory. (The relevant cases are in the embedded clauses in [7-13] since root null subjects are more liable to be identifiable through discourse and may tell us little about grammatically licensed null subjects.)[6]

(7-13)   a. (?ani xošev   še-)   tixtəvi   sipur.
       (I   think(BENONI)-MS that-) 2FS-write(FUT) story
       '(I think that) you will write a story.'

       b. *(?ani xošev   še-)   yixtəvu   sipur.
       (I   think(BENONI)-MS that-) 3PL-write(FUT) story
       '(I think that) they will write a story.'

(7-14)   (?ani xošev   še-)   hem yixtəvu   sipur.
       (I   think(BENONI)-MS that-) they 3PL-write(FUT) story
       '(I think that) they will write a story.'

The first thing to note with respect to these examples, is that pro is formally licensed in Hebrew tensed clauses, for the obvious reason that pro is available in

(7-13a). Since licensing is a parametric option for a given head, it suffices that pro be possible for a given tense setting to conclude that Infl (i.e., T^0) must be taken to be a proper licensing head, in accordance with the principles of the Pro Module in (7-10). Consequently, the split in the paradigm cannot be attributed to a negative setting of the formal licensing parameter for T^0.

If the availability of referential null subjects is correlated with the availability of discrete inflectional affixes for the feature [person], how is one to explain the split in the paradigm in (7-12) between the first or second person, on the one hand, and the third person, on the other? In both of the examples in (7-13), person features are clearly distinct, yet (7-13a) is a grammatical case of pro-drop and (7-13b) is not.

Let us examine in greater detail the relation between the phonetic realization of affixes and the availability of null referential subjects, observing first the past tense paradigm in (7-12). This inflectional paradigm reveals that there is no overt affix designating third person; for the sake of the argument, take the -*a* of *katv-a* 'she wrote' and the -*u* of *katv-u* 'they wrote' to mark feminine gender and plural number, respectively. This gap can be taken to mean either that there is no affix corresponding to the feature third person, or that the affix is phonetically null. Whichever option one selects (I have chosen the latter—cf. note 12, chapter 1—since it permits a homogenous treatment of both the past and future paradigms), it is clear that no ambiguity arises for the identification of the null subject if a verb inflected for third person is employed. Since there is only one null or unpronounced form, the null affix identifies pro as third person precisely and unambiguously.[7]

Consideration of the future tense paradigm renders the correlation of the paradigm split in (7-12) with morphological explicitness even more tenuous. The [3MS] verbal form is marked by a distinct prefix *y(i)-*, and yet null subjects are not permitted in its company.

This is further evidenced by the fact that, while the verbal forms manifesting [2MS] and [3FS] are identical in the future tense paradigm, (7-15) can only have the first and not the second interpretation.

(7-15)   ti-xtov.
         'You-MS will write.'
         *'She will write.'

One wonders why the system does not work the other way around—namely, why speakers do not allow a null subject with the second rather than the first interpretation, or why both forms are unacceptable with a null subject?

What the Hebrew facts seem to be telling us is that the paradigm split in (7-12) is not, at least directly, related to the third person verbal inflection, in particular, that the unavailability of a third person pro has little or nothing to do with morphological richness or explicitness. The Hebrew inflectional paradigm is as formally explicit as that of Italian and Spanish.

A comparative glance at neighboring Palestinian Arabic, the inflectional paradigm of which is given in (7-16), further confirms this conclusion.[8]

(7-16)   Palestinian Arabic Inflectional Paradigms: *ktb* 'write'

	Imperfect "Dependent" Form		Perfect Form	
	Singular	Plural	Singular	Plural
1	ʔa-ktub	(m)nu-ktub	katab-t	katab-na
2m	tu-ktub	tu-kutb-u	katab-t	katab-tu
2f	tu-kutbi-i	"	katab-ti	"
3m	yu-ktub	yu-kutb-u	katab	katab-u
3f	tu-ktub	"	katb-at	"

Palestinian has referential null subjects in conjunction with third person inflection, as shown in (7-17).[9]

(7-17)   a. fakkar-t   ʔinno b-(y)u-ktub   riwaaye.
               think-PERF-1S that   ASP-3MS-write-(IMPERF) story
               'I thought that he will write a story.'

          b. fakkar-t   ʔinno katb-at   riwaaye.
               think-PERF-1S that   write-(PERF)-3FS   story
               'I thought that she wrote a story.'

The paradigm of the Palestinian imperfect is practically identical to that of the Hebrew future tense. The paradigm of the Palestinian perfect, is, if anything, less explicit than that of Hebrew, since the forms [1S] and [2MS] are realized by a syncretic affix. Yet referential null subjects are possible in all three persons in Palestinian and only in the first two persons in Hebrew.[10] Given the extraordinary similarity between Hebrew and Palestinian agreement inflection, the more restricted occurrence of null subjects in the former cannot be associated with an overt morphological difference.[11]

It would be too hasty, however, to conclude that morphological richness plays no role in sanctioning the admissibility of pro in Hebrew. While the past and future tense paradigms allow a referential pro in conjunction with first and second person inflection, Benoni verbs resist a referential pro entirely. None of the examples in (7-18) is grammatical.

(7-18)   a. *kotev   sipurim.
               write(BENONI)-MS   stories
               'I (M)/you (MS)/he write(s) stories.'

          b. *kotvim   sipurim.
               write(BENONI)-MPL stories
               'We (M)/you (MPL)/they (M) write stories.'

          c. *kotevet   sipurim.
               write(BENONI)-FS   stories
               'I (F)/you (FS)/she write(s) stories.'

          d. *kotvot   sipurim.
               write(BENONI)-FPL stories
               'We (F)/you (FPL)/they (F) write stories.'

The Benoni paradigm, repeated in (7-19), distinguishes two numbers and two genders. As pointed out in Borer (1986), Person distinctions are entirely absent. The split between the past/future and the *Benoni* inflection shows that Person features are crucial for the identification of null subjects, as predicted by Rizzi's approach.

(7-19)   Inflectional Paradigm
          of the Benoni

	Singular	Plural
Masc.	kotev	kotv-im
Fem.	kotev-et	kotv-ot

I have argued that the Benoni inflection is participial agreement associated with an Agr position lower than TP (Chapter 2). When the Benoni occurs as the only visible verb in a present-tense sentence, it can either raise to T^0 directly or be raised to $AgrS^0$ following incorporation into a a null auxiliary, the latter—on the null hypothesis—fully inflected for person, number, and gender. The impossibility of referential null subjects, even under the analysis of present-tense sentences as incorporating a null auxiliary, shows not only that person features have to be represented but also that they must meet some criterion of morphological distinctness.

We thus see that the mystery of Hebrew referential null subjects does not lie in their being insensitive to considerations of morphological explicitness. On the contrary, Rizzi's claim to the effect that, in addition to formal licensing, pro must be in the domain of an Agr node rich enough to identify its features, holds for Hebrew as for other inflecting languages. For referential pro to be licit, [person] must be represented on Agr in a discrete fashion.

7.2.5 The Internal Structure of Pronouns

The task, then, is to identify the factor that renders referential pro inadmissible in conjunction with a third person Agr, despite the discrete fashion in which the third person is represented. I have shown that the identification procedure proposed by Rizzi and the claim that the availability of person features on Agr is a necessary condition for the identification of a referential pro must be maintained for Hebrew. It should be concluded, therefore, that manipulation or revision of the Pro Module will not yield a satisfactory answer to the puzzle posed by Hebrew.

This conclusion leads me to abandon the search for an answer in terms of the factors that enter into the identification of pro and turn my attention to the internal structure of the pronominal element itself. The basic idea I wish to develop in this section is that third person pro is inherently impersonal in nature, and hence incompatible with a referential interpretation. Following Ritter (1995) to a large extent, I propose a structural implementation of this idea, leading to some consequences regarding the structure of pronominal elements in general.

Ritter (1995) observes that first and second pronouns in Hebrew are in complementary distribution with the definite determiner *ha-*. Compare (7-20a) with (7-20b).

(7-20) a. *ha-ʔani /*ha-ʔanaxnu /*ha-ʔat   /*ha-ʔata   /*ha-ʔatem
           *the-I   /the-we   /the-you-F /the-you-M /the-you-PL

        b. ha-ʔiš̌
           the-man

This fact leads her to argue that first and second person pronouns are D heads, and thus compete with the determiner *ha-*, itself a D⁰ element.

Third person pronouns, however, can combine with *ha-* to yield demonstrative pronouns, as shown in (7-21).

(7-21)   ha-hu /ha-hi   /ha-hem
            the-he   the-she   /the-she
            'that-M'/ 'that-F'/ 'those'

The logic by means of which the examples in (7-20a) are ruled out suggests that third person pronouns are not D⁰ elements but instantiate a different category, which Ritter labels Num⁰ (containing the features [number] and [gender]). In configurational terms, the DPs in (7-20) and (7-21) have the structures in (7-22). (Assume that the pronominal forms are intransitive heads—that is, that they have no complement.)

(7-22)   a. = (7-20a)

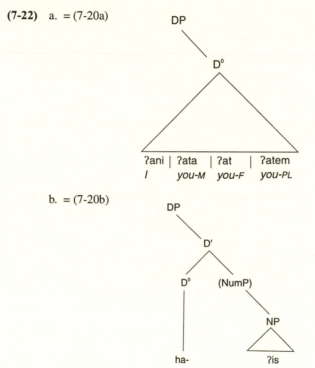

c. = (7-21)

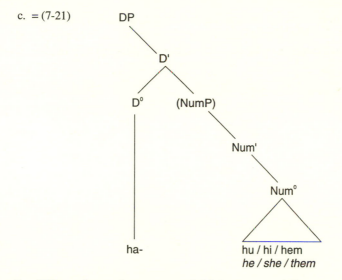

Given the different internal structure of third person and first or second person pronouns, the question arises as to how to analyze the third person pronoun when it is a *personal* pronoun, as in (7-23), and not a demonstrative.

(7-23)   hu   katav   sipurim.
         he   write(PAST)-3MS   stories
         'He wrote stories.'

The pronoun *hu* ('he') in (7-23) differs from the demonstrative in (7-21) in two respects: it lacks a determiner, and it is specified for the feature [person]. Ritter proposes that this φ-feature belongs to the category D^0. The D-structure of the pronoun in (7-23), and more generally of nondemonstrative third person pronouns is thus as in (7-24).

(7-24)

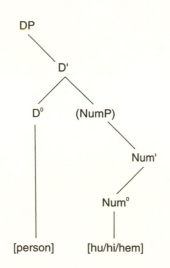

The feature [person] is a φ-feature. Let us say that it is an N-related head, and as such requires checking with an appropriate nominal head. Let us conjecture that checking is implemented by raising and adjoining Num⁰ to D⁰, yielding (7-25).[12]

(7-25)

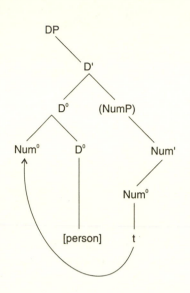

Assume further that the feature [person] entails definiteness. In the demonstrative *ha-hu* 'the-he', the definiteness feature is contributed by the article. Where personal *hu* 'he' appears, this feature is contributed by [person].

We are now in a position to tackle the question why (7-23) is grammatical only with an overt pronoun—that is, why (7-26) is ungrammatical (see also the contrast between [7-13b] and [7-14]).

(7-26)   *katav   sipurim.
           write(PAST)-3MS   stories
           'He wrote stories.'

The internal structure of the null subject in (7-26) is diagrammed in (7-27).

(7-27)

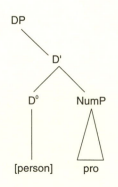

NumP in (7-27) is a null category, a pro. Now, the derivation diagrammed in (7-25) is only licit when there is lexical material in Num^0 capable of checking or supporting the [person] feature or affix in D^0. In (7-27), however, Num^0 cannot serve to check or support [person] in D^0. PronNumP can be taken to be an intrinsically featureless category—if the contents of pro is *assigned* rather than *recovered* by its licensing head (see [7-10b]). Alternatively, if pro is taken to be specified for at least some features, as in the discussion of expletives in §7.2.8., then Num^0 may simply be inaccessible to (head) movement when it occurs internally to pro.

Pro is indeed formally licensed by T^0 ("external licensing") and identified by coindexation with $AgrS^0$ in (7-26). However, the feature [person] occupying D^0, the head of the pronominal DP, cannot be sanctioned internally to DP. Hence the DP cannot have a personal reference.[13]

Palestinian Arabic (like Spanish and Italian) has referential pro in company with third person agreement in the past and future. Not surprisingly, Arabic third person pronouns cannot be preceded by a determiner, as shown by the ungrammaticality of (7-28). I take that to mean that third person pronouns in this language are D^0 elements, and can be represented like a Hebrew first and second person pronoun; cf. (7-22a).

(7-28) *l-hu/*l-hi/l-hinni
  the-he/the-she/the-they

First and second person pronouns cannot be impersonal, they are intrinsically fully referential. There are no first or second person expletives, only "third" person expletives. Benveniste makes the typological claim that in many languages "the 'third person' is not a 'person'; it is really the verbal form whose function is to express the *non-person*" (1966: 198). It is tempting to cast this claim into a structural mold and claim that, in the unmarked case, first and second person pronouns are D^0 elements, and the remaining pronoun an element of the class Num^0. In languages such as Italian and Spanish, which admit a third person pro alongside an impersonal one, there are two "third" person pros—the personal one, which is a D^0 head, and the impersonal one, which is a Num^0 head. This is perhaps not surprising, given the fact that French uses the same morphological form, namely *il*, for both types of pronouns.[14]

7.2.6 Nonreferential Pro

The immediate prediction of the foregoing analysis is that impersonal null subjects of various sorts should be perfectly licit in the company of past/future tense verbs inflected for third person since they do not require a specification for [person]. Example (7-29a) illustrates a quasi-argumental 'atmospheric' pro, and (7-29b) a pro with arbitrary reference.

(7-29) a. haya   kar.   b. maxru   šam   kartisim.
          be(PAST)-3MS cold   *sell(PAST)-3PL there tickets*
          'It was cold.'   'They sold tickets there.'

Number specification is a necessary condition for the identification of quasi-referential null subjects—see (7-11). Since all verb types in Hebrew—past, future, and Benoni—manifest number distinctions (i.e., singular and plural), this condition is satisfied with all types of Agr. It is therefore not surprising that these instances of pro can occur in conjunction with Benoni verbs, as in (7-30).

(7-30)   a. kar.   b. moxrim   šam   kartisim.
              cold   *sell(BENONI)-MPL there   tickets*
              'It is cold.'   'They sell tickets there.'

Pleonastic null subjects are nonreferential and, in accordance with (7-11), require no identification of φ-features (see, however, §7.2.8, where this assumption is challenged). They are subject only to the formal licensing condition, (7-10a). Since Hebrew T^0 is a licit formal licensing head for null subjects, we expect pleonastics to show up with all verb classes. Example (7-31a) illustrates a *there*-type (DP-associated) expletive, and (7-31b) an *it*-type (CP-associated) expletive.

(7-31)   a. hitxolela   ba-xuc   səʕara.
              rage(PAST)-3FS   in-the-outside   storm
              'A storm raged outside.'

             b. barur me-ʔelav   še-   mediniyut ha-memšala   mutʕet.
              evident-MS from self-3MS that- policy   the-government   erroneous.
              'It is self-evident that the policy of the government is erroneous.'

To conclude, nonreferential instances of pro are available in all tenses in Hebrew. This is due to the fact that they require coindexation only with the feature [number] with which Agr heads in all tenses in Hebrew are endowed.

7.2.7   The Internal Structure of Nonreferential Pronouns

The question to be addressed in this section concerns the internal structure of nonreferential pro. Consider again the illicit structure of a third person referential pro in Hebrew. Recall that this structure is ill formed because the feature [person] cannot be supported or checked when NumP is pro.

Nonreferential pro falls into two main types: quasi referential (of which arbitrary pro and atmospheric pro are two subcases), and expletive pro. The latter has no referential value and is assigned no θ-role. Take that to be structurally represented by the absence of a DP layer. Assume, in other words, that D^0 is the locus of the features contributing to the determination of the reference of a DP (Longobardi 1994 and Stowell 1991a), so that when this layer is missing, the nominal in question cannot bear a θ-role. Expletive pro thus has the structure of a "bare" NumP with an intransitive head, as in (7-32).

(7-32)

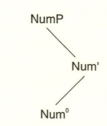

Atmospheric pro has a fixed reference. For lack of a better term, let us say that it refers to the "atmosphere." Take 'atmosphere' to be a semantic feature in D^0. Crucially, "atmosphere" is not a φ-feature; it is not morphologically represented, but it has a status similar to semantic features such as [human] and [generic] which, at least in the languages under consideration here, are not inflectional affixes. Since D^0 of an atmospheric pro is not an inflectional element like [person], its content does not require checking or lexical support internally to DP. It can consequently coexist with a phonetically null (nonlexical) NumP.

Arbitrary pro receives a similar analysis in this system. Its reference is a combination of semantic feature values (e.g., [+human], [+generic]), which we can simply abbreviate by *arb*. Like 'atmosphere', the semantic features making up *arb* are not φ-features (although *arb* may and typically is associated with a fixed set of φ-features), and hence do not require checking by a lower head.[15] Hence, Num^0 does not need to raise to D^0 to check any features and the pronominal DP is well formed. Putting together atmospheric pro and pro_arb, we arive at the following structure for a quasi-referential pro.[16]

(7-33)

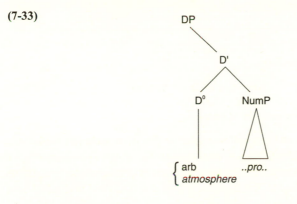

7.2.8 Reconsideration of the Feature Identification Procedure

We are now in a position to provide a principled explanation for why different types of pro require different degrees of feature identification. If Rizzi (1986) is correct, example (7-11) stands as a valid generalization. The question is why this generalization holds. Let us take the identification procedure of pro to consist of coindexation of all of pro's φ-features with those of Agr^0. Thus, whatever features are manifested by the pronoun, those features must be coindexed with the same features on Agr^0. If the pronominal DP is endowed with person features, then the relevant Agr^0 must also be endowed with person features. If pro only has number features, then Agr must be specified for number and so forth. Strictly speaking, then, it is not the case that different types of pro require different degrees of identification. Rather, all instances of pro require coindexation with an Agr endowed with all of pro's features.

The referential force of a referential pro is represented by means of the feature [person] in D^0. Thus, the Agr with which pro is coindexed must contain person features. Quasi-referential pro lacks a fully referential D^0—that is, the feature person is not represented in the pronominal DP. Consequently, the identifying Agr need not contain person features. Both referential and quasi-referential instances of pro are endowed with a number specification, because pro is of the category NumP.

I have argued that expletive pro is devoid of the DP layer altogether, that it is a bare NumP. This means that expletive pro has no person features, and hence can be associated with an Agr node lacking this feature. However, since expletives belong to the category NumP, they are endowed with a number specification and must be associated with an Agr node containing number features.

That expletives are specified for number seems rather clear, although difficult to discern in languages such as Hebrew or Italian. This is so for the simple reason that, in such languages, verbal agreement features in structures of subject inversion—where the subject position is arguably filled by an expletive—always match those of the postverbal subject, as illustrated in (7-34). The verb is inflected for singular number in (7-34a), where the postverbal subject is singular and for plural number in (7-34b), where the subject is plural.[17]

(7-34)   a. pro kart a   kan   teʔuna.
                 occurred(PAST)-3FS here   accident
             'An accident occurred here.'

         b. pro kar u   mikrim ka-ʔele   ba-ʕavar.
                 occurred(PAST)-3PL events like-these in-the(-past)
             'Events such as these occurred in the past.'

Let us say that the contents of Num^0 of an expletive pro is variable in (7-34). It is singular in (7-34a), and in (7-34b) it is plural.

In many languages, the value for the number feature is invariable. This seems to be the case in many dialects of Northern Italy (viz., Poletto 1993 and references cited therein), and if Mohammad (1990) is correct, this is also true in Standard Arabic. In (7-35), the postverbal plural subject *ʔaḥdaaθ* 'events' appears in conjunction with a verb in the singular (the verb is also marked for feminine gender, as are all verbs whose subject is inanimate, an irrelevant detail). Mohammad (1990) argues that the verb in (7-35) agrees with a singular expletive.

                 ↓agreement↓
(7-35)   pro   jarat   ʔaḥdaaθ ka-haaði-hi fi-l-maadi.
                 occur(PERF)-FS   events   such-this   in-the-past
             'Events such as these occurred in the past.'

Note that the mere fact that the number specification of expletive pro can vary across languages means that this instance of pro is specified for number—that is, it contains a NumP. The parameter distinguishing languages such as Standard Arabic from languages such as Hebrew seems to have little consequence for the grammars of these languages as a whole. What seems to be at stake, rather, are minor lexical differences: Standard Arabic has expletive pronouns (i.e., pro-NumPs), whose value for the feature number is [+ singular] (or [- plural]), while the value for Hebrew expletive pro is not fixed: it is [± singular] (or [± plural]).

One might think of a pro with a fixed number specification as actually having no specification for number, the value [Ø] being realized as default [+singular] agreement on the verb. This is independently motivated by the fact that verbal agreement is singular when the postverbal subject is (an extraposed) CP, and hence lacks φ-features of its own. This seems to be true even in grammars endowed with a variable expletive.

For languages like Hebrew with a variable expletive, a further mechanism is necessary to ensure that the number specification on pro match that of a postverbal nominal subject. One can think of this matching as necessary up to availability: when the feature number is specified (as either '+' or '–'), it must match that of the postverbal subject. When [number] is [Ø], such a matching is trivially satisfied, in the sense that there is no positively specified number feature on the expletive.

Note, finally, that expletives have number specification because they are nominal expressions, not because of any semantic requirement. Reference, to recall, is tied up with the [person] feature in D^0. In languages such as English or Dutch, expletives are locative expressions such as 'there'. Locative expletives lack a specification for number since their structure includes no NumP. Insofar as there are null locative expletives, they require no feature identification simply because they have no φ-features.

7.2.9 Summary

Close observation of the Hebrew inflectional paradigms yielded two major consequences. First, that the generalization in (7-11) holds for Hebrew—that is to say, referential pro in Hebrew requires association with an Agr specified for person. This consequence explains the contrast between the distribution of pro in the past/future tense and in the Benoni. Second, we saw that an explicit morphological representation of [person] is a necessary condition for the identification of referential pro, but is insufficient to characterize the contrast internal to the past and future paradigms, namely, the availability of pro with first and second person inflection and its unavailability in conjunction with third person inflection.

I then pursued a different angle, and looked at the internal structure of the pronouns in question. Following Ritter's work, I argued that third person pronouns in Hebrew have a deficient structure with respect to first and second person pronouns, and the unavailability of third person pro followed from the inability to license the referential content of D^0, embodied in the feature [person]. A proposal was then advanced that the three major classes of pronouns—viz., referential, quasi referential, and expletive—have somewhat differing internal structures. I attempted to derive the feature content of pro from its structure and explain the generalization in (7-11). It was argued that the lack of the feature [person] on some instances of pro is a consequence of its deficient structure, in particular of the fact that it either lacks a DP layer altogether (expletive pro) or that D^0 does not contain the feature [person] or, for that matter, any inflectional feature, but a combination of semantic features (quasi-referential pro).

7.3   THE POSITION OF NULL SUBJECTS

In the framework of a theory in which Infl is both the source of nominative Case and the locus of φ-features, it is predicted that null subjects must occur in Spec/I since they must occur in a Case-marked position and Spec/I is the nominative position.

Here, however, it is shown that the nominative Case assigner (the locus of nominative Case features) is not to be equated with the head containing φ-features. I have identified the head-checking nominative Case with T^0. If T^0 is incorporated into $AgrS^0$ in the syntax, as Chomsky (1993) proposes for English, and the language lacks a Spec/T position, then indeed, formal licensing and feature identification are implemented in the same position. However, we have seen that not all languages or constructions make use of this option. In particular, the Hebrew *?eyn* construction shows that nominative Case can be assigned independently of subject agreement matching: subjects may occur at S-structure in Spec/T, in their Case position, without requiring access to AgrSP.

The study of null subjects in environments where nominative Case (formal licensing) and agreement (feature identification) are dissociated thus raises the question of where pro may occur in the clausal structure. A present tense sentence such as (7-36) contains a Benoni verb and may, as I have shown, have the structure of a bare TP.

(7-36)   moxrim   kan   kafe.
              sell(BENONI)-MPL   here   coffee
              'They sell coffee here.'

In the absence of an AgrSP layer, the highest possible subject position in the clause is Spec/T. We have argued that lexical subjects may occur in Spec/T at S-structure. Does this carry over to pro? Is (7-37) a proper representation of (7-36)? (The representation of the adverb *kan* 'here' is suppressed.)

(7-37)

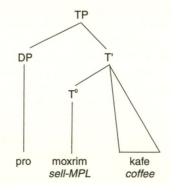

The impersonal quasi-referential pro in (7-36) can presumably be Case marked in Spec/T and identified in a position lower than TP.

I believe that the analysis adumbrated here is basically tenable. It hinges, however, on the claim that the present tense sentence in (7-36) is indeed analyzed as a TP, and not as an AgrSP. The option of projecting AgrSP is always available, however, as we have seen, since the occurrence of a null auxiliary in (7-36) cannot be ruled out.

In order to ensure that pro is trapped, so to speak, in Spec/T, we must turn to a structure that does not admit a null auxiliary and, consequently, forbids the occurrence of the AgrSP layer. The *Ɂeyn* negative structure and, in particular, the brand of *Ɂeyn* sentences that involve no agreement on the negative head and hence do not project AgrSP, permit a closer scrutiny of the positional options of pro.

7.4   NULL SUBJECTS IN *Ɂeyn* SENTENCES

In *Ɂeyn* sentences lacking an AgrSP layer, lexical and overt pronominal subjects occur in Spec/T, as in the examples in (7-38).

(7-38) a. Ɂeyn Rina   kotev et   sipurim.
           neg   Rina   write(BENONI)-FS   stories
           'Rina does not write books.'

     b. Ɂeyn hi   kotev et   sipurim.
           neg   she   write(BENONI)-FS   stories
           'She does not write books.'

The question arises as to which types of null subjects may occur in the absence of an AgrSP layer. Consider first the examples in (7-39).

(7-39) a. Ɂeyn mitxolel ot   kan   sufot.
           neg   occur(BENONI)-FPL   here   storms
           'Storms don't occur here.'

     b. Ɂeyn maɁarixim   Ɂet   ha-truma   šela.
           neg   value(BENONI)-MPL   ACC   the-contribution   her
           'People don't value her contribution.'

An expletive pro in a structure of subject inversion appears in (7-39a), and an arbitrary pro with generic human reference in (7-39b). The acceptability of these sentences indicates, first, that pro is formally licensed under *Ɂeyn*, and second, that a pro with a specification for number can be properly identified in the structure. We have assumed that the formal licensing head of subject pro is T^0. We now have empirical evidence to support that assumption, since the other conceivable licensing head, namely $AgrS^0$, is simply not projected in (7-39).

But how is pro's number feature identified in the absence of an $AgrS^0$? Recall that the Benoni forms are endowed with participial agreement. More to the point, sentences such as those in (7-39) contain a structurally low subject agreement projection, namely, AgrPartP. The head of this projection discretely manifests features of number and gender, and pro can be identified in a Spec-head configuration with it. We can schematize the manner in which pro is rendered licit under *Ɂeyn* by means of the following tree diagram.

(7-40)

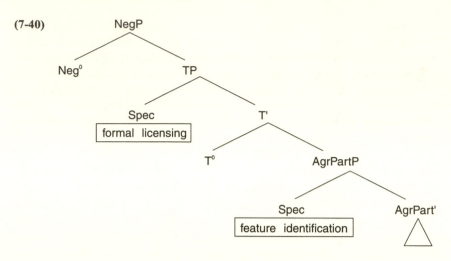

Since only [number] and [gender], but not [person], are manifested by AgrPart^0—the latter feature occurring only on AgrS^0—referential pro is predictably barred from occurring under *ʔeyn*, as shown by the ungrammaticality of (7-41).

(7-41)   *ʔeyn   kotev   /kotev-et   /kotv-im
    neg   *write(BENONI)-MS /write(BENONI)-FS /write(BENONI)-MPL*

/kotv-ot   sipurim.
/write(BENONI)-FPL   stories
'I/You/He/She/We/You/They doesn't/don't write stories.'

The picture that seems to emerge from this discussion is that all types of non- and quasi-referential null subjects are sanctioned under *ʔeyn*, in Spec/T. Formal licensing is satisfied through nominative Case assignment by T^0, and number features on AgrPart^0 can serve to identify pro's-feature content.

Matters are more complex, however. We shall see that in contrast to a DP-associated expletive as in (7-39), an expletive associated with an extraposed clause does not seem to be available under *ʔeyn*. I shall also discuss the fact that only an arbitrary pro with generic reference can occur under *ʔeyn*, while an existentially quantified arbitrary pro cannot; see §7.4.2 where the difference between the two arb interpretations is explained. The other quasi-referential pro, the atmospheric one, is also unavailable under *ʔeyn*, as we shall see in §7.4.3.

Since these instances of pro do not form a coherent natural class in terms of their feature content, an analysis exploiting only the devices afforded by the Pro Module cannot account for their distribution. I shall attempt to show that other considerations, primarily related to the particular syntax of *ʔeyn* sentences, can be invoked to provide a satisfactory, albeit not a unified, analysis of the data.

7.4.1   Expletives, Extraposition, and Sentential Subjects

We have seen one case of expletive pro under *ʔeyn*, namely, in sentences with inverted subjects. The postverbal subject in (7-39) is a DP. Let us now see what happens in sentences where the postverbal subject is an extraposed clause. Consider the contrast in (7-42).

(7-42) a. kaše   li-lmod   polanit.   b. *ʔeyn kašc   li-lmod   polanit.
          difficult to-learn Polish   *neg difficult to-learn Polish*
          'It is difficult to learn Polish.'   'It isn't difficult to learn Polish.'

Extraposition of a CP is perfectly licit in (7-42a), but gives rise to strong ungrammaticality in (7-42b). In order to understand this contrast, it should first be observed that (7-43) is perfectly acceptable.

(7-43) ʔeyn ze kaše   li-lmod   polanit.
         neg it difficult to-learn Polish
         'It isn't difficult to learn Polish.'

Sentence (7-43) differs minimally from (7-42b) in the presence of the pronoun *ze* 'it'. The nature of this pronoun is clarified several paragraphs below, but no matter how we analyze it, the three-way contrast between (7-42a), (7-42b), and (7-43) demonstrates that what is at stake is not the occurrence of an extraposed clause as such in the structure, since a postverbal "subject" CP is represented in all three examples.[18] I shall show that the variable factor is the manner by which the expletive or the element occupying Spec/T in these sentences is associated with the extraposed clause.

I approach this question by noting that the ungrammaticality of (7-42b) poses something of a theoretical problem, when taken in tandem with the full acceptability of (7-39a). Both examples involve a postverbal subject; both exploit a null expletive in Spec/T. Many accounts for the relationship between expletives and their associates consider *there-* and *it-*type expletives to be similar. Both are taken to be associated with the postverbal argument by means of a CHAIN; that is, the two are coindexed and in LF the argument moves to replace the expletive which, being contentless, cannot meet the principle of Full Interpretation. The derivation of two example sentences is given in (7-44).[19]

(7-44) a. There arrived [three girls].

    ↑_____|

   b. It is obvious [that the earth is round].

    ↑_____|

While expletive replacement raises no particular difficulties in the case of (7-44a), substitution or adjunction of the extraposed CP into a position occupied at S-structure by a DP, as in (7-44b), raises a question concerning structure preservation.

Indeed, a number of authors have argued that subject clauses are never actually in Spec/I—that is, they are never literally subjects, even in the intraposed version of (7-44b), namely (7-45). (See, e.g., Emonds 1976, Koster 1978, and Stowell 1981.)

(7-45) [cpThat the earth is round] is obvious.

Emonds (1976) and Stowell (1981) argue that sentential subjects are Topics (Koster 1978 uses the term "satelites," which we can also take to mean topics of some sort.) The syntax of Hebrew sentential subjects, examined in greater detail in the following subsections, argues in favor of these approaches and yields an explanation for the ungrammaticality of (7-42b).

7.4.1.1   *Sentential Subjects in Hebrew*

Hazout (1994) notes that sentences with sentential subjects occur in one of the three forms illustrated in (7-46).

(7-46)   a. kaše   li-lmod   polanit.
             difficult to-learn Polish
             'It is difficult to learn Polish.'

       b. ze kaše   li-lmod   polanit.
             it difficult to-learn Polish
             'It is difficult to learn Polish.'

       c. li-lmod   polanit ze kaše.
             to-learn Polish it difficult
             'To learn Polish is difficult.'

When the clausal subject is extraposed, the subject position is either filled by a null expletive, (7-46a), or by the pronoun *ze*, (7-46b). When the clausal subject is intraposed, however, *ze* is still obligatory. Example (7-46c) contrasts with (7-47).[20]

(7-47)   *li-lmod   polanit kaše.
             to-learn Polish difficult
             'To learn Polish is difficult.'

In order to better understand the syntax of sentential subjects and extraposition in Hebrew, I first summarize Hazout's (1994) analysis of *ze*.

7.4.1.2   *The Pronoun* ze

Hazout (1994) argues that *ze* is not an overt expletive.[21] He observes that *ze* is barred from sentences in which the subject position is nonthematic—personal and impersonal passives, for example. The sentences in (7-48) are ungrammatical, he claims, because *ze* requires but is not assigned a θ-role.

(7-48)   a. *ze carix   la-ʕavod.
             it   must   to-work
             'One has to work.'

       b. *ze nimsar   še- Dan higiʕa.
             it   was communicated that- Dan arrived.
             'It was communicated that Dan arrived.'

       c. *ze nišmaʕ   cilcul   paʕamon.
             it   was heard   ringing   bell
             'The ringing of a bell was heard.'

All of the examples in (7-48) can be rendered grammatical if a null subject appears in lieu of *ze*. This leads Hazout to conjecture that *ze* is a pronoun to which a θ-role is assigned.

He then proceeds to discuss the alternation exhibited in (7-46). Prima facie, the alternation between *ze* and a null subject in (7-46a,b) could be taken to indicate that *ze* is indeed an overt variant of pro. Hazout notes, however, that the postverbal CP should be taken to occupy different positions in these two examples. He shows that extraction from a CP associated with pro yields a grammatical output, as in (7-49a), and an ungrammatical one when *ze* occupies the subject position, as in (7-49b).

(7-49) a. ma   kaše   li-lmod?   b. *ma   ze kaše   li-mod?
           what difficult to-learn   *what it difficult to-learn*
           'What is difficult to learn?'   'What is it difficult to learn?'

This contrast can be accounted for, he argues, if the clause is in an argument position—an L-marked position in Chomsky's (1986) terminology—in (7-49a) in conjunction with pro, a true pleonastic. The extraposed clause is in an adjunct position when *ze* appears, as in (7-49b). In the latter example, the postverbal CP must occur in an adjunct position in order not to violate the θ-criterion (if the clause were in an argument position, it would require a θ-role, but the single θ-role of a predicate like *kaše* 'difficult' is assigned to *ze*). Being a clausal adjunct, its CP node constitutes a barrier to wh-movement for elements internal to it, which is why (7-49b) is ungrammatical.

7.4.1.3 *Sentential Subjects in ʔeyn Sentences*

Let us interpret the options illustrated in (7-46) in the following way: in (7-46a), the clause is the sole argument of the adjective *kaše* 'difficult' %0, and the subject position is filled by an expletive pro. In (7-46b), the clause is an adjunct and the sole θ-role is assigned to *ze*, which then raises to the subject position. Example (7-46c) shows that a clausal "subject" is in a Topic position and *ze* is like a resumptive pronoun.

Suppose, further, that (7-46a) must be transformed into (7-46c) in LF. We can think of this requirement in the following terms: the expletive subject of (7-46a) must be licensed in LF in order for the Principle of Full Interpretation to be satisfied. Replacement of the nominal expletive by the clausal argument is not a viable option, given the plausible assumption that substitution must be structure-preserving. Suppose that anteposition of the clausal argument into a Topic position in the Comp domain is followed by adjunction of the expletive. A derivation such as the one schematized in (7-50) cannot be excluded on principled grounds: the expletive is licensed by adjunction to the argument and structure preservation is not violated.

(7-50)

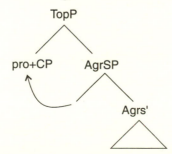

The preceding discussion was motivated, as we recall, by the ungrammaticality of (7-42b), repeated here:

(7-42) b. *ʔeyn kaše   li-lmod   polanit.
  neg   difficult   to-learn   Polish
  'It isn't difficult to learn Polish.'

The suggestion I would now like to make is that this sentence is ruled out because there is no Topic position available under *ʔeyn* to host the fronted CP in LF and to permit the subsequent adjunction of pro. In §4.4.2, it was shown that Topicalization, even of a direct object, is not possible under *ʔeyn*, whereas it is perfectly acceptable when *ʔeyn* is absent. Contrast (7-51a) and (7-51b), the latter containing an embedded Topic.

(7-51) a. *ʔeyn tapuxim Dani   ʔohev.
  neg   apples   Dani   likes
  'Apples, Dani doesn't like'

  b. ʔani xošev še-   tapuxim Dani   ʔohev.
  I   think   that-   apples   Dani   likes
  'I think that apples, Dani likes.'

I submit that (7-42b) is ruled out for the same reason as (7-51a). The presence of *ʔeyn* in Neg^0 marks the upper boundary of IP, and there is no CP projection, and hence no Topic position, under NegP.[22]

The contrast in (7-42) and (7-43) is thus explained in structural terms and has nothing to do with the conditions under which pro is admitted under *ʔeyn*: (7-42a) is acceptable since the clausal argument can be moved to a Topic position in the CP layer in LF. Example (7-43) is grammatical since it does not include a clausal subject; indeed, there is no clausal argument since the extraposed CP is an adjunct and *ze* a referential pronoun. Topicalization of the CP is hence not called for. Example (7-42b), on the other hand, involves LF-movement of the CP argument to Topic position, an option unavailable under *ʔeyn*, due to the absence of a CP layer. Finally, we can straightforwardly exclude (7-52) on the same grounds as (7-42b): example (7-52) includes an S-structure Topic and (7-42b) a Topic formed in LF. Both can be excluded by the absence of an available Topic position.[23]

(7-52) *ʔeyn li-lmod   polanit   ze kaše.
  neg   to-learn   Polish   it   difficult
  'It isn't difficult to learn Polish.'

7.4.2 Two Types of Pro$_{arb}$

Let us reconsider sentence (7-39b), repeated here as (7-53).

(7-53) ʔeyn maʔarixim   ʔet   ha-truma   šela.
  neg   value(BENONI)-MPL   ACC   the-contribution   her
  'People don't value her contribution.'

Example (7-53) illustrates the occurrence of pro with arbitrary interpretation under *ʔeyn*. Pro is interpreted generically in (7-53), as indicated by the English translation of pro as *people*. Following Cinque (1988), let us term this variety of pro$_{arb}$ *quasi universal* (abbreviated arb$_\forall$).

Another variety of arb interpretation has been discussed in the literature and is illustrated by (7-54); see, e.g., Authier (1989), Belletti and Rizzi (1988), Cinque (1988), and Jaeggli (1986).

(7-54)   dofkim   ba-delet.
        knock(BENONI)-MPL on-the-door.
        'Someone is knocking on the door.'

Unlike the arb$_\forall$ of (7-53), the subject of (7-54) has the force of existential quantification, as indicated, once again, by the English translation. Call this variety of pro$_{arb}$ quasi-existential (arb$_\exists$).[24] Interestingly, only a quasi-universal occurrence of arb is sanctioned under *?eyn*. Compare (7-53) with (7-55).

(7-55)   *?eyn dofkim   ba-delet.
        neg   knock(BENONI)-MPL on-the door
        'No one is knocking on the door.'

There is no obvious semantic reason for this contrast since (7-55) is rendered grammatical when *?eyn* is replaced with the clitic negative head *lo*, yielding the synonymous (7-56).

(7-56)   lo   dofkim   ba-delet.
        neg knock(BENONI)-MPL on-the door
        'No one is knocking on the door.'

The contrast between (7-55), on the one hand, and (7-54), (7-56), on the other, is thus syntactic in nature and is linked to the particular structural configurations embedding *?eyn* and to the position occupied by pro. While the subject in (7-54) and (7-56) can be in Spec/AgrS, since both sentences are compatible with a null auxiliary analysis of the Benoni, the subject of (7-55) can only be as high as Spec/T. In what follows, the ungrammaticality of (7-55) will be shown to follow from this difference.

Let us make explicit some assumptions regarding the syntactic representation of the two varieties of arbitrary pro. Assume, with Rizzi (1986), that arb is some sort of θ-role but that the arbitrary DP contains an open position bound by a quantifier in LF. In other words, the suggestion is to invoke Heim's (1982) analysis of indefinites and apply it to arbitrary pro.[25]

For Heim, indefinites are semantic variables that receive their quantificational force (e.g., generic or existential) through binding by an appropriate operator. The generic interpretation is brought about when the variable is bound by a generic operator or a quantificational adverb. The existential interpretation is due to a quantificational mechanism called *existential closure*. Indefinite DPs, however, are also arguments and bear θ-roles. Suppose that pro$_{arb}$ is subject to a similar analysis. Arb interpretation is assigned along with a θ-role, but the more precise interpretation of arb as generic or existential is contributed by the type of operator that binds the variable within it.

Recent studies in the syntax and semantics of indefinite DPs converge on the idea that the two interpretations, namely, the generic and the existential one, are associated with different structural positions of the bound indefinite (see, e.g., Diesing 1992a,b, Heim 1982, and Kratzer 1989). Diesing (1992a) argues that the existential interpretation requires that the subject variable lie within the scope of existential closure, which she identifies with the VP (her "inner subject position"), while the generic interpretation is only possible if the subject cannot be existentially bound and must occupy a position higher than VP, Diesing's "outer subject position," or Spec/I.

Let us now reconsider the data in (7-53)–(7-56). The fact that a generic interpretation is available to a subject occupying Spec/T, as in the *ʔeyn* sentence in (7-53), means that Spec/T lies outside the scope of existential closure.[26] This is further corroborated by (7-57), where an individual-level predicate (in the sense of Carlson 1977) imposes a generic reading on the subject, and the latter appears under *ʔeyn*.

(7-57) ʔeyn zamarei opera yodʃim   italkit.
        neg singers opera know(BENONI)-MPL Italian
        'Opera singers don't know Italian.'

Whatever mechanism allows for the generic interpretation in (7-57) sanctions this interpretation in (7-53). The subject *zamarei opera* 'opera singers' in the former and pro_{arb_V} in the latter can both be bound by a generic operator when they are in Spec/T.

Let us turn to $pro_{arb_∃}$ relating it to the existential interpretation of indefinites. Recall that existential closure applies to material internal to VP. When the subject of a sentence such as (7-58) is interpreted existentially, there must be some device that allows the subject to be interpreted in its θ-position in VP and not in its Case position in Spec/I.

(7-58) Firemen are available.

Following Diesing (1992a), I take this mechanism to be Lowering, in the sense of May (1985). Seen in these terms, we can reformulate the problem posed by (7-55) in the following terms: why is Lowering permitted in (7-58), but prohibited in (7-55)?

Invoking once more the structural limitations imposed by the presence of *ʔeyn* in (7-55), consider the following reasoning: LF-lowering leaves an empty category that must be properly governed. I am not aware of any means by which antecedent government can be satisfied by the trace of a lowered constituent, for the simple reason that the antecedent does not c-command the trace. Indeed, it itself is c-commanded by the trace. Assume, therefore, that antecedent government does not have to be met by traces formed by lowering.[27]

Empty categories, even those produced by Lowering, must be licensed. If antecedent government is irrelevant, a likely alternative is the other component of the ECP module, namely Head Government. Let us then ask how head government is satisfied in (7-58). In order for a trace to be head-governed, it must be c-commanded by licit head governor. Suppose that in LF, $AgrS^0$ can raise to C^0 or to some head position in the CP layer, giving rise to a representation such as (7-59), where the trace of *firemen* is head-governed by the $AgrS^0$ complex *are*, and the subject is in the VP, c-commanded by $\exists$, the existential quantifier.[28]

(7-59) [$_{CP}$ are [$_{AgrSP}$ t$_i$ . . . $\exists$[$_{VP}$ firemen$_i$ available]]]

We have seen that traces are not licit in the subject position under *ʔeyn*, that is, that Neg^0 is not a licit head governor (see §4.8). Moreover, *ʔeyn*, unlike C^0, cannot be substituted for in LF by a raised verb, since such substitution would result in the irrecoverable deletion of the negative head. Likewise, if the verb in (7-59) does not substitute for C^0, but moves to some other position within CP, then the impossibility of such an operation in (7-55) is due to the absence of a CP layer under *ʔeyn*.

We can therefore rule out the existential interpretation of pro$_{arb}$ in (7-55) by appealing, in the final analysis, to the ECP. The conditions on the licensing and identification of pro are satisfied, but the trace of the lowered subject cannot be head-governed in Spec/T, when *ʔeyn* marks the upper boundary of IP.

7.4.3 Atmospheric Pro

A no less intriguing case is that of quasi-referential atmospheric pro, which, as (7-60) shows, is not sanctioned under *ʔeyn*.

(7-60) *ʔeyn kar.
     neg   cold
     'It isn't cold.'

Note that negation has nothing to do with the ungrammaticality of (7-60), since (7-61) is perfectly well formed.

(7-61) lo   kar.
     neg cold
     'It isn't cold.'

The appearance of a different negative head in (7-60) and (7-61) disguises a profound difference in the structure of the two sentences. While the former is, and can only be, a bare NegP, the latter may include an AgrSP projection. To recall, *lo* is a clitic and as such, it is transparent to verb movement, in the manner discussed in §1.3.3 and §5.3.1. Example (7-61) is thus compatible with an analysis of present tense sentences as containing a null present tense auxiliary which raises to AgrSP and is structurally equivalent to the past and future tense sentences illustrated in (7-62), where the auxiliary is overt.

(7-62) a. lo   haya   kar.   b. lo y hye   kar.
        neg be(PAST)-3MS cold   *neg 3MS-be(FUT) cold*
        'It was cold.'   'It will be cold.'

In (7-60), on the other hand, AgrSP cannot be projected due to the barrierhood of the non-clitic head *ʔeyn*. The structures of the two sentences are schematized in (7-63).

(7-63)

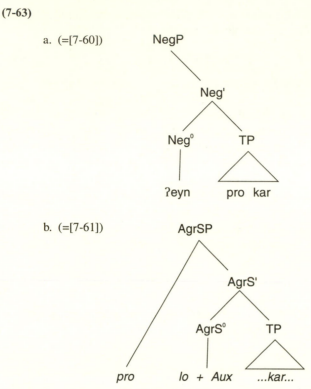

a. (=[7-60])

```
            NegP
               \
              Neg'
              /  \
          Neg⁰    TP
            |    /  \
          ʔeyn  pro kar
```

b. (=[7-61])

```
           AgrSP
           /    \
          /     AgrS'
         /      /   \
        /    AgrS⁰   TP
       /       |    /  \
     pro   lo + Aux  ...kar...
```

The contrast between (7-60) and (7-61) shows that an auxiliary must be present in the structure. The ungrammaticality of (7-60) is due to the fact that auxiliaries cannot occur in sentences incorporating *ʔeyn*.

The requirement that an auxiliary be present is not imposed by the predicate adjective, since a fully referential subject is possible as the subject of, for example, *kar* 'cold':

(7-64) ʔeyn ha-gufa   kara.
        neg   the-corpse   cold-FS
        'The corpse is not cold.'

The obligatory appearance of the auxiliary seems to be linked to the particular θ-role borne by atmospheric subjects, since a fully referential θ-role is sanctioned under *ʔeyn*. Suppose that the θ-role "atmosphere" is assigned jointly by the auxiliary and the predicate adjective in a manner reminiscent of θ-roles assigned by idioms: take "be + cold" to be an idiom of sorts which assigns a particular role to its subject. "Be + cold" requires access to $AgrS^0$, unprojected in (7-60).

The conclusion that can be drawn from this discussion is that both the formal licensing and the feature identification conditions are met by an atmospheric pro: the former through nominative Case assignment by T^0, and the latter through agreement coindexation with $AgrPart^0$. The unavailability of atmospheric null subjects under *ʔeyn* is due to a factor orthogonal to the Pro Module, to the fact that the particular quasi referential θ-role assigned to pro must be sanctioned by the presence of an auxiliary which is barred from occurring under *ʔeyn* for purely syntactic reasons.

7.4.4 Summary

Section 7.3 considered the position of pro in *ʔeyn* clauses against the background both of an explicit theory of pro (embodied in [7-10]) and a structural characterization of *ʔeyn* clauses (see chapter 4). It was shown that pro is formally licensed in Spec/T, the nominative Case position, and identifiable (up to the feature [number]) in Spec/AgrPart. Table (7-65) lists the subtypes of pro and summarizes their distribution under *ʔeyn*.

(7-65) The Distribution of pro Under *ʔeyn*

Pro Type	Available under *ʔeyn*
pro_{ref}	–
$pro_{exp\text{-}DP}$	+
$pro_{exp\text{-}CP}$	–
$pro_{arb_\forall}$	+
$pro_{arb_\exists}$	–
pro_{atmos}	–

Since person features are not manifested by AgrPart, referential pro is predictably unavailable under *ʔeyn*. Referential pro requires access to Spec/AgrS because only $AgrS^0$ contains the [person] feature necessary for its identification. Referential pro is thus excluded from occurring under *ʔeyn* for reasons directly linked to its identification. The distribution of other instances of pro cannot, however, be explained in terms of (7-10), the availability of number features rendering identifiable all types of quasi- and nonreferential pro. Yet, as we have seen, only DP-linked expletives and quasi-universal pro_{arb} licitly occur under *ʔeyn*.

It was argued that atmospheric pro does not occur under *ʔeyn* because the θ-role *atmosphere* is assigned to pro conjointly by the adjectival predicate and an auxiliary. For independent syntactic reasons, an auxiliary cannot occur under *ʔeyn*. The reason for this, discussed at length in chapter 4, is that auxiliaries are intrinsically endowed with $AgrS^0$ head features and must therefore incorporate to $AgrS^0$. *ʔeyn*, however, forms a barrier for head movement to $AgrS^0$. Raising of the auxiliary over *ʔeyn* thus violates the ECP.

The prohibition against CP-linked expletives under *ʔeyn* requires a different explanation. I argued that extraposed subjects are topicalized in LF and expletive pro adjoins to the Topic. Topicalization requires an appropriate landing site in the CP layer. Such a layer is surely available in *ʔeyn* clauses, but above and not below NegP. Topicalization and the subsequent incorporation of the expletive to the topicalized CP cannot cross NegP, again for reasons directly related to the ECP.

Finally, the descriptive generalization concerning the distribution of pro_{arb} under *ʔeyn* is that only if arb is quasi universal or generic, it can occur under *ʔeyn*. Quasi-existential pro_{arb} is not licit in that position. The generalization can be expressed in a more articulate way by associating the quasi-existential interpretation with a VP-internal position, to which pro must lower in LF. Lowering from

Spec/T, like other movement operations which leave a trace in Spec/T, is barred by the head government clause of the ECP, *?eyn* not being a proper head governor.

Before bringing this chapter to an end, it is of interest to take a look at the distribution of pro in *?eyn* sentences in which an AgrSP is projected. We have looked at "bare *?eyn*" sentences. Let us now turn our attention to sentences in which *?eyn* manifests subject agreement.

7.5   NULL SUBJECTS IN AGREEING *?eyn* SENTENCES

Recall that when *?eyn* bears agreement, the subject must precede it, and cannot follow it, as shown in the contrast in (7-66).

(7-66)   a. ha-yladim   ?eyn-am   kotv im   sipurim.
                  the children   neg-3MPL   write(BENONI)-MPL   stories
                  'The children do not write / are not writing stories.'

          b. *?eyn-am ha-yladim   kotvim   sipurim.
                  neg-3MPL   the-children   write(BENONI)-MPL   stories
                  'The children do not write / are not writing stories.'

We have argued that the subject in (7-66a) is in Spec/AgrS to which it raises from Spec/T, its case position. Subject agreement (AgrS^0 features) is checked in the Spec-head configuration established in AgrSP between the subject and the agreeing negative head *?eyn*.

Lexical pronouns must also occur in Spec/AgrS when *?eyn* bears agreement, as shown in (7-67).

(7-67)   a. hem   ?eyn-am   kotv im   sipurim.
                  they   neg-3MPL   write(BENONI)-MPL   stories
                  'They do not write / are not writing stories.'

          b. *?eyn-am hem   kotvim   sipurim.
                  neg-3MPL   they   write(BENONI)-MPL   stories
                  'They do not write / are not writing stories.'

All things being equal, it is predicted that pro in agreeing *?eyn* sentences should also be licit in Spec/AgrS. Indeed, when *?eyn* is specified for first or second person agreement, a referential null subject may occur in the structure, as in (7-68).

(7-68)   ?eyn -(en)i /-xa   /-ex   /-enu kotev/et/im   sipurim.
                  neg   -1S   /-2MS /-2FS /-1PL   write(BENONI)-MS/-FS/-PL   stories.
                  'I/you-m/you-f/we write stories.'

When *?eyn* is specified for third person, however, a referential pro is not acceptable. The suffix *-o* in (7-69) is a discrete representation of the features [3MS], yet a null subject is not tolerated.

(7-69)   *?eyn-o kotev   sipurim.
                  neg-3MS   write(BENONI)-MS   stories
                  'He doesn't write stories.'

The contrast between (7-68) and (7-69) reproduces a by now familiar bifurcation: that of first and second person versus third person in the past and future tense paradigms, as discussed in §7.2.4. The fact that the same split recurrs in the inflectional paradigm of *ʔeyn* demonstrates that the split is not related to tense, since *ʔeyn* sentences are present tense and, in this respect, are just like the Benoni forms; yet they pattern with the past/future paradigms as far as the distribution of referential null subjects is concerned.

In the discussion of the inflectional paradigms of the past and future tenses, I argued that the absence of pro drop when the verb is inflected for third person is not in any way related to the morphological "poverty" of the third person affix. The paradigm of *ʔeyn* inflection in (7-70) independently argues against such an approach to the null subject person split. In (7-70), each and every combination of person and number is associated with a unique affix.

(7-70) Inflectional Paradigm of *ʔeyn*

	Singular	Plural
1	ʔeyn-(en)i	ʔeyn-enu
2m	ʔeyn-xa	ʔeyn-xem
2f	ʔeyn-ex	ʔeyn-xen
3m	ʔeyn-o	ʔeyn-am
3f	ʔeyn-a	ʔeyn-an

Given the fact that some instances of pro (i.e., with first and second person, cf. [7-68]) are available, we can conclude both that pro is formally licensed and that it is identifiable when it occurs as the subject of agreeing *ʔeyn*. The unacceptability of (7-69) should be related, I suggest, to the same considerations that rule out third person referential pro in the company of tensed verbs, namely, to the impossibility of licensing [person] in D^0, when NumP is nonlexical. Referential pro is therefore available in the agreeing *ʔeyn* construction to the degree that the pronominal DP is itself a syntactically well-formed referential expression.[29]

When we turn our attention to quasi- and nonreferential pro, a surprising picture emerges. (7-71) shows that not a single subtype of these instances of pro is allowed in *ʔeyn* sentences.

(7-71) a. *ʔeyn-an mitxolelot kan   sufot.   DP-linked expletive pro
    neg-3PL   occur   here   storms
    'Storms don't occur here.'

  b. *ʔeyn-o kaše   li-lmod   polanit   CP-linked
    neg-3MS difficult to-learn   Polish
    'It isn't difficult to learn Polish.'

  c. *ʔeyn-am dofkim   ba-delet.   pro$_{arb_\exists}$
    neg-3PL   knock(BENONI)-MPL   on-the door
    'No one is knocking on the door.'

  d. *ʔeyn-am maʔarixim   ʔet
    neg-3PL   value(BENONI)-MPL   ACC

    ha-truma   šela.   pro$_{arb_\forall}$
    the-contribution   her
    'People don't value her contribution.'

  e. *ʔeyn-o kar.   pro$_{atmos}$
    neg-3MS cold
    'It isn't cold.'

The generalization that appears to underlie the distribution of pro in the agreeing *?eyn* construction is that the agreement on *?eyn* is only compatible with a fully referential subject. This explains why only a referential (first and second person) pro may appear as the subject of agreeing *?eyn* and why all of the sentences (7-71) are unacceptable. (Recall that the unavailabilty of third person pro is not related to properties of verbal agreement but to the internal structure of the pro DP itself.)

The requirement that the subject of agreeing *?eyn* be fully referential holds whether the subject is pro or a lexical pronoun. Recall that Hebrew is endowed with the pronominal form *ze*, which is associated with extraposed clauses. The ungrammaticality of (7-72) shows that *ze* cannot occur as the subject of agreeing *?eyn* sentences.[30]

(7-72)   *ze ?eyn-o   kaše   li-lmod   polanit.
        it   neg-3MS   difficult   to-learn   Polish
        'It isn't difficult to learn Polish.'

The reason that the agreement on *?eyn* bars all nonreferential subjects could, prima facie, be related to some constraint requiring the Spec/AgrS to contain a DP with specific reference. All instances of pro in (7-71)—with the possible exception of pro_{arb} in (7-71c)—are not only non- or quasi-referential, but they are also nonspecific.

If a specificity constraint were at work here, the agreement affixes on *?eyn* could conceivably be assimilated to clitics. In terms of Sportiche's (1996) approach, clitics are heads that agree in specificity with their specifiers. Their specifiers may be null pronominals or overt DPs (when both the clitic head and its specifier are phonetically realized, a configuration of clitic-doubling is manifested). Under this approach, the affixal head of AgrSP manifested on *?eyn* would be a nominative clitic head and the clausal subject in Spec/D would be the clitic's "double."

The difficulty with this assimilation of *?eyn* agreement to clitics is that the constraint imposed on the subjects of agreeing *?eyn* is actually not one of specificity. Recall that (7-71c) is unacceptable, despite the fact that the clausal subject, a pro_{arb}, can have specific reference, as in the following discourse fragment.

(7-73)   *?ani xošev še-   dofkim   ba-delet.   ze kanir?e Dani.
        I   think that- knock(BENONI)-MS on-the door   It probably Dani*
        'I think that someone is knocking on the door. It's probably Dani.'

Conversely, agreeing *?eyn* can occur with an overt subject which is nonspecific. This is brought out clearly in (7-74), where the bare plural subject has generic, nonspecific reference.

(7-74)   *zamarei opera   ?eyn-am   yodſim   italkit.
        singers   opera   neg-3PL   know(BENONI)-MPL   Italian*
        'Opera singers don't know Italian.'

I believe that the relevant factor is indeed reference and not specificity. In all of the examples in (7-71) pro is not referential—that is, it is either quasi- or nonreferential. These sentences are ruled-out because the agreement affixes on *?eyn* require a fully-referential subject. Thus, the factor we are searching for has to do with properties of the Agr bundle expressed on *?eyn*. *?eyn* agreement can be seen as specified [+referential], thus requiring co-indexation with a [+referential] subject. I have adopted Longobardi's (1994) and Stowell's (1991a) idea that the referential properties of a DP are represented on D^0: a DP is fully referential when D^0 is filled either by the determiner ha- 'the', or by the feature [person], bearing the values [1 person], [2 person], and so on.

Let us suppose that, in addition to being specified for one of the three persons, the [person] component of Agr can fail to be manifested. Call such an agreement bundle *impersonal* Agr. (The homonymy between third person Agr and impersonal Agr is due to a morphological rule spelling out the lack of person as third person, by default.) An impersonal Agr can enter into a Spec-head relationship with a DP subject which lacks a person feature altogether. Recall that pleonastic subjects lack a person feature because they are not endowed with a DP layer and quasi-referential subjects contain a semantic non-φ feature in D^0. Impersonal Agr cannot, however, be coindexed with a referential subject, since the latter's [person] specification cannot be matched on an Agr lacking [person].

There are thus two major differences between examples (7-75a) and (7-75b).

(7-75)   a. maxr u   kan   kafe.
sell(PAST)-3PL   here   coffee
'Coffee was sold here.' *or* 'One sold coffee here.'

b. hem   maxr u   kan   kafe.
they   sell(PAST)-3PL   here   coffee
'They sold coffee here.'

In (7-75a), the head of the null pronominal DP subject does not contain the feature [person]. In addition, the verbal agreement bundle is not specified for person, but is impersonal. Thus, all the examples in the preceding text, where agreement on a verb whose subject is quasi- or nonreferential subject were glossed as '3 (person)' should now be replaced with glosses in which [person] is not specified. In (7-75b), both the subject and the verbal agreement bundle contain an explicit representation of third person.

The problem posed by the ungrammaticality of (7-71) can be resolved by saying that the third person affixes in the *ʔeyn* agreement paradigm—namely -*o*, -*a*, and -*am*—contain genuine third person marking, which cannot be used as a default mark for impersonal Agr. Note the morphological difference between the agreement affixes on *ʔeyn* in (7-70) and those in the verbal paradigm in (7-12). Compare, in particular, the absence of an overt suffix for third person in the (suffixal) past tense paradigm and -*o* in the (also suffixal) *ʔeyn* paradigm in (7-70). My conjecture is, therefore, that within the bounds of *ʔeyn*'s inflectional paradigm, there is no way to morphologically express an impersonal Agr. Agreement on *ʔeyn* must express [person]; hence, it can only be construed with a subject with like features. This means that only referential DPs, lexical pronouns, and pro marked for first or second person can enter into a coindexing relationship with agreeing *ʔeyn*, while subjects containing a D^0 bereft of a specification for [person] cannot.

EIGHT

Subject-Verb Inversion

8.1 INTRODUCTION

This chapter deals with the conditions under which the marked order VS(O) is obtained in Hebrew.[1] The earliest work on subject "inversion" relied primarily on Romance and distinguished "free" inversion from what I term Triggered Inversion. The former was thought to involve subject lowering and the latter V-Raising. (See e.g., Rizzi 1982, Jaeggli 1982, Shlonsky 1987, and Torrego 1984, among many others.)

The VP-Internal Subject Hypothesis opened up the possibility of analyzing all varieties of inversion as involving a VP-internal subject over which the verb raises to I^0 or to C^0. In what follows, I try to show that Hebrew subjects may remain in VP only when the verb belongs to the ergative class or appears in passive voice. An inversion configuration with both transitive and unergative predicates is produced when the verb raises to Comp over a subject in Spec/I.

The question arises as to why subjects of nonergative, i.e., transitive and unergative, predicates cannot remain in VP. This is a rather unique state of affairs, if my description is valid, since the possibility of leaving a subject in its θ-position is usually taken to be a consequence of the positive setting of the *Pro-Drop Parameter* (Rizzi 1982). Hebrew, as we have seen, is positively set for this parameter (§7.2.4). In particular, null expletives are formally licensed in subject position.

I shall try to show that the availability of null expletives , while perhaps a necessary condition for the occurence of a postverbal subject in its thematic position at S-structure, is not a sufficient condition. In order to remain in VP, the subject must be (Case) licensed in that position. I shall demonstrate that only subjects of ergative and passive verbs are licensed in VP. Due to a structural property of the Hebrew clausal skeleton, the functional head responsible for assigning Case to a

VP-subject does not immediately govern VP, Case cannot be assigned, and the subject is forced to raise out of VP.

8.2 TWO STRATEGIES OF INVERSION

I consider a subject to be *inverted* when it appears to the right of the verb. The following examples illustrate inversion in Hebrew.

(8-1) a. ba-pšita   ha-leilit   ʕacra   ha-mištara peʕilim   rabim.
   in-the-raid   the-nightly   detain(PAST)-3FS the-police   activists   many
   'The police detained many activists in the nightly raid.'

   b. matai   ʕacra   ha-mištara ʔet ha-peʕilim?
   when   detain(PAST) 3FS   the-police   ACC the-activists
   'When did the police detain the activists?'

   c. lo   tamid   mešalem   Dani   misim ba-zman.
   NEG always   pay(BENONI)-MS Dani   taxes   on-time
   'Dani doesn't always pay taxes on time.'

   d. xaser   xelek ba-mxona.
   lack(BENONI)-MS part   in-the-machine
   'There is a part missing in the machine.'

   e. xala   ʕaliya ba-temperatura.
   come   about(PAST)-FS rise   in the temperature
   'The temperature has risen.'

The examples in (8-1) fall into two major categories. In (8-1a–c), the verb is not the first element in the clause—it is preceded by some constituent. In fact, the verb may not appear in initial position. Contrast the examples in (8-2a–c) with those in (8-1a–c).

(8-2) a. *ʕacra   ha-mištara peʕilim   rabim ba-pšita   ha-leilit.
   detain(PAST)-3FS the-police   activists many in-the-raid   the-nightly
   'The police detained many activists in the nightly raid.'

   b. *ʕacra   ha-mištara ʔet ha-peʕilim   ʔetmol.
   detain(PAST)-3FS the-police   ACC the-activists yesterday
   'The police detained the activists yesterday.'

   c. *mešalem   Dani   tamid   misim ba-zman.
   pay(BENONI)-MS Dani   always   taxes   on-time
   'Dani always pays taxes on time.'

I shall refer to the type of inversion illustrated in (8-1a-c) as *Triggered Inversion*, thus making explicit the observation that verb > subject word order requires a trigger, in the form of some preverbal constituent.[2] The second category of inversion will be referred to as *Free Inversion*, implying, first and foremost, that it requires no trigger, as shown by the examples in (8-1d,e).

8.3   TRIGGERED INVERSION (TI)

8.3.1   The Nature and the Position of the Trigger

Triggers can be sentential adverbs, PPs and preopoosed clauses, direct and indirect objects of the verb, clausal complements, certain negative phrases, wh expressions and (null) relative operators. A partial classification is given in (8-3).

(8-3)   a. Temporal Adverb
ʔetmol   ʕacra   ha-mištara harbe peʕilim.
yesterday detain(PAST)-3FS the-police many activists
'The police detained many activists yesterday.'

b. Prepositional Phrase
ba-pšita   ha-leilit   ʕacra   ha-mištara peʕilim   rabim.
in-the-raid the-nightly detain(PAST)-3FS the-police activists many
'The police detained many activists in the nightly raid.'

c. Clausal Adverb
mi-bli   lə-kabel ʔišur   mi-gavoha
without   to-get   authorization from-higher up

ʕacra   ha-mištara peʕilim   rabim.
detain(PAST)-3FS the-police activists many
'The police detained many activists without getting authorization from higher up.'

d. Direct Object
peʕilim   rabim ʕacra   ha-mištara ba-pšita   ha-leilit.
activists many   detain(PAST)-3FS the-police in-the-raid the-nightly
'The police detained many activists in the nightly raid.'

e. Indirect Object
la-taxana   šalxa   ha-mištara ʔet ha-ʕacurim.
to-the-station send(PAST)-3FS   the-police ACC the-detainees
'The police sent the detainees to the station.'

f. Clausal Complement
lo   lə-daber be-mešex ha-nesiʕa tavʕa   ha-mištara
NEG   to-talk   during   the-ride demand(PAST)-3FS the-police

min   ha-ʕacurim.
from   the-detainees
'The police asked the detainees not to speak during the ride.'

g. Negative Phrase
lə-ʕolam lo   taskim   ha-memšala   lə-farek   hitnaxaluyot.
never   NEG   3FS-(FUT)agree the-government to-dismantle settlements
'The government will never agree to dismantle settlements.'

h. Wh-Expression
matai ʕacra   ha-mištara ʔet ha-peʕilim?
when   detain(PAST)-3FS the-police ACC the-activists
'When did the police detain the activists?'

i. Relative Operator

ha-šir	še	katav	Bialik	bə-sof	yam-av	moce xen
the-poem	*that*	*write(PAST)-3MS*	*Bialik*	*at-end*	*life-3MS*	*pleases*

bə-ʕein-ai.
in-eyes-1S

'The poem that Bialik wrote at the end of his life pleases me.'

In short, just about any constituent that may appear clause-initially preceding the subject can act as a trigger for inversion. Conversely, if a constituent cannot appear clause-initially (in SVO orders), it cannot serve as a trigger.

One such class of elements is that of manner adverbs which, as (8-4) shows, can neither occur clause-initially in SVO orders nor trigger inversion, i.e., VS order.

(8-4) a. *li-rvaxa /bə-ʕadinut /ləgamrey Dani patax ʔet ha-delet.
       wide /gently /completely Dani open(PAST)-3MS ACC the-door
       'Dani opened the door wide/gently/completely.'

    b. *li-rvaxa /bə-ʕadinut /ləgamrey patax Dani ʔet ha-delet.
       wide /gently /completely open(PAST)-3MS Dani ACC the-door
       'Dani opened the door wide/gently/completely.'

The ungrammaticality of these sentences is due to the fact that the positioning of manner adverbs is quite restricted: they may only occur in VP edge positions. Assume further that adverbs typically do not move (in the audible syntax), so that if they occur in clause-initial position, they are base-generated there.

Clausal complements may act as triggers (viz. [8-3f]), as well as occur clause-initially in SV orders, as in (8-5).

(8-5) lo lə-daber be-mešex ha-nesiʕa ha-mištara tavʕa min
     NEG to-talk during the-ride the-police demand(PAST)-3FS from

ha-ʕacurim.
the-detainees

'The police asked the detainees not to speak during the ride.'

Small clause complements, however, cannot be preposed. Consider the contrast between (8-6a) with the small clause in situ and (8-6b,c) where the small clause occurs in clause-initial position, with and without inversion.

(8-6) a. kulam xošvim ʔet šulamit le-gaʔon.
      everyone think(BENONI)-MPL ACC Shulamit to-genius
      'Everyone considers Shulamit a genius.'

    c. *ʔet šulamit le-gaʔon xošvim kulam.
      ACC Shulamit to-genius think(BENONI)-MPL everyone
      'Everyone considers Shulamit a genius.'

    b. *ʔet šulamit le-gaʔon kulam xošvim.
      ACC Shulamit to-genius everyone think(BENONI)-MPL
      'Everyone considers Shulamit a genius.'

I would like to explain this contrast in terms of Case theory. The subject of a small clause complement is (accusative) Case-licensed through government by the matrix verb (or, alternatively, by movement into Spec/AgrO). When a direct object is fronted to clause-initial position (viz. [8-3d]), its trace can be Case licensed. Fronting of a small clause, however, leaves a small clause trace, and the subject within it is inaccessible to Case-licensing.[3]

TI is not a manifestation of the V2 constraint, familiar from the Germanic languages. First, TI can be freely embedded in the presence of an overt complementizer. Second, embedded TI is oblivious to the nature and type of matrix verb. In German, in contrast, embedded V2 is only possible under bridge verbs and the complementizer must be absent. These two properties of Hebrew are illustrated by the example in (8-7), where TI occurs inside a clause-initial adjunct CP, containing an overt complementizer (the clausal adjunct appears in square brackets).

(8-7) [mipney še   ba-pšita   ha-leilit   ʕacra   ha-mištara
       because that in-the-raid the-nightly detain(PAST)-3FS the-police

       peʕilim   rabim], hexlatnu   lə-ʔargen   hafgana.
       activisits   many   decide(PAST)-1PL to-organize   demonstration
       'Because the police arrested many activists in the nightly raid, we decided to
       organize a demonstration.'

A third difference between TI and the V2 phenomenon is that TI does not obligatorily place the verb in second position. In example (8-8), the verb is preceded by two constituents and occupies the third and not the second position from the left.

(8-8) ʔet   ha-paʕil   ha-ze   matai   ʔacra   ha-mištara ?
       ACC   the-activist   the-this   when   detain(PAST)-3FS   the-police
       'When did the police detain this activist?' lit. 'This activist, when did the police
       detain?'

I assume that the unifying feature of triggers is that they appear in the Comp domain. To recall, CP is a multilayered projection, containing positions for topics, focalized constituents, fronted negative expressions, wh-operators, relative operators, and perhaps other elements as well (see §1.2.2). Under this approach, different types of triggers occupy different specifier positions within the CP layer. Since the study of the Comp domain lies beyond the scope of this essay, I will continue to use the label CP as a cover term for Comp-internal projections.[4]

8.3.2 Triggered Inversion as Movement of I to C

The next point to make is that inversion, or rather the positioning of the verb to the left of the clausal subject, is brought about when the inflected verb raises into the head position of which the trigger is the specifier, as diagrammed in example (8-9).

(8-9)

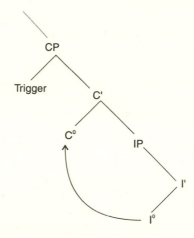

With many, if not most trigger types, inversion is optional. Compare (8-10a = 8-3b) with (8-10b); cf. also (8-3f) and (8-5).

(8-10) a. ba-pšita   ha-leilit   ʕacra   ha-mištara   peʕilim rabim.
          in-the-raid   the-nightly detain(PAST)-3FS the-police   activists many
          'The police detained many activists in the nightly raid.'

         b. ba-pšita   ha-leilit   ha-mištara ʕacra   peʕilim   rabim.
          *in-the-raid   the-nightly the-police   detain(PAST)-3FS many
                                                   activists*
          'The police detained many activists in the nightly raid.'

I believe the optionality in these cases reflects register or dialectal differences: formal written Hebrew requires inversion—this is particularly clear when the trigger is a wh-expression or a relative operator—while colloquial spoken Hebrew eschews it. In a strict sense, then, triggered inversion is not an optional process but results from a blend of dialects.

An interesting exception is negative inversion, which is obligatory on all registers. Thus, it does not alternate with (8-11). This means that whatever require-ment must be satisfied by moving the verb to Comp, it must be stated independently for different types of triggers. I return to the obligatoriness of inversion in (8-11) later in this section.

(8-11) ??lə-ʕolam ha-memšala   lo   taskim   lə-farek   hitnaxaluyot
         never   the-government NEG 3FS-(FUT)agree to-dismantle settlements
         'The government will never agree to dismantle settlements.'

8.3.2.1 *Feature Checking versus the Satisfaction of Licensing Criteria*

Movement of I to C under a trigger results in the establishment of a Spec-head relation between the trigger and the inflected verb that is expressed through coindexing. This is the typical configuration of feature checking in Chomsky's (1993) sense, extended to operator and operator-like features (wh, focus, and the like.) Within the A′ system, a Spec-head configuration can also be taken to satisfy the representational criteria proposed by Rizzi and others (the Wh-Criterion, the Neg-Criterion, the Focus-Criterion, etc.; see Haegeman and Zannuttini 1991, Puskas 1993, Rizzi 1991, among others).[5] The feature checking and the criterial approaches imply different approaches to syntactic licensing. As Rizzi (class lectures, 1994) points out, feature checking can be satisfied derivationally (a verb can check features with an object in Spec/AgrO, for example, and then raise to T^0 of AgrS^0), while the licensing criteria are satisfied representationally. Thus, feature checking and criterion satisfaction are not notational variants, but constitute different conceptions of syntactic well-formedness.

Viewed from the perspective of feature checking, I→C movement under a trigger is required to check the features of the trigger against those on the inflected verb, the idea being that V, or I, is endowed with topic, focus, or wh head features that must be coindexed with a specifier bearing the appropriate feature or features. Under this approach, the difference between the two registers or dialects of Hebrew, the one where I→C occurs and the one where it does not, can be plausibly viewed as consequences of the weakness or strength of the features in question. In the dialect where inversion occurs, those features are strong and thus in need of pre-Spellout-checking, whereas in the dialect in which inversion does not occur, those features are weak. Hence, under this view, the absence of inversion is only an indication that *overt* I→C does not take place. In order for the weak features to be checked, I→C occurs in LF. The feature checking approach has nothing particularly illuminating to say about (8-11), where inversion is obligatory in both dialects. The feature that triggers I-movement should be taken to be strong in both dialects. There is no real reason, under this approach, why the one element triggering inversion in both dialects is a focalized negative constituent such as *ləʕolam* 'never'.

Under a generalization of the criterial approach, verb raising to C is needed to satisfy a criterion according to which a Spec containing elements bearing a certain set of operator or operatorlike features must be coindexed with a head bearing like features, and vice versa.

8.3.2.2 Why Can't Traces of Triggers License Inversion?

An important facet of triggered inversion, first discussed in Borer (1984), is that traces of triggers do not license inversion. Thus, inversion is only possible in the topmost clause of "long" interrogatives, as in the contrast in (8-12): inversion applies in the CP containing the actual wh-word, as in (8-12a), and not in the lower CP, as in (8-12b).

(8-12) a. ʔet   mi   maʔamin   Dani   še   Rina   makira?
           ACC   who   believe(BENONI)-MS   Dani   that   Rina   know(BENONI)-FS
           'Who does Dani believe that Rina knows?'

        b. ???ʔet   mi   maʔamin   Dani   še   makira   Rina?
           ACC   who   believe(BENONI)-MS   Dani   that   know(BENONI)-FS   Rina
           'Who does Dani believe that Rina knows?'

These facts can be straightforwardly construed, once we take into account that traces of operators are not operators in themselves (a wh-trace does not transform the CP in which it appears into an indirect question), so that even if such features could be freely sprinkled on heads and specifiers, they would have to enter a checking configuration or meet the relevant criterion only in the Comp where they are interpreted. The pattern illustrated in (8-12) can be directly handled by a criterial approach to licensing, admitting the reasonable generalization of this approach to the gamut of syntactic operators and affective constituents.

Chomsky's feature checking approach is formulated so as to apply essentially to inflectional features. While its extension to operator features is not inconceivable, it would consist of viewing inversion and similar processes in other languages as driven by considerations of morphological or phonological well-formedness. Such an approach can handle the root-embedded asymmetry of Hebrew inversion—that is, the pattern in (8-12)—by imposing a ban on multiple checking. If a feature is checked in an embedded context, it is no longer around to check or be checked in the root sentence. If movement of I to C occurs in the embedded clause, there would be no motivation for such movement in the higher one.

There is no principled reason, however, in the feature checking approach, for inversion or feature checking to take place in the root clause. While some languages allow inversion in both root and embedded clauses (e.g., Spanish, viz. Torrego 1984), the checking approach entails the prediction that there should exist a class of languages with the opposite property of Hebrew—namely, languages in which inversion *only* occurs in the lowest clause of a multiply embedded sentence and *never* in higher clauses. This is so since the features in question would be checked in the embedded clause, rendering redundant further checking (inversion) in the matrix. In such a language, (8-12a) would be ungrammatical; only (8-13) would be possible (it is not possible in Hebrew). Under the criterial approach, on the other hand, the sentence in (8-13) is, ceteris paribus, predicted to be unavailable on principle.

(8-13) ?et mi Dani ma?amin še makira Rina?
ACC who Dani believe(BENONI)-MS that know(BENONI)-FS Rina
'Who does Dani believe that Rina knows?'

The pattern in (8-12) further suggests that triggered inversion is crucially tied up with verb movement. A conceivable alternative (pursued to some degree in Shlonsky 1987), claiming that triggered inversion involves the failure to raise the subject over the verb (or lower it, in the manner in which, for example, Italian Free Inversion was thought of in Rizzi 1982), would be at pains to relate the option of raising or not raising the subject within IP to the lexical status of a trigger in CP. Indeed, one of the main differences between French Stylistic Inversion—which does not involve V-movement to Comp—and Hebrew TI, is that traces trigger the former, but not the latter (viz. note 2). Since French inversion is not driven by the need to satisfy a licensing criterion, there is no reason why the mere presence of an element in Comp would be sufficient to allow for inversion. The criterial approach to Hebrew TI thus has the merit that it establishes a link between I→C movement and the failure of traces to trigger inversion.

8.3.2.3   *Negative Inversion in the Criterial Approach*

The criterial approach can also shed some light on the fact that inversion under a focalized negative trigger (as in [8-3g]) is obligatory, even in the dialect where inversion is unavailable with other triggers (cf. the discussion surrounding [8-11]). To see this, let us first see if we can characterize the two dialects of Hebrew more precisely. Let us say that inversion takes place whenever the features that must be coindexed with the trigger are *not* generated in the head of the trigger phrase, but on the verb or one of the verb-related inflectional heads, for example, I^0. I→C movement is then necessary in order to raise the relevant feature to the Comp domain in order for the criterion to be satisfied. For instance, when inversion occurs in interrogative phrases, the [wh] feature is base-generated on I^0 and raised to C^0. This is diagrammed in (8-14) (see Rizzi 1991).

(8-14)

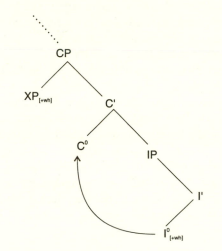

Under this approach, the most natural way of characterizing the dialect in which inversion does not take place is to say that the [wh] feature is generated in C^0, as in (8-15). The Wh-Criterion can be satsified in CP without recourse to I→C movement.

(8-15)

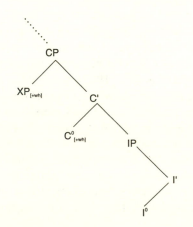

Returning now to (8-3g) and (8-11), we are led to say that the reason for which (8-3g) is the only option in Hebrew—that is, the fact that Negative Inversion is not subject to dialect or register variation—is a consequence of the fact that the feature [+neg], unlike, say, [+wh], cannot be base-generated in Comp, as a matter of dialectal option and can only be generated on Neg^0. Thus, in (8-3g), Neg^0 must be raised to Comp and since the negative head *lo* incorporates the inflected verb, I→C movement must occur in order for the Neg-Criterion to be satisfied.

8.3.2.4 *Inversion in Relative Clauses*

Before concluding this section, let us dwell on one other consequence. The example in (8-3i) shows that inversion is triggered in relative clauses. Borer (1984) shows that this type of inversion is only possible in the highest Comp of the relative clause, thus recapitulating the pattern manifested by other types of inversion. Contrast the two relative clauses in (8-16).

(8-16) a. ha-ʔadam   še   xašav   Dani   še   Rina   pagša . . .
       the-person   *that*   *think(PAST)-3MS*   *Dani*   *that*   *Rina*   *meet(PAST)-3FS*
       'The person that Dani thought that Rina met . . .'

     b. ??ha-ʔadam   še   xašav   Dani   še   pagša   Rina . . .
       the-person   *that*   *think(PAST)-3MS*   *Dani*   *that*   *meet(PAST)-3FS*   *Rina*
       'The person that Dani thought that Rina met . . .'

It is not immediately clear what serves as the inversion trigger in (8-16a). If it is the relative operator, then the fact that inversion occurs under the complementizer *še* means that the operator occupies a Spec-position below *še*. The inflected verb then moves into the head position of this "relative" Comp. Such a derivation is schematized in (8-17).

(8-17)

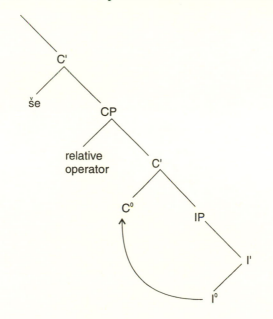

This approach to TI in relative clauses is observationally adequate, but it presupposes that the relative operator in Hebrew occupies a different position than it does, say, in English, where relative operators appear in the Spec of *that* and not of a lower head. There is an alternative, however, to positing this otherwise unmotivated difference between the two languages (see Shlonsky 1985 for empirical arguments against a derivation such as [8-17]). I discuss this alternative in the following paragraphs.

Hebrew disposes of two relativization strategies. In one, the relativized position is a gap, in the other, it is a resumptive pronoun. The two strategies are illustrated in (8-18) for object relatives.[6]

(8-18) a. ha-ʔadam   še   Rina pagša . . .
            the-person that Rina meet(PAST)-3FS
            'The person that Rina met . . .'

        b. ha-ʔadam   še   Rina pagša   ʔoto . . .
            the-person that Rina meet(PAST)-3FS him
            'The person that Rina met . . .' *Lit:* 'The person that Rina met him . . .'

I assume that when the resumptive strategy is employed, the relative operator is base-generated in Comp, in a canonical position to the left of *še* (see Shlonsky 1992).

There exists a variant of (8-18b) in which the resumptive pronoun is topicalized and appears in a position to the immediate right of the complementizer *še*. This variant is illustrated in (8-19) and the relevant aspects of its derivation are schematized in (8-20).

(8-19) ha-ʔadam   še   ʔoto Rina   pagša . . .
        the-person that him   Rina   meet(PAST)-3FS
        'The person that Rina met . . .'

(8-20)

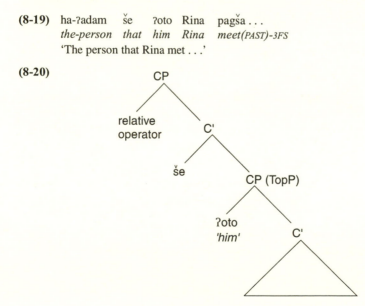

Being a topic, the resumptive pronoun in (8-19) can act as a trigger for inversion, as in (8-21), which I take to be derived by moving I^0 to the C^0 of which the fronted resumptive pronoun is the specifier.

(8-21) ha-ʔadam   še   ʔoto   pagša   Rina . . .
        the-person   that   him   meet(PAST)-3FS   Rina
        'The person that Rina met . . .'

I would like to now suggest—reviving and updating Borer's (1984) "deletion in Comp" idea—that when inversion occurs in the highest Comp of a relative clause containing no overt fronted resumptive pronoun, as, for example, in (8-3i) or in (8-16), there is a covert trigger—namely a phonetically unrealized resumptive pronoun. This covert pronoun, or pro, is only licensed in Comp—that is, in a position where it is identifiable by the relative operator and cannot, for example, occur in situ.[7]

8.3.3   The Position of the Subject under TI

In (8-1a), the subject occurs between the verb and the object. Positioning it to the right of the object, as in (8-22), leads to ungrammaticality.[8]

(8-22) *ba-pšita   ha-leilit   ʕacra   peʕilim   rabim ha-mištara.
        in-the-raid   the-nightly   detain(PAST)-3FS   activists   many   the-police
        'The police detained many activists in the nightly raid.'

It is thus reasonable to assume that the subject occupies some left-hand Spec position within IP.

I have shown that Hebrew verbs raise out of VP before S-structure. The basic diagnostic for verb movement involves the positioning of VP-adverbials between the verb and the direct object, as in (8-23).

(8-23) ha-mištara   ʕacra   be-koʔax   peʕilim   rabim.
        the-police   detain(PAST)-3FS   with-force   activists   many
        'The police forcefully detained many activists.'

The fact that (8-23) is well formed can be taken as evidence to the effect that the verb raises out of VP before S-structure.

When occurring in an inverted sentence, the adverbial PP *be-koʔax* 'with force' appears between the subject and the object. It cannot precede the subject. Consider the contrast between (8-24a) and (8-24b).

(8-24) a. ba-pšita   ha-leilit   ʕacra   ha-mištara be-koʔax
          in-the-raid   the-nightly   detain(PAST)-3FS   the-police   with-force

          peʕilim   rabim.
          activists   many
          'The police forcefully detained many activists in the nightly raid.'

       b. ??ba-pšita   ha-leilit   ʕacra   be-koʔax   ha-mištara
          in-the-raid   the-nightly   detain(PAST)-3FS   with-force   the-police

          peʕilim   rabim.
          activists   many
          'The police forcefully detained many activists in the nightly raid.'

It should be stressed that (8-24b) is not ruled out simply because an adverb intervenes between the verb and the subject. Sentential adverbs, for example, can freely occur exactly in the context where VP-adverbials may not. Compare (8-24b) with (8-25).

(8-25)   ba-pšita   ha-leilit   ʕacra   ka-nirʔe   ha-mištara
          in-the-raid   the-nightly   detain(PAST)-3FS   apparently   the-police

          peʕilim   rabim.
          activists   many
          'The police apparently detained many activists in the nightly raid.'

The adverbial diagnosis strongly suggests that the subject is not in VP in contexts of Triggered Inversion, but has moved higher, above VP-edge adverbs and below sentential ones.

We can cull further evidence to support the hypothesis that the subject in TI is not in VP, when we turn attention to postverbal subjects in clauses containing an auxiliary and a verb in the Benoni.

(8-26)   ba-pšitot   ha-leiliot   hayta   ha-mištara
          in-the-raid-PL   the-nightly-PL   be(PAST)-3FS   the-police

          ʕoceret   peʕilim   rabim.
          detain(BENONI)-FS   activists   many
          'On the nightly raids, the police used to detain many activists.'

I have argued that the Benoni in such compound tense constructions is raised to AgrPart^0 before S-structure (see chapters 2–3). Since the subject occurs to its left, I am led to conclude that it cannot be in VP.[9]

This conclusion is further confirmed by the presence of a floating quantifier in a position between the Benoni verb and the direct object, as in (8-27).

(8-27)   bə-yaldut-am   hayu   ha-studentim   mesaxkim   kul-am
          in-youth-3MPL   be(PAST)-3MPL   the-students   play(BENONI)-MPL   all-3MPL

          maxboʔim.
          hide and seek
          'In their youth, the students used to all play hide and seek.'

The auxiliary verb is raised to the Comp layer in (8-27). The subject should thus be taken to occupy a Specifier position not lower than Spec/AgrPart and no higher than Spec/AgrS. We must consider three potential surface subject positions: Spec/AgrPart, Spec/T, and Spec/AgrS. Let us see if one or more of these options can be ruled out.

I have argued that present tense sentences are structurally ambiguous. Example (8-28) can be analyzed either as containing a null auxiliary to which the Benoni incorporates, moving along with the auxiliary to AgrS^0, as shown in the tree diagram in (8-29), or as lacking an auxiliary, as in (8-29b). Under the former structural description, AgrSP is projected, and the subject raises to Spec/AgrS; in the latter, AgrSP is not projected and, as (8-29b) illustrates, the subject occupies Spec/T. (The argument in favor of this view is developed in

§4.7 and §4.8, and is based on the position of the subject in agreeing and nonagreeing *ʔeyn* sentences).

(8-28) Daniela   toferet   smalot.
       Daniela   sew(BENONI)-FS   dresses
       'Daniela sews / is sewing dresses.'

(8-29)   a.

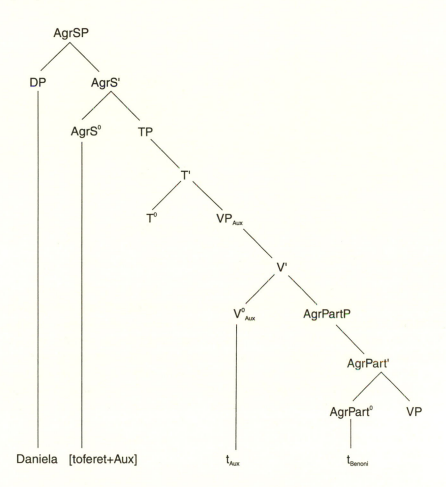

(8-29) b.

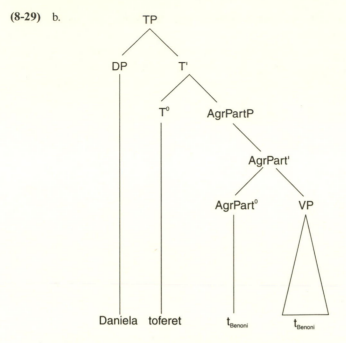

Consider what happens when Triggered Inversion applies to a Benoni sentence that does not contain an auxiliary. TI involves movement of the verb to Comp. In this particular instance, it is the Benoni which is raised to CP. It then follows that the subject in (8-28) is in Spec/T, just as in (8-29b).

When an auxiliary is present in the structure, then it is the complex head containing the Benoni and the null auxiliary which is raised to Comp. The subject, in this case, should be taken to occupy Spec/AgrS and not Spec/T. The reasoning leading up to the conclusions of this and the preceding paragraph is that TI does not effect the subject, but only alters the position of the verb relative to the subject.

If we now reflect a bit on this analytical sketch, several conclusions emerge. First, the subject is never in Spec/AgrPart under triggered inversion, a conclusion that was independently reached in the discussion of Benoni sentences in chapters 2, 3, and 4. Second, the postverbal subject of a Benoni sentence can be either in Spec/T or in Spec/AgrS. Notice that the choice is not free, but is determined by whether the AgrSP layer is generated or not.

We are thus led to (8-30).

(8-30)   Clausal subjects in Hebrew occupy the highest available Specifier position (within IP).

This statement expresses the observation that the subject is never found at S-structure—neither in the base, VP-internal position, nor in Spec/AgrPart. In Benoni sentences, the subject raises to Spec/AgrS when AgrSP is projected; otherwise, it raises to Spec/T. Finally, in sentences in which the verb is in the past or future tense form and AgrSP is projected, the subject is in Spec/AgrS.

The rest of this chapter is designed to explain the descriptive generalization embodied in (8-30). The following sections investigate the position of postverbal subjects in two Romance languages, French and Italian. I hope to show that Romance postverbal subjects are in VP, while the Hebrew ones obey (8-30). I then turn to discuss Free Inversion in Hebrew, which will be shown to differ from TI in, among other things, the position of the postverbal subject. A comparison of the two inversion strategies will allow us to explain (8-30) and account for the difference between Hebrew and French/Italian with respect to the positioning of postverbal subjects in purely structural terms.[10]

8.3.3.1 *Position of the Postverbal Subject in French*

Consider French Stylistic Inversion, illustrated in (8-31).

(8-31) Le jour où   sont arrivés les enfants . . .
        the day   where   are   arrived   the children
        'The day on which the children arrived . . .'

French speakers find sentences in which the postverbal subject is not adjacent to the verb to be very marginal. Although inversion is possible with transitive verbs, the object must be cliticized in order to meet the "adjacency requirement" between the verb and the subject. The order VSO is unacceptable in French. The sentences in (8-32) illustrate these points.

(8-32) a. Le jour où   l'ont   vu   les enfants . . .
           the day   where   it-have   seen   the children
           'The day on which the children saw it . . .'

        b. ??Le jour où   ont   vu   ce film   les enfants
           The day   where   have   seen   this film   the children . . .
           'The day on which the children saw this film . . .'

        c. *Le jour où   ont   vu   les enfants   ce film . . .
           the day   where   have   seen   the children   this film . . .
           'The day on which the children saw this film . . .'

These properties of French Stylistic Inversion render rather difficult any attempt to determine the precise position of the subject using the familiar diagnostics of adverbial positioning and relative word order. Nevertheless, Friedemann (1992, 1995) has argued that postverbal subjects in French are in Spec/V, and that Spec/V is linearly on the right of V′ so that the structure of the French VP is as in (8-33).

(8-33)

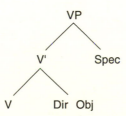

It is clearly the case that floating quantifiers must be c-commanded by the DP with which they are associated.[11] This requirement is a trivial consequence of Sportiche's (1988) analysis, according to which floating quantifiers mark NP traces.

For example, they can appear in position between the auxiliary and the participle, c-commanded by the subject.

(8-34)   Les enfants   sont tous arrivés.
      the children   are   all   arrived
      'The children have all arrived.'

Note, however, the ungrammaticality of (8-35).

(8-35)   *Le jour où   sont tous arrivés   les enfants . . .
      the day   where   are   all   arrived   the children
      'The children have all arrived . . .'

We should interpret (8-35) to mean that the floating quantifier is not c-commanded by the postverbal subject. More generally, (8-35) shows that a postverbal subject in French is located in a position lower than that of the lowest possible position of the floating quantifier.

There is some rather compelling evidence that subject floating quantifiers in French cannot appear in VP—that is, contra Sportiche (1988), floating quantifiers cannot be taken to mark the base position of the subject in VP, but only an intermediate subject position. Consider the sentence in (8-36), which contains both a subject floating quantifier and the leftward-moved bare quantifier *tout* (cf. Kayne 1975).

(8-36)   Les enfants   ont   tous tout   mangé.
      the children   have   all   everything   eaten
      'The children have all eaten everything.'

Following Friedeman and Siloni (1993), assume that the hierarchy of projections in French is as in (8-37); see §8.4, where the different position of AgrOP in Hebrew is discussed.

(8-37) $\text{AgrSP} > \text{TP} > \text{AgrOP} > \text{VP}_{\text{Aux}} > \text{AgrPartP} > \text{VP}_{\text{Past Participle}}$

The direct object *tout* in (8-36) has been moved leftward from its base position in the VP to a position lying to the left of the past participle. Take this position to be Spec/AgrOP, as suggested in Friedemann (1992); I leave open the question of whether the object undergoes further A'-movement (cf. Kayne 1975). The auxiliary verb is in AgrS^0 (Belletti 1990), and the subject, lying to its left, cannot be lower than Spec/AgrS. The only available position for the floated subject quantifier, *tous*, therefore, is Spec/TP. Adoption of (8-37) precludes the other logical option—namely, that the floating quantifier is in Spec/AgrPartP since it is located to the left of, and hence higher than, AgrOP.

The discussion of the preceding paragraphs quite clearly establishes the position of the subject in French Stylistic Inversion as lower than Spec/T. This leaves two remaining positional options: Spec/AgrPart and Spec/V. The former can be eliminated on the basis of the ungrammaticality of (8-38). If the subject were in Spec/AgrPart, it would perforce follow the auxiliary and *precede* the participle, which can be no higher than AgrPart^0.

(8-38) *Le jour où   sont les enfants   arrivés . . .*
        the day   where   are   the children   arrived
        'The day on which the children arrived . . .'

I thus concur with Friedemann (1992, 1995) that postverbal subjects in French are in their base VP-internal position at S-structure.

Further evidence to this effect is provided by an observation by Obenauer (1984) to the effect that postverbal subjects give rise to what we would, following Rizzi (1990), call Relativized Minimality effects. He shows that the quantifier *combien*, which is extractable from inside a postverbal subject, cannot be so extracted when the participle is preceded by the adverb *beaucoup*, which occupies a relatively low position in the clause, its occurrence immediately to the left of the participle suggesting that it is a VP-edge or AgrPartP-edge adverb. The contrast in (8-39) should be treated on par with the similar pattern observed in the extraction from object position, analyzed in Rizzi (1990).

(8-39) a. *Le jour où   ont   beaucoup telephoné   d'étudiants.*
        the day where   have   many   telephoned   of students
        'The day on which many students telephoned.'

      b. *Combien   ont   telephoné   d'étudiants?*
        how many   have   telephoned   of students
        'How many students have telephoned?'

      c. **Combien   ont   beaucoup telephoné   d'étudiants?*
        how many   have   many   telephoned   of students

The effect studied by Obenauer shows that a postverbal subject in French occupies a position that is lower than, and hence c-commanded by, *beaucoup*.

8.3.3.2 *The Position of the Postverbal Subject in Italian*

Unlike French Stylistic Inversion, Italian inversion requires no trigger. A further difference between the two is that the adjacency constraint on postverbal subjects is weaker in Italian. This is manifested in two ways. First, the intervention of a direct object between a verb and a postverbal subject renders the clause marginal, and not, as in French, ungrammatical. This is shown in (8-40) (data from Rizzi 1991).[12]

(8-40) a. *?Ha risolto il   problema   Gianni.*   b. *?Ha vinto la corsa   Gianni.*
        has solved the   problem   Gianni   *has won   the race   Gianni*
        'Gianni solved the problem.'   'Gianni won the race.'

Second, certain adverbs and quantifiers may occur between the verb and the subject without giving rise to any sort of marginality. Rizzi (1991) provides examples with *sempre* 'always' and *tutto* 'everything', among others.

(8-41) a. *Vince sempre   Gianni.*   b. *Ha   fatto   tutto   Gianni.*
        wins   always   Gianni   *has   done   everything   Gianni*
        'Gianni always wins.'   'Gianni did everything.'

Other adverbs, however, cannot licitly intervene between the verb and subject. This is shown in (8-42) with *bene* 'well' and *ieri* 'yesterday'.

(8-42) a. ?Ha giocato bene Gianni.   b. ??Ha telefonato   ieri   Gianni.
       has played   well   Gianni   *has   telephoned yesterday Gianni*
       'Gianni played well.'   'Gianni telephoned yesterday.'

Rizzi (1991) argues that the adverbs that cannot intervene between the verb and the postverbal subject are those whose natural position is on the margin of VP. An a priori possible interpretation of these facts is that the Italian postverbal subject, like its Hebrew counterpart, is in a position higher than that of VP-edge adverbs and lower than that of adverbs such as *sempre* 'always'. Italian would then be like Hebrew.[13]

However, if the subject were indeed as high as Spec/AgrPart or Spec/T in (8-41) and (8-42), we would expect it to naturally occur between an auxiliary and a participle in a compound tense construction. This is patently not the case. In Italian, as in French, the postverbal subject must follow the participle; (8-43) is strictly ungrammatical.[14]

(8-43) *ha Gianni   giocato.
      has Gianni   played
      'Gianni played.'

If Italian postverbal subjects are in VP at S-structure, how should one explain the facts in (8-41) and (8-42)? Rizzi notes that, when adverbial intervention results in ungrammaticality, the adverbs in question rupture the adjacency not between the verb and the subject but between the latter and the first inflectional head above VP, which he takes to be responsible for the assignment of nominative Case. The adverbs that licitly breach the adjacency are attached higher than the first inflectional head above VP. Under Rizzi's approach, the adjacency requirement is not a constraint on the linear ordering of the verb and the subject (cf. the near acceptability of the sentences in [8-40]); instead, it reduces to Stowell's (1981) and Chomsky's (1981) condition of adjacency between a Case-assigning head (or, rather, the trace of one) and a Case-marked argument.

8.3.3.3 Conclusion

Let us conclude §8.3.3. The two languages I have briefly examined, French and Italian, allow for a subject to occur in postverbal position. Although the conditions for such inversion are different in each grammatical system, as well as in comparison with Hebrew, they split along a very clear line: French and Italian postverbal subjects occur in a very low position in the clause, presumably in their base, VP-internal position. Subjects in Hebrew TI in contrast, must move out of VP before S-structure, as expressed by (8-30). This generalization, when taken in tandem with the subsequent discussion, leads to a further, perhaps related conclusion—namely, that postverbal subjects are not *licensed* in their base position at S-structure. If we follow Rizzi (1991) and take licensing to be essentially the assignment of Case, we can state the restriction imposed on TI in the following terms.

(8-44)   Hebrew subjects are not Case-licensed in their θ-position.

In order to better understand why (8-30) and (8-44) hold, I turn to another inversion construction where, contrary to TI, subjects *are* Case-licensed in their θ-position.

8.4 FREE INVERSION (FI) AND VP-SUBJECTS

FI, to recall, is so named because the order verb > subject is licit without the presence of a preverbal trigger. FI is restricted to occur with verbs that do not assign an external θ-role—that is, unaccusative and passive predicates.[15] Consider (8-45).

(8-45)   neʕelmu   harbe   sfarim mə-ha-sifriya.
        disappear-PASSIVE(PAST)-3PL   *many*   *books*   *from-the-library*
        'Many books disappeared from the library.'

The postverbal subject of FI must be indefinite, as observed in Borer (1984). Thus, example (8-45) contrasts sharply with example (8-46), which contains a definite subject.

(8-46)   *neʕelmu   ha-sfarim   mə-ha-sifriya.
        disappear-PASSIVE(PAST)-3PL   *the-books*   *from-the-library*
        'The books disappeared from the library.'

Example (8-46) can be "saved," as it were, and rendered grammatical by the addition of a preverbal trigger, as in (8-47).

(8-47)   ba-šavuʕa   še-ʕavar neʕelmu   ha-sfarim
        on-the-week   *the-last*   *disappear-PASSIVE(PAST)-3PL*   *the-books*

           mə-ha-sifriya.
           from-the-library
        'Last week, the books disappeared from the library.'

I would like to analyze the pattern exemplified in (8-45)–(8-47) in the following terms. (8-45) and (8-46) illustrate the Definiteness Effect on postverbal subjects. This familiar constraint bars definite or strong DPs from the object position of ergative and passive verbs. It is familiar from English (e.g., Milsark 1974, Safir 1985), and Italian (Belletti 1988), and it has been observed in many languages and studied from a variety of perspectives (see e.g. the papers in Reuland and ter Meulen 1989). The fact that Hebrew FI gives rise to the Definiteness Effect constitutes rather robust evidence that the postverbal subject in, for example, (8-45) occupies a position internal to VP, under V'— namely, its θ-position.

When a trigger appears clause-initially, as in (8-47), the conditions for TI are met. The subject can and, as I have argued, must be raised from its θ-position. Hence, it is no longer in VP at S-structure and the Definiteness Effect is circumvented, allowing a definite subject to occur postverbally. Thus, although the linear order of the IP-internal constituents is the same in (8-45) and (8-47), the position of the subject is different.

In order to demonstrate the sensitivity of Italian to the Definiteness Affect, Belletti (1988) cites examples in which the postverbal subject is followed by an adverbial PP, as in (8-48).

(8-48)   a. All' improvviso   è   entrato   un uomo dalla   finestra.
            suddenly   is   entered   a man   from-the window
            'Suddenly, a man came in through the window.'

      b. *All' improvviso è   entrato   l'uomo   dalla   finestra.
            suddenly   is   entered   the-man   from-the window
            'Suddenly, the man came in through the window.'

When the clause-final PP *dalla finestra* 'from the window' does not appear, the equivalent of (8-48b) becomes grammatical.

(8-49)   E'   entrato   l'uomo.
            is   entered   the-man
            'The man entered.'

The reason for this difference is that the clause-final PP is necessary to "trap" the subject in its base position under V'. When the PP is absent, the postverbal DP *il uomo* is raised out of V' to some Specifier position on the right of V'. Thus, the absence of a clause-final PP in (8-49) serves the same role as the presence of a trigger in Hebrew. Both allow a thematic object to raise out of V' and escape the Definiteness Effect.

A question arises as to the nature of this position in Italian. A possibility that comes to mind is that it should be identified with Spec/V, which, in the case of ergative verbs, would be a nonthematic position.[16]

Following rather standard assumptions, I take the representation of a sentence with FI to be as in (8-50).

(8-50)

The postverbal subject appears in its base (object) position, and Spec/AgrS is filled by an expletive pro. Recall from Chapter 7, section 7.4, that when AgrSP is not projected, for example, in nonagreeing *ʔeyn* sentences, pro appears in Spec/T. The relevant example and the associated structural description are given in (8-51).

(8-51) a. ʔeyn   mitxolelot   kan
            NEG   occur(BENONI)-FPL   here
            'Storms don't occur here.'

b.

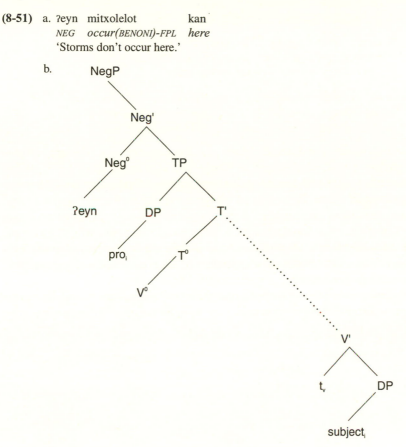

In chapter 7, it was shown that expletive pro is formally licensed in Hebrew. It was also assumed that the basic function of pro is to check the nominative features of T^0 (Chomsky 1993). Chomsky (1982) and others have argued that the expletive serves to transmit nominative features to the postverbal DP by a mechanism of cosuperscripting. This view is challenged in Belletti (1988), who demonstrates that the postverbal subject must be licensed independently of pro. She takes the licensing mechanism to be the assignment of inherent (partitive) Case (see also Lasnik 1992). Thus, in contexts of FI, the postverbal argument is licensed internally to VP, while the nominative Case features of T^0 are checked by pro. Hebrew FI can thus be analyzed on a par with, for example, Italian inversion with ergative predicates.

Nevertheless, Hebrew is not entirely like Italian. If it were, we would expect FI to be possible with verbs of other classes, in particular with unergative predicates. This is so because, to stress this point again, pro is licensed in both languages. The problem, then, is why the parity of the examples in (8-52) does not extend to those in (8-53).

(8-52) a. È avvenuto   un incidente in via Gramsci.
        is   occurred   an accident   in street Gramsci
        'An accident occurred on Gramsci street.'

        b. karta   teʔuna   bi-rxov   ʔaxad-ha-ʕam.
        occur(PAST)-3FS accident   on-street Axad-ha-ʕam
        'An accident occurred on Axad-Haʕam street.'

(8-53) a. ha   suonato la campana.   b. *cilcel   ha-paʕamon.
        has   rang   the bell   *ring(PAST)-3MS the-bell*
        'The bell rang.'   'The bell rang.'

Let us assume, with Belletti (1988), that the assignment of inherent partitive Case licenses a postverbal subject at S-structure (see also Lasnik 1993). When inversion takes place with a nonergative verb, partitive Case is not available since nonergative verbs lack the option of assigning partitive. Recall Rizzi's (1991) argument that Italian postverbal subjects (of nonergative verbs) must be Case-marked by the first functional head above VP, which he identifies with T^0 in simple clauses and with the head bearing participial morphology in compound tenses. This analysis allows a straightforward explanation of the nuanced adjacency condition on verbs and postverbal subjects discussed in §8.3.3.

We can be more precise about the nature of the Case-assigning head. In chapter 3, I argued that in Hebrew compound tenses, as in Italian ones, VP is dominated by an aspectual phrase, and the latter is associated with a dominating agreement phrase, as in (8-54).

(8-54)

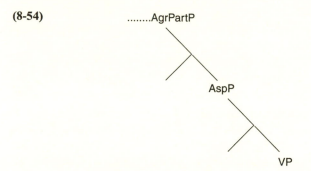

I would now like to suggest that the head responsible for nominative assignment to a VP-internal subject is Asp^0 (or rather its trace, via the *Government Transparency Corollary*). Rather than invoking a different head for nominative assignment in simplex clauses, I would like to claim that Asp^0 is the unique head assigning nominative Case through government. This suggestion implies that an AspP is generated in both simplex and in complex clauses, the difference being that in the former it lacks the associated participial agreement projection, there being no participial morphology in need of licensing on a tensed verb.

Universal Grammar makes available a fixed hierarchy of contentful functional projections. I have also argued that AgrPs differ from contentful projections such as TP and AspP in that AgrPs are not configured by Universal Core Structure (see chapter 1, §1.2). Thus, one predictable axis of architectural variation among languages concerns the generation of agreement projections.

I would, consequently, like to conjecture that the crucial difference between Hebrew and Italian, the factor ultimately responsible for the positioning of postverbal subjects in the two languages, is the projection of the AgrP in which accusative Case is checked. As we shall soon see, the position of AgrOP in the Hebrew clausal hierarchy renders impossible the assignment of Case by Asp^0 to a VP-internal subject.

Considering compound tenses, Friedemann and Siloni (1993) argue that AgrOP is the agreement phrase associated with the VP of the participle in Hebrew (and in Romance constructions with the auxiliary *be*) and with the VP headed by the auxiliary *have* in French and Italian. For instance, they note that object clitics are attached to the participle in Hebrew and never to the auxiliary, while the inverse holds for Romance. This is illustrated by the following paradigm.

(8-55) a. Dani haya mazmin -eni li-mʕon-o yom yom.
         Dani be(PAST)-3MS invite(BENONI)-MS -1S to-home-3MS every day
         'Dani used to invite me to his home every day.'

      b. *Dani haya -eni mazmin li-mʕon-o yom yom.
         Dani be(PAST)-3MS -1S invite(BENONI)-MS to-home-3MS every day
         'Dani used to invite me to his home every day.'

(8-56) a. *Gianni ha invitato-mi.   b. Gianni mi ha invitato.
        Gianni has invited-me   *Gianni me has invited*
        'Gianni invited me.'   'Gianni invited me.'

In chapter 9, I argue that so-called object clitics in Hebrew, such as *-eni* in (8-55), constitute the phonetic realization of $AgrO^0$, to which the verb, the participle in the example at hand, raises and to which it adjoins in the audible syntax. The contrast in (8-55) shows that Agr^0 is accessible to the Benoni participle, but never to the auxiliary. This then implies that AgrOP is lower than the VP headed by the auxiliary. Combining this result with the hierarchy of projections defended in the preceding chapters, we arrive at (8-57), which is essentially Friedemann and Siloni's suggestion.

(8-57)   (TP)

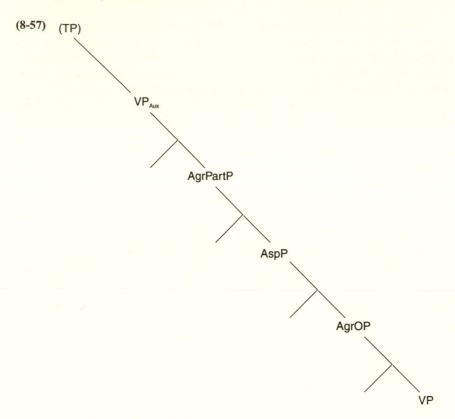

In Italian, however, clitics are attached to the auxiliary and never to the participle in compound tenses. This, and other considerations, lead Friedemann and Siloni to argue that AgrOP is located above the auxiliary, as in (8-58).

(8-58)

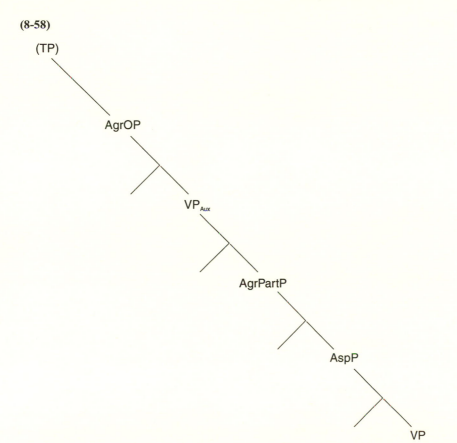

Let us now consider simplex tenses. These differ from complex ones in the absence, notably, of the VP housing the auxiliary and of the participial agreement projection. The natural assumption is that these are the only differences between the two types of clauses. In particular, AspP is represented in both simplex and complex tenses, and the relative position of AgrOP (with respect to VP and AspP) does not vary. I further hold, with Friedemann and Siloni and others, that AgrOP is projected not only in the company of transitive verbs but also of unergative ones (the latter subcategorized by a null, perhaps cognate, object).

The structural description of simplex tense clauses in Hebrew and Romance would thus contain the following hierarchy of projections.

(8-59) a. <u>Hebrew</u>

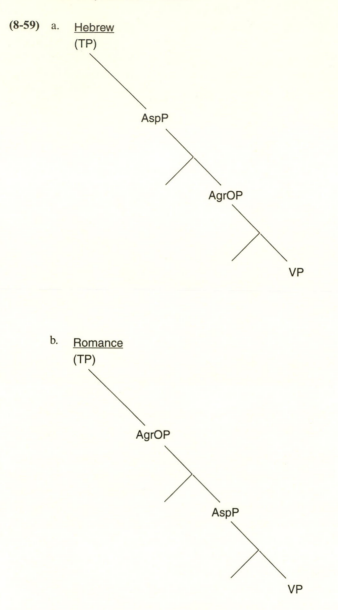

The relative positioning of AgrOP in the two language types is crucial to an explanation of why postverbal subjects may remain in VP in Romance language but not in Hebrew. In the former, but not in the latter, Asp^0 immediately dominates VP. Consequently, Asp^0 (exceptionally) governs Spec/V, and nominative Case can be assigned to the subject in VP. In Hebrew, on the other hand, AspP does not immediately dominate VP; rather, it dominates AgrOP, rendering nominative Case unassignable by Asp^0 to a subject in VP.

It thus transpires that postverbal subjects in Hebrew may not remain in VP because they are not licensed in that position, nor can they raise to Spec/AgrO since that position is reserved for objects. The statement in (8-30), however, expresses a stronger claim—namely, that the subject must not just raise out of VP; it must raise to the highest available subject position in the clause (i.e., Spec/T or Spec/AgrS).

I would like to now argue that the first condition actually implies the second— that is, if the subject must raise out of VP, then it must raise all the way up and cannot remain at S-structure in an intermediate position, higher than its -position in VP and lower than Spec/AgrS when AgrSP is projected. What we need to rule out, in other words, are subjects occurring in Spec/AgrPart in complex tenses and in Spec/T when AgrSP is projected.

Let us first consider Italian and make the explicit suggestion that the assignment of Case is always optional, leaving open the question of whether the optionality resides in the lexical entry of the Case-assigning head or whether the actual assignment of this Case is optional. Note, now, that even though there are several potential subject positions in the clause (as evidenced, for instance, by the distribution of floating quantifiers), Italian subjects are either in VP or in Spec/AgrS. If they could occupy intermediate positions, we would expect them, for example, to be able to occur above VP-edge adverbs, which is plainly not the case, as shown in (8-42).

Suppose the option of assigning Case to a VP-subject is taken. Then the subject remains in VP and an expletive pro appears in Spec/AgrS. Let us call this the "pro stratagem." Alternatively, Case is not assigned to the subject by Asp^0. The subject then raises all the way up, and the pro stratagem is not made use of. A state of affairs that is never found consists of combining the pro stratagem with partial raising of the subject. For example, it is never the case that the subject moves to Spec/T and remains there while pro is generated in Spec/AgrS.[17]

Recall the assumption that an argument associated with pro replaces it or adjoins to it in the LF component. Thus, combining the pro-stratagem with partial NP-movement leads to the formation of an A-chain in two steps: one in the audible syntax, and one in LF. I suggest that we express the incompatibility of the pro stratagem with partial NP-movement by means of the following statement:

(8-60)   A-movement must be terminated in the component in which it is initiated (S-structure or LF).

A slight modification or adjustment of (8-60) is necessary to account for the fact that thematic objects of ergative verbs can move to Spec/V to escape the Definiteness Effect (viz. the discussion surrounding the Italian examples in [8-48] and [8-49]). It appears that when a DP undergoes A-movement but remains within one maximal projection, this does not count as a violation of (8-60).[18]

Let us now return to Hebrew TI. The fundamental difference between Hebrew and Italian is that a postverbal subject cannot be Case-licensed in its base position. Therefore, the subject must raise out of VP. We have seen, however, that it always raises to the highest available subject position in the clause. It cannot, for example, raise to Spec/T and remain there, adjoining or replacing an expletive pro in Spec/AgrS only in LF. Excluded, for instance, is an S-structure representation such as (8-61).

(8-61)

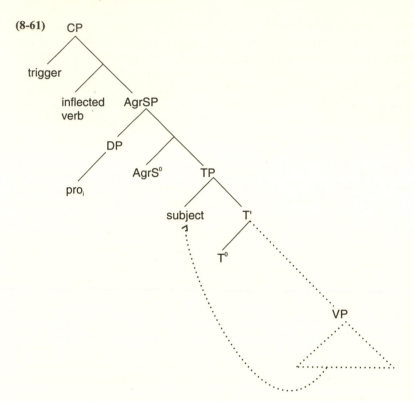

Example (8-61) would be a case of partial NP-movement, violating (8-60). The difference between Hebrew and Italian is that, in Hebrew TI, only the option of S-structure movement is available to a postverbal subject, while Italian allows A-movement to take place either at S-structure or in LF (expletive replacement). In contexts of FI, inherent partitive assigned by V to its sister under V' can serve to license a postverbal subject and the latter may hence remain in its base position.

8.5 CONCLUSION

To conclude this chapter, let us consider an interesting twist. There is some evidence in Hebrew that under TI, postverbal subjects of ergative and passive verbs may remain lower than VP-edge adverbials and, unlike subjects of other verb classes, are not obligatorily raised to the highest potential subject position in the clause.

Recall the observation that manner adverbials must follow the subject in TI configurations (viz. the discussion surrounding the sentences in [8-24]). There is something of a contrast, in my judgment, between (8-62a) and (8-63a), which illustrate this observation, and (8-62b) and (8-63b), where manner adverbials precede a definite subject of an ergative/passive verb under TI. If an adverbial such as *be-šeket* 'quietly' marks the upper edge of VP, then thematic objects of ergative predicates do not raise out of VP. They do, however, move out of V′, since they escape the Definiteness Effect. Subjects of nonergative predicates cannot remain inside VP and must raise higher than 'quietly'.

(8-62) a. ??ha-boker   patax   be-šeket Dan ʔet delet xadr-o.
this-morning open(PAST)-3MS   quietly Dan ACC door room-3MS
'This morning, Dan slowly quietly opened the door to his room.'

b. (?)ha-boker   niftexa   be-šeket ha-delet.
this-morning opened(PAST)-PASS-3FS quietly   the-door
'This morning, the door opened quietly.'

(8-63) a. ??ha-boker   hecig   be-ʔofen   mešaxneʕa Dani ʔet
this-morning present(PAST)-3MS in-manner convincing Dani ACC

ha-pitaron   šel-o.
the-solution of- 3MS
'This morning, Dani presented his solution in a convincing manner.'

b. (?)ha-boker   hucag   be-ʔofen   mešaxneʕa
this-morning present(PAST)-PASS-3MS in-manner convincing

ha-pitaron   šel-o.
the-solution of-3MS
'This morning, his solution was presented in a convincing manner.'

Reflecting a bit, we can see that these sort of data are actually predicted to be valid in the framework of the present analysis. This is so since only in the company of ergative/passive verbs is there no, nor can there be, an AgrO projection in the clause. Plainly, if there were one, the (single) argument chain would come to be associated with both accusative and nominative Case—the former assigned in AgrOP, the latter via expletive replacement in AgrSP. If AgrOP is indeed absent in (8-62b) and (8-63b), then Asp^0 comes to immediately dominate VP. We arrive at (8-64), where, crucially, Asp^0 can Case-license a subject in Spec/V.[19]

(8-64)

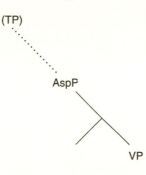

PART III

THE PRONOMINAL SYSTEM

The final part of this work studies the pronominal system of Hebrew and Arabic. Chapter 9 considers the pronominal suffixes that appear on all of the lexical and some functional categories in these languages. These have been analyzed in the generative tradition either as clitics or as incorporated pronouns. The analysis presented in the following pages revives a more traditional view, one that considers these pronominal endings to be inflectional suffixes. I argue that such inflection signals the presence of an AgrP, to which a lower head adjoins in the audible syntax. Various consequences follow, perhaps the most spectacular of which is the existence of an abundance of Agr phrases, each associated with a contentful functional or lexical head. The status of AgrP is brought under closer examination, and it is concluded that it is a fundamentally different type of projection from other functional heads.

Chapter 10 is a study of pronouns in particular in Hebrew. Independent pronominal forms have been analyzed variously as freestanding pronouns and as clitics, and the literature suffers from a certain degree of confusion as to their nature. I hold that independent pronouns in Hebrew are phonetically ambiguous between strong and weak but not clitic forms. Much of the chapter is dedicated to a study of the weak forms of these pronouns. I argue that the three-way distinction between strong, weak, and clitic pronouns may be reduced to a binary one. If cliticization like that of Romance involves a combination of XP movement and head movement, then weak pronouns can be characterized as LF-clitics: they accomplish XP movement in the audible syntax and undergo X^0 movement in Logical Form.

Finally, the appendix discusses X^0 incorporation to heads of projections that are not Agr. It is shown that, while incorporation to Agr takes the form of (left) adjunction, incorporation to a subcategorizing head is best treated as selected substitution.

NINE

Semitic Clitics

9.1 INTRODUCTION

This chapter is concerned with the enclitic pronouns of Arabic and Hebrew, illustrated by the examples in (9-1) with the clitic underlined.[1]

(9-1) a. kaan   b ixayyṭ   <u>-ha.</u>
       be(PAST)-3MS   *3MS-(IMPERF)sew*   *3FS*
       'He was sewing it.'   Palestinian Arabic

       b. ʕašaan   <u>-ha</u>   b-itxayyṭ   l-fisṭyaan . . .
        because   *3FS*   *3FS-(IMPERF)sew*   *the-dress*
        'Because she sews the dress . . .'   Palestinian Arabic

       c. tmunot   <u>-eha</u>   tluyot   ʕal   ha-kir.
        picture   *-3FS*   *hang(PASSIVE BENONI)-FS*   *on*   *the-wall*
        'Her pictures hang on the wall.'   Hebrew

       d. xašavnu   ʕal   <u>-eha.</u>
        think(PAST)-1PL   *about*   *-3FS*
        'We thought about her.'   Hebrew

An adequate analysis of these clitics must account for the fact that they are manifested on all lexical categories (i.e., on V in (9-1a), on P in (9-1b,d), and on N in (9-1c).) The analysis must also explain why Semitic clitics are, without exception, enclitics, and why they manifest no overt distinctions of Case.

These three properties and others to be presented here sharply distinguish Semitic clitics from Romance ones, as can be immediately discerned by comparing the expressions in (9-1) with the French examples in (9-2).

(9-2) a. Elle l'a   cousu.   b. Elle lui   donne un cadeau.
　　　　she it-has sewn　　　　　*she 3S-DAT gives a   present*
　　　　'She has sewn it.'　　　　　　'She gives her/him a present.'

Clitics in French, and Romance languages generally, appear only on verbs; they manifest case distinctions (viz. the different forms of the accusative clitic in [9-2a] and the dative one in [9-2b]), and they are either proclitics or enclitics. In French, they are proclitics on tensed verbs and negative imperatives, and enclitics on other verbal forms—for example, on affirmative imperatives, as shown in (9-3).

(9-3) Donne -lui un cadeau!
　　　　give   -3S   a present
　　　　'Give him/her a present!'

9.2 PROPERTIES OF SEMITIC CLITICS

The French object clitic in (9-2a) is attached to the auxiliary, while the Semitic one in (9-1a) is attached to the main verb. Romance clitics are typically attached to the auxiliary in compound tenses.[2] This is never the case in Semitic. Semitic clitics are invariably attached to the main verb in periphrastic constructions. Insofar as the generalization underlying clitic placement in French or Italian is that the clitics are attached to the highest verbal head in the clause—that is, the auxiliary in compound tenses and the main verb in simple ones—the generalization holding for Semitic should be stated as in (9-4).

(9-4) Clitics are always attached to the closest c-commanding head.

Object clitics are thus attached to a verb, oblique ones to a preposition, and so forth.

Insofar as clitics are X^0 categories, incorporated to another head, then the chain connecting the clitic to its base position appears to violate the Relativized Minimality clause of the ECP in Romance, but not in Semitic. Consider (9-2a), for example. The object clitic can presumably be taken to be the head of the object DP at D-structure. In its surface position, however, it is attached to the auxiliary. This means that it is moved from its original position, crossing over several potential antecedents (the main verb and several functional heads) and creating at least a potential Minimality violation. In the Semitic (9-1a), in contrast, the clitic is attached to the verb—that is, the chain it forms with its base position is a perfectly licit one, in terms of Relativized Minimality.

The Romance case can be dealt with by assuming that clitics undergo head movement only as a final step. They are generated and move as XPs to some intermediate Spec position, perhaps Spec/AgrO, from where the head of this XP incorporates to the higher head to which the verb is adjoined (viz. Kayne 1989, Sportiche 1990, and much current work). Such a derivation is illustrated in (9-5).[3]

(9-5)

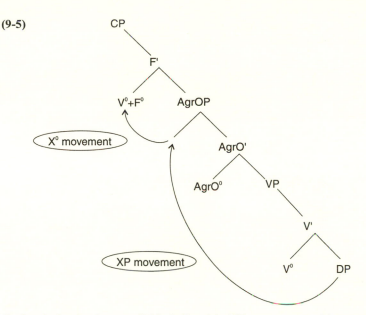

Such a derivation is unavailable in Semitic. If it were, we would expect object clitics to have the option of appearing in positions higher than that occupied at S-structure by the main verb.

A second difference evident from the comparison of the sentences in (9-1) with the one in (9-2a) is that Romance clitics may appear to the left of their hosts (proclisis), while in Semitic, as noted above, they are without exception enclitics. In Eastern Romance, the choice between proclisis and enclisis is determined by the tense and mood of the verb.[4] No such pattern can be found in Semitic.

A third important difference is that while Romance clitics appear on verbs and auxiliaries, Semitic clitics appear on all lexical and some of the functional categories, as in the Palestinian Arabic paradigm in (9-6).

(9-6) a. Verb + Object:

fhimt l-mʕalme.
understand(PERF)-1S *the teacher*
'I understood the teacher.'

fhimt-ha.
(I) understood her

b. Noun + Possessor:

beet l-mʕalme
house the-teacher
'the teacher's house'

beet-ha
her-house

c. Preposition + Object:

min l-mʕalme
from the-teacher

min-ha
from-her

d. Complementizer + Subject:

ʔinnu l-mʕalme
that   the-teacher

ʔin-ha
that-she

e. Quantifier + DP:

kull l-mʕalmaat
all the-teachers

kull-hin
all-them

A fifth property of Semitic clitics that distinguishes them from Romance ones is that there are no clitic clusters in Semitic. The relevant case involves clitics in the double object construction.[5] Arabic causative verbs and a small number of noncausative verbs alternate between a double accusative and an accusative-dative complement alignment pattern (see Hazout 1991, Hoyt 1989, Mouchaweh 1986). Consider the following paradigm from Cairene Arabic (Kenstowicz and Wahba 1980).

(9-7) a. ?il-mudarris   fahhim   l-dars   li-l-bint.
          the-teacher   *understand(PERF-CAUS)-3MS*   *the-lesson*   *to-the-girl*
          'The teacher explained the lesson to the girl.'

       b. ?il-mudarris   fahhim   l-bint   l-dars.
          the-teacher   *understand(PERF-CAUS)-3MS*   *the-girl*   *the-lesson*

       c. ?il-mudarris   fahhim   -u   li-l-bint.
          the-teacher   *understand(PERF-CAUS)-3MS*   *-3MS*   *to-the-girl*

       d. ?il-mudarris   fahhim   -ha   l-dars.
          the-teacher   *understand(PERF-CAUS)-3MS*   *-3FS*   *the-lesson*

       e. ?il-mudarris   fahhim   -u   laa-ha.
          the-teacher   *understand(PERF-CAUS)-3MS*   *-3MS*   *to-3FS*

       f. *?il-mudarris   fahhim   -ha-u   /-u-ha
          the-teacher   *understand(PERF-CAUS)-3MS*   *-3FS-3MS*   */3MS-3FS*

Examples (9-7a,b) illustrate the dative alternation. In the first sentence in this pair, there is a direct object and an indirect (prepositional dative) one. The second, dative-shifted sentence, illustrates the double object variant. The second pair of sentences, (9-7c,d), illustrate pronominalization of one of the complements. In (9-7c), the theme is cliticized on the verb, and in (9-7d) the causee, or the shifted object. The crucial data are found in the third pair in (9-7). When both complements are pronominalized, only one can show up as a clitic on the verb, and the other one must find another host. In the first member of this pair, (9-7e), the direct object is cliticized on the verb and the indirect one on the preposition. Example (9-7f) shows that cliticizing both complements on the verb in any order is unacceptable. Put differently, only the prepositional dative construction can be the source for pro-nominalization of both complements. If clitic clusters are disallowed in Cairene, then (9-7e) is the only option when both objects are pronominalized, because only in the prepositional dative construction is there a second host for the second clitic.

A final property distinguishing Semitic clitics from Romance ones to be noted at this point is that certain Romance clitic forms have a morphological affinity with determiners: French *la* is the third person accusative feminine clitic and the feminine definite determiner (see, e.g., Cardinaletti 1994a). No such affinity can be observed in Semitic.

To conclude this descriptive section, I list the relevant properties of Semitic clitics as discussed, noting that for each and every one of them, Romance clitics have the opposite property.

(9-8) *Properties of Semitic clitics*
       a. They occur on the right of their host, never on the left.

       b. They are always attached to the closest c-commanding head.

c. They appear on all lexical categories and on certain functional ones.

d. They do not manifest case distinctions.

e. They never cluster—that is, there is a single clitic per host.

f. They bear no morphological resemblance to nominal determiners.

9.3   THE INCORPORATION ANALYSIS

One thread running through generative research on Semitic has been the view that the enclitic pronouns are heads affixed to their governor under linear adjacency. Thus an object clitic on a verb is affixed in the configuration in (9-9a), and a prepositional object is affixed to a preposition in the configuration (9-9b).

(9-9)   a.   b.

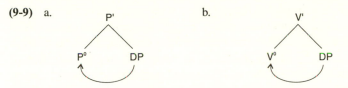

Broselow (1976) argued that the clitic is right-adjoined to its host. Fassi Fehri (1993) espouses a similar view, based on Baker's (1985) theory of Incorporation.

This approach is consistent with the locality of cliticization—that is, the choice of host. In several respects, however, it is insufficient. First, it fails to explain why Romance clitics, which are also presumably X^0 categories, do not give rise to a consistent pattern of local affixation to their governor. The difference between Romance and Semitic under the Incorporation approach would have to be reduced to something like the following. While in both language families clitics are incorporated heads, Incorporation in Romance can only take place once the clitic has moved out of its base position, in particular to a position immediately governed by the highest verb in the clause; Semitic clitics cannot avail themselves of this possibility.

This would in turn lead one to say that the difference between the two language families has to do with the licensing conditions on pronouns. Romance clitics are presumably licensed only once they are incorporated into AgrS, while Semitic pronouns can be licensed by affixation directly onto the category governing them. It is not clear why this should be the case: whether it constitutes a primitive difference between pronouns in the two language families or whether it is due to the setting of some parameter.

A further difficulty with the approach to Semitic cliticization in terms of local affixation/incorporation is that it provides no explanation why the clitic appears always on the right and never on the left of its host. It could be that, *pace* Kayne (1989, 1994), there is a fundamental (perhaps parametric) difference between Semitic and Romance in the direction of incorporation of heads to heads, such that, in Semitic, head movement always yields right adjunction. If this were the case, we would expect other types of incorporation to follow the same pattern. However, to the degree that one can find examples of overt incorporation in Semitic, left adjunction rather than right adjunction seems to be the rule.

A particularly illuminating example is provided by Hebrew Copula Inversion, a construction studied in chapters 2 and 3 and illustrated here in (9-10b).

(9-10) a. Dani   haya   tofer   smalot.
           Dani   *was(PAST)-3MS*   *sew(BENONI)-MS*   *dresses*
           'Dani was sewing dresses.'

        b. Dani   tofer   haya   smalot.
           Dani   *sew(BENONI)-MS*   *was(PAST)-3MS*   *dresses*
           'Dani was sewing dresses.'

In this construction, a participle appears to the left of the auxiliary. Following Borer (1995), it was shown that the participle incorporates to the auxiliary, forming an inseparable unit with it (viz. §3.1.3). The relevance of this construction to the present discussion is that, insofar as the participle raises to adjoin to the auxiliary, it adjoins on the left of the auxiliary and not on the right. If one maintains that clitics are incorporated to their heads, then one must perforce complicate the description of Semitic incorporation by adding an exception clause affecting the direction of the attachment of clitics (or conversely, of inverted participles). A further set of difficulties with this family of proposals is signaled by an observation of Broselow's that, while postverbal direct objects can and must be encliticized onto the verb, postverbal subjects cannot. Let us reflect on this matter in greater detail.

Consider the following Hebrew example. Recall that Hebrew verbs may precede their subjects and follow a trigger; see chapter 8. Example (9-11a) illustrates inversion of a nonpronominal subject and (9-11b) of a pronominal one.

(9-11) a. bə-yaldut-o   raxav   Dani   ʕal   gamal.
           in-youth-3MS   *ride(PAST)-3MS*   *Dani*   *on*   *camel*
           'In his youth, Dani rode a camel.'

        b. bə-yaldut-o   raxav   hu   ʕal   gamal.
           in-youth-3MS   *ride(PAST)-3MS*   *he*   *on*   *camel*
           'In his youth, he rode a camel.'

The following example shows that the postverbal pronoun cannot be cliticized onto the verb.

(9-12) *bə-yaldut-o   raxav   -o   ʕal   gamal.
         in-youth-3MS   *ride(PAST)-3MS*   *3MS*   *on*   *camel*
         'In his youth, he rode a camel.'

One might argue that the ungrammaticality of (9-12) is due to structural reasons—namely, that clitics must be sisters to their host, as in (9-9), and that a subject is never a sister to a verb. This argument is belied, however, by the following consideration.

Clitics in Semitic, as we have seen, occur on nouns. In particular, they occur on derived nominals, as in (9-13b).

(9-13) a. ktivat   Dan   ʔet   ha-maʔamar   hirgiza   ʔet   Miriam.
           writing   *Dan*   *ACC*   *the-article*   *anger(PAST)-3FS*   *ACC*   *Miriam*
           'Dan's writing of the article angered Miriam.'

b. ktivat   -o   ?et   ha-ma?amar   hirgiza   ?et   Miriam.
   writing *3MS* *ACC* *the-article*   *anger(PAST)-3FS*   *ACC* Miriam
   'His writing of the article angered Miriam.'

The order of constituents in (9-13) strongly favors a Noun-Raising account, according to which a D-structure representation, in which the agent of writing is the specifier of the NP, is transformed into a head-initial one by the raising of N^0 across it to some functional projection (D^0 or perhaps Agr^0—cf. Fassi-Fehri 1989, 1993, Ritter 1988, 1995 and Siloni 1994). In the derived S-structure representation, the agent argument is not a sister to N. Rather, it is exceptionally governed by it, as in (9-14) (for the sake of concreteness, I take head movement to target D^0).

(9-14)

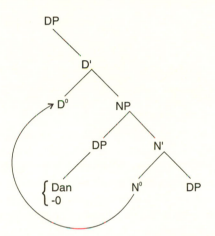

The structural relationship between a verb and a postverbal subject in, for example, (9-12), is identical to the one schematized in (9-14), with the appropriate change of category labels: the inflected verb moves to C^0 over the clausal subject in Spec/AgrS. The full acceptability of (9-13b) should be interpreted to mean that there is no *structural* constraint as such blocking incorporation of a (postverbal) subject onto a verb. Put differently, a nonstructural explanation should be sought for the ungrammaticality of (9-12).

I would like to suggest an explanation of this type and develop the idea that (9-12) is ungrammatical simply because there are no clitics in Semitic, that is, no pronominal arguments whose heads are raised and incorporated to a host. I approach this matter by first arguing against the view that subject *agreement* is itself a clitic in Semitic. Then, in §9.4, I argue that whereas the pronominal suffixes in Semitic are all instances of agreement, or Agr^0 elements, subject agreement is an exception: it is not associated with a verb through the latter's incorporation to an affixal Agr head, but rather, is associated with the verb in the Lexicon, prior to syntactic projection.[6]

9.3.1 Is Subject Agreement a Clitic?

Fassi-Fehri (1993) argues that subject agreement is an incorporated pronoun. According to this view, the subject pronoun in a VSO language such as Standard

Arabic is incorporated to the verb, exactly like an object pronoun. Thus, in the following example, first the subject, then the object, is incorporated into the the the verbal stem.

(9-15)   raʔai   -tu   -hu.
             see-PERF *-1S*   *3MS*
             'I saw him.'

For reasons that will become clear in a moment, the Arabic VSO pattern does not provide sufficient evidence to evaluate this claim. Consideration of a residual VSO effect in Hebrew can shed some light on the issue. Recall from chapter 4 that the negative head *ʔeyn* can be followed by a subject pronoun, as in (9-16a); *ʔeyn* can also be followed by a suffix, identical in form to the clitics under discussion in this chapter, as in (9-16b).

(9-16)   a. ʔeyn ʔani ʔohev   xacilim.
               NEG   I   like(BENONI)-MS   *eggplants*
               'I don't like eggplants.'

             b. ʔeyn (ən)i ʔohev   xacilim.
                NEG   1MS   like(BENONI)-MS eggplants
                'I don't like eggplants.'

Under the incorporation approach, (9-16b) is a variant of (9-16a) with the postnegation pronoun incorporated into it. This, however, falls short of explaining the following paradigm, which shows that, when the suffixal form of the third person pronoun appears, the sentence is ungrammatical without an overt subject; contrast (9-17b) with (9-17c).

(9-17)   a. ʔeyn hu ʔohev   xacilim.
               NEG   he   like(BENONI)-MS eggplants
               'He doesn't like eggplants.'

             b. *ʔeyn -o ʔohev   xacilim.
                NEG   3MS   like(BENONI)-MS   eggplants
                'He doesn't like eggplants.'

             c. hu ʔeyn -o ʔohev   xacilim.
                he NEG   3MS   like(BENONI)-MS   eggplants
                'He doesn't like eggplants.'

The paradigm in (9-17) strongly suggests that the suffix on *ʔeyn* should not be analyzed as an incorporated pronoun but, rather, as an inflectional marker, a manifestation of subject agreement. This is so since it patterns with all other instances of third person inflection in Hebrew in failing to appropriately identify a referential null subject (viz. §7.2.4 ff.). With pro unidentified, an overt subject must be realized, as in (9-17c).

The semi-pro-drop properties of Hebrew thus make it possible to distinguish between an inflectional affix and an incorporated pronoun. The *ʔeyn* construction gives rise to the agreement pattern characteristic of the VSO~SVO alternation in Standard Arabic where verbs fully agree only with preverbal subjects. However, since referential null subjects are licensed in the company of third-person inflection in Standard Arabic, one is at pain to decide whether *-uu* in (9-18) is an Agr⁰ licensing a null subject or whether it is a pronoun incorporated into the verb.

(9-18)   ʔakal   -uu   l-taʕaam.
   ate(PERF)   *-3MPL*   *the-food*
   'They ate the food.'

The markers of subject agreement on *ʔeyn* are unique in that they are taken from the class of suffixal inflection. When occurring on verbs however, subject agreement in Semitic is expressed by morphologically distinct paradigms. Subject agreement is both suffixal and prefixal, varying in accordance with the Tense and Aspect specification of the verb. Furthermore, agreement manifests person, number, and gender distinctions only in the nonparticipial forms; the latter, to recall, are inflected only for number and gender. Subject agreement in Semitic is discussed in §1.3.2. To recapitulate, (9-19) provides the paradigm of subject agreement in the Palestinian Arabic imperfect form and, for the sake of comparison, (9-20) tabulates the forms of the "pronominal suffixes" in this language (there are minor differences when the clitic is attached to a vowel-final stem).

(9-19) Inflectional paradigm of √*šwf* 'see' in Palestinian Arabic

	Singular			Plural		
	Prefix	Stem	Suffix	Prefix	Stem	Suffix
1	ʔa-	šuuf		n-	šuuf	
2m	t-	šuuf		t-	šuuf	-u
2f	t-	šuuf	-i	t-	šuuf	-u
3m	y-	šuuf		y-	šuuf	-u
3f	t-	šuuf		y-	šuuf	-u

(9-20) Clitic Forms in
     Palestinian Arabic

Singular		Plural	
1	-(n)i	1	-na
2m	-ak	2m	-ko
2f	-ik	2f	-ko
3m	-o	3m	-hin
3f	-ha	3f	-hin

Alongside the syntactic and morphological considerations that cast doubt on the view that subject agreement is an incorporated pronoun, a comparative angle further suggests that subject agreement is not a clitic. I discuss this angle briefly in the following section.

9.3.2   Clitics and Agreement in Berber

Berber is a non-Semitic language of the Afroasiatic family, but it shares with Semitic a number of morphological properties. In both types of languages, a word's consonantism identifies its root and basic meaning, while particular vowel-consonant sequences (templates) provide derivational information. This sort of non-concatentative morphology does not, however, carry over to inflection. The coding of inflectional information—person, number, and gender—is, concatenative in both Semitic and Berber. An inflectional paradigm of the Ait-Seghrouchen dialect of Tamazight Berber is provided in example (9-21). Notice that the inflectional markers in Berber, exactly as in the Palestinian Arabic paradigm in (9-19), are composed of either prefixes, suffixes, or both (data from Guerssel 1985).

(9-21)   Inflectional Paradigm of √*wdf* 'enter' in Tamazight Berber

	Singular				Plural		
	Prefix	Stem	Suffix		Prefix	Stem	Suffix
1		wdf	-x	1	n-	wdf	
2	t-	wdf	-t	2m	t-	wdf	-m
3m	y-	wdf		2f	t-	wdf	-nt
3f	t-	wdf		3m		wdf	-n
				3f		wdf	-nt

The direct object pronoun in Berber, as in Semitic, is an enclitic layered on the outside of subject agreement, viz. (9-22b).

(9-22) a. ttci   -x   aysum.   b. ttci   -x   -tt.
  eat(PERF) -1S   meat   *eat(PERF)   -1S   -3MS*
  'I ate meat.'   'I ate it.'

On the basis of (9-22) alone, it is hard to determine whether the suffixed form -*x* '-1s' is a bound pronoun or an agreement marker. One crucial difference between Berber and Semitic, however, demonstrates that subject agreement is not a bound pronoun, as opposed to the object suffix -*tt* glossed as '-3MS' in (9-22b).

Berber clitics, but not subject agreement, must occupy the second position in the clause. That is to say, they appear to the right of the verb (as a suffixed form) when the verb is string-initial (in VSO orders) but appear to its left, when the verb is preceded by a member of a certain class of elements, which Ouhalla (1989) characterizes as the class of X^0 categories. For example, in embedded sentences with an overt complementizer, the clitics appear to the immediate right of the complementizer. Contrast the position of -*tt* '3MS' in (9-23a) and (9-23b); data from Guerssel (1985).

(9-23) a. y-   uzn   -tt   Mohand i   Tifa.
    3MS   send(PERF)   3MS   Mohand to   Tifa
    'Mohand sent it to Tifa.'

  b. ssən   -x   is   -tt   y-   uzn   Mohand i   Tifa.
    know(PERF) -1S   that -3MS   3MS-   send(PERF)   Mohand to   Tifa
    'I think that Mohand sent it to Tifa.'

If subject agreement were a clitic, we would expect it to also vary in its position and appear as a verbal affix in verb-initial CPs and as a suffix on Comp in embedded clauses. This is patently not the case. Subject agreement in Berber is a conjugation, while object clitics are second position clitics, the analysis of which lies beyond the scope of this work (see Ouhalla 1989). I will assume that subject agreement in Berber patterns like the Semitic one. The clitic system of Berber, however, is different from the Semitic one.

I have tried to show that subject agreement in Semitic is not an incorporated pronoun, that is to say, a D-structure DP whose head is incorporated to some host. In the next section, I argue that the pronominal suffixes, the so-called Semitic clitics, are forms of agreement. I return to the question of subject agreement in §9.4.1.

9.4   SEMITIC CLITICS AS AGR^0 ELEMENTS

The hypothesis I would like to submit is that Semitic clitics are Agr^0 elements to which a lower head adjoins as it raises out of the complement of Agr^0. Let us first consider object clitics. Suppose that in Semitic, AgrO^0 may contain an affix—that is, have an overt head. When the verb raises out of VP, for example, over negation, (9-24), it must adjoin to AgrO^0 on its path upward, simply because AgrOP lies above VP and below NegP.

(9-24)   bitxayyṭ   -o   -š.
      3FS-(IMPERF)sew   -3MS   -NEG
      'She does not sew it.'

In Hebrew Copula Inversion, an object clitic is carried along with the Benoni form when the latter adjoins to the auxiliary, as discussed in Friedemann and Siloni (1993). Contrast (9-25a) and (9-25b).

(9-25)   a. Dani   tofr   -am   haya.
         Dani   sew(BENONI)-MS -3MS   be(PAST)-3MS

       b. *Dani   tofr   haya   -am.
          Dani   sew(BENONI)-MS be(PAST)-3MS   -3MS
         'Dani was sewing them.'

In fact, an object clitic is the only element that may intervene, so to speak, between the inverted participle and the copula. This means that the clitic cannot be anything but an incorporated X^0 category, since a category of a different level cannot be embedded inside a head. The analysis of CI which I have in mind is diagrammed by the phrase marker in (9-26), where AgrPart^0, itself a complex head containing AgrO^0 and V^0, is incorporated to V^0$_{Aux}$ (see chapter 8 for a justification of the order AgrPartP > AgrOP > VP).

(9-26)

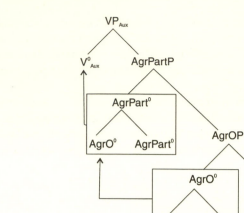

The position of the clitic on the right of the verb—the fact that clitics are invariably enclitics—is a trivial consequence of this analysis, since it is the verb that incorporates into $AgrO^0$, and not vice versa. The pattern of strict enclisis evidenced in Semitic thus results from the process of left adjunction, which invariably yields the surface order [incorporated head > Agr].

The strict locality on clitic attachment—the fact that an object clitic is attached to the main verb and never to the auxiliary—is a consequence of the Head Movement Constraint. The contents of $AgrO^0$ must appear on the main verb because AgrO c-commands the main verb and not the auxiliary. One major difference between Romance and Semitic clitics thus emerges: Romance clitics are XPs at some level of representation; Semitic clitics are affixal (Agr) heads at all levels.

9.4.1   Extensions and Consequences

9.4.1.1   *Subject Agreement Reconsidered*

Let us now return to the problem of subject agreement. If so-called object clitics are manifestation of $AgrO^0$, and if subject agreement is the contents of $AgrS^0$, we expect object agreement to be closer to the verbal stem than subject agreement, for the simple reason that the adjunction of the verb to $AgrO^0$ is derivationally prior to its adjunction to $AgrS^0$. This is never the case.

I would therefore like to suggest that we abandon the assumption that $AgrS^0$ in Semitic contains an overt affix. Rather than taking subject agreement morphology on a verb to constitute the affixal contents of $AgrS^0$, I suggest that we consider it to be base-generated features on the verb itself which are checked in $AgrS^0$. Thus, the actual affixes constituting subject agreement are not base-generated independently of the verbal stem and attached to it as a consequence of verb movement and adjunction. Rather, a verb is selected from the Lexicon bearing subject agreement. Object agreement, on the other hand, and as we shall momentarily see, all other subcases of agreement, are generated as independent heads (Agr⁰s), and their attachment or cliticization is a product of syntactic movement and adjunction.

The positioning of subject agreement closer to the verbal stem than object agreement should therefore be taken to reflect the fact that subject agreement is lexical and is therefore attached to the verb prior to the latter's movement to AgrO⁰. A hallmark of the inflectional morphology of Semitic is that the form of subject agreement affixes depends on the aspectual or temporal specification of the verb. In Arabic and Hebrew, subject agreeement in the perfect or past form is without exception suffixal, while agreement in the imperfective or future forms contains a combination of prefixes and suffixes. Object agreement markers, however, are invariably suffixal. I take this fact to further support the view that the so-called clitics are syntactically attached (and the directionality of head-to-head adjunction imposes the order stem > clitic), while subject agreement affixes are lexical. We expect their ordering with respect to the stem to thus be somewhat arbitrary, as lexical properties often are.

I have tried to argue that, while AgrO⁰ may contain an overt head (the so-called object clitic), AgrS⁰ does not contain an affix. However, it would be wrong to associate this difference with the intrinsic contents of the Agr head in question. Put differently, there is no principled reason why AgrS⁰ should fail to contain an affix. Indeed, if morphological form is a clue, then the the the fact that the subject agreement markers on the negative head *ʔeyn* are identical to those of direct object and prepositional agreement (and hence differ from prototypical subject agreement) should be taken to mean that when *ʔeyn* is present in the structure, AgrS⁰ does contain an affix; compare the pattern of *ʔeyn* inflection and that of Hebrew object agreement on a verb such as *hizmin* 'invite (PAST)-3MS' tabulated in (9-27).[7]

(9-27)	a.	Agreement Paradigm of ʔeyn		b.		Hebrew Object Agreement	
		Singular	Plural			Singular	Plural
	1	-(ən)i	-enu		1	-(ən)i	-enu
	2m	-xa	-xem		2m	-xa	-xem
	2f	-ex	-xen		2f	-ex	-xen
	3m	-o	-am		3m	-o	-am
	3f	-a	-an		3f	-a	-an

9.4.1.2 *Agr, Agr Everywhere*

The fact that clitics appear on all lexical and some of the functional categories should now be taken to indicate that all these categories may have associated Agr projections, so that a PP or a CP can appear dominated by Agr phrases. We should thus think of the preposition + clitic sequence in, for example, (9-1d), the noun + clitic sequence in (9-1c), or the complementizer + clitic sequence in (9-6d) as incorporating the following structures. The arrows indicate head movement. The existence of further dominating structure—e.g., a DP projection in (9-28b)—is of course not precluded.

(9-28) a.

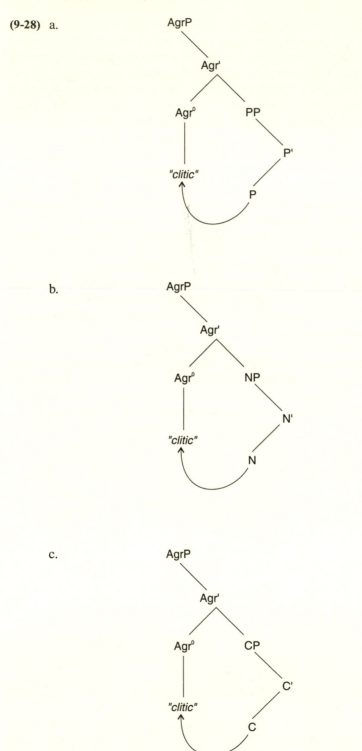

The proliferation of Agr categories might be construed as a problem for selection. If a verb selects a proposition, for instance, a CP, how can selection be satisfied if CP is dominated by AgrP? I think the answer is that Agr phrases are simply not visible for selection, so that when, say, C^0 selects IP, it selects a TP, AgrSP being in some sense invisible. Contrary to other functional projections (such as TP, DP, AspP, or NegP), AgrP plays no coherent semantic role. Chomsky (1991), for example, crucially requires that AgrP delete in LF. But whether AgrP is inserted or deleted (essentially a theory-internal question), it plays no part in categorial or semantic selection. AgrPs have one role to play: they enable feature checking to be carried out in a Spec-head configuration. Beyond that they are entirely redundant.

Let us further assume, with Chomsky (1993), that AgrSP, AgrOP, and so on, are heuristic labels. AgrSP is the Agr category accessed by the subject, while AgrO is targeted by the direct object. The association of $AgrS^0$ with subjects and of $AgrO^0$ with objects is due to the operation of derivational constraints (e.g., the need to respect Equidistance; see §1.2 and the discussion in §9.4.2), and not a consequence of some intrinsic connection between the Agr category and the nominal expresssion in its Spec. The content of Agr^0 is constituted of a particular choice of agreement or φ-features, but the labels AgrSP, AgrOP, and so on, do not refer to different categories, but to different instantiations of AgrP. This explains the absence of Case distinctions on these Agr heads. One expects Case distinctions to show up on nominals—on XPs—and Standard Arabic indeed manifests a robust system of morphological Case, but on DPs, not on clitics.

Proceeding, let us suppose that, whenever an affix appears in an Agr head, a DP bearing the appropriate nominal features agrees with it and appears in its Spec, raising from some thematic position. Take this DP to be a referential pro, as in the schema in (9-29), where X is a member of the class of clitic-bearing heads and XP is a thematic domain.[8]

(9-29)

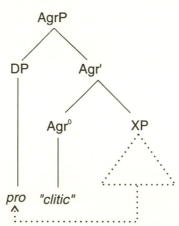

The formal similarity between clitics and determiners in Romance suggests that they belong to one and the same category, namely D^0 (Cardinaletti 1994, Uriagereka 1994). By a similar token, the absence of any such similarity in Semitic is just what one expects if clitics are Agr^0 elements and determiners belong to the category D^0.

9.4.2   On the Absence of Clitic Clusters

I now turn to another salient property of Semitic clitics, the absence of clitic or agreement clusters. The relevant paradigm to examine is one in which a verb has more than a single object. Such a test case is provided by the double object construction, manifested in numerous Arabic dialects.

Recall the Cairene Arabic paradigm in (9-7). In particular, (9-7f) illustrates the ungrammaticality of clusters. The view that Arabic clitics are Agr heads allows us to formulate succinctly the restriction violated in this example.

(9-30)   There is only a single AgrP immediately above VP.

Consideration of (9-7c,d) shows that the single Agr projection associated with VP can be headed by an affix corresponding to either the direct object (9-7c) or the indirect object (9-7d). This shows that there is no inherent link between AgrOP and *direct object* agreement (recall that there are no Case distinctions on the Agr heads). In principle, any argument can make use of Spec/AgrOP.

This fact, as well as the restriction stated in (9-30) receive a natural interpretation in terms of Chomsky's (1993) notions of domain and equidistance. In order to see this, let us consider a possible structure where (9-30) does *not* hold—where VP is dominated by two Agr projections (as, for example, in Ouhalla 1993a).

Example (9-31) diagrams a VP-shell—two stacked VPs, the lower one containing the two objects, and the higher one containing the subject. Unlike Larson's (1988) proposal, however, the indirect object in (9-31) is mapped onto a hierarchically higher position than the direct object, for reasons discussed in Belletti and Shlonsky (1995).[9]

(9-31)

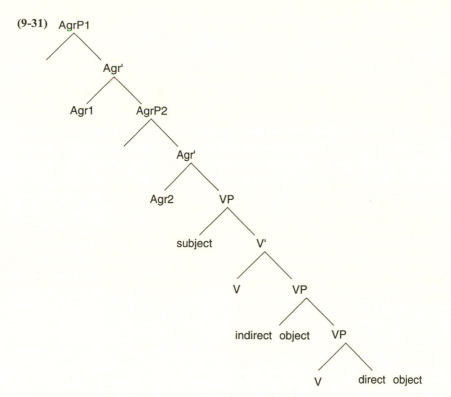

In a nutshell, Chomsky's (1993) proposal is that A-movement of a DP can skip the closest c-commanding Spec position if V has adjoined to a higher head and extended its domain. This is so because the extraction site and the intermediate Spec position are rendered equidistant from the target Spec. This system allows for objects to raise to Spec/AgrO crossing over the base subject position and for subjects to raise over objects in Spec/AgrO. Crucially, however, only one Spec can be thus skipped with every step of domain extension. At the same time, one must assume that movement within the VP shell itself is free, for otherwise the direct object would never be able to leave VP, independently of the number and position of AgrPs above VP, since its trajectory crosses over two consecutive Specs, one occupied by the indirect object and the other by the subject.[10]

In a structure like (9-31), one argument is bound to be trapped within VP. Suppose that the direct object raises to Spec/Agr2 and the indirect object to Spec/Agr1; then the subject would be stranded in VP. Similarly, if one object moved to Spec/Agr2 and the subject to Spec/Agr1, the second object would be stranded. It thus follows that VP may be associated with a single AgrP. Hence, a verb may be associated with a single Agr affix and the absence of clitic clusters is explained.[11]

Pronominalization of both objects in Cairene Arabic requires the prepositional dative construction. One clitic shows up on the verb, indicating that the single AgrP above VP has been triggered and its Spec is occupied. The other clitic is manifested on the preposition, indicating that the preposition's associated AgrP has been used and that P has raised to its respective Agr (see (9-28a)). Such a derivation is fully consistent with Chomsky's approach, since the two AgrPs are within the domains of two distinct heads.

An independent question now arises with respect to the actual derivation of (9-7b)—namely, that of the double-object construction. In particular, the conclusion that VP is associated with a single AgrP raises the obvious question of how two (accusative) objects can be licensed if there is only one Spec/AgrO and a single accusative Case feature. Rather than discussing this question in abstract—the objects in (9-7b) are in situ at S-structure and provide no evidence as to where they are raised in LF—I propose to take up this question in the context of a discussion of the movement properties of Semitic weak pronouns. These provide overt evidence for movement out of VP. In chapter 10, I argue that the trajectory of the LF-movement of nonpronominal DP objects is patterned, at least in part, after the trajectory of weak pronoun raising in the overt syntax.

Finally, note that no problem arises for extracting a subject over Spec/AgrO. In Simplex tenses, for example, verb movement to AgrO^0 makes Spec/AgrO available as a landing site. The object pro thus raises into it. Then, the verb raises to T^0 and the subject can move directly from Spec/V to Spec/T, respecting Equidistance.

9.4.3 Predictions Concerning Clitic Doubling

If Semitic "clitics" are X^0 categories, then there should be no principled ban on clitic doubling, since for every X^0 there will always be a YP (Spec) position associated with it (viz. [9-29]; in fact, there are two, Spec/Agr and the θ-position of the argument). This is quite clearly confirmed. The following Palestinian paradigm illustrates that clitic doubling is found in all categories in which "clitics" are found.[12]

(9-32)　a. fhimt　　　　　　　　-ha　　la　l-mʕalme.
　　　　　　　understand(PERF)-1S -3FS　to　the-teacher.
　　　　　　　'I understood the teacher.'

　　　　b. beet　-ha　　la　l-mʕalme . . .
　　　　　　　house -3FS　to　the-teacher.
　　　　　　　'the teacher's house . . .'

　　　　c. min　-ha　　la　l-mʕalme . . .
　　　　　　　from -3FS　to　the-teacher.
　　　　　　　'from the teacher . . .'

　　　　d. ʔin　-ha　　l-mʕalme　　btiiji.
　　　　　　　that -3FS　the-teacher　3FS-(IMPERF)come
　　　　　　　'. . . that the teacher is coming/will come.'

Notice, first, that the expressions in (9-32a–c) all manifest a preposition, [*la*], preceding the doubled argument. In (9-32d), however, there is no preposition, and the doubled argument, the clausal subject, follows directly the agreeing C^0 (i.e., the C^0 bearing the clitic).

9.4.3.1   *Why the Preposition [la] Is Required*

This preposition has been viewed as a dummy Case marker inserted once the Case typically assigned by the head of the phrase to its complement is absorbed by the clitic.[13] I think that this idea is fundamentally correct and can explain the occurrence of [la] in (9-32a–c) as well as its obligatory absence in (9-32d).

Let us consider again the clitic configuration in (9-29) and ask what position is occupied by the doubled DP. There are two possibilites, Spec/Agr or the θ-position of the argument, NP/XP. These are diagramed in (9-33a,b), where, in addition, the lexical head is adjoined to Agr^0. In (9-33a), the argument is raised to Spec/Agr and comes to be coindexed with Agr^0 by virtue of the configuration. In (9-33b), the argument remains in situ, and an expletive pro is inserted in Spec/Agr. An agreement configuration is then established between Agr^0 and the expletive.

(9-33) a.

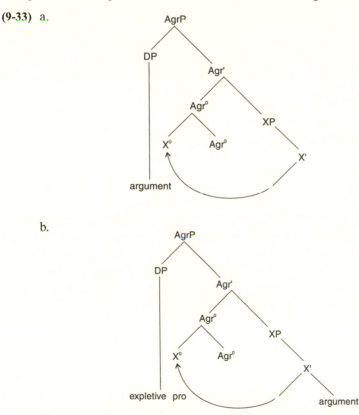

In (9-32a), the verb+Agr^0 complex moves further up into the higher inflectional domain of the clause. Thus, the fact that the doubled argument *follows* the verb provides no real indication of which one of (9-33) is correct. One might also assume that the N^0 host of Agr in (9-32b) is moved higher than AgrP, presumably into the DP projection (Ritter 1995 and Siloni 1994) so that, once again, surface word order is of no help in determining whether the doubled argument is in situ or in Spec/Agr. The revealing example is (9-32c), for only when $X^0 = P^0$ (and XP =

PP) are there no grounds to believe that the head raises higher than Agr^0. Given the order of consituents in (9-32c), we can conclude that the doubled argument remains in situ, since it lies to the right of Agr^0. Generalizing (9-32c) to the other cases seems natural and allows us to hypothesize that (9-33b) is the correct representation of clitic doubling in Semitic.

One might reason that, if the possibility exists for an expletive to fill Spec/Agr, allowing the doubled argument to remain in situ, this possibility is always to be preferred on grounds of derivational economy. In any event, the DP which remains in situ must somehow be licensed independently of Agr^0, since it is not in an agreement (or Checking) relationship with it in (9-33b). One should then take the dummy preposition, the [la] of (9-32a-c), to be a Case assigner inserted so as to govern and Case-mark the argument in its base position.[14]

With the exception of Standard Arabic, subjects in the languages under discussion in this work differ from other arguments in that the option of raising them to Spec/Agr is, if not the unmarked option, at least the common one. Direct objects, oblique objects, and adnominal complements do not typically raise to their respective Spec/Agr Case positions. In the preceding paragraphs I suggested that this is due to considerations of economy. If this is indeed the case, then one should explain why subjects do not abide by this condition—that is, why clausal subjects do not as a rule choose to remain in VP in null subject languages. The problem is rather general, and it arises not just under the assumptions made here. In many grammatical systems, subject raising is either obligatory or highly preferred but overt object raising (*object shift*) is ungrammatical. While many languages do manifest subject raising but no object shift, there are few, if any, that manifest the opposite case—namely, object shift without subject raising.

To sum up, I have tried to make use of the old idea that clitics "absorb" Case, and the argument needing Case must therefore find some other means of licensing in order to explain the occurrence of the preposition *la* in clitic doubling constructions. In terms of the discussion here, Semitic "clitics" do not literally absorb Case. Rather, they assign it to an expletive in Spec/Agr, and Case is no longer available for the doubled argument. This is why the preposition, essentially a Case-assigning head, must be inserted (but see note 14).

9.4.3.2   *Clitic Doubling without [la]*

The present analysis entails a prediction that is not entailed by the Case absorption idea in its classical guises. Suppose there were a situation in which a clitic-doubled argument had to move to or through Spec/Agr in the syntax—that is, a situation in which NP-movement from the argument's θ-position could not be postponed to LF. In such a situation, a clitic-doubling structure would resemble (9-33a): an expletive would not appear, and the doubled argument would be in, or will have moved, through Spec/Agr and will thus be assigned Case directly. The prediction is that, in such cases, the dummy preposition would not appear; *la* would be absent since the argument would be in a Case configuration with Agr^0. The prediction, in other words, is that overt object shift to the Spec of an activated $AgrO^0$ would give rise to a clitic-doubling configuration without what we might call "prepositional support."

I would like to examine two such cases. In the first, the doubled argument is itself a pronoun. Consider first the contrast between the grammatical (9-34a), with no overt pronominal object, but only a clitic (and a pro object, cf. [9-29]), the ungrammatical (9-34b), in which a full object pronoun appears, and the grammatical (9-35), which manifests both a full object pronoun and a clitic (examples are from Palestinian).

(9-34)   a. šuft   -ik   mbeeriḥ.
          see(PERF)-1S -2FS   yesterday
          'I saw you yesterday.'

        b. *šuft   ʔinti   mbeeriḥ.
          see(PERF)-1S you-F   yesterday
          'I saw you yesterday.'

(9-35) šuft   -ik   ʔinti   mbeeriḥ.
          see(PERF)-1S -2FS   you-F   yesterday
          'I saw you yesterday.'

The ungrammaticality of (9-34b), compared with the full acceptability of (9-35), illustrates a phenomenon familiar to students of clitic doubling—namely, its obligatoriness with pronominal arguments. In all varieties of Spanish, for example, clitic doubling with pronominal objects is obligatory, as in (9-36), while there is substantial dialectal variation with respect to its acceptability with nonpronominal objects.[15]

(9-36) *(La) vi   a   ella.
          her   (I) saw   to   her
          'I saw her.'

Whatever may be the reason for this (see the cited literature for suggestions), it is interesting to note that Semitic clitic doubling and Romance share this important feature.[16] But what is striking about (9-34) is not only that clitic doubling is obligatory with pronominal direct objects, but that the dummy preposition *la* is absent. In fact, *la* is barred from appearing in such examples, as the ungrammaticality of (9-37) clearly attests. Example (9-37) contrasts sharply with examples such as (9-32a), in which a clitic doubles as a non-pronominal object.

(9-37) *šuft   -ik   la   ʔinti   mbeeriḥ.
          see(PERF)-1S -2FS   to   you-F   yesterday
          'I saw you yesterday.'

Arabic pronouns can be classified into essentially two categories, which, following and adapting Kayne (1975), I call "weak" and "strong." The distribution of pronouns in Semitic is discussed at greater length later in chapter 10. To anticipate that discussion, let us make the following assumptions regarding object pronouns, following in essence Cardinaletti and Starke (forthcoming).

- Weak pronouns must raise in the overt syntax at least as high as the Spec/Agr in which they are Case-marked.

- Strong pronouns do not raise in the syntax, and are employed where weak ones cannot (i.e., as a last resort.)

The pronoun *ʔinti* in the examples here is thus weak in the unmarked case. Being a weak pronoun, it raises to Spec/Agr in the overt syntax. The absence of *la* is now accounted for straightforwardly, since the S-structure representation of, for example, (9-35) is as in (9-33a) and not as in (9-33b), which is the representation associated with clitic-doubled nonpronominal arguments. The sketch in (9-38) recapitulates the relevant part of the derivation of (9-35): the verb raises and adjoins to AgrO⁰, and the the direct object moves to Spec/AgrO. In this configuration, the pronoun can be Case-marked directly through agreement with AgrO⁰. Subsequently, the boxed verbal complex is further raised to the higher inflectional domain of the clause, giving rise to the observed word order.

(9-38)

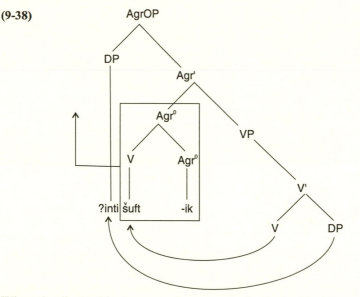

When the direct object pronoun is contrastively stressed and hence focalized, it is strong and not weak, as we shall see very clearly in chapter 10. I shall assume that, in this case, the pronoun is not moved to Spec/Agr.

I would like to suggest that the absence of the dummy preposition in the context of clitic doubling of a strong pronoun is due to the availability of alternative means of identification or licensing of the doubled pronoun. Contrastive stress may be precisely such a device.

The second case I examine concerns the distribution of clitic doubled QPs. I shall base my discussion on the following paradigm from Palestinian.

(9-39) a. šuft   -hin   kul -hin.
              see(PERF)-1S   -3PL   all   -3PL
              'I saw them all.'

         b. *šuft   kul   -hin.
              see(PERF)-1S   all   -3PL
              'I saw them all.'

c. *šuft   -hin   kul   l-wlaad.
   see(PERF)-1S   *-3PL*   *all*   *the-children*
   'I saw all the children.'

d. šuft   kul l-wlaad.
   see(PERF)-1S   *all*   *the-children*
   'I saw all the children.'

Note, first, that the quantifier in, for example, (9-39a) itself contains a clitic. The universal quantifier is the word *kul*, to which a clitic is suffixed. This clitic indicates that the quantifier is associated with an agreement projection. Shlonsky (1991) analyzes the quantifier as a functional head taking a DP complement (see also Benmamoun 1992). When the DP raises over the quantifier, it agrees with it. Thus, we have (9-40a) without agreement and (9-40b) with agreement. Examples are from Hebrew.

(9-40)   a. ra?iti   ?et   kol ha-yladim.
             see(PAST)-1S   *ACC*   *all*   *the-children*
             'I saw all the children.'

         b. ra?iti   ?et ha-yladim   kul -am.
            see(PAST)-1S   *ACC*   *the-children*   *all*   *-3MPL*
            'I saw all the children.'

I take the relevant part of the derivation of (9-40b) to be as in (9-41).

(9-41)

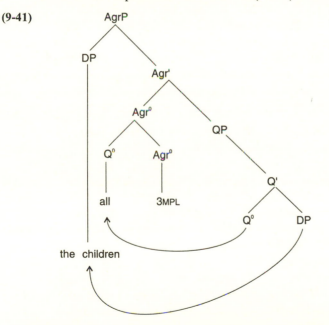

Returning now to (9-39a), note that both the quantifier and the verb bear agreement. Benmamoun (1992) argues that, in such cases, the quantified DP, a pro, is moved from the complement position of the quantifier to Spec/AgrO, triggering agreement twice.

The analysis I would like to pursue is slightly different. I would like to propose that, indeed, the quantified DP is raised to what we might call Spec/AgrQ (the

Agreement phrase associated with the quantifier), but then the entire QP is raised to Spec/AgrO. In other words, I suggest that we assimilate the movement of *kul-hin* in (9-39a) to that of a weak pronoun, for instance, *ʔinti* in (9-35). The clitic doubling attested in (9-39a) is a doubling of the entire QP. Example (9-39b) shows that the parallelism between weak object pronouns and QP is not spurious. Both require clitic doubling: (9-39b) is on a par with (9-34b).

Contrast (9-39d) with (9-39b). The two sentences differ in that the former does not contain a "bare" QP, or a quantifier lacking a lexical argument, but has a QP that contains a lexical quantified DP. The difference with respect to clitic doubling can be explained by reference to the difference in the status of QP. When, and only when, the QP is "bare," does it behave like a weak pronoun, raising to Spec/AgrO obligatorily. When the complement of Q^0 is a lexical DP, the QP functions like a strong pronoun, and movement to Spec/AgrO does not occur.

If bare QPs behave like weak pronouns, we have an immediate explanation for the absence of the preposition *la* in examples such as (9-39a). When QP is raised to Spec/AgrO, a configuration basically identical to that of (9-38) is brought about; Case marking can proceed in a Spec-head configuration, and the preposition is superfluous.

Fronting of QPs to some middle-field position is not unique to Arabic. A similar phenomenon was noted in Kayne (1975) for French. Examples (9-42a,b) show that a bare quantifier must surface to the left of the past participle. One is tempted to consider the position of leftward-moved *tout* in French to be Spec/AgrO (this is the position I took in §8.3.3 ff). The difference between French and Arabic is that French $AgrO^0$ does not contain an affix. When *tout* is not bare (or when it is stressed), judgments are reversed, as in (9-42c,d).

(9-42) a. J'ai   tout   vu.   c. *J'ai   tous   les enfants   vu.
            I-have   all   seen   *I-have   all   the children   seen*
            'I saw everything.'   'I saw all the children.'

        b. ??J'ai   vu   tout.   d. J'ai   vu   tous les enfants.
            I-have   seen   all   *I-have   seen all the children*
            'I saw everything.'   'I saw all the children.'

The consequence that can be drawn at this point is that a preposition is required in clitic-doubling structures only when the doubled DP is not in an agreement configuration with the clitic at S-structure.[17]

9.4.3.3 *Clitic Doubling in the Comp Domain*

This subsection considers (9-32d), repeated here as (9-43).

(9-43) ... ʔin -ha   l-mʕalme   tiiji.
            that   -3FS   the-teacher   3FS(IMPERF)-come
            '... that the teacher is coming / will come.'

In (9-43), a clausal subject is clitic-doubled and the clitic is attached to C^0. The analysis developed in this chapter forces us to assume that the Agr head filled by the affix *-ha* in (9-43) is accessed by C^0. We should therefore assume (9-44), where an AgrP, call it AgrCP, dominates CP (cf. [9-28c]).

(9-44)

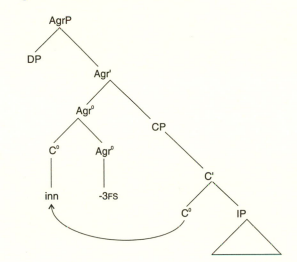

Example (9-43) differs from the other cases of clitic doubling in that the doubled argument here is not the complement of the head which incorporates into Agr^0, but the specifier of this complement. Compare (9-45a), which is the standard case of doubling, where X = P, N, or V, with (9-45b), where YP, the doubled DP, is not a sister to the head which incorporates into Agr^0, but rather the specifier of that head, X = C and Z = I.

(9-45) a.

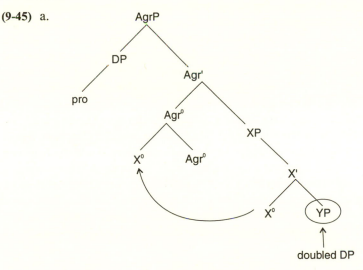

b.

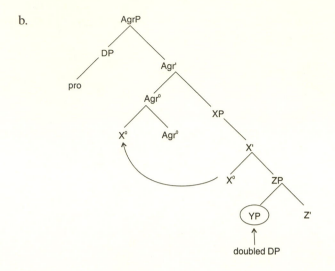

Clearly, the reason the doubled DP cannot be the complement of C^0 is that C^0 does not take a DP complement but an IP complement. Yet if the doubled DP can be the specifier of ZP, one wonders whether there is any principled reason why clitics in the Comp domain may not double DPs which are even further embedded. Put plainly, can the doubled DP in (9-43) be a nonsubject? Can it, for instance, be a direct object?

I have assumed that with the exception of the cases discussed in §9.4.2.2, clitic doubling configurations involve agreement with an expletive pro in Spec/Agr, while the doubled DP remains in situ. Yet, clearly, the expletive and the doubled DP are associated. The simplest thing to say is that the relation between pro and its associate is of exactly the same formal nature as that which holds between an expletive and a postverbal subject (viz. the discussion in chapter 8). Following standard assumptions regarding expletive-argument pairs, let us take this relationship to be a chain, formed in LF. Take the doubled DP to move in LF to the position occupied by pro. LF movement to Spec/AgrC must abide by standard conditions on chain formation, among them Relativized Minimality. We should further assume that Spec/AgrC, like all specifiers of agreement projections, is an A-position. It is now clear why the expletive in (9-43) must take the subject as its associate: LF movement to Spec/AgrC by any other DP would give rise to a Minimality effect or, in more traditional terms, a violation of the Specified Subject Condition. This is so since the clausal subject position in Spec/AgrS is the closest A position to Spec/AgrC. Any DP in a more deeply embedded position would have to cross over Spec/AgrS on its way to Spec/AgrC.[18]

The last question to ask in this context is why clitic doubling in (9-43) does not trigger the insertion of *la*, the dummy preposition responsible for Case marking doubled arguments. We have seen that *la* is manifested when the doubled DP remains in its θ-position where it is not Case-licensed at S-structure. Yet the clausal subject in (9-43) is not in its base position; it lies to the left of the verb. The subject in (9-43) is in Spec/AgrS—that is, it is already in a Case position—so that the insertion of *la* would be entirely superfluous.[19]

9.5 FINAL REMARKS

I have argued that Semitic clitics are Agr^0 heads while Romance clitics are not, so that the differences between Semitic and Romance clitics essentially reduce to this variation (see §9.2 for the view that Romance clitics are X^0 heads; cf. Sportiche 1990, 1996 and Franco 1993). Let us now ask why this difference exists. This issue encapsulates two distinct queries: why Semitic languages lack Romance-type clitics and, conversely, why Romance lacks the Semitic type.

I have basically adopted in this work the view that Romance clitics are D^0 categories that undergo head movement—functional heads lacking a lexical restriction (Cardinaletti 1994, Uriagereka 1995). One might then search for the absence of Romance-like clitics in Semitic in properties of the Semitic determiner system.

Definite determiners in Semitic are themselves dependent morphemes: they always appear attached to the noun they determine, and they are phonotactically conditioned by it. They are endowed with two other properties that distinguish them from Romance ones: they never agree with the noun they determine, and they are manifested not only on the head noun, but obligatorily on all its modifiers, even those that are conjoined; viz (9-46). However one analyzes this type of determiner, it seems clear that it cannot be detached from the noun it determines: it is not a free standing functional head as its Romance counterpart.[20] This leads to the conclusion that the absence of Romance-type clitics in Semitic correlates with the non-separatability of D^0 (on which, see also Borer 1989a).

(9-46) ha-šulxan   ha-xum   ve-   ha-ʔarox
        the-table   the-brown   and   the-long
        'the brown and long table'

As for the second question—the absence of Semitic-type clitics in Romance—I would like to simply point out that it is self-evident to every student of Semitic that clitics morphologically resemble pronouns, and it is pretty clear that they are diachronically derived from them. The question to pose is then why atonic free-standing pronouns are reanalyzed as Agr heads. I refer the reader to Roberts and Shlonsky (1996), where precisely this question is taken up and a correlation is attempted between the consistent pattern of enclisis observed in Semitic (and, incidentally, Celtic) and the fact that the Semitic languages in question are all (at least diachronically) VSO languages.

TEN

Pronouns

10.1 THE INTERNAL STRUCTURE AND DISTRIBUTION OF "UNATTACHED" PRONOUNS

Alongside the agreement suffixes or "clitic" forms discussed in chapter 9, both Hebrew and Arabic possess sets of unattached or free standing pronouns. The internal structure of nominative pronouns is discussed in chapter 7, where it is argued, following Ritter (1995), that first and second person pronouns are D^0 elements while third person (or more precisely, nonperson) pronouns belong to the category Num^0. Example (10-1) below lists the forms of the nominative series in Hebrew.

(10-1) Paradigm of Nominative Pronouns

	Singular	Plural
1	?ani	?anaxnu
2m	?ata	?atem
2f	?at	?aten
3m	hu	hem
3f	hi	hen

Consider now the paradigms of direct object or accusative pronouns in Hebrew and those of indirect or dative pronouns, tabulated in (10-2) and (10-3), respectively.

(10-2) Paradigm of Accusative Pronouns

	Singular	Plural
1	?ot-i	?ot-anu
2m	?ot-xa	?et-xem
2f	?ot-ax	?et-xen
3m	?ot-o	?ot-am
3f	?ot-a	?ot-an

(10-3)   Paradigm of Dative Pronouns

	Singular	Plural
1	l-i	l-anu
2m	l-xa	la-xem
2f	l-ax	la-xen
3m	l-o	la-hem
3f	l-a	la-hen

In sharp contrast to subject pronouns, the nonnominative ones are, as a rule, constructed around a lexical base—a preposition or Kase particle, perhaps a morpheme of *support*, in the terminology of Cardinaletti and Starke (forthcoming)—to which the inflectional suffixes, the "clitics" of chapter 9, are suffixed (see chapter 1 for a discussion of *ʔet* and of the KP constituent). The Kase particle *ʔet* in (10-2) and the P^0/K^0 *l(ə)* in (10-3) are followed by an agreement suffix. The discussion in the previous chapter leads me to argue that the internal structure of these pronominal forms is as in (10-4a), where the projection headed, for example, by *ʔet*, is itself dominated by an agreement projection. Example (10-4b) schematizes the derivation of the surface form of the pronoun: *ʔet* is raised and adjoined to the c-commanding Agr^0, and the DP complement of *ʔet*, a referential pro, is moved to Spec/Agr where its agreement is checked against Agr^0.

(10-4)   a.

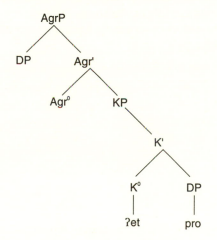

b.

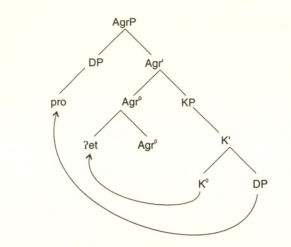

Hebrew differs from Arabic in that direct object pronouns are typically expressed by means of complex forms such as those in (10-2); as we recall, pronominal suffixes (the Semitic clitics of chapter 9) on verbs are confined to a stylistically marked register or dialect (see chapter 9, note 1). While Standard Arabic renders 'I saw her' by generating an affix in AgrO⁰ and incorporating the verb to it, as in (10-5a), colloquial modern Hebrew employs the freestanding form *?ota*, viz. (10-5b); (10-5c) is the stylistically marked form. I take the reason for this difference to be a lexical one: the dialect of colloquial Hebrew in question does not generate an affix in AgrO^0, while Arabic does.

(10-5) a. ra?aitu   -ha.
            see(PERF)-1S   *-3FS*
            'I saw her.'

        b. ra?iti   ?ota.
            see(PAST)-1S   *her*
            'I saw her.'

        c. rəiti   -ha.
            see(PAST)-1S   *-3FS*
            'I saw her.'

Literally speaking, then, these freestanding pronouns are AgrPs and not, say, DPs or P/KPs. It is perhaps useful to make explicit once again one of the themes of the present essay—namely, that Agr projections enter neither into semantic nor into categorial selection, so that from a selectional point of view, IPs are TPs and not AgrSPs. By parity of reasoning, an indirect pronoun such as *lo* 'to him' is a PP/KP and not an AgrP.[1]

Direct and indirect object pronouns in Hebrew contain a pro that is licensed and assigned features by coindexation with the Agr head dominating KP. In a strict sense, then, nonnominative pronouns in Semitic are always null: The difference between the unattached forms and the clitic configurations—that is, the difference between (10-5b) and (10-5a)—is, minimally, the position and manner of the licensing of pro. In (10-5a), pro is raised from complement position to Spec/AgrO and enters into a coindexing relationship with AgrO^0. In (10-5b), pro is licensed and identified by moving into the specifier position of the K^0-associated Agr. If Hebrew, in its colloquial varieties, does not project an overt affix in AgrO^0, there is no way for pro (notably a referential pro) to be identified in Spec/AgrO.

I thus contend that the projection of an AgrP above the particles *?et* and *lə*- serves to create a licensing and identification configuration for object pro. These AgrPs are not projected when the object is not pro, so that direct and indirect objects such as *?et Dani* '*ACC Dani*' and *lə-Rina* 'to Rina' are not associated with a complex structure such as that in (10-4). The unique property of Semitic is that AgrPs can be associated with practically all contentful projections, lexical and functional, as we saw in chapter 9. The pronominal system benefits from this property in that these AgrPs—projected immediately above the particles governing objects and containing, as they do, overt affixes endowed with rich morphology—can serve to license pro. When there is no pro in the structure, there is no need to project this structural layer, since non-null objects do not require licensing and identification through this particular mechanism.

We have seen that in dialects endowed with a productive rule of dative shift, the indirect object may come to be associated with the affix in AgrO^0. Recall the Cairene Arabic paradigm introduced in §9.2. I repeat the relevant examples in (10-6) here. Note, in particular, the example in (10-6b), where an indirect object is dative-shifted and comes to be associated with the affix *-ha*.

(10-6) a. ?il-mudarris fahhim   -u   li-l-bint.
           the-teacher   *understand(PERF-CAUS)-3MS*   *-3MS* *to-the-girl*
           'The teacher explained it to the girl.'

       b. ?il-mudarris fahhim   -ha   l-dars.
           the-teacher   *understand(PERF-CAUS)-3MS*   *-3FS* *the-lesson*
           'The teacher explained the lesson to her.' *Lit:* 'The teacher explained her the lesson.'

The Cairene "response," as it were, to a situation where both objects are pronominalized, is to associate the direct object with AgrO^0 and to express the indirect one by means of a freestanding form structured around a preposition and an associated Agr. This is shown in (10-7).

(10-7) ?il-mudarris fahhim   -u   laa-ha.
         the-teacher   *understand(PERF-CAUS)-3MS*   *-3MS* *to-3FS*
         'The teacher explained it to her.'

I argued that (10-7) illustrates a stratagem for avoiding multiple clitics, or ungrammatical sequences of multiple agreement on a verb, as in (10-8).

(10-8) *?il-mudarris fahhim   -ha-u   /-u-ha
         the-teacher   *understand(PERF-CAUS)-3MS*   *-3FS-3MS* */3MS-3FS*

Yet (10-7) is not the only conceivable stratagem for circumventing the ban on multiple agreement. Other dialects of Arabic work differently. In Palestinian, for example, it is the indirect object that comes to be associated with Agr^0, and the direct object shows up as a complex pronoun, the lexical base of which is the morpheme *yya* (*ʔiyya* in clause-initial position and in citation), to which a pronominal suffix is attached. Thus, compare the Cairene example in (10-7) with the Palestinian sentence in (10-9).[2]

(10-9) ʔil-mudarris fahham -ha yya-a.
the-teacher understand(PERF-CAUS)-3MS 3FS YYA-3MS

The *yya* series is structured like the complex pronouns in (10-4). *yya* is the head of a KP projection which itself is dominated by an Agr projection. The full paradigm of the *yya* series is tabulated in (10-10).

(10-10) Palestinian Arabic
Paradigm of Unattached
Accusative Pronouns

	Singular	Plural
1	ʔyya-ni	ʔyya-na
2m	ʔiyya-k	ʔiyya-kum
2f	ʔiyya-ki	″
3m	ʔyya-a	ʔyya-hin
3f	ʔiyya-ha	″

The distribution of *yya* pronouns is restricted in comparison with, say, the Hebrew *ʔet* series. While in Hebrew, the freestanding pronoun is used in the unmarked case, Palestinian Arabic licenses the use of the *yya* pronoun in a very limited set of contexts. Essentially, *yya* pronouns are used only when there is no accessible AgrO affix with which a null object can be associated. One such case is illustrated in (10-9): the AgrO affix is associated with the indirect object (which has been dative-shifted and raised as a pro to Spec/Agr). Pronominalization of the direct object leads to the generation of a pronoun format in which *yya* figures as the lexical base supporting an Agr projection. The absence of the *yya* form in Cairene renders impossible the association of the indirect object with AgrO when the direct object is also pronominalized.

Another context in which *yya* appears is as the pronominal direct object of the verb *want*, as in (10-11b).

(10-11) a. bidd-i   jariide.   b. bidd-i   yya-ha.
want-1S   newspaper-F   *want-1S   YYA-3FS*
'I want a newspaper.'   'I want it.'

The verb *bidd* is morphologically defective. It has no morphological tense specification, no past or future (perfect and imperfect) form. Past versus nonpast tense distinctions are manifested by the choice of auxiliary, as in (10-12). Moreover, *bidd* does not inflect for subject agreement like a verb, but rather like a noun or a preposition, in that it is associated with pronominal suffixes that resemble the agreement suffixes or clitics of the previous chapter (cf. in this respect, the agreement pattern of Hebrew *ʔeyn* in chapter 4, §4.2, table 4-6).

(10-12) kunt   bidd-i   jariide.
be(PERF)-1S   want-1S   newspaper
'I wanted a newspaper.'

Given its morphological deficiency, it is plausible that *bidd* lacks the option of supporting an associated affix in AgrO^0, so that a pronominal object must be realized as a freestanding form, independent of AgrOP.[3]

10.2 PRONOUNS WEAK AND STRONG

Much of the literature on Semitic pronouns classifies some or all of the unattached forms discussed in previous sections as clitics. This label is meant to imply that these pronouns obey a rather strict adjacency condition. For example, while a VP-adverbial such as *ʔanušot* 'mortally' can appear between a verb and a direct object, as in (10-13a), it cannot occur in a position between a verb and an *ʔet* pronoun, as indicated by the ill-formedness of (10-13b).[4]

(10-13) a. Dani   paca   ʔanušot   ʔet   šlomo.
             Dani   injure(PAST)-3MS   mortally   ACC   Shlomo
             'Dani injured Shlomo mortally.'

         b. *Dani   paca   ʔanušot   ʔoto.
             Dani   injure(PAST)-3MS   mortally   him
             'Dani injured him mortally.'

The only grammatical output consists of placing the pronoun immediately to the right of the verb and hence to the left of the adverb, as in (10-14).

(10-14) Dani   paca   ʔoto   ʔanušot.
          Dani   injure(PAST)-3MS   him   mortally
          'Dani injured him mortally.'

Belletti and Shlonsky (1995) show that in a double complement construction, the indirect object may either precede or follow the direct object. The two permutations are exemplified in (10-15).

(10-15) a. natanu   lə-Rina   matana.   b. natanu   matana   lə-Rina.
             give(PAST)-1PL   to-Rina   present   *give(PAST)-1PL   present   to-Rina*
             'We gave Rina a present.'   'We gave a present to Rina.'

When one of the complements is a pronoun, however, the order is immutable. The pronoun precedes the nonpronominal complement and must appear linearly adjacent to the verb. The adjacency requirement, illustrated by the contrast in (10-16), as well as in the preceding examples, does, indeed, suggest that these pronouns are clitics, much like the Romance variety.

(10-16) a. natanu   l-a   matana.   b. *natanu   matana   l-a.
             give(PAST)-1PL   to-her   present   *give(PAST)-1PL   present   to-her*
             'We gave her a present.'   'We gave her a present.'

An additional clitic-like property of Semitic pronouns is that when both direct and indirect objects are pronominalized, they seem to form a cluster. They rigidly respect the order indirect object > direct object, and nothing can intervene between them. Consider (10-17).

(10-17) a. natanu   l-a   ʔota.
             give(PAST)-1PL to-her it
             'We gave it to her.' *Lit.* 'We gave her it.'

          b. *natanu   ʔota l-a.
             give(PAST)-1PL it   to-her
             'We gave it to her.' *Lit.* 'We gave it her.'

Yet these same pronouns also behave as nonclitics. For instance, they can be left-dislocated and coordinated.

(10-18) a. ʔoto, lo   raʔinu   ʔetmol.
             him, NEG see (PAST)-1PL yesterday
             'Him, we didn't see yesterday.'

          b. lo   raʔinu   ʔet Dani ve- ʔoto.
             NEG see(PAST)-1PL ACC Dani and- him
             'We didn't see Dani and him.'

These two properties sharply distinguish clitics from strong pronouns in a language such as French. Compare the (a) sentences in (10-19) and (10-20) with the (b) ones (*le* is the clitic form, *lui* is the strong form).

(10-19) a. *Le,   on   n'a   pas vu   hier.
             him (CL) one NEG-has NEG seen yesterday
             'Him, we didn't see yesterday.'

          b. Lui, on   n'a   pas vu   hier.
             him, one NEG-has NEG seen yesterday
             'Him, we didn't see yesterday.'

(10-20) a. *On n'a   pas vu   Jean et   le.
             one NEG-has NEG seen Jean and him
             'We didn't see Jean and him.'

          b. On n'a   pas vu   Jean et   lui.
             one NEG-has NEG seen Jean and him
             'We didn't see Jean and him.'

A further, rather telling property of Hebrew pronouns is that they cannot, under any circumstances, be carried along by a Benoni verb when it undergoes Copula Inversion (CI, see chapter 3). Compare (10-21a) without inversion with (10-21b), where the Benoni verb inverts with the auxiliary.[5]

(10-21) a. Dani haya   tofer   ʔotam.
             Dani was(PAST)-3MS sew(BENONI)-MS them
             'Dani was sewing them.'

          b. *Dani tofer   ʔotam haya.
             Dani sew(BENONI)-MS them was(PAST)-3MS
             'Dani was sewing them.'

This latter property can be taken as a starting point for an analysis. Since CI clearly involves head-to-head incorporation (see §3.1.3 ff.), the ungrammaticality of (10-21b) shows that Hebrew pronouns are not X^0 categories. Recall that the only element that can intervene between the Benoni verb and the auxiliary is AgrO^0, realized as the affix *-am* in (10-22).

(10-22)   Dani   tofer   -am   haya.
         Dani   sew(BENONI)-MS   -3FPL   was(PAST)-3MS
         'Dani was sewing them.'

I shall make the standard assumption that clitics, in the Romance sense, are X^0 categories (although they start out as maximal projections; see the discussion in §9.1, based on Kayne 1989 and much other work). This definition thus excludes Hebrew pronouns from the family of clitics. Having clarified the terminology, we must now turn to an explanation of the adjacency requirement on Hebrew pronouns.

10.2.1   The Weak-Strong Distinction

Following Cardinaletti and Starke (forthcoming), I take pronouns to belong to one of three classes: clitics, weak pronouns, and strong pronouns. Using diagnostics proposed originally in Kayne (1975), these authors provide diagnostic criteria to distinguish the three classes of pronominal elements. I summarize their results in table (10-23).

(10-23)   Cross Classification of Pronoun-types

	Contrastive Stress	Modification	Coordination	Animacy	Attached
Clitic	−	−	−	+	+
Weak	−	−	−	+	−
Strong	+	+	+	−	−

The descriptive generalization embodied by (10-23) is that weak pronouns are like clitic pronouns except that they are unattached. They cannot be contrastively stressed, they cannot be modified or coordinated, and they may have inanimate referents. Strong pronouns are also freestanding; they may be stressed, modified, or coordinated, but they cannot have inanimate referents.

Hebrew pronouns, I would argue, are lexically ambiguous between strong and weak. The key to understanding the mixed or even contradictory behavior of Hebrew pronouns is to realize that there is no phonetic or overt morphological distinction between the two: both types are rendered by the same form. Thus, *?oto* is weak in, for example, (10-13b), but strong when stressed or coordinated, as in the examples in (10-18).[6]

Among the characteristics distinguishing strong and weak pronouns is the fact that only the latter can have inanimate referents. This is brought out clearly in the contrast in (10-24): (10-24a) is well-formed, whether *?oto* refers to a person or to a film; in (10-24b), however, only the first interpretation is possible, the focalized strong pronoun permitting only an animate denotation.

(10-24) a. raʔinu   ʔoto be-festival ha-sratim.
               see(PAST)-1PL him   in-festival   the-films
               'We saw him/it at the film festival.'

         b. ʔoto, raʔinu   be-festival ha-sratim.
            him   see(PAST)-1PL   in-festival   the-films
            'Him/*It, we saw at the film-festival.'

Cardinaletti and Starke argue at length that weak pronouns constitute the unmarked choice and that strong pronouns are used only where weak ones cannot be used. Underlying this claim is the proposal that weak pronouns, like clitics, but unlike strong pronouns, must move in the syntax to their appropriate Spec/Agr (I propose a modification of this view in §10.3). In Chomsky's (1993) terminology, weak pronouns cannot procrastinate movement to LF. The difference between clitics and weak pronouns in this system is that clitics move as XPs to their appropriate Spec/Agr position, and then continue to raise as heads. Weak pronouns, on the other hand, effect only XP movement and stop in Spec/Agr. The two derivations are diagrammed in (10-25a,b) for direct objects.

(10-25)   a. Cliticization   AgrSP

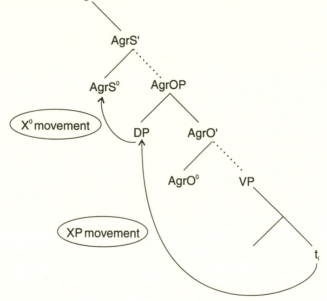

b. Weak pronoun movement

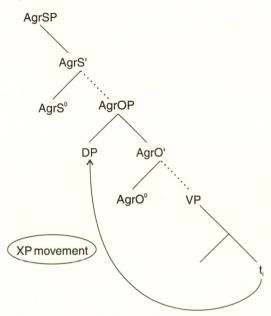

The ill-formedness of (10-13b), the fact that weak pronouns must occupy a position higher than VP adverbs, now falls out naturally, since the AgrP serving direct objects is AgrOP, which is higher than VP. (This point is made by Friedemann and Siloni 1993.)

When they are forced to be strong—for example, when they are assigned focal stress—the adjacency requirement no longer holds, and object pronouns pattern with nonpronominal DPs, in that they can be separated from the verb by an intervening adverb. Contrast (10-13b) with (10-26).

(10-26) Dani paca   ʔanušot ʔoto.
      Dani injure(PAST)-3MS mortally him
      'Dani injured <u>him</u> mortally.'

Similarly, *ʔoto* can be modified when strong, as in (10-27).

(10-27) Dani paca   ʔanušot rak ʔoto.
      Dani injure(PAST)-3MS mortally only him
      'Dani mortally injured only him.'

Another syntactic context or construction that distinguishes weak and strong pronouns is that of derived nominals. Consider first the fact—discussed in Borer (forthcoming) and Siloni (1994)—that nonpronominal DPs may occur as themes of action nominalizations preceded by *ʔet*, while weak pronouns may not.

(10-28) a. kri?at ha-kacin ?et Dan lə-seder hifti?a   ?et
         calling the-officer ACC Dan to-order surprise(PAST)-3FS ACC

    š?ar ha-xayalim.
    other the-soldiers
    'The officer's calling Dan to order surprised the other soldiers.'

   b. *kri?at ha-kacin   ?oto lə-seder hifti?a
    calling the-officer him to-order surprise(PAST)-3FS

    ?et š?ar ha-xayalim.
    ACC other the-soldiers
    'The officer's calling him to order surprised the other soldiers.'

Siloni (1994) argues that the unacceptability of examples such as (10-28b) is due to the absence of an AgrOP in derived nominals, or what amounts to the same thing, the absence of a checking position for accusative Case; see also Borer (forthcoming). Weak pronouns, which must raise to Spec/AgrO, are hence unlicensed in nominal constructions.

Notice, now, that strong pronouns may occur as themes of derived nominals. Consider (10-29a), where the intensifying particle *rak* 'only/just' modifies the pronoun, and (10-29b), where the pronoun is coordinated with a full DP.

(10-29) a. kri?at ha-kacin rak ?oto lə-seder hifti?a   ?et š?ar
         calling the-officer only him to-order surprise(PAST)-3FS ACC other

    ha-xayalim.
    the-soldiers
    'The officer's calling only him to order surprised the other soldiers.'

   b. kri?at ha-kacin ?et Dan ve- ?oto lə-seder hifti?a
    calling the-officer ACC Dan and- him to-order surprise(PAST)-3FS

    ?et š?ar ha-xayalim.
    ACC other the-soldiers
    'The officer's calling Dani and him to order surprised the other soldiers.'

The analysis developed thus far leads me to concur with Friedemann and Siloni (1993) and Cardinaletti and Starke (forthcoming) and claim that Hebrew pronouns are weak in the unmarked case and must raise to their respective Spec/Agr position in the audible syntax. Otherwise, these pronouns are of the strong variety.

10.2.2 SUBJECT PRONOUNS

The context in which weak subject pronouns show up most clearly is when they follow a verb that has undergone Triggered Inversion. Consider the examples in (10-30).

(10-30) a. lə-?eize min situacia mesarevet   ?at lə-hikanes?
         into-what kind situation refuse(BENONI)-FS you-F to-enter
         'What sort of situation do you refuse to enter into?'

   b. matai yaca   hu la-sadot?
    when go out(PAST)-3MS he to-the-fields
    'When did he go out to the fields?'

That these pronouns are weak can be evidenced by the fact that they must be adjacent to the verb. Contrast the unacceptable (10-31a), where *bəderex klal* 'usually' appears between the verb and the pronominal subject with grammatical (10-31b,c). In (10-31b), the subject is not a pronoun, and in (10-31c) it is a strong pronoun (underlined).

(10-31) a. *lə-ʔeize   min   situacia   mesarevet   bə-derex klal ʔat
            into-what *kind* *situation* *refuse(BENONI)-FS* *usually*   *you-F*

           lə-hikanes
           to-enter
           'What sort of situation do you usually refuse to enter into?'

         b. lə-ʔeize   min   situacia   mesarevet   bə-derex klal Rina
            into-what *kind* *situation* *refuse(BENONI)-FS* *usually*   *Rina*

           lə-hikanes?
           to-enter
           'What sort of situation does Rina usually refuse to enter into?'

         c. lə-ʔeize   min   situacia   mesarevet   bə-derex klal ʔat
            into-what *kind* *situation* *refuse(BENONI)-FS* *usually*   *you*

           lə-hikanes?
           to-enter
           'What sort of situation do you usually refuse to enter into?'

The AgrP which serves subjects is AgrSP. It thus follows that the weak pronoun in (10-31a) is in Spec/AgrS. Note that this provides independent evidence that Triggered Inversion involves movement of the verb over the subject into the Comp domain, as opposed to movement to I^0 over an unraised subject, as in Doron (1983) and Borer (1995), a point argued for in §8.3.2.

Consider now the fact that postverbal pronouns are illicit when the verb is inflected for first and second person. Doron (1988) considers the contrast between the acceptable (10-32a), with the verb inflected for third person, and (10-32b), where it is inflected for second person.

(10-32) a. ʔetmol   šamʕa   hi   harcaʔa.
            yesterday *hear(PAST)-3FS* *she* *lecture*
            'Yesterday, she heard a lecture.'

         b. *ʔetmol   šamʕat   ʔat   harcaʔa.
            yesterday *hear(PAST)-2FS* *you-F* *lecture*
            'Yesterday, you heard a lecture.'

Doron's view is that the unacceptability of (10-32b) is due to the fact that the inflected verb and the pronoun form what she calls a "clitic configuration": the content of (subject) Agr is identical to that of the pronoun. Agr is assigned Case, which is then no longer available to the pronoun. In (10-32a), Agr is not specified for the feature [person]; hence, it is not identical to the pronoun, a clitic configuration is not established, and Case may be assigned to it.

The sentences in (10-33) are well-formed, according to Doron, because the postverbal pronoun is not identical in content to Agr. In (10-33a) it bears the feature [contrast], and in (10-33b) it is part of a coordinate DP.

(10-33)   a. ʔetmol   šamʕat   ʔat   harcaʔa.
               yesterday hear(PAST)-2FS you-F   lecture
               'Yesterday, <u>you</u> heard a lecture.'

          b. *ʔetmol   šamʕatem   ʔat   ve-   Dani   harcaʔa.
               yesterday hear(PAST)-2MPL you-F   and- Dani   lecture
               'Yesterday, you and Dani heard a lecture.'

Finally, Doron argues that, when the pronoun precedes the inflected verb, i.e., when inversion does not take place, it does not form a clitic configuration with Agr, whence the grammaticality of (10-34).

(10-34)   ʔetmol   ʔat   šamʕat   harcaʔa.
              yesterday you-F   hear(PAST)-2FS lecture
              'Yesterday you heard a lecture.'

Doron's analysis is incompatible with a number of assumptions I have made and argued for in the course of this work. Let us see how the facts in (10-32)–(10-34) can be handled within the analytic framework developed in this chapter.

What the contrast between (10-32b) and the sentences in (10-33) clearly shows is that *weak* pronouns are unacceptable in postverbal position in company with first and second person verbal inflection. When these pronouns are strong, as in the sentences in (10-33), they are perfectly licit. I would like to argue that the ungrammaticality of (10-32b) follows from the Avoid Pronoun Principle of Chomsky (1981). Specifically, assume that whenever there is a choice between a null subject and an overt one, the null one is always selected.[7] Null pronouns are by definition weaker than overt pronouns, so the choice between pro and *ʔat*, in (10-32b) boils down to a choice between a stronger and a weaker form.

The acceptability of (10-32a) poses no problem since it is precisely in the company of third person inflection that null subjects are not permitted in Hebrew (viz. §7.2.4 ff.) An overt weak pronoun thus appears.

I take postverbal weak pronouns, as in (10-30b), to appear in Spec/AgrS. However, this is not the only position they may occupy. In a sentence headed by the negative head *ʔeyn*, exemplified by (10-35), weak subject pronouns are licensed in Spec/T when AgrSP is not projected (see the discussion in §7.4).

(10-35)   ʔeyn hi   kotevet   sipurim.
              NEG   she   write(BENONI)-FS stories
              'She does not write books.'

Spec/T is the position in which nominative Case features are checked. What (10-35) shows, then, is that weak pronouns must check a Case feature at S-structure. This holds for object pronouns as well as subject ones, but only in the case of subject pronouns are the checking positions for agreement and Case distinct.[8]

As for the licit occurrence of a preverbal pronoun in (10-34), I am led to believe that this pronoun is strong and not weak. If the Avoid Pronoun principle bars overt pronouns where null ones are available, it must be the case in (10-34) that a null pronoun is not licit. What looks like free variation between (10-34) and (10-36) below, with a pro subject, should thus be reconsidered.[9]

(10-36)   ʔetmol   šamʕat   harcaʔa.
              yesterday hear(PAST)-2FS lecture
              'Yesterday, you heard a lecture.'

10.3 THE SYNTAX OF HEBREW WEAK PRONOUNS RECONSIDERED

In this section, I first show that weak pronouns do not have a fixed position in Hebrew. Under certain circumstances, they raise higher than Spec/AgrO, and under other circumstances, they remain in Spec/AgrO. I then draw the empirical generalization that weak pronouns must always be adjacent to a verb associated with agreement features, and I attempt to explain why this should be the case by reconsidering the nature of weak pronouns. The discussion is centered first on direct object pronouns, and the discussion of indirect object pronouns is taken up in the context of an analysis of weak pronoun clusters.

10.3.1 Weak Pronouns Can Appear Higher than AgrOP

First, the requirement that weak pronouns be adjacent to the verb holds more generally than in cases where the intervening constituent is a VP adverb. The contrast in (10-37) illustrates the intervention effect of a "high" adverb, whose natural position is higher than AgrOP.

(10-37)   a. Rina   tazmin   bə-hexlet ʔet   Dani la-msiba.
                 Rina 3FS-(FUT)invite certainly ACC Dani to-the-party
                 'Rina will certainly invite Dani to the party.'

              b. *Rina tazmin   bə-hexlet ʔoto la-msiba.
                 Rina 3FS-(FUT)invite certainly him   to-the-party
                 'Rina will certainly invite him to the party.'

Only (10-38) is grammatical.

(10-38)   Rina   tazmin   ʔoto bə-hexlet la-msiba.
              Rina 3FS-(FUT)invite   him   certainly to-the-party
              'Rina will certainly invite him to the party.'

Second, postverbal subjects, which can occupy no position lower than Spec/TP (viz. §8.3.3), may not intervene between a verb and a weak pronoun. This is shown in (10-39), where Triggered Inversion raises the verb over the subject.

(10-39)   a. maxar   tazmin   Rina ʔet Dani la-msiba.
                 tomorrow 3FS-(FUT)invite Rina ACC Dani to-the-party
                 'Tomorrow, Rina will invite Dani to the party.'

              b. *maxar   tazmin   Rina ʔoto la-msiba.
                 tomorrow 3FS-(FUT)invite Rina him   to-the-party
                 'Tomorrow, Rina will invite him to the party.'

Only (10-40) is acceptable, with the pronoun preceding the subject.

(10-40)   maxar   tazmin   ?oto Rina la-msiba.
          tomorrow 3FS-(FUT)invite him   Rina to-the-party
          'Tomorrow, Rina will invite him to the party.'

In the preceding sections, it was shown that weak pronouns may occur no lower than Spec/AgrO. The examples in (10-38) and (10-40) suffice to show that they appear in an even higher position. Yet, the position of Hebrew weak pronouns is not fixed. I now turn to examples which show that, under certain circumstances, these pronouns do remain in Spec/AgrO.

10.3.2 Weak Pronouns Can Appear in Spec/AgrO

Weak pronouns appear in Spec/AgrO when the main verb does not raise. This is exemplified by structures containing an auxiliary and a Benoni participle.

(10-41)   Dani haya   kotev   ?oto.
          Dani be(PAST)-3MS write(BENONI)-MS it
          'Dani was writing / used to write it.'

The pronoun may not appear to the left of the verb—that is, in a position adjacent to the auxiliary.

(10-42)   *Dani haya   ?oto kotev.
          Dani be(PAST)-3MS it   write(BENONI)-MS
          'Dani was writing / used to write it.'

Following Friedemann and Siloni (1993), I take the pronoun in (10-41) to occupy Spec/AgrO. The Benoni participle, to recall, is raised to AgrPart⁰, thereby appearing to the left of the pronoun. The derived positions of the verb and the pronoun in (10-41) are diagrammed in (10-43).

(10-43)

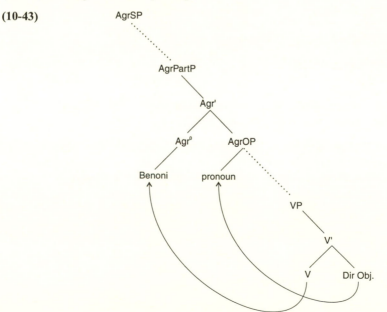

The discussion in this and the preceding sections leads to two empirical generalizations:

(10-44)   a. A weak pronoun must raise to Spec/AgrO.

   b. A weak pronoun must be adjacent to the first verb on its left.

Property (10-44a) restates the idea that pronouns cannot procrastinate Case checking (Cardinaletti and Starke, forthcoming). The following section considers (10-44b).

10.3.3   The Nature of Hebrew Weak Pronouns

French object clitics always move to the same position. They show up on the auxiliary when there is one, and on a tensed verb in an analytic tense construction. Since both auxiliaries and tensed verbs raise to the same position in the audible syntax, the hypothesis that the clitic's host is always the same is quite plausible.[10]

Hebrew weak pronouns do not have a stable position. Example (10-44b) implies that they appear in a position relative to that of the verbal form preceding them. Since the position of the participle is different from that of a tensed verb, it follows that the position of the pronoun is different as well.

A number of authors have suggested that Hebrew weak pronouns are phonetic clitics. That is to say that their adjacency to the verb is brought about by a process of postsyntactic cliticization (see, e.g., Borer 1983, Friedemann and Siloni 1993). In Friedemann and Siloni's view, Hebrew object pronouns move to Spec/AgrO in the syntax and then undergo cliticization in the PF component.

Let us consider again the sentence in (10-40), repeated as (10-45).

(10-45)   maxar   tazmin   ?oto Rina la-msiba.
   tomorrow   3FS-(FUT)invite   him   Rina   to-the-party
   'Tomorrow, Rina will invite him to the party.'

If the pronoun is in Spec/AgrO in the syntax, it must be taken to move to a position to the left of the subject in PF. Under this view, the derivation of (10-45) would look something like (10-46).

(10-46)

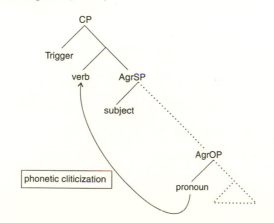

Figure (10-46) diagrams a case of nonlocal movement. If phonetic cliticization is subject to familiar locality constraints, then (10-46) ought be excluded. If it is not subject to syntactic constraints, but only to a requirement of linear adjacency between the host and the clitic (see Marantz 1988), then (10-46) must be ruled out on grounds of non-adjacency.

While I do not wish to deny that Hebrew weak pronouns are phonetic clitics since they form an intonational group with the verb, I would like to suggest that their trailing character—that is, the property listed under (10-44b)—is first and foremost a consequence of the need to satisfy an LF condition. I argue that the movement of the pronoun as indicated by the arrow in (10-46) is effected in the audible syntax in order to establish a syntactic configuration favoring the satisfaction of this condition.

The proposal I submit is that weak pronouns are LF clitics and that their host is a verb-related Agr^0. If genuine clitics, in a language like French, accomplish XP movement as well as X^0 movement in the audible syntax, then Hebrew weak pronouns effect the former in the syntax and the latter in LF. Following Rizzi (1993), let us assume that clitic heads are D^0 elements endowed with V-features that are strong in Romance. By analogy, take the K^0/P^0 heads *ʔet* and *lə* to possess V-features, though of a weak variety, requiring checking only in LF.

Head movement from Spec/AgrO to the position occupied by the verb clearly violates Relativized Minimality, which holds in LF. Indeed, the combination of strong XP features and weak X^0 ones seems to give rise to a paradox: the pronoun must move to Spec/Agr^0 qua XP, but once this is accomplished it cannot incorporate to a verb-related Agr^0 in LF since the verb has moved too far away for head movement to be licensed (and traces of heads are not licit hosts; cf. Kayne 1989b).

The paradox can, however, be resolved, once we give up the idea that the pronoun must remain in Spec/AgrO. What we need to say is that the pronoun must move, qua XP, high enough in the tree so as to be, in LF, in a position from which head movement can be licitly launched. The various specifier positions lying in between Spec/AgrO and C^0—the position of the verb—are not available as landing sites for an object since they are all occupied by subject traces or by the subject itself. Let us therefore assume that the pronoun raises by adjunction, as opposed to substitution, and attaches to the maximal projection immediately c-commanded by the Agr-bearing verbal head. What I have in mind is an S-structure representation for (10-45) such as (10-47), where the arrow indicates syntactic XP-movement.

(10-47)

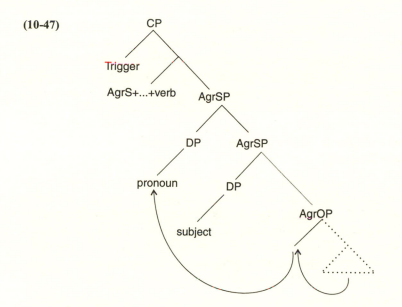

The lower arrow in (10-47) indicates movement to Spec/AgrO. This step is obligatory. The higher arrow shows the extra step undertaken by these pronouns in order to enable head movement in LF.

In (10-48), the verb is in AgrS⁰ and the pronoun *?oto* is therefore adjoined to TP.

(10-48)   Rina   tazmin   ?oto   la-msiba.
   Rina   3FS-(FUT)invite   him   to-the-party
   'Rina will invite him to the party.'

The extra movement step(s) undertaken by the pronoun in (10-45) and (10-48) are a "last resort" operation: they are effected whenever the potential host is not in a local configuration with the pronoun (it does not immediately c-command it). This second step of movement is not effected in complex tense structures, where the host, namely the Benoni verb, is in a position to which the clitic can incorporate from Spec/Agr⁰ without violating Relativized Minimality.[11]

The question arises as to why XP movement must occur entirely in the audible syntax. Why, for example, can the pronoun not raise to Spec/AgrO and carry out both the next step of XP movement as well as head movement entirely in LF? We came across a similar case in §8.4, where it was shown that at S-structure subjects can either occur in their base position or raise all the way to their final landing site. Ruled out are cases of partial subject raising—for instance, raising to Spec/AgrPart and subsequent movement to Spec/AgrS in LF. To account for the ban on partial movement, I proposed the following statement, which I repeat in (10-49), to capture the absence of partial pronoun movement as well.

(10-49)   A-movement must be terminated in the component in which it is initiated (S-structure or LF).

This proposal handles the examples in (10-41) and (10-45). With respect to the latter, my analysis explains why the weak pronoun must occur to the left of the clausal subject. But this is only one aspect of the adjacency requirement observed by verbs and weak pronouns. The other aspect concerns the position of adverbs. On the assumption that adverbs are base-generated in a position adjoined to some XP, it follows that adjoining the pronoun to an XP to which an adverb itself is base-adjoined results in the order pronoun > adverb and not adverb > pronoun. This is at the root of the contrast between, for example, (10-37b) and (10-38).

10.3.4   Indirect Object Weak Pronouns and Pronoun Clustering

The analysis of direct object pronouns in the preceding section carries over directly to indirect or oblique ones. They, too, trail and must be adjacent to the verb in the manner described. the following examples recapitulate these points: The contrast between (10-50a) and (10-50b) illustrates the adjacency requirement, the sentences in (10-51) show the trailing character of pronouns; and those in (10-52) manifest a pronoun in Spec/Agr under a Benoni participle. In all relevant respects, then, indirect pronouns are weak in the same sense as are direct object ones.

(10-50)   a. Rina tišlax   l-o   maxar   sefer.
                Rina   3FS-send(FUT)   to him   tomorrow   book
                'Rina will send him a book tomorrow.'

        b. *Rina tišlax   maxar   l-o   sefer.
                Rina   3FS-send(FUT)   tomorrow   to him   book
                'Rina will send him a book tomorrow.'

(10-51)   a. maxar   tišlax   l-o   Rina   sefer.
                tomorrow   3FS-(FUT)send   to him   Rina   book
                'Tomorrow, Rina will send him a book.'

        b. *maxar   tišlax   Rina   l-o   sefer.
                tomorrow   3FS-send(FUT)   Rina   to him   book
                'Tomorrow, Rina will send him a book.'

(10-52)   a. Dani haya   šoleʔax   l-a   sfarim.
                Dani   be(PAST)-3MS   send(BENONI)-MS   to her   books
                'Dani used to send her books.'

        b. *Dani haya   l-a   šoleʔax   sfarim.
                Dani   be(PAST)-3MS   to her   send(BENONI)-MS   books
                'Dani used to send her books.'

Indirect pronoun movement poses a number of technical problems. I will make certain proposals regarding these, if only for the sake of providing a coherent and adequate description of the facts. I have argued that there is only a single Agr phrase above VP serving objects. This raises the immediate problem of Case-checking in examples such as (10-53), in which the indirect object is a weak pronoun, *la*, and the direct object is a full DP.

(10-53)   natanu   l-a   sefer.
           give(PAST)-1PL   to-her   book
           'We gave her a book.'

The pronoun *la* must first move to Spec/Agr. In doing so, however, it fills the position into which the direct object *sefer* 'book' must move in LF. The indirect object, being a weak pronoun, moves to Spec/Agr^0 in the audible syntax (and then continues its movement to the pre-cliticization site). The direct object, I suggest, adjoins to AgrOP in LF (see Friedemann and Siloni 1993 for a similar view).

Underlying this claim is Chomsky's (1993) idea that adjunction is "broadly L-related" in the sense that an element adjoined to an XP is still within the domain of feature checking. It must, in any case, be assumed that both the verb and AgrO^0 contain accusative *and* dative features. Thus, compare (10-53) with (10-54), where the weak pronoun is the direct object and the full XP is the indirect one. Here, the direct object raises to Spec/AgrO in the overt syntax, and the indirect one adjoins to AgrO in LF.

(10-54) natanu   ?oto lə-Rina
         give(PAST)-1PL it   *to-Rina*
         'We gave it to Rina.'

A more transparent instance of multiple raising to Spec/AgrO is manifested in sentences in which both direct and indirect objects are pronouns. Recall the example in (10-17a), repeated here as (10-55).

(10-55) natanu   l-a   ?ota.
         give(PAST)-1PL to-her it
         'We gave it to her.' *lit.* 'We gave her it.'

I propose that, in (10-55), the direct object is raised to Spec/AgrO and the indirect object adjoins to it. What needs to be explained is that the two pronouns form a cluster, in that no element can split the adjacency of the two pronouns, as shown in (10-56) with the intervening adverb *?etmol* 'yesterday'.

(10-56) *natanu   l-a   ?etmol   ?ota.
         give(PAST)-1PL to-her yesterday it
         'We gave it to her yesterday.' *lit.* 'We gave her yesterday it.'

We can account for this observation by having the direct object adjoin to the indirect one in Spec/AgrO, and not, as in (10-53) or (10-54), to AgrOP.

How can we make sense of these distinct derivational patterns? Let us assume that adjunction of one pronoun to the other is the unmarked case: both pronouns percolate their features to the highest dominating DP, and feature checking can be carried out in one fell swoop. In (10-53) or (10-54), however, this option is unavailable. Movement of the nonpronominal DP in LF cannot result in adjunction to the pronoun in Spec/AgrO for the simple reason that the pronoun is not in Spec/AgrO at this level, but has raised to a precliticization site. If adjunction to traces is not an available option, then the non-pronominal DP must find an alternative checking site. Adjunction to AgrOP thus serves to check the DP's features. Note that if adjunction to an AgrP were an option for checking on a par with movement to Spec/Agr, then there would be no reason for arguments (e.g., subjects) to typically move into the latter position. It seems that an element is moved to a broadly L-related position only if the L-related position is unavailable.

Note, now, that the pronominal cluster formed in, for example, (10-55) observes a strict ordering constraint: the indirect object precedes the direct one. Under the analysis proposed here, this should be interpreted to mean that the indirect object is adjoined to the direct object, and not vice versa. Indeed, the reverse order of operations—that is, adjunction of the direct object to the indirect one—results in ungrammaticality; cf. the discussion surrounding (10-17).

(10-57)   *natanu   ʔota l-a.
          give(PAST)-1PL   it   to-her
          'We gave it to her.'

The reason for the observed pattern is the following: in line with Belletti and Shlonsky (1995), I assume that the indirect object is generated in a structurally higher position than the direct one, within VP. The D-structure complement alignment proposed in Belletti and Shlonsky (1995) is diagrammed in (10-58), adapting proposals of Kayne (1985) and Larson (1988).

(10-58)

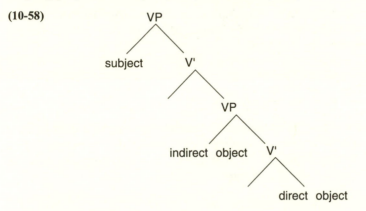

When both objects raise in the overt syntax, the lower object moves first, creating a position to which the higher (indirect) object can adjoin. I take this choice to be dictated by the Cycle Condition. Since LF movement always involves "recycling," as it were, movement of the indirect object at S-structure does not constrain LF-raising of the direct object in LF, accounting for the reverse order of operations in (10-54). The sketch in (10-59) diagrams the essential part of the derivation of (10-55): the dotted arc indicates verb movement, and the straight arcs stand for DP or pronoun movement.

(10-59)

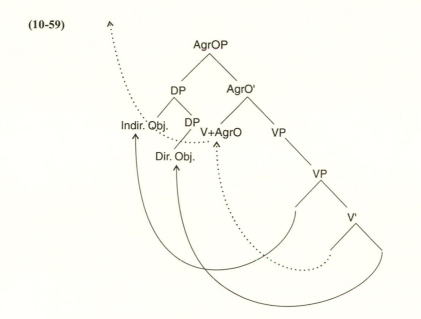

Let us finally consider how pronominal clusters of direct and indirect objects behave in the presence of weak subject pronouns.[12] Consider (10-60), which illustrates the only acceptable ordering of the pronouns, namely subject > indirect object > direct object.

(10-60) ʔetmol   natna   hi   l-o   ʔoto.
yesterday *give(PAST)-3FS* *she* *to-him* *it*
'Yesterday, she gave it to him.'

The three pronouns form a cluster. I have argued that the cluster of the indirect and direct object is formed in Spec/AgrO (by adjunction of, for example, *lo* to *ʔoto,*), and that this cluster raises as a unit to adjoin to the maximal projection immediately c-commanded by the verb. Since the verb is in C⁰, this cluster should be taken to be adjoined to AgrSP. The subject pronoun, however, is to be found to the left of the cluster of object pronouns, and it clusters with them. A plausible suggestion is that the subject pronoun is itself raised from Spec/AgrS and adjoined to the object cluster. I have in mind a derivation such as (10-61).

(10-61)

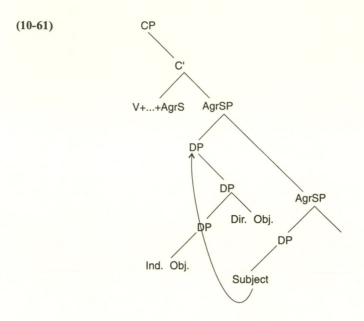

10.4 CONCLUSION

Let us review the main points of this chapter. The problem posed by Hebrew weak pronouns such as *ʔoto* or *lo* is that they share properties both of clitics and of unattached or freestanding forms. I argued that they should be classified as *weak pronouns*—as pronouns driven to raise to their Case position in the audible syntax. However, this characterization was shown to be insufficient in explaining the fact that these pronouns are always positioned to the immediate right of the lowest overt Agr-bearing verb in the clause (the Benoni participle, when there is one; otherwise, the inflected verb). While not ruling out that *in addition* to being weak pronouns, Hebrew pronouns are phonetic clitics, it was shown that their movement to verb-adjacent position cannot be explained purely in terms of phonetic clustering. I argued that Hebrew weak pronouns differ from Romance-like clitics in the level of application of head movement. Weak pronouns, I suggested, are best characterized as LF clitics: they raise in the syntax as XPs to a position from which head movement can be successfully launched. It would be highly desirable if this characterization of weak pronouns could be shown to hold universally. If that were the case, the notion of weak pronouns could be dispensed with entirely for all but purely descriptive purposes. There would then be two classes of pronouns, XPs, or strong ones, and X^0s, or clitics.[13]

  Finally, I attempted to account for pronominal clustering in Hebrew by means of a number of explicit hypotheses regarding their trajectory and form of movement. The assumption that there is a single AgrOP above VP, even in the presence of several complements in VP, gives rise to a situation in which one pronoun is moved to Spec/AgrO and the other(s) must adjoin to it, thereby forming a pronominal cluster. It is of some interest to note that such clustering of weak pronouns is not unique to Hebrew. Pronouns in the Mainland Scandinavian languages, for example, typically raise out of VP in the overt syntax (Holmberg 1986). This phenomenon, known as Object Shift, has been argued to involve raising of, for example, the accusative pronoun to Spec/AgrO (see Vikner 1995). Vikner notes that, when both the direct and the indirect object undergo object shift, they observe a unique order and pattern as a cluster. It is suggestive to think of Scandinavian weak pronouns also as LF clitics.

Appendix:
Nonpronominal Incorporation

Chapter 9 dealt with the so-called pronominal clitics in Arabic and Hebrew. The basic argument was that the suffixal endings on verbs, prepositions, nouns, and so on are affixal heads of Agr projections situated above VP, PP, NP, and so on, respectively. "Cliticization" under this view is really inflection, and it occurs when the lexical head in question raises and left-adjoins to Agr^0.

Here we are concerned with the contrast between pronominal cliticization and another phenomenon of cliticization that is quite widespread in Semitic. This phenomenon is characterized by the merger of a lexical stem (with or without an agreement affix) with a contentful functional head. An good example of this is the association of the definite determiner, Hebrew *ha-*, Standard Arabic *ʔal-*, with the nominal stem, as in the examples in (A-1).

(A-1) a. ha-　bayt　　　　b. ʔal- bayt
　　　　the- house　　　　*the house*
　　　　'the house'　　　　　'the house'

It is not a mere orthographic convention that these determiners are merged with the following noun. Rather, the orthography here mirrors a process of morphological merger which, I will argue, involves syntactic incorporation. The attachment of the determiner triggers phonological processes that typically do not occur across word boundaries: the /l/ of Arabic *ʔal* is assimilated to a following coronal (compare *ʔal-bayt* 'the house', as in (A-1b), with *ʔad-daar* 'the apartment'). In biblical Hebrew, the definite determiner *ha-* causes the gemination of a following nonguttural consonant (compare *nasi* 'leader' with *ha-nnasi* 'the-leader').

Other examples attest to the widespread occurrence of this merger phenomenon. A future tense reading of a sentence with a verb in the imperfect in Standard Arabic is signaled by the particle *sawfa*. This morpheme has a reduced variant, *sa-*, which appears as a proclitic on the verbal stem (see §6.2.1).

(A-2) a. sawfa ʔaktubu.　　　　b. sa-　ʔaktubu.

FUT   1S-write(IMPERF)   FUT   1S-write(IMPERF)
'I will write.'   'I will write.'

In Moroccan Arabic, the future tense is also formed synthetically, by means of the auxiliary *γadi*, of which there are three variants. Two are relevant for the present discussion—the full form *γadi* and the reduced form *γa*. These are exemplified in (A-3); the data and part of the discussion are taken from Benmamoun (1992).

(A-3) a. lə-wlaad γadi yemši w.
      the-boys FUT   3MPL-leave(IMPERF)
      'The boys will leave.'

   b. lə-wlaad γa yemši w.
      the-boys FUT 3MPL-leave(IMPERF)
      'The boys will leave.'

Like Palestinian (viz. §1.3.3 and §5.3.1), Moroccan disposes of a bimorphemic NegP, of which *ma* is the specifier and *-š* is the head. When the sentences in (A-3) are rendered negative, the following pattern emerges. When the reduced form *γa* is employed, the negative head *-š* is encliticized onto the main verb (which I have argued to be a participle in §6.2.1). This is shown in (A-4).

(A-4) a. lə-wlaad ma γa yemši w   š.
      the-boys NEG FUT 3MPL-IMPERF-leave -NEG
      'The boys will not leave.'

What (A-4) demonstrates, in fact, is the incorporation of the verbal stem into the auxiliary and their movement as a unit to a position to the left of negation.

When the full form *γadi* is employed, the grammar of Moroccan disposes of two options: either incorporation does not take place, in which case Neg^0 is cliticized onto the auxiliary, or it does occur, in which case the pattern exemplified by (A-4) is reproduced, with *-š* encliticized onto the verbal stem. The two options are illustrated in (A-5).

(A-5) a. lə-wlaad ma γadi -š   yemši w.
      the-boys NEG FUT   -NEG 3MPL-leave(IMPERF)
      'The boys will not leave.'

   b. lə-wlaad ma   γadi yemši w   š
      the-boys NEG FUT 3MPL-leave(IMPERF) NEG
      'The boys will not leave.'

I would like to argue that *γadi* is ambiguous between an incorporating and a nonincorporating form (the short form *γa* is thus a morphological variant of the incorporating *γadi*.)[1] These Moroccan data exemplify incorporation in a rather clear fashion, due to the relative positioning of the verbal elements with respect to negation.

A further example of nonpronominal incorporation is provided by Palestinian Arabic, in which nonpast indicative mood is realized by the particle *b-*, a proclitic on the imperfect or *dependent* verbal stem. Compare the "subjunctive" use of the imperfect in (A-6a) with the indicative one in (A-6b), where the proclitic *b-* is manifested. Attachment of *b-* to the verbal stem causes elision of the stem-initial consonant.

(A-6) a. ṭalab   min-ni   ʔinno ʔaruuḥ   maʕ-ak.
       ask(PERF)-3MS from-1S that   1S-go(IMPERF)   with-2MS
       'He asked me to go with you.'

   b. xabbar   l-mudiir   ʔinno b- (ʔ)aruuḥ   maʕ-ak.
       notify(PERF)-3MS the-principal that   B   1S-go(IMPERF)   with-2MS
       'He notified the principal that I will go with you.'

A further case of this sort of incorporation is illustrated by the merger of the Hebrew negative head *lo* and the verbal stem. In chapter 5, I argued that Neg-cliticization in Hebrew involves incorporating T^0 (which includes the verbal stem) to Neg^0, and that this is brought about by selected substitution of the former into a slot in the morphological subcategorization frame of the latter (see §1.3.3 and §5.3.1 for discussion).

I take all the above cases to exemplify syntactic incorporation (which to differing degrees is correlated with morphological rebracketing). The regularity of the proclitic pattern across Arabic and Hebrew strongly suggests that the incorporation is syntactically effected and that the complex forms are not derived as such from the Lexicon.

Let us consider what is at stake here. If this sort of incorporation were patterned like the "cliticization" of the previous chapter, then we would expect the incorporating head, for example, N^0, to be left-adjoined to the host, D^0. Yet the pattern that emerges is one where the incorporating head appears to the right and not to the left of the host.[2] The descriptive conclusion that emerges from this discussion is the following.

(A-7) Incorporation to an Agr head involves left adjunction while incorporation to a contentful functional head involves right adjunction.

There is an important difference between the two types of hosts under discussion. Functional heads such as T^0 and Neg^0 have a fixed position in the clausal hierarchy and dominate a unique complement type. Agr heads, on the other hand, do not enter into selection and cannot be said to subcategorize for any particular category.

Suppose that the contentful functional heads requiring incorporation of a lower head are endowed with a morphological subcategorization frame containing a slot into which the subcategorized head substitutes in the syntax (in the sense of Rizzi and Roberts 1989). I have argued that this is the case of Hebrew *lo*. I would now like to generalize this idea to the other cases exemplified here. In abstract terms, I have in mind something like (A-8).

(A-8)

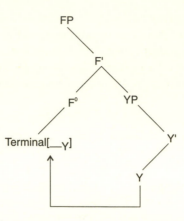

Now consider (A-9).

(A-9) Selected substitution mirrors the parametric setting of the head-complement ordering parameter.

In Arabic and Hebrew, the slot into which the subcategorized head substitutes,
is always to the right of the host because these are head-initial languages.[3] Postulate
(A-9) implies that the subcategorization slot should be on left of the host in an OV
language. The Ethio-Semitic languages, which are by and large head-final, therefore constitute a test case for this claim. To the degree that the "tense markers" in,
say, Chaha (a Gurage language studied in Rose 1996, from which the data are taken)
constitute the equivalent of Standard Arabic *sa(wfa)* or Moroccan *ɣa(di)*, then, if
(A-9) is valid, they should occur to the right of the verbal stem. This is the patently
the case, as Rose shows. This is shown by the examples in (A-10), with the tense
markers underlined (a similar state of affairs holds in Amharic, as D. Perrett informs
me). Set for Guarage, then, (A-9) takes the form shown in (A-11), its mirror image.

(A-10) a. zäkärxᵂɨ   -m.
        jump(PERF)-1S   PAST
        'I jumped.'

      b. äzgär   -šä.
        1S-jump(JUSS)   IRREALIS FUT
        'I might be going to jump.'

      c. äzägɨr   -te.
        1S-jump(IMPERF)   REALIS FUT
        'I will jump.'

(A-11)

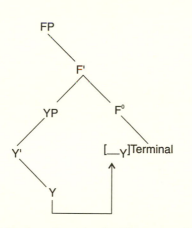

Incorporation to an Agr head, on the other hand, cannot take the form of selected substitution, for the simple reason that Agr does not select for anything. The only way it can host an incorporating head is for the latter to adjoin to it.

Adjunction, when it does take place, is always left adjunction. I have argued in this appendix that apparent cases of right adjunction in Semitic are cases of selected substitution. This conclusion reinforces Kayne's (1994) proposal to the effect that UG does not permit right adjunction.

Notes

CHAPTER 1

1. These are nontrivial in two senses: they can be formulated only on the basis of highly complex syntactic relations and interactions and they constitute generalizations drawing together facts which are observationally unrelated.

2. Grammars are objects in the *individual* mind/brain. The Hebrew of two native speakers may be very similar, but it is nevertheless not identical (there are no identical human beings). It is by explicit abstraction away from individual differences and by idealization that one can talk about the grammars of Modern Hebrew, Palestinian Arabic, and so forth. See Chomsky (1965) for discussion.

3. The notion "native speaker" is inappropriate when discussing Standard Arabic, since it is a language learned by school-age children and does not enter into the primary linguistic data available to the child. I have come to be convinced that, with the exception, perhaps, of what one might call "canonical facts," listed in grammar books or otherwise explicitly taught, the tacit knowledge of Arabs of the standard written language reflects the grammars of their native dialect. Thus, there is a Cairene Standard Arabic, a Beyrouti Standard Arabic, and so on.

4. For discussion of TP, of particular relevance for the study of the Benoni in Part 1, see Déchaine (1993). See Starke (1994) for the view that small clauses are CPs with TP.

5. The exception to this is AgrOP which serves as the locus of legitimation of Accusative Case features. I will argue that Nominative Case features are associated with T^0 so that AgrSP, like AgrPartP, serves only to license agreement features.

6. A head is taken to subcategorize for its complement, yet I am assuming that IP, the complement of C^0, is an AgrSP phrase and not a projection of T^0. This is precisely the sort of case which shows that AgrPs are "invisible" for selection.

7. Matters become notoriously complex once it is admitted that overt morphology is not a very reliable tool for determining the strength or weakness of an inflectional feature. Although it can be shown, I believe, that certain functional heads contain an overt affix, such as $AgrO^0$ in Arabic, while others do not, such as $AgrS^0$ in Hebrew and Arabic (see chapter 9), one cannot conclude that the presence of an affix renders a head strong while its absence renders it weak. The weakness or strength of an affix might be better approached by looking

at verb movement: if it occurs, then the feature is strong; if it does not, then it is weak. Yet this transposition stands the danger of being circular: An affix is strong if it leads to overt verb movement, and overt movement occurs whenever an affix is strong.

8. The view that VSO word order is a derived order is quite well established. The analysis of its derivation in terms of verb movement over the subject harks back to Emonds (1979). More recent studies include Fassi Fehri (1989), Koopman and Sportiche (1991), Sproat (1985), and Woolford (1991), to cite only a handful.

9. In some languages, GP = FP, so that the subject and the verb are under the same node immediately dominating XP. Whether this is true of Hebrew and Palestinian Arabic is discussed in subsequent chapters.

10. For discussion and various points of view, see, e.g., Ayoub (1981), Bakir (1980), Benmamoun (1992), Demirdache (1988), Doron (1996), Fassi-Fehri (1989, 1993), Mouchaweh (1986), Mohammad (1989, 1990), and Ouhalla (1991).

11. See §4.6 for a more detailed discussion of verb movement in Hebrew.

12. I assume throughout this work that the third person singular masculine form in the suffixal pattern (i.e., *tafar* in [1-14]) contains a phonetically null suffix, [3MS]. This permits a unified view of the suffixal pattern and is motivated, inter alia, by the fact that [3MS] is phonetically realized in the prefixal pattern, by *yi-*. See chapter 6 for further discussion.

As the reader can plainly tell, the agreement paradigm is a rich one in the sense that all forms but two, namely, the forms for the future 2M and 3F, are discrete. One then expects the languages that utilize these verbal patterns to be null subject languages. This expectation is met when it comes to the various dialects of Arabic. Hebrew is a peculiar case, as I show in chapter 7.

13. The Arabic system is representative of the Western Semitic pattern:

> The 'tense' system presents one of the most complicated and disputed problems of Semitic linguistics. In the West Semitic area, Arabic and most of the other languages exhibit, according to the traditional approach, two conjugations which are usually called "tenses." But this nomenclature must be considered improper, as different temporal concepts converge in each of these two conjugations; it would be more appropriate to speak of "aspects." One of these conjugations uses prefixes and generally indicates an incomplete action which correspond, according to circumstances, to our future, present or imperfect . . . The other conjugation employs suffixes . . . and generally indicates a completed action." Moscati et al. 1980:17)

14. The system of tense, mood, and aspect in Standard Arabic is dealt with in Fassi-Fehri (1993), chapter 4. A very detailed study of Jerusalem (Palestinian) Arabic, rich in examples, is that of Piamenta (1964) of which Piamenta (1966) is a shortened English version. See also Eisele (1988) on Cairene and for an extensive bibliography.

15. There are some remarkable similarities with the modern Balkan languages. I will not pursue this comparative angle. See, e.g., Terzi (1992).

As the reader can plainly tell by scrutinizing the glosses to (1-18), subject agreement morphology may occur in numerous places in the clause. This matter harks back to §1.2.1 and is discussed at length in chapter 9.

16. See Fassi-Fehri (1993) for discussion of Standard Arabic participles and Piamenta (1964) for Jerusalem Palestinian. In Palestinian, the use of the participle as a present tense verb is by and large restricted to stative and perceptual verbs. I am inclined to agree with Harrell (1962:176) who writes that in Moroccan "for those verbs of which the durative form [Palestinian *b-*. U.S.] indicates only habitual or repetitive action but not progressive action, the active participle has a progressive meaning." Thus we find (ia) but not (ib).

(i) a. hiy   naaime   /qaaʕde /saamiʕa   muṣiiqa
    she   sleep-FS   sit-FS   listen-FS   music
    'She is sleeping *or* asleep/sitting *or* seated/listening to music.'

  b. *hiy   raaqisa   /kaatbe.
    she   dance-FS   write-FS
    'She is dancing/ writing.'

17. I will not dwell here on some of the criticism that has been leveled against this analysis for Italian. See, e.g., Zanuttini (1991) for pertinent discussion.

18. Pron occurs in the following environments:

* In identity statements, such as (i).

  (i) A hu   B.
    B Pron-MS B
    'A is B.'

* When the predicate assigns a permanent property (an "individual-level" predicate; see Carlson 1977, Diesing 1992b, Kratzer 1995) to the subject, as in (iia) (compare [iib] where the predicate is "stage-level").

  (ii) a. Dani   hu   šikor.   b. Dani   šikor.
    Dani   Pron-MS   drunk   *Dani   drunk*
    'Dani is a drunk(ard).'   'Dani is drunk.'

* In inverted copular sentences, (see Moro 1993), as in (iii).

  (iii)   marca   tova   hi   Dina.
    lecturer-F good-F Pron-FS Dina
    'Dina is a good lecturer.'

For further discussion see Déchaine (1993), Doron (1993), Penner (1988), Rapoport (1987), and Rothstein (1995).

19. To render incorporation of T^0 to Neg^0 compatible with (even a weak version of) Greed (Chomsky 1993), suppose that T^0 is lexically endowed with Neg features, requiring head to head checking.

21. In some dialects, only one of the two morphemes is phonetically spelled out. Thus, in certain subdialects of Palestinian (perhaps substandard), *ma* can be optionally left out, while in, for example, Syrian Arabic, the morpheme *š* is not pronounced. Compare (ia) and (ib):

(i) a. biddi   š.   Palestinian
    want-1s   neg
    'I don't want.'

  b. ma biddi.   Syrian
    neg want-1s
    'I don't want.'

This sort of variation is familiar from Romance dialects. See Zanuttini (1991) for discussion.

21. Benmamoun considers *walu* and *ḥedd* to be negative polarity items. I am not entirely convinced that they are not negative quantifiers. See Zanuttini (1991) for arguments to the effect that negative quantifiers should be distinguished from negative polarity items.

22. Manner adverbs in Hebrew *may not* occur between the subject and the verb, as shown by the ungrammaticality of the sentences in (i). This fact constitutes further evidence that the verb raises out of VP in Hebrew, to a position higher than that of manner adverbs.

(i) a. *Dani ʔanušot   hika   ʔet šlomo.
        Dani mortally   hit(PAST)-3MS ACC Shlomo
        'Dani hit Shlomo mortally.'

    b. *Dani bə-ʕadinut   patax   ʔet ha-delet.
        Dani gently   open(PAST)-3MS ACC the-door
        'Dani opened the door gently.'

23. The order V > direct object > adverb is also consistent with the view that the direct object raises over the adverb, perhaps to Spec/AgrO. I hypothesize, however, that this is not a valid S-structure derivation in Hebrew. For further discussion of object positions in Hebrew, see chapter 10 and Belletti and Shlonsky (1995).

24. See Lamontagne and Travis (1987) for a discussion of Kase projections.

25. As for the subjects of small clauses which, as Belletti shows, cannot be assigned Partitive Case by a governing verb in Italian since the latter does not θ-mark them, assume, with Lasnik (1992), that inherent Case does not universally require θ-role assignment and that Hebrew, like English but unlike Italian, allows inherent Case to be assigned structurally.

CHAPTER TWO

1. Three comments are in order here. First, the unmarked use of the participial past in (2-1a,c) is to express habitual aspect (Berman (1978)). This is indicated as an option in the translation. Second, Hebrew lacks the auxiliary *have*, and thus has no compound tenses in the Indo-European sense. I shall, however, continue to call (2-1a,c) compound past constructions since they involve two verbal categories, an auxiliary and a participle. Third, the auxiliary *be* followed by a present participle also expresses the conditional, as in this example.

ʔilu Dani haya   kotev   sipurim, ʔaz . . .
if Dani be(PAST)-3MS write(BENONI)-MS stories   then . . .
'If Dani were to write stories, then . . .'

2. Hebrew lacks a present tense form for the verb 'be', whence the absence of a copula in (2-5a). This matter is discussed at length in §2.4.1.

3. For a partial classification of Hebrew verbs as strongly or weakly transitive, see Glinert (1989).

4. *Construct state* is a genitive construction found throughout Semitic. Detailed discussions can be found in Borer (1983, 1989a, 1996), Fassi-Fehri (1993), Hazout (1991), Ritter (1988), (1995), and Siloni (1991, 1994).

5. Benoni participles can also be ambiguous with adjectives. Example (i) is ambiguous between a verbal and an adjectival passive, as discussed in Borer and Wexler (1987). Adjectival predicates are considered in a different context in §3.3.

ha-yalda mesoreket.
the-girl comb(PASSIVE BENONI)-FS
'The girl is being combed.' *or* 'The girl is combed.'

6. A lexicalist approach to the derivation of action nominalizations in Hebrew is defended in Siloni (1994). A syntactic derivation of nominals from underlying verbs is proposed in Borer (forthcoming), Fassi-Fehri (1993), and Hazout (1991). Hazout (1991, chapter 5) also discusses agent nominalizations of the sort discussed in the text, arguing that an underlying verb is nominalized through incorporation to a nominalizing head. There are some genuine issues to be resolved here, and the controversy is quite lively.

7. I abstract away from the differences between past and present participles, as well as the distinction between gerunds and participles. See note 14.

8. Floating quantifiers in Hebrew are studied in detail in Shlonsky (1991), to which the reader is referred for discussion of, for example, their inflection.

9. The relative positioning of participles and floating quantifiers in English (i) and French (ii) indicates that participles do not raise out of VP. Italian participles, however, like Hebrew ones, must precede floating quantifiers, as Belletti (1990) shows; see (iii). Hence, Hebrew is like Italian in this respect, requiring participle raising out of VP.

(i) The children have all left / were all leaving.

(ii) Les enfants sont tous partis.

(iii) I bambini sono partiti tutti.

10. For an analysis of negation in small clauses and the idea that small clauses do not contain NegP, see Cardinaletti and Guasti (1994).

11. Some speakers accept (2-28b). Friedemann and Siloni (1993) suggest that this split in judgments reflects the existence of two distinct dialects. They argue that, for those who accept this sentence, the subject remains in VP.

It is interesting to note that a manner adverbial—which I take to delimit the upper edge of VP—cannot precede the subject, but must follow it, even for speakers who accept (2-28b). This is shown by the contrast in (i). The ungrammaticality of (ib) is thus something of a problem for the view that subjects in this dialect remain in VP. I speculate on an alternative explanation of this dialect split in chapter 3, note 13.

(i) a. %ʔetmol   haya   tofer   Dani bə-yad-av   smalot.
        yesterday *be(PAST)-3MS* *sew(BENONI)-MS* *Dani* *with-hands-3MS* *dresses*
        'Yesterday, Dani was sewing dresses with his hands.'

    b. *ʔetmol   haya   tofer   bə-yad-av   Dani smalot.
        yesterday *be(PAST)-3MS* *sew(BENONI)-MS* *with-hands-3MS* *Dani* *dresses*
        'Yesterday, Dani was sewing dresses with his hands.'

12. The unacceptability of inversion in (2-33) is also compatible with a different analysis—one holding that the matrix verb *see* must be adjacent to the small clause subject, either because it Case marks it (Stowell 1981) or because the small clause predicate undergoes reanalysis with the matrix predicate (Stowell 1991b). See also Rizzi (1982). Inversion disrupts this adjacency, whence the ungrammaticality of (2-33).

It is of interest, then, to contrast (2-33) with (i) below, which shows that an adverb may intervene between *see* and the small clause subject.

(i) raʔi-ti   ʔetmol   ʔet ha-yaladim   tofrim   smalot.
    see(PAST)-1S *yesterday* *ACC* *the-children* *sew(BENONI)-MPL* *dresses*
    'Yesterday, I saw the children sewing dresses.'

The contrast can be explained as follows: the matrix verb *raʔiti* '(I) saw' raises out of VP and over the adverb, positioned on the left margin of the matrix VP. The verbal trace, though not the verb itself, is adjacent to the small clause subject. In (2-33), however, the small clause predicate occupies a position between the trace of the verb in the matrix VP and the subject, disrupting the linear adjacency of the trace of the matrix verb and the small clause subject. Note that if the accusative Case borne by the small clause subject is checked in LF by moving it to Spec/AgrOP of the matrix clause, as Chomsky (1993) would argue, the adjacency requirement cannot be directly linked to Case assignment and must be rethought.

13. It was shown that *lo* can function as a negative adverbial attaching to some category lower than TP and imposing a contrastive reading on the negated constituent. In particular, the order *lo* > Benoni is found internal to AgrPartP. Semirelatives are an exception: *lo* may not precede the participle. This leads me to modify somewhat Siloni's (1994) analysis and claim that the

Benoni is incorporated into D^0 (cf. Siloni 1990). The impossibility of inserting any sort of lexical material between *ha-* and the Benoni in semirelatives is likewise accounted for.

14. It is possible that what I have termed small clause adjuncts are also endowed with a CP node, as in the bracketed segment of (i).

(i) [When sick], John stays at home.

The difference between (2-50a) and (2-50b) should then be treated, not as a difference between a small clause (TP-less and CP-less) adjunct and a clausal one, but as a difference in the nature of T^0. In both (2-50a) and (i), T^0 is non-finite and C^0 is null, while in (2-50b), T^0 is finite as the presence of the finite complementizer *še* attests. The presence of a NegP in (at least some) gerundive clauses—and hence of a TP and a CP—is further motivated by the fact that the French example in (iia) can occur with clausal negation (iib), and the English adjunct in (iiib) can contain polarity items.

(ii) a. Parlant   de mes problèmes ...
        speaking of my problems
        'Speaking about my problems ...'

    b. Ne   parlant   jamais de mes problèmes ...
        NEG speaking   never of my problems
        'Never speakng about my problems ...'

(iii) a. Aware of the problem ...   b. Not aware of any problems ...

CHAPTER THREE

1. Borer (1995) shows that adjectival predicates also undergo CI. This is further discussed in §3.3. Borer also develops an argument in favor of a lowering derivation of CI, in which the auxiliary is adjoined to the participle in its base position. I discuss this alternative in note 7.

2. Only tensed auxiliaries can undergo CI. Example (i) shows that the nonfinite auxiliary must precede the predicate *mugešet* 'served', indicating the absence of CI.

(i) a. ha-ʕuga   ʕasuya   li-hyot mugešet   bə-ševaʕ.
      the cake   likely(PASSIVE BENONI)-FS to-be   served(PASSIVE BENONI)-FS at-seven
      'The cake is likely to be served at seven.

    b. *a-ʕuga   ʕasuya   mugešet   li-hyot bə-ševaʕ.
      the cake   likely(PASSIVE BENONI)-FS served(PASSIVE BENONI)-FS to-be   at-seven
      'The cake is likely to be served at seven.

If CI is triggered by a clitic auxiliary, then the absence of CI with nonfinite instances of Aux should be taken to mean that the nonfinite form does not have a clitic or weak variant.

Infinitives are formed by affixing the preposition *l(ə)-* 'to' to a verbal stem. Suppose that the infinitive is not formed lexically—that is, that the affixation of *l(ə)-* to the stem occurs in the syntax by, for example, raising the stem to a functional head containing *l(ə)*. If the auxiliary stem itself has a weak form to which the participle adjoins, then the complex head formed by CI would have to raise to *l(ə)* as a unit, yielding a head bracketed as *lə* + [participle + stem], which is most likely ruled out on purely morphological grounds—that *l(ə)* morphologically selects nonfinite tense. If the nonfinite stem is raised to *l(ə)-* prior to incorporating the participle, then the complex word formed by *l(ə)* + nonfinite stem cannot, qua complex word, have a clitic variant, thus eliminating the trigger for syntactic incorporation.

3. The ECP is violated derivationally in (3-9), though perhaps not representationally. One can imagine an analysis of (3-9) consistent with a representational ECP. Such an analysis

would resemble Belletti's (1990) and Moritz's (1989) treatment of the relationship between verb movement and negation in Italian.

4. See Cardinaletti and Starke (forthcoming) and chapter 10 for arguments to the effect that weak forms are the default forms.

5. The reason for the caveat *in principle* is that the most natural interpretation of compound tense sentences involving an auxiliary and a participle is that of habitual past (see also chapter 2, note 1). Participles that cannot be interpreted as continuous, such as *knowing,* are only marginally acceptable under an overt auxiliary, (i).

(i) ?(?)Dani haya   yodeʕa   polanit.
    Dani   be(PAST)-3MS know(BENONI)-MS Polish.
    'Dani was knowing Polish.'

Such participles are possible, however, when the auxiliary is used to express the conditional mood, as in (iia), in which case they may freely undergo CI, (iib).

(ii) a. ʔilu Dani haya   yodeʕa   polanit, ʔaz . . .
       if   Dani be(PAST)-3MS know(BENONI)-MS Polish, then . . .
       'If Dani knew Polish, then . . .'

     b. ʔilu Dani yodeʕa   haya   polanit, ʔaz . . .
       if   Dani know(BENONI)-MS be(PAST)-3MS Polish, then . . .
       'If Dani knew Polish, then . . .'

PP and DP predicates, however, while occurring under conditional *be*, (iiia), cannot invert, (iiib).

(iii) a. ʔilu Dani haya   ʕal ha-gag   / more, ʔaz . . .
       if   Dani be(PAST)-3MS on the-roof teacher, then . . .
       'If Dani were on the roof / a teacher, then . . .'

      b. *ʔilu Dani ʕal ha-gag   / more haya,   ʔaz . . .
        if   Dani on the-roof teacher, be(PAST)-3MS then . . .
        'If Dani were on the roof / a teacher, then . . .'

6. In §3.3 I discuss CI in Polish. R. Borsley informs me that nominal, adjectival, and prepositional predicates cannot incorporate to the auxiliary in Polish. This suggests that these predicates lack an associated AgrPartP so that there is no suitable host for the clitic auxiliary. This line of reasoning tackles the ungrammaticality of (3-11b) and (3-12b) from the auxiliary's angle.

7. Borer argues that CI is also subject to a derivation in which the auxiliary is either base-adjoined or lowered and adjoined to the participle. She notes that a certain class of adverbial modifiers, such as *yoter midai* 'too much' or *paxot midai* 'too little', which can appear between the auxiliary and the participle, as in (ia), cannot precede the auxiliary when the order is auxiliary > participle, as in (ib). However, these adverbs may precede an inverted participle (i.e., when the order is participle > auxiliary), as in (ic).

(i) a. ha-ʕuga   hayta   paxot midai ʔafuya.
       the-cake be(PAST)-FS too little   baked(PASSIVE BENONI)
       'The cake was not baked enough.'

     b. *ha-ʕuga paxot midai hayta   ʔafuya.
        the-cake too little   be(PAST)-FS baked(PASSIVE BENONI)
        'The cake was not baked enough.'

     c. ha-ʕuga   paxot midai ʔafuya.   hayta.
       the-cake too little   baked(PASSIVE BENONI) be(PAST)-FS
       'The cake was not baked enough.'

She argues that this three-way contrast shows that the adverb occupies a position between that of the auxiliary and the participle. When the auxiliary and the participle form a complex head, the adverb must precede the auxiliary, suggesting that the complex head occupies the same position as the participle. This can be interpreted to mean either that the base-generated complex head is not raised or that the independently generated auxiliary is lowered across the adverb and right-adjoined to the participle. The existence of such an operation raises a number problems in the context of an Economy approach to derivations, as in Chomsky (1991, 1993), and I am reluctant to accept this analysis.

The hypothesis that CI involves raising of Asp^0 to T^0 can be used to sketch an alternative analysis of the data in (i). Suppose that *paxot midai* 'too little', an aspectual adverb, must c-command Asp^0. When CI does not apply, the adverb appears between the auxiliary and the participle, as the contrast between (ia) and (ib) suggests. When CI applies, Asp^0 is raised to toT^0 and T^0 becomes the site of aspectual features. The adverb must then c-command T^0 and must therefore occur to the left of the auxiliary-participle complex, as in (ic).

In more general terms, let us assume that there are two distinct aspectual loci in the clause, Asp^0 and T^0. This seems to be independently necessary, since in many languages, participial aspect must be distinguished from the aspectual properties of the auxiliary. (It is not inconceivable that there is a second AspP above TP. I will continue to assume, however, that higher aspect is part of the T^0 complex, if only for the sake of simplicity.) The two aspects are merged, so to speak, when CI applies, allowing adverbs that modify the "lower," participial aspect, to occur in a position c-commanding the "higher" aspect.

Borer also shows that these adverbs cannot precede the auxiliary-participle complex when inversion takes place. When I raises to C, *paxot miday* must follow the verb. The contrast in (ii) shows that the positioning of the adverb is indeed restricted to a position c-commanding aspect, be it Asp^0 or T^0 when CI applies overtly.

(ii) a. *bə-yaldut-o   paxot midai kore   haya   Dani.
         in-youth-3MS   *too little   read(BENONI)-MS be(PAST)-3MS   Dani*
         'In his youth, Dani used to read too little.'

      b. bə-yaldut-o   kore   haya   Dani paxot midai.
         in-youth-3MS   read(BENONI)-MS   be(PAST)-3MS   Dani   too little
         'In his youth, Dani used to read too little.'

8. The hypothesis that individual-level adjectives do not raise to T^0 has repercussions elsewhere in the grammar of Hebrew. T. Siloni points out (personal communication) that individual-level adjectives cannot occur as predicates in semirelative constructions (these are discussed in chapter 2, §2.3.4), while no such restriction holds of stage-level adjectival predicates. Compare the following pair of semirelatives:

(i) a. yladim   ha-ayefim mi-lexet   b. *yladim   ha-xaxamim
        children   the-tired   from-walking   *children   the-smart*
        'Children who are tired from walking'   'Children who are smart'

If the predicate in a semirelative must raise to D^0—the functional head generated in lieu of T^0 in this construction—then the ungrammaticality of individual-level adjectives in semi-relatives follows from their inability to raise.

That individual-level adjectives do not raise is further signaled by the fact that they co-occur with Pron in copular constructions (see chapter 1, §1.3.3), while stage-level predicates do not (but see Greenberg 1994 for discussion of the rather complex distribution of Pron). The contrast between the two following examples is typical of this state of affairs.

(i) a. */??Dani hu   ʕayef.   b. Dani hu   xaxam.
   Dani PRON-MS *tired*   *Dani* PRON-MS *smart*
   'Dani is tired.'   'Dani is smart.'

To recall, Pron is the phonetic realization of I^0. With I^0 thus filled with non-affixal lexical material, no head can raise to it. A predicate such as *ʕayef* 'tired' must raise to I^0, while a predicate such as xaxam 'smart' cannot. The pattern of grammaticality in (i) is hence accounted for. The distribution of Pron is further discussed in chapter 5. See, in particular, §5.3.

9. A question arises as to how participle raising is effected in LF, given that, in the input to LF, the auxiliary is in $AgrS^0$ and the participle in $AgrPart^0$. This is a problem familiar from analyses of Restructuring (on which, see §3.4). There are two options, as far as I can see: either the participle undergoes what has been called Long Head Movement (Rivero 1994 and references cited therein), skipping over the traces of the auxiliary, or it undergoes successive adjunction to traces (or copies, viz. Chomsky 1993). Kayne's (1989) ban on adjunction to traces may only thus hold for movement in the overt syntax.

A further technical problem concerns the status of Chomsky's (1993) Greed principle which would ban raising of the participle to Aux in the audible syntax. It is possible that Greed must be weakened, perhaps along the lines suggested in Lasnik (1993). One should also consider the possibility that Checking theory and the principle of Greed are too weak to capture the entire gamut of cases handled by Support theory.

10. The idea that the participle raises out of complement small clauses is not novel: it is proposed in Stowell (1991b); see also note 13).

11. Another auxiliary triggering participle incorporation in the conditional *byś*. Borsley and Rivero argue that unlike *(e)ś*, *byś* is not a phonetic clitic. It is suggestive to think of *byś* as being homophonous between a clitic and a full form, much like the Hebrew auxiliary.

12. In at least some cases of Restructuring—as from an embedded small clause or in causative constructions—the lower clause is a structurally deficient: it lacks a TP (see Guasti 1993 for discussion). In this respect, these small clauses are quite similar in structure to the clausal unit I have termed AgrPartP.

13. Alternatively, suppose that restructuring predicates never assign a θ-role and always trigger T-raising. The optionality of restructuring can then be taken to reflect the level of its application, S-structure or LF, just like participle raising in Hebrew.

Stowell (1991b) extends Rizzi's analysis of restructuring to English, arguing that English small clause predicates undergo Romance-like Restructuring in LF. I do not wish to dwell here on Stowell's arguments, but only to mention that, while Stowell could only speculate on why such restructuring takes place, the discussion here provides us with a reasonably principled explanation: small clause predicates restructure because their aspectual features must be associated with T^0, by LF. Stowell also claims that small clause predicates raise out of adjuncts, and he notes the serious problem this engenders from the standpoint of the ECP, since adjuncts constitute islands to movement. Suppose that adverbial adjuncts, as opposed to small clause complements, contain a CP layer and hence a TP. The Benoni predicate could then raise to T^0 within the adjunct clause, satisfying the need to associate Asp^0 with T^0 internally to the adjunct. See note 14, chapter 2. Not implausibly, this might extend to absolute constructions in Romance. Raising of Asp^0 to T^0 in semirelatives suggests that participle incorporation to the D^0 *ha-*, mentioned in chapter 2, note 13, is driven by the need to check aspectual features in D^0, requiring a revision of Siloni's (1994) analysis.

Guasti (1993) argues that at least some cases of restructuring apply in the overt syntax. The dialect of Hebrew mentioned in chapter 2, note 11, speakers of which accept a constituent order in which the auxiliary is raised to Comp, but the clausal subject, rather than occurring in a position between the auxiliary and the Benoni, follows the latter, can perhaps be analyzed as involving the syntactic participle-raising allowed in this dialect without CI.

CHAPTER FOUR

1. *ʔeyn* is also used to negate possessive constructions such as (i) which are not discussed in this work. For recent treatments, see Borer (1983), Hermon (1984), and Shlonsky (1987).

(i) **ʔeyn** l-i   kesef.
     neg   to-me money
     'I don't have money.'

2. This agreement pattern recalls the familiar pattern of subject-verb agreement in Classical and Standard Arabic, where a verb does not agree with a following subject but must agree with a preceding one. The substantial difference between the Hebrew *ʔeyn* construction and the Arabic paradigm is that clause-initial verbs in the latter manifest gender agreement and a singular (perhaps default) number affix, whereas clause-initial *ʔeyn* manifests no agreement whatsoever. The *ʔeyn* construction can be seen as giving rise to a "residual" VSO effect in much the same way as English subject-auxiliary inversion is a "residual" V2 effect; cf. Rizzi (1990b).

3. L. Haegeman (personal communication) observes that this argument is belied by the fact that there are negative concord grammars in which a specifier of NegP may cooccur with a negative adverb. A case in point is Québecois French, as discussed in Déprez (1996).

4. When *lo* follows *ʔeyn*, as in (i), the sentence is acceptable only under a contrastive reading of *lo*. See §2.3.1.

(i) **Ruti ʔeyn-a**   lo   yodaʕat   ʔet   ha-tšuva.
     Ruti neg-3FS   neg   know(BENONI)-FS   ACC   the-answer
     'Ruti doesn't <u>not</u> know the answer.'

5. I return to the discussion of *lo* incorporation in §5.3.1, contrasting it with the incorporation of negative heads in Palestinian Arabic.

6. In §7.5, I discuss why an expletive pro is unavailable in (4-7a)—that is, why the following representation is illicit.

(i) ***pro ʔeyn-a   Ruti yodaʕat   ʔet   ha-tšuva.**
     pro   neg-3FS   Ruti know(BENONI)-FS   ACC   the-answer
     'Ruti does not know the answer.'

7. Hebrew provides few straightforward diagnostics to distinguish embedded topics from embedded (contrastive) focus. For example, in lacks the Italian-type *Clitic left Dislocation* construction (see Cinque 1990). I will assume that fronted topics and fronted foci are both positioned in the Comp layer, leaving open the question of the internal structure of CP.

8. See Shlonsky (1990) for further examples concerning the consumption of raw eggplants, and Crawford and Poutaraska (1985:44-45) for empirical justification.

9. Negative imperatives cooccur with *ʔeyn*, as in (i).

(i) **ʔeyn** lə-ʕašen   ba-sifriya.
     neg   to-smoke   in-the-library
     'It is forbidden to smoke in the library.'

Like many languages, Hebrew has two imperative forms, one that is morphologically derived from the future tense, and another that utilizes the nonfinite verb form. Rather than an expression of negation, *ʔeyn* in (i) has the force of a root modal. It basically means 'It is forbidden to smoke in the library.' At this point, I do not know how to handle such cases.

10. This genre of analyses has been explicitly propounded for VSO orders by numerous authors since it was first proposed in Emonds (1979). See Woolford (1991) for a recent discussion of VSO-hood in a variety of languages, McCloskey (1991) on Irish, and Benmamoun (1992), Fassi-Fehri (1993), Mohammed (1990), and Ouhalla (1993a) on Standard Arabic.

The earliest work on subject "inversion" in Romance distinguished "free" inversion from what I term Triggered Inversion (chapter 8). The former was thought to involve subject lowering and the latter V-Raising. See, e.g., Rizzi (1982), Jaeggli (1982), Shlonsky (1987), and Torrego (1984), among many others.

11. Spec/AgrPart is not a Case position, since PRO can occur there. See the discussion of adjunct small clauses in §2.3.3.

12. Chomsky (1993) claims that English lacks Spec/T. A more nuanced view has been elaborated by Jonas and Bobalijk (1993) and adopted in Chomsky (1994). Jonas and Bobalijk argue that Spec/T is projected in the syntax only when Spec/AgrO is projected. They point to a correlation between the existence of transitive expletive constructions, where an indefinite subject occurs in Spec/T and Object Shift (where the direct object precedes the verb). Hebrew is clearly an exception to that generalization, since it lacks object shift. Finnish may also be an exception since it has transitive expletive constructions, but no Icelandic-like object Shift. See Holmberg and Nikanne (1994).

13. The class of intrinsic head governors—namely X_{lex}, Agr, and T—is not a natural class. A suggestion that comes to mind, prompted by Chomsky's checking theory, is that the presence of Agr features renders a head a proper head governor for traces. In this theory, Agr features occur on two heads: once on the Agr head itself, and once on the head that checks those features. Thus, lexical heads can be taken to be head governors in virtue of possessing Agr features. T^0 is also endowed with Agr, since it either raises to $AgrS^0$ for checking or incorporates an Agr-bearing verb. If this approach is adopted, some interesting questions arise with respect to the proper formulation of the ECP and the distribution of functions between the two requirements of head government and antecedent government. See Moro (1993a) for some interesting developments.

14. Notice, moreover, that if (4-47) and (4-52) are analyzed on a par with (4-51), then there literally are no such things as a "that-trace effect" or a "que-qui rule" (Pesetsky 1982). These are but manifestations of a more general phenomenon which is not restricted to complementizers.

15. The visible alternation in the position of the subject in the *ʔeyn* construction suggests a certain modification of Rizzi's theory. In his system, *qui* is a lexical variant of *que*, endowed with Agr. However, the *ʔeyn* construction shows that the manifestation of Agr on Neg^0 leads to the projection of an AgrSP to the head of which Neg^0 is incorporated and to the Spec of which the subject is raised.

Generalizing the idea that inflectional morphology must be checked in an appropriate inflectional head leads us to argue that if C^0 can be endowed with Agr, then there must also be an Agr projection in the CP system where these Agr features may be checked. The proposal that CP contains an Agr projection is developed in Shlonsky (1994b) and utilized to explain the distribution of complementizer agreement and subject clitics in West Flemish.

16. There is a slight technical difficulty here since literally speaking, t_k, the trace of Neg^0, is not itself endowed with Agr features. A plausible solution is to invoke the idea that in order for Neg^0 to be able to raise to $AgrS^0$ it must itself have abstract AgrS features to check.

17. As pointed out by a reviewer, the analysis of wh in situ from under *ʔeyn* (and of QR in the following subsection) pose a serious challenge to the view of head government developed in Aoun, Hornstein, Lightfoot, and Weinberg (1987).

18. Example (i) is marginally acceptable, but only under a group or referential interpretation of the quantifier.

(i)   ??eyn   kol   ha-studentim   yodʕim   ʔet   ha-tšuva.
    neg   all   the-students   know(BENONI)-MPL   ACC   the-answer
    'It is not the case that all the students know the answer.'

When a quantificational reading is forced, for example, when there is a bound pronominal DP c-commanded by the subject quantifier, it can no longer appear under *ʔeyn*. Example (ii) patterns with (4-56a) and not with (i).

(ii)   *ʔeyn   kol   ha-studentim$_i$ xošvim   še   hem$_i$ intiligentim.
    neg   all   the-students   think(BENONI)-MPL   that   they   intelligent
    'It is not the case that all the students think they are intelligent.'

I am grateful to G. Lanconi for bringing up the question of the status of (i).

19. This means that pace, e.g., Kroch (1974), quantifiers may not be interpreted in situ. If *kol student* 'every student' in (4-56) could be interpreted in its S-structure position, on the basis, say, of its c-command domain at that level, then the sentence would not be ungrammatical, since no empty category in need of head government would be created, but only admit of a narrow scope interpretation of the quantifier.

20. One is now led to wonder about the grammaticality of (ia), or its French equivalent in (ib).

(i)   a. I   think   that   everyone   knows   the   answer.

    b. Je   pense   que   tout le monde   connaît la   réponse.

As noted in Moro (1993a), sentences such as (ia,b) pose a problem for Rizzi's (1990a) version of the ECP in which *that* and, similarly, *que* are not proper head governors. Rizzi's system seems to have the undesirable consequence of ruling out QR as a violation of the ECP.

A possibility that comes to mind is to relate the ungrammaticality of QR in (ia,b) to the contrast in (ii).

(ii)   a. ?Who thinks that who left?

    b. *Who do you think that left?

The fact in need of explanation in both (i) and (iia) is that, while the presence of *that* and *que* block proper government of a subject trace formed in the overt syntax, they are compatible with a trace formed in LF.

Lasnik and Saito (1992) propose a plausible account. Their idea is that *that* may delete in LF allowing Infl (AgrS^0) to raise to C^0. (Their proposal that Infl may also adjoin to IP in, for example, *everyone left*, can be reinterpreted to mean that Infl raises to a head position within the CP layer, lower than the canonical position of complementizers. If QR does not involve adjunction to IP, but raising into the specifier position of a Topic-like projection within the CP layer, the raised Infl could occpy the head of that projection.) Raising of AgrS^0 to C^0 provides a proper governor for the subject trace. The LF-representation of (ia) and (iia) would therefore be as in (iiia,b).

(iii)   a. I think [$_{CP}$ knows$_{[+AGR]}$ [$_{AgrsP}$ everyone$_i$ [$_{AgrsP}$ t$_i$ the answer . . .]]]

    b. Who thinks [$_{CP}$ who$_i$ left$_{[+AGR]}$ [$_{AgrsP}$ t$_i$ . . .]]

Note that only a semantically inert C^0 may delete in LF. Example (iv) is ungrammatical even under the assumption that *whether* is in Spec/C, since C^0, in this case, is marked [+wh] and its deletion would be irrecoverable.

(iv) *John wonders whether who left?

In the case of quantifiers under *ʔeyn*, we can now see that the only way that the system would allow for the trace of QR to be head-governed is if *ʔeyn* were deletable in LF and its position could be filled by an appropriate head governor. However, *ʔeyn* is not semantically inert and therefore undeletable, patterning in this respect with a [+wh] C^0. Alternatively, if QR is a form of topicalization, involving substitution rather than adjunction, QR under *ʔeyn* is ruled out due to the absence of Topic or Topic-like projections between NegP and TP.

Example (iiib) requires further comment, since it contrasts with the ill-formed (v), where AgrS^0, embedded in the auxiliary verb *do*, is raised to C^0 in the overt syntax.

(v) *Who did leave?

If AgrS^0 were free to move to an empty C^0, (v) should be acceptable. Rizzi (1991) argues that movement of the inflected verb to C^0 is not required in cases of subject extraction, because the Wh-Criterion may be satisfied representationally. Phonetically null C^0 is an Agr coindexed with *who*. *Who* is coindexed with its trace and the latter with AgrS^0, which contains the *wh* feature. If Rizzi is correct, then (v) violates Economy, since the satisfaction of the Wh-Criterion representationally is more economical then its satisfaction through movement.

There is rather robust evidence, however, that even when permitted by Economy, an AgrS^0 raised to Comp cannot license a subject trace (see also McCloskey 1992). Consider (vi).

(vi) *who$_i$ do you think that never in his life would t$_i$ travel to Paris?

The cases where Infl→Comp does seem to provide head government for a subject trace all involve LF movement. Let us tentatively suggest, then, that LF raising of AgrS^0 to C^0 can license a trace, while similar raising at S-structure does not. One can think of this idea in the following terms: suppose that S-structure raising of AgrS^0 invariably involves adjunction to C^0. The Government Transparencey Corollary of Baker (1985) allows for the complex head to govern all the positions governed by AgrS in its original position. However, no new government possibilities are created. Specifically, the complex head does not become a proper head governor for the subject trace. When occurring in LF, take AgrS^0 raising to involve substitution into C^0, rather than adjunction. Substitution into C^0 permits a recon-figuration of the government domains because it does not involve incorporation in Baker's sense. Thus, in LF, a raised AgrS^0 can and does head-govern a subject trace.

CHAPTER FIVE

1. In §7.4.2, we shall see that a generic interpretation is available to an arbitrary pro under *ʔeyn*. Assuming that the mechanism by which a generic interpretation is assigned is the same for both indefinite subjects of individual level predicates and generic pro, then the problem is why a bare plural cannot occur within the scope of a generic operator under *ʔeyn*, while pro may do so. I leave this matter open.

2. Readers with some familiarity with Hebrew syntax might consider the idea of treating *beʒ* as the covert variant of *yeš*—namely, the verbal particle that occurs in affirmative existential/locative (as well as possessive) sentences. (For a discussion of *yeš*, see Borer 1983, Hermon 1984, and Shlonsky 1987.) *Yeš* has sometimes been treated as simply the positive counterpart of *ʔeyn* (see, e.g., Borer 1983). Clearly this cannot be the case if *ʔeyn* is the head of NegP. Borer is in fact led to argues that there are two *ʔeyn*s in Hebrew, a negative existential verb, or verboid, and a clausal negator. Much perspicuity can be gained, I believe, by treating *ʔeyn* uniformly as a negative head and attributing the existential import of, say, (1b) to other components of the construction.

In affirmative existential/locative sentences, *yeš* is obligatory, imposing a definiteness restriction on its subject and recapitulating the extraction pattern of (6) and (7). Consider the sentences in (i)–(iv).

(i) a. yeš yladim   ba-gina.
    be children in-the-garden
    'There are children in the garden.'

    b. *yeš ha-yladim   ba-gina.
    be the-children in-the-garden
    'There are the children in the garden.'

(ii) a. ma   yeš ba-gina?
    what be in-the-garden
    'What is there in the garden?'

    b. *mi   yeš ba-gina?
    who be in-the-garden
    'Who is there in the garden?'

(iii) a. yeš harbe   yladim   ba-gina.
    be many children in-the-garden
    'There are many children in the garden.'

    b. *yeš kol   yeled ba-gina.
    be every child in-the-garden
    'There is every child in the garden.'

(iv) a. yeš <u>yladim</u>   ba-gina.
    be <u>children</u> in-the-garden
    'There are <u>CHILDREN</u> in the garden.'

    b. *yeš <u>ha-yladim</u>   ba-gina.
    be <u>the-children</u> in-the-garden
    '<u>The children</u> are in the garden.'

Yeš cannot be phonetically realized as in the presence of *ʔeyn*, as (v) shows. Yet the evidence does seem to suggest the presence of the verb 'be' in such sentences. (Ben-Shoshan's Hebrew dictionary gives some examples of the sequence *ʔeyn > yeš* from poetry, but there are no examples attesting to the opposite order. This is consistent with the suggestion in this note.)

(v) a. *yeš ʔeyn yladim   ba-gina.
    be NEG children in-the-garden

    b. ʔeyn yeš yladim   ba-gina.
    NEG be children in-the-garden

There is thus some plausibility to the view that *be* has two surface realizations, *yeš* and [Ø].

3. If the argument of be_3 is a small clause containing the locative phrase as a predicate, as in Stowell (1978), then Belletti's analysis must be modified to allow partitive case to be assigned across a (small) clausal boundary (see Lasnik 1992 and Shlonsky 1987). Belletti's original account can be maintained if the postverbal subject is a direct argument of be_3 and the locative phrase is an adjunct (see Moro 1993b).

4. The sentences in (11) are slightly odd. If the wh-expression *ma* 'what' is replaced with one requesting an answer in the form of a specific indefinite DP, such as *ʔeize hafgana* 'which demonstration', this oddity disappears.

5. Agr^0 elements do not have subcategorization frames, as I have argued elsewhere in this work. It follows that they are not endowed with morphological subcategorization frames. Hence, they only host incorporation through adjunction. I assume that in Hebrew only nonlexical and clitic heads can be adjoined to.

6. I am assuming here that auxiliaries cannot procrastinate movement. This seems to be a rather solid cross-linguistic generalization. See Chomsky (1993) for one explanation. See also note 9.

7. The question arises as to why the null auxiliary can move independently to T^0 and $AgrS^0$ *only* when a predicate nominal is present in the structure. Put differently, what rules out precisely the same derivation when a Benoni predicate is generated? A plausible answer is that raising the auxiliary independently is only possible if, indeed, there is a functional head higher in the structure which can provide it with lexical support. In Benoni sentences, there is no such head, since T^0 and $AgrS^0$ are not lexicalized. The one exception to this, namely Neg^0, is considered later in this chapter.

8. Example (5-17) is acceptable when the subject is topicalized and *hi* is not Pron, but a subject resumptive pronoun. When the subject is a quantifier phrase, as in (i), its topicalization yields an ungrammatical output.

(i) ?af ?axat hi   ?eyn-a   manhigat ha-kita.
   no one   pron-3FS   neg-3FS   leader   the-class
   'No one is the leader of the class.' *lit.* 'No one, she is the leader of the class.'

9. The question arises as to why the auxiliary, incorporated to *lo*, may procrastinate movement to AgrS^0, contrary to the claim made in note 6. I would like to suggest that the incapability to procrastinate holds of bare auxiliaries and auxiliaries incorporated into nonlexicalized functional heads. If Chomsky (1993) is right in arguing that auxiliaries are deleted in LF or are otherwise invisible to LF movement, then we might say that incorporation of an auxiliary to a lexicalized head—for example, to *lo*—protects it, as it were, from deletion and renders it visible to LF operations.

In chapter 3, §3.2, it was argued that the null auxiliary in Benoni present-tense sentences is lexically supported by the Benoni verb that incorporates into it. The discussion of Pron in the present chapter has led me to suggest that the null auxiliary can be lexically supported by raising to AgrS^0 and adjunction to Pron, or by adjunction to *lo* in Neg^0. The shared features of V (or, more precisely, AgrPart^0), AgrS^0, and Neg^0 is that they are all "verbal," or V-related heads. Auxiliary support, whether involving CI or raising of the auxiliary itself, thus bears the hallmarks of syntactically constrained head movement. In this respect, this process must be distinguished from auxiliary-cliticization in Slavic (Polish, for example; see Borsley and Rivero 1994), where "support" often takes the form of adjacency to any phonologically strong constituent.

CHAPTER SIX

1. Since they add nothing to the discussion, I omit morphological Case marking in the Arabic examples except in cases where users require them. In this, I follow the practice of many contemporary editors.

2. Ayoub contends that the semantic distinction between what Western grammarians label "moods,"—that is, indicative, subjunctive, and jussive—is somehow neutralized under negation; "Les trois désinences correspondent à l'indicatif " (1995). I will henceforth omit the glosses for mood and put aside the question of why these distinctions are nevertheless maintained morphologically.

3. Examples (6-8a,c) are from Fassi-Fehri (1993:147–148), where other, more complex examples are given. In particular, the perfect form can appear under an auxiliary, and the sentence is interpreted as a pluperfect. This is illustrated in (i). Note the presence of the particle *qad* in (i), which somehow licenses the perfect form in a position subordinated to the auxiliary. I put such examples aside.

(i) kaana   ?al-walad qad   lasiba.
   be(PERF)-3MS   the boy   PARTICLE   play(PERF)-3MS
   'The boy had been playing.'

4. In §10.3.3, I tentatively suggest that the participial Benoni is endowed with covert person features (see, in particular, chapter 10, note 11).

5. "The most revolutionary change between Biblical Hebrew and Mishnaic Hebrew occurred in the area of the tenses and moods. Here the verb was entirely reorganized. The short imperfect lost its aspectual function, now denoting future action. . . The perfect now denotes only past action; the participle is employed to denote present or future action" (Kutscher 1982), §218. For discussion of Mishnaic (postbiblical Palestinian) Hebrew, see Segal (1927); for a comparison of biblical and postbiblical Hebrew, see Bendavid (1971, in Hebrew).

It is interesting, in this context, to note that the biblical Hebrew imperfect, which like its Arabic counterpart expresses nonpast tense, can be transformed into a past tense verb when preceded by a particle called the "conversive *waw*." Thus, *wa-yixtov* means 'he wrote' and has the same tense specification as *katav*, whereas *yixtov* means 'he writes / will write'. This suggests that the imperfect form in biblical Hebrew, like its counterpart in Arabic, is unmarked for tense.

6. In other respects, too, Arabic is more conservative than Hebrew: it has overt Case marking, dual number, and a verbal diathesis encoding a rich system of aspect. All three are missing in Modern Hebrew and the first two are also absent in the colloquial dialects.

7. See Benmamoun (1994) and Moutaouakil (1991) for a discussion of this adjacency effect.

8. See Rizzi (1995) for the view that Do-Support in English proceeds in a similar fashion: *do* is a base-generated auxiliary with T and (unlike the Arabic cases, also with AgrS features). Neg features are base-generated on T^0 and T^0 (which comes to host *do*) raises to Neg^0 to meet the Negative Criterion in, for example:

John did not do this.

9. The question arises as to why incorporation of T^0 to Neg^0 in Arabic or of T^0 to Hebrew *lo* do not take the form of left adjunction, contrary to Hebrew CI. The answer is to be found precisely in the different type of head incorporation involved in the two cases. When T^0 incorporates to Neg^0, it undergoes *substitution* into a subcategorization slot. CI, on the other hand, is a case of adjunction of the Benoni to the auxiliary. The basic generalization is that adjunction of X^0 to Y^0 yields the linear sequence x^y while subsitution of X^0 to Y^0 is realized as y^x. In the appendix, we shall see that this generalization can account for a variety of incorporations in Semitic.

10. If V_{IMPERF} is incorporated to T^0, T^0 to Neg^0, and Neg^0 to $AgrS^0$, then it follows that the verb is brought up to $AgrS^0$ through a series of head incorporations. Why, then, is a verb in the perfect form unable to undergo these processess, raising up to $AgrS^0$ and checking its features with those of $AgrS^0$? If such a derivation were licit, we would be derprived of an explanation of why *laa* cannot occur with perfect verbs. Put more generally, such a derivation would render the barrier status of *laa* inconsequential.

Recall that T^0 raising to *laa* is driven by the need to raise the neg features of T^0 to a position where these features are in a Spec-head configuration with a negative operator. The impossibility of raising to Neg^0 a T^0 which hosts a verb in the perfect can be due to the absence of neg features on the T^0 associated with the perfect form. In this way of seeing things, the inability of the perfect verb to occur under *laa* is indeed not due to the barrier status of *laa*.

In order to maintain an ECP-based explanation, the following possibilities suggest themselves. First, one might suppose that even if the derivation were licit, there would be two measures of AgrS features to be checked: those of the verb (in the perfect form), and those of *laa*. One might plausibly assume that one measure would remain unchecked, if checking is carried out on a one to one basis.

Alternatively, one might assume that a head substituted into a subcategorization slot is not visible for checking (perhaps because it occupies an X^{-1} position (cf. Roberts 1993). Thus, even if T^0 is substituted into the slot on Neg^0, and Neg^0 adjoins to $AgrS^0$, the features of the verb are not accessible to checking. If this approach is adopted, one must explain why substitution of a verb into the Hebrew negative head *lo* does not block checking of the verb's AgrS features. Here, appeal can be made to an independent difference between *lo* and *laa*. The latter is not a clitic. Take this to mean that *laa* is an X^0, so that substitution into its subcategorization frame takes the form of movement into an X^{-1} position. Because *lo*, on the other hand, is itself an X^{-1} element, the subcategorization slot is an X^0 position.

11. Only imperfectives but not active participles can occur in sentences negated by *laa*, as shown by the ungrammaticality of (i). One is led to think that *laa* can only negate verbal categories, while *laysa* negates nonverbal ones.

(i) *Mona laa ḍaaribatan   Zayd.*
   Mona   neg   hit(BENONI)-FS   Zayd
   'Mona is not hitting Zayd.'

12. Many traditional descriptions of Arabic treat preverbal subjects as topics. Let us suppose that this is in fact the case and that preverbal subjects are not in Spec/AgrSP at S-structure, but in a higher Comp-like position. We must now ask why Topicalization cannot move the subject directly from Spec/TP, but must do it stepwise via Spec/AgrSP. (This is the interpretation I would like to give to the obligatoriness of agreement in S > V orders in Arabic, a well-known fact.)

If a subject were topicalized from its Case position in Spec/TP, its trace would not be properly head-governed, under the assumptions of the present work, since the closest head c-commanding would be C^0 or Top^0, as shown in (i).

(i)

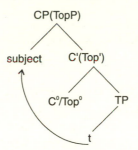

The suggestion that comes to mind is that, whenever a subject is topicalized, AgrSP is projected so as to provide an appropriate head governor for the trace in Spec/TP. See §4.8 for discussion of the role of Agr in the theory of head government.

13. See, however, Ouhalla (1993b) for the view that *maa* spells out focus as well as negation features.

PART II

1. Hebrew differs from a typical null-subject language in yet another respect: it does not allow subjects to be extracted directly from their VP-internal position, even from configurations in which subjects *are* licensed in that position (Free Inversion). I have dealt with this fact in Shlonsky (1990) under somewhat different assumptions.

CHAPTER SEVEN

1. See, however, Cardinaletti (1994b) for a proposal regarding the position of subject pro in Italian.

2. The literature on Null Subjects is immense. Some of the more familiar works are Borer (1986), Chomsky (1981), Huang (1984), Jaeggli (1982), Perlmutter (1971), Rizzi (1982), Roberge (1990), Safir (1985), and Travis (1984), as well as the other works cited in this chapter.

3. It is of anecdotal interest that in Palestinian Arabic the subject of climatological verbs is not a (null) pronoun, but the expression 'the universe', as in (i).

(i)   l-dinya   bitšit.
     the-universe   rains
     'It rains.'

4. French has null objects and prepositional objects, as in (ia,b). Italian has null subjects and objects, as in (ii).

(i) a. Ceci amène *pro* à conclure   que . . .   b. Il a   diné   avec *pro*.
     this leads   to conclude that   *he has eaten with*
     'This leads one to conclude that . . .'   'He dined with them.'

(ii) a. *pro* fuma.   b. Questo conduce pro a concludere che . . .
       smokes   *this   leads   to conclude   that*
       'He smokes.'   'This leads one to conclude that . . .'

5. These facts were first discussed in Borer (1980). See also the following works, on which I draw heavily in the ensuing discussion: Borer (1983, 1986, and 1989b), Doron (1983), Ritter, (1995), and Shlonsky (1987).

6. Borer (1989b) shows that pro can occur with third person inflection, when it is c-commanded by a controlling DP in the matrix clause, as in (i). Pro in (i) can be coreferential with any of the two matrix DPs, but cannot have independent reference.

(i) Tal$_i$?amar   lə-?itamar$_j$ še-   pro$_{i/j/*k}$ ya cli?ax.
     Tal say(PAST)-3MS to-Itamar   that-   3MS-succeed(FUT)
     'Tal said to Itamar that he, Tal or Itamar, will succeed.'

Noting that this option is only available when the licensing I^0 is past or future, and is unavailable when the subordinate verb is in the Benoni, Borer concludes that the third person marker in Hebrew is anaphoric, thus requiring binding by the higher DP. How this binding is effected is hard to say. It is an atypical A-binding relationship since embedded topics or foci and wh-elements seem to block it, as in (ii).

(ii) a. *Tal ?amar   lə-?itamar$_j$ še-   ba-bxinot   pro$_{*i/*j/*k}$
       Tal   say(PAST)-3MS to-Itamar   that- in-the-exams

     yacli/ax.
     3MS-succeed(FUT)
     'Tal said to Itamar that in the exams, he will succeed.'

   b. ??Tal$_i$ ša?al   ?et   ?itamar matai pro$_{i/*j/*k}$ ya cli?ax.
     Tal   ask(PAST)-3MS ACC   Itamar when   3MS-succeed(FUT)
     'Tal asked Itamar when he will succeed.'

There is clearly some sort of anaphoric dependency here, but the blocking effect induced by the interference of A′ elements is at odds with Borer's idea that pro is (A)-bound in these contexts. The generalization suggesting itself is that pro must be bound by the closest A′-antecedent. In the absence of one, pro must be A-bound.

7. Moreover, if the absence of an affix could not be taken to be a distinctive feature, we would be led to the absurd consequence that the Hebrew Benoni forms arguably have no number specification, since they lack an overt singular (masculine) affix. See the discussion surrounding the examples in (7-18).

8. See §1.3.2 for a discussion of the different aspectual and temporal specifications of the these forms in Arabic.

9. Some speakers prefer the nonnull subject version of (7-17b), with the subject pronoun appearing as an enclitic on the complementizer, as in (i).

(i)   fakkar t   ?inn-ha   katb at   riwaaye.
think(PERF)-1S   that-2FS   write(PERF)-3FS   story
'I thought that she wrote a story.'

These speakers attribute the text example with the null subject to a more colloquial register. For a discussion of subject clitics in Palestinian Arabic, see §9.3 and §9.4.3.3.

10. The fact that only five out of the six forms are discretely represented in Palestinian suggests that a one-to-one correspondence between persons and affixes is not a necessary condition for the identification of referential pro. What makes an inflectional paradigm "rich"—what the the threshhold of richness is that such a paradigm must go beyond in order for referential pro to be identified—is a question that remains to be answered. See Jaeggli and Safir (1989), for a recent proposal.

Note that the Palestinian paradigm is formally equivalent to that of Rumanian and Icelandic (cf. Platzack 1987), in that there is a syncretic form expressing two persons. While Rumanian is a robust null subject language, Icelandic does not admit referential pro, but only the nonreferential varieties. The conjugation of Italian *essere* 'be' also gives rise to a single syncretism. More data must be collected to determine whether the threshold of identifiability of a null subject is up to a single syncretism.

11. My informants on Palestinian Arabic differ in their judgments from those who informed Kenstowicz (1989). In that article, as we recall, Palestinian Arabic was argued to be nonnull subject. At my request, M. Kenstowicz has reconfirmed those judgments with his informants. One might appeal to regional dialectal differences to account for this disparity (my informants are from northern Palestine; his were predominantly from the center and south). Lebanese Arabic patterns with the variety of Palestinian described in this work, as shown in Aoun, Benmamoun, and Sportiche (1994). See also their note 6.

12. Alternatively, take [person] to be an inflectional affix in need of lexical support, implemented by raising Num^0 to D^0.

13. It has been argued that Romance clitics, in particular direct object clitics, such as *le* in *je le mange* 'I eat it' are D^0 heads (see, e.g., Cardinaletti 1994a and Uriagereka 1995). This explains their homophony with definite determiners. Uriagereka takes the structure of a clitic to be as in (i). (In clitic-doubling constructions, the doubled DP is in Spec/D in this approach).

(i)

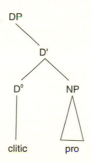

Cliticization of the determiner obtains when D^0 is incorporated to $AgrS^0$. The similarity between (i) and the structure Ritter proposes for third person pronouns in Hebrew is worth noting. Unlike a Romance clitic, however, [person] is not licensed by incorporation to the clausal Agr, but must be sanctioned internally to the DP projection. Let us suppose, with Rizzi (1993), that the drive for Romance cliticization, that is, of the incorporation of D^0 to $AgrS^0$, is that a clitic D^0 has verbal features (in the sense of Chomsky 1993) which it must check with an appropriate verbal head. A nonclitic D^0—a definite determiner—has nominal features which it checks with a nominal head. In this way of seeing things, Hebrew [person] is not a V-related but an N-related head. Indeed, the Semitic languages in general lack Romance-like clitics, perhaps because they lack V-related D^0 heads. For more discussion, see chapter 9.

14. If French pronouns can be Num^0 (as well as a D^0) heads, we can perhaps draw an analogy between the Hebrew demonstratives in (7-21), formed by raising Num^0 to a D^0 containing the determiner, and the French series, consisting of the D^0 form *ce* and a pronoun: *celui, celle, ceux, celles*. Interestingly, only the tonic form of the pronoun can appear here; forms such as *ce(i)l* are excluded. This might have to do with the fact that *il* is a clitic and must be attached to a verbal head (e.g., $AgrS^0$). The presence of a determiner such as *ce* would then block cliticization (i.e., head movement) of *il* out of DP.

In a number of ergative languages, the split between an ergative/absolutive and an accusative/nominative case marking system bifurcates the pronominal system (Silverstein 1986). Thus, in, for example, Punjabi, first and second person subject pronouns block ergativity (Mahajan 1994). It is tempting to speculate that this phenomenon and the *person split* in the distribution of Hebrew null subjects are related. I will not pursue the matter here. See Mahajan (1994) for some suggestions.

15. Rizzi argues that arbitrary pro in object position is assigned the role *arb* by its governing verb and that θ-role assignment *formally licenses* pro in the sense of (7-10a). Since (7-10a) and (7-10b) are linked, in Rizzi's view, in that the licensing head is also the identifying head, it follows that an arbitrary object pro must be both θ-marked and Case-marked by the verb. The two are dissociated in the case of subjects of small clause complements: these are indeed Case-marked by the matrix verb, but they are θ-marked by the small clause predicate, predicting that an arbitrary pro cannot occur in the subject position of small clauses. This turns out to be only partially true: a small clause subject can be an arbitrary pro if two conditions are met: the small clause predicate undergoes reanalysis with the matrix verb, and the small clause subject is an *affected* theme (in the sense of Anderson 1979) of the reanalyzed complex. For further discussion see the cited work.

The claim that the assigner of the θ-role and the Case assigner must be the same head cannot be maintained in its original formulation if Case assignment—accusative Case included—is always implemented in a Spec-head configuration with an Agr head ($AgrO^0$), as Chomsky (1991) proposes. Needless to say, the empirical force of Rizzi's approach and, in particular, the analysis of pro_{arb} small clause subjects is lost under current assumptions about Case theory. (See also the text discussion following the example in [7-10] as well as Cardinaletti and Guasti 1991)

A more serious problem for this approach concerns arbitrary pro in subject position, since the θ-marker and the Case assigner are dissociated, even under a more traditional approach to Case assignment. Belletti and Rizzi (1988) suggest that Infl (the feature identifier) serves to also transmit the relevant θ-role to the subject, thus unifying licensing and identification under a single head. Yet this idea is practically unstatable, given the widely held assumption that Spec/I is not a θ-position. As Chomsky has often remarked, this is a typical state of affairs: theoretical advances frequently entail a loss of empirical coverage. Authier (1989) pursues a different path and argues that arbitrary pro in object position has the status of a variable bound by a nonrestrictive operator, in the sense of Lewis (1975) and Heim (1982). But see Delfitto (1990) for an implicit critique. It is not inconceivable that the two approaches can be reconciled, and I will indeed suggest a mixed approach in §7.4.2. I put these matters aside in the text discussion since my concern is with the identification of φ-features which I take pro_{arb} to be endowed with, independent of other considerations.

16. Pro$_{arb}$ is typically plural in Hebrew, as in the text example in (7-30b). With some predicates, however, it is singular.

(i) carix   la-ʕavod.
     must   to-work
     'One has to work.'

Whatever the factor that determines the number specifiction of pro$_{arb}$, it has little or no impact on the system proposed since [plural] or [singular] are φ-features and hence must be identified by an appropriately inflected Agr.

What rules out a representation such as in (ii), where *hu*, a Num^0 element, occurs in a DP whose head contains *arb* or *atmosphere*? Put differently, why can *hu*, or, for that matter, any overt personal pronoun, never be interpreted as quasi referential?

(ii)

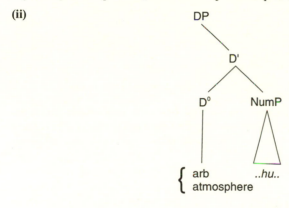

Overt personal pronouns only occur either as the second component of demonstrative pronouns, in which case they are complements of the definite article *ha-*, or as complements of the abstract feature [person] in D^0. In the latter case, we have argued that Num^0 incorporates to D^0. There are firm grounds to believe that Num^0 (or AgrGen^0—see Siloni 1994)—also incorporates to D^0 when the latter contains *ha-*. When D^0 contains the features making up, say, *arb*, Num^0 does not incorporate to it, as I have argued. The empirical generalization which excludes (ii), is, therefore (iii).

(iii) A lexical Num^0 must incorporate to D^0.

This can be interepreted in Checking-theoretic terms: a lexical Num^0 must check its head features with an apprporiate head internally to DP. The definite determiner *ha-* and [person] are endowed with the relevant features; *arb* and *atmosphere* are not. The latter are only compatible, therefore, with a nonlexical Num^0—that is, with pro.

17. In some subdialects of Hebrew, sentences such as those in (7-34) can be rendered with the verb in the masculine singular form (viz. e.g. Hermon 1984). These dialects are reminiscent of the general situation in Standard Arabic.

18. Ze, in the text examples, should be distinguished from demonstrative *ze* in such examples as (i), as well as from the *ze* which occurs as a subject of copular constructions such as (ii). In the latter guise, *ze* has feminine and plural counterparts, *zot* and *ele/elu*, respectively.

(i) ze   kaše   lə-ʔaxila.   (ii) zot   šgiʔa.
     this   difficult   to-eating   *this   mistake*
     'This is difficult to eat.'   'This is a mistake.'

19. Chomsky (1991) modifies his analysis of expletives somewhat and argues that the associate does not eliminate the expletive by replacing it, but rather that the expletive is an LF-clitic which adjoins to the associate in Spec/AgrS after the latter has raised to that position.

20. Some factors contribute to an amelioration of sentences such as (7-47). When the intraposed clause (or some part within it) receives contrastive stress and is interpreted as a focus, *ze* is optional, as in (i).

(i) <u>li-lmod</u>   polanit (ze) kaše   (ʔaval šave   ʔet   ha-maʔamac).
     to-learn   Polish (it) difficult (but   worth   ACC   the-effort).
     'To <u>learn</u> Polish is difficult (but worth the effort).'

Possibly, when the postverbal subject is moved to a focus position in the Comp domain, and is not topicalized, it can do so from a clause with a null expletive subject, as well as from a clause with *ze* as subject. (Thanks to L. Rizzi for pointing out this option.)

Another factor contributing to an amelioration of (7-47) is the "heaviness" of the predicate: (ii) is substantially better than (7-47).

(ii) ?li-lmod polanit (ze) meʔod kaše.
      to-learn   Polish (it) very   difficult
      'To learn Polish is very difficult.'

Finally, some verbs, such as *le-hoxiax* 'to prove', *le-harʔot* 'to indicate', and *lešaxneʕa* 'to persuade' do not seem to require *ze* at all, as shown in (iii). See Emonds (1976: 123) for some discussion of the problem raised by verbs with sentential subjects and objects in English and Zaring (1994) on similar data from French.

(iii) še   Dani ʔaxal xacilim   lo   mevušalim moxiʔax še-   hu metoraf.
       that Dani ate   eggplants not cooked   proves   that- he mad
       'That Dani ate raw eggplants proves that he is mad.'

21. Hazout's arguments are quite similar to those in Bennis's (1986) study of Dutch expletives and Zaring's (1994) of French. See also Grange and Haegeman (1992) on West Flemish, and Vikner (1995) for a detailed discussion of the position of postverbal "subject" clauses.

22. Even in English, where clausal subjects occur without a pronoun such as *ze*, it is not implausible that they are dependent on the presence of a CP layer in the clause. The contrast in (i), which illustrates the exclusion of "sentential subjects" from small clauses, can be taken to mean that the intraposed clause is not in subject position but in CP, the latter being absent in small clauses.

(i) a. That John is a good linguist is obvious

     b. *I consider that John is a good linguist obvious.

Similarly, if complements to causative verbs lack a CP layer, as argued in Guasti (1993), then the absence of embedded topics can be accounted for in a similar vein.

(ii) a. I made [John eat an apple] / [John believe that the earth is round].

      b. *I made [an apple John eat] / [that the earth is square John believe].

The grammaticality of (iii), however, demonstrates that the extraposed clause is not topicalized in LF. If it were, we would expect it to have the same grammaticality status as (7-42b).

(iii) I consider it obvious that John is a good linguist.

Since (iii) is unquestionably grammatical, it might be better analyzed on par with (7-43). This would then imply that English *it* in extraposition contexts is not or does not have to be an expletive but may, like Hebrew *ze*, be analyzed as a referential pronoun. I leave this and related matters for further research.

23. T. Siloni (personal communication) points out that (i) is an acceptable variant of (7-52).

(i) li-lmod   polanit   ?eyn   ze kaše.
to-learn   Polish   neg   it difficult
'It isn't difficult to learn Polish.'

In (i), the CP appears to the left of NegP. Recall that clauses with a bare *?eyn* lack an AgrSP layer but may, of course, be embedded under C⁰. I take the structure of (i) to be as in (ii), where the clausal subject is topicalized to the matrix CP.

(ii)

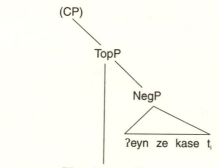

(CP)

TopP

NegP

?eyn ze kase t$_i$

[lilmod polanit]$_i$

Example (iii), however, is entirely unacceptable.

(ii) *lilmod   polanit   ?eyn   kaše.
to-learn   Polish   neg   difficult
'To learn Polish is not difficult.'

As in (ii), *lilmod polanit* in (iii) is in a Topic position, to the left of *?eyn*. I have argued that intraposed clauses without *ze* implicate an expletive pro in the subject position, namely Spec/T in (iii). Now, LF movement of pro from Spec/T to adjoin to the CP topic conceivably leaves a trace which must be properly governed. Yet, as we have seen, Spec/T is not a head-governed position under *?eyn*; see §4.7.

Another construction involving a postverbal subject which resists embedding under *?eyn* is locative inversion, as in (i), suggesting that the preposed locative is not in subject position but is a topic of sorts, as argued originally in Stowell (1981). But see Bresnan and Kanerva (1989) and Hoekstra and Mulder (1990) for the view that preposed locatives are in subject position.

(i) a. (?ani xošev še-)   ba-pina   ʕomed xatul šaxor.
   (I   think   that-) in-the corner stands   cat   black
   '(I think that) In the corner stands a black cat.'

   b. ?eyn ba-pina   ʕomed xatul šaxor.
   NEG   in-the corner stands   cat   black
   'It is not the case that in the corner stands a black cat.'

24. As Cinque (1988) notes, only *and arb₃* is compatible with the existence of a single individual satisfying the description; contrast (ia) and (ib).

(i) a. ?ani xošev še-   ma?arixim   ?et ha-truma   šela. (ze
   I   think   that- value(BENONI)-MPL ACC the-contribution her   (It

   kanir?e   Dani.)
   probably   Dani)
   'I think that people value her contribution. (It's probably Dani.)'

b. ʔani xošev še-   dofkim   ba-delet.   (ze kanirʔe   Dani.)
I   think that- knock(BENONI)-MS on-the door (It probably Dani)
'I think that someone is knocking on the door. (It's probably Dani.)'

Among the other properties distinguishing *arb₃* and *arb𝑉*, Cinque (1988: 546) notes the following:

- Only *arb₃* is compatible with specific time reference.

- Only *arb𝑉* is compatible with generic time reference.

- *Arb₃* is restricted to external arguments but *arb𝑉* can be both an external and an internal argument.

25. This way of looking at things allows us to maintain the gist of both Rizzi's (1986) and Authier's (1989) approaches. See also Cinque (1988), note 29, crediting L. Rizzi.

26. See chapter 5, note 1, for a brief discussion of the differences between generically bound bare plurals under *ʔeyn* and pro$_{arb}$.

27. This might be strengthened to the claim that antecedent government is in general not an independent requirement and may be reduced to a more elaborate notion of head government, as suggested in Moro (1993a).

28. Movement of AgrS^0 to C^0 and consequent head government of a subject trace must be limited to LF, because when effected at S-structure such an operation does not rescue a subject trace, as discussed at length in Rizzi (1990). See also note 20, chapter 4.

To get around this problem, as well as around the set of problems posed by lowering derivations, L. Rizzi (personal communication) suggests an alternative analysis, whereby the quantificational properties of pro$_{arb₃}$ are handled by a regular quantifier that undergoes Quantifier Raising in LF, rather than by existential closure, the option I have taken. The advantage of this analysis is that it permits us to rule out (7-55) on a par with, for example, (i), which, I have argued, leaves an ungoverned trace in Spec/T in LF. See the discussion of the sentences in §4.8.

(i) *ʔeyn šloša yladim   yodʕim   ʔet ha-tšuva.
    NEG   three children know(BENONI)-MPL ACC the-answer
    'Three children don't know the answer.'

29. The agreement paradigm of *ʔeyn* is identical to the inflection found on verbs and prepositions, in my view, erroneously called clitics. This inflection is discussed at length in chapter 9, where I argue that the object and oblique "clitics" in Semitic are realizations of Agr heads to which the lexical head in question (V, P, etc.) is incorporated in the syntax. The complement of *see* in sentence (i) is a referential pro in Spec/AgrO.

(i)   reʔiti   -v.
    pro see(PAST)-1S   -3MS
    'I saw him.'

If agreement on *ʔeyn* is to be assimilated to these Agr elements, as the morphological parallelism strongly suggests, we must explain why only Spec/AgrS cannot be filled by a third person referential pro (viz. [7-69]). The difference, I believe, does not lie in the nature of the Agr head but in the different internal structures of null subjects and null objects.

I have argued that null subject pronouns cannot be interpreted as referential because third person pronouns in Hebrew are Num heads and the [person] feature on D^0 is only licensed when NumP is lexical or non-null. Hebrew (and Arabic) are only endowed with overt nominative pronominal forms: *hu, hi, hem* etc. . . . are *subject* pronouns. Nonsubject pronouns, it will be shown in chapter 10, are always pro (although pro may be integrated into a more complex structure; see §10.1). If Hebrew indeed has two sets of pronouns—nominative ones and nonnominative ones—we can posit a lexical difference between the two sets: third person pronouns in the nominative series (including pro) are Num^0s, while third person pronouns in the nonnominative set are D^0s.

30. When *ze* is used as a demonstrative pronoun or as the pronominal subject of a copular construction, it can appear as the subject of agreeing *ʔeyn*, as in the following examples. Such pronouns are fully referential expressions, unassociated with an extraposed CP.

(i) a. ze   ʔeyn-o   kaše   lə-ʔaxila.   b. zot   ʔeyn-a   tšuva.
         this-M neg-3MS difficult to-eating   *this-F neg-3FS answer*
         'This isn't difficult to eat.'   'This is not an answer.'

CHAPTER EIGHT

1. The present chapter builds on earlier work of mine; see Shlonsky (1987) and Shlonsky and Doron (1992). A very different analysis is developed in Borer (1995). See following note 4.

2. See Shlonsky (1987). Borer (1984, 1995) labels this process *Stylistic Inversion*, suggesting an affinity with French (cf. Kayne and Pollock 1978, Friedemann 1995 and § 8.3.3). However, since Hebrew triggered inversion crucially involves raising the inflected verb to the Comp domain—as I argue later in §8.3.2—while French *Stylistic Inversion* does not, I choose to employ a different terminology. This fundamental difference between the two inversion strategies underlies their divergent behavior in four empirical domains. First, French inversion does not require an overt trigger. Traces of wh-movement, for instance, can trigger it (§8.3.2). This is patently not the case in Hebrew, where the inversion trigger cannot be a trace. Second, the class of inversion "triggers" in French is restricted in comparison with Hebrew, where just about any clause-initial constituent permits inversion. Certain wh-elements, notably *pourquoi* 'why', do not trigger inversion in French. No such restriction is found in Hebrew. Third, French inversion is sharply degraded when the verb is transitive, whereas such a degradation is not characteristic of Hebrew. Finally, inverted subjects in French occupy a position on the right margin of the clause, whereas in Hebrew they occupy a clause-medial position, appearing to the left of a complement if there is one.

3. Two consequences to this analysis are worth mentioning. First, this account presupposes that movement leaves a veritable trace and not a copy (cf. Chomsky 1993). If a moved small clause were to leave a copy, then its subject within the copy would presumably be accessible for Case assignment. Second, the analysis shows that the accusative marker *ʔet* is indeed only a Case *marker* and not the source of accusative features. This is so since *ʔet* is fronted along with the entire small clause in (8-6b,c). If it were capable of assigning case directly, the small clause subject would be licensed. See also §1.3.4.

4. A different view of inversion is advanced in Borer (1995). She argues that triggers occupy Spec/I, which she takes, following Diesing (1992a), to be a position capable of hosting both A and A′ elements. In her view, the verb in TI raises to I^0 and the subject remains inside VP. The existence of multiple topics, as Borer labels the preverbal constituents in TI—for example, in (8-8)—lead her to suggest that topics may be adjoined to IP. In the analysis pursued here, multiple "topics" indicate the presence of several positions within the Comp domain.

5. The basic format for a licensing criterion is: *An XP marked [+F] must be in a Spec-head configuration with an X^0 marked [+F] and vice-versa.*

6. The syntax of Hebrew resumptive pronouns is studied in the following works, to which the reader is referred for more detailed discussion: Borer (1984), Demirdache (1991), Doron (1982), Hayon (1974), Sells (1984), and Shlonsky (1992).

7. In Shlonsky (1992), I discuss one case where a phonetically null resumptive pronoun can occur in situ: in Standard Arabic relative clauses, where C^0 agrees in φ-features with the relative operator.

8. The order Trigger > V > O > S is only possible if the subject is heavy and constitutes a case of *Heavy NP Shift*, on which see Belletti and Shlonsky (1995).

9. The reader is referred to chapter 2, note 11, and to chapter 3, note 13, for discussion of a dialectal variety of Hebrew which permits the subject to occur in a position linearly to the right of the Benoni verb.

10. For the sake of completeness, I mention a fact which my anaysis of TI cannot account for. Weak Crossover effects are substantially weakened under TI, as shown in (i). (For a discussion under different assumptions, see Shlonsky 1987 and Borer 1995.)

(i) a. ?*?et mi   ?im-o
        ACC   who   mother-3MS love(BENONI)-3FS?
        'Who does his mother love?'

     b. ??et mi   ?ohevet   ?im-o?
        ACC   who   love (BENONI)-3FS   mother-3FS
        'Who does his mother love?'

If TI involves movement of the verb over the subject, it follows that the relative position of the subject and the object trace are the same in both (ia) and (ib). The contrast between them is hence surprising.

11. I thank L. Rizzi for bringing the following argument to my attention.

12. For a recent discussion of the adjacency condition in Italian, see Belletti and Shlonsky (1995), the conclusions of which differ from the ones reached in this book.

13. We shall see that this interpretation is untenable. It is also doubtful, given the ungrammaticality of (i), with *bene* to the right of the subject. Predictably, the Hebrew equivalent of (i)—namely, (ii) with TI—is perfectly grammatical.

(i) *Ha giocato Gianni bene.
     has played Gianni well

(ii) ?etmol   sixek   Dani heitev.
     yesterday play(PAST)-3MS Dani well

14. Note than no adjacency requirement as such holds of the auxiliary and the participle, as floating quantifiers and adverbs may licitly occur between them in Italian (Belletti 1990). In this respect, Italian differs from Spanish, where string adjacency between the auxiliary and the participle must be observed.

15. More subtle restrictions, hinging on the tense of the verb and the extent to which it is interpreted as a presentational verb, are discussed in detail in Shlonsky (1987). I put them aside in this volume.

16. The idea that the same position serves derived postverbal subjects both of thematic objects and of thematic subjects is not a new one. It harks back to Rizzi (1982), where both positions were taken to be derived ones. Belletti (1988) argues that both types of subjects are in a VP-adjoined position. Belletti and Shlonsky (1995) argue that this position should be identified with the specifier position of a Focus position located above VP and lower that the head Case-marking the subject.

17. Note that this is another way of saying that Italian and Hebrew lack transitive expletive constructions. These are discussed in Jonas & Bobalijk (1993), for example.

18. Such a modification is independently needed to account for VP-internal Dative Shift in Larson's (1988) analysis.

19. An outstanding problem remains, however. If the postverbal subjects in (8-62b) and (8-63b) are in VP, why is TI—namely, movement of the inflected verb to C^0—still necessary to allow the verb to precede the subject? The following consideration suggests that the possibility of leaving clausal subjects in Spec/V at least partially depends on I→C movement and cannot be entirely explained by appeal to Case-licensing of the postverbal subject.

Inversion is not possible under *ʔeyn*, as shown in (ib); example (ia) shows the grammatically possible constituent order. This is a predictable consequence of the text analysis, since the lowest possible subject position in the sentences in (i) is Spec/T and hence the subject must linearly precede the verb (the highest possible position of which is T^0; see chapter 4).

(i) a. ʔeyn ha-yladim   kotvim   sipurim.
         NEG   the-children   write(BENONI)-MPL   stories
         'The children are not writing stories.'

      b. ???ʔeyn kotvim   ha-yladim   sipurim.
         NEG   write(BENONI)-MPL   the-children   stories
         'The children are not writing stories.'

However, inversion becomes marginally acceptable when a topic precedes *ʔeyn*, as in (ii) (T. Siloni, personal communication).

(ii) ʔba-kitot   ha-nəmuxot ʔeyn kotvim   ha-yladim   sipurim.
          in-the-classes   the-lower   NEG   write(BENONI)-MPL   the-children   stories
          'In the lower grades, children don't write stories.'

Example (ii) is rather mysterious. For example, it does not manifest I→C movement. However (ii) is analyzed, it shows that the possibility of leaving the subject in VP depends on some other factor that is tied up with the presence of the topic.

CHAPTER NINE

1. The (phonologically conditioned) sets of these suffixed pronouns are basically stable, in the sense that they do not vary with the change of host, as shown in the pairs (9-1a,b) and (9-1c,d). I put aside what I think are minor qualifications of this general statement (e.g., the fact that cliticized first person singular direct objects on regular verbs in Hebrew and in certain dialects of Arabic manifest the consonant [n], which is generally absent when the clitic host is a preposition or a noun). It should also be mentioned that clitics on verbs in Hebrew are stylistically marked and many forms are learned or nonexistent. The intuitions of Hebrew speakers with respect to the sort of questions posed in this chapter are nonetheless firm.

2. There are some exceptions, e.g., Brazilian Portuguese (Bianchi and Figueiredo-Silva 1993, Galician (Uriagereka 1995), Val d'Otain Franco-Provençal (Roberts 1993). See also Kayne's (1975) discussion of French *en* in *pour en parler*.

3. For the sake of concreteness, I take cliticization in (9-5) to involve head movement from inside a DP in Spec/AgrO and incorporation to the auxiliary. It is plausible that the clitic moves higher and actually attaches to a functional head higher than V^0_{Aux}, and that subsequent incorporation of the auxiliary to the same functional head renders the chain representationally licit, as in Belletti's (1990) treatement of the cliticization of Neg^0. The literature on French clitics is enormous. My discussion is based to a large degree on the following relatively recent work: Belletti (forthcoming), Rizzi 1993, Sportiche 1990, 1996.

4. In the Western Romance languages, notably Portuguese, clitics occur in second position, as they do in Berber, cf. §9.3.2.

5. Fassi-Fehri (1993, chapter 3, section 1.2) documents counter examples to this claim, from Classical Arabic:

(i) a. ?aʕtaytu   -ka   -hu.   b. darbu   -ka   -hu . . .
       give(PERF)-1S -2MS -3MS   *beating -2MS -3MS*
       'I gave you it.'   'your beating him . . .'

I believe that the status of these examples is controversial. J. Ouhalla (personal communication) informs me that, in any event, they are not to be found in Modern Standard Arabic.

The Classical Arabic Double Object construction presents other peculiarities discussed in Mouchaweh 1986 (chapter 5) and Ouhalla 1993a. For example, contrary to English and many, if not all, of the modern Arabic dialects where the order of complements is Goal/Beneficiary > Theme, there is a preference in Classical Arabic for the reverse order, as in (ii).

(ii) a. ?aʕtaytu   ?al-kitaab-a   Zayd-an.
        give(PERF)-1S the-book-ACC Zayd-ACC
        'I gave Zayd the book.' *lit.* 'I gave the book Zayd.'

      b. ?aʕtaytu   -hu   ?al-taalib-a.
        give-(PERF)-1S -3MS the-student-ACC
        'I gave it to the student.' *lit.* 'I gave it the student.'

In addition, the Goal/Beneficiary argument may be wh-moved, as in (iii) (Moucheweh 1986, chapter 5, note 5).

(iii) man   ?aʕtayta   kitaab-ak?
        Who give(PERF)-2MS book-2MS
        'To whom did you give your book? *lit.* 'Who did you give your book?'

Given these peculiarities of the Classical Arabic construction, it seems hasty to regard (ia,b) as counterexamples to the claim that clitic clusters are not permitted in Semitic. A more detailed study of the syntax of the double object construction in Classical Arabic is required before the relevance and status of these examples can be determined.

6. A second family of analyses of Semitic clitics, represented by Borer's (1983) study of Hebrew clitic doubling, should be mentioned at this point. Borer reasons that since clitics (in particular on Hebrew nouns) can be doubled, the clitic and the doubled NP cannot be taken to occupy the same base position. She proposes that the clitic is base-generated on its host where it must, for reasons that need not concern us here, be coindexed with the NP it doubles. The structure she proposes for clitic constructions is given in (i), where X = N in Hebrew.

(i)

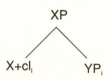

This approach raises problems similar to those mentioned in connection with the Incorporation theory of Semitic clitics. Among other things, the base-generation approach provides no explanation for the locality of cliticization. That there cannot be an inherent link between the possibility of clitic doubling and the locality of clitics is evidenced by the fact that at least some Romance languages manifest both clitic doubling and clitic climbing (Spanish, Rumanian). Like the Incorporation approach, the base-generation theory of clitics provides no clue as to why Semitic clitics are enclitics and never proclitics.

7. The alternative would be to say that the agreeing form of *ʔeyn* is lexically formed and checked in Agrs^0. While this is perfectly conceivable, the formal affinity with object agreement is harder to explain if this option is taken.

8. While the Agr heads in question are basically identical in terms of their feature content, the same cannot be said for the pro occupying their Spec position. Third person Null subjects in Hebrew, for example, are NumP categories since they are modeled after the overt pronouns; see §7.2.5. I argued that this fact lies at the core of the unavailability of third person null referential subjects. Object pro, however, is not so restricted. Third person pro is as legitimate as a second or first person one. Subject pro is a NumP; object pro is a DP and hence perfectly compatible with an Agr^0 bearing third person features.

9. The Arabic examples in (9-6) are of causative sentences. Certain types of causatives are often analyzed as involving clause union. I believe there is no evidence for treating Arabic causatives as biclausal in the base component. The causative verb is an affix (or a template) and not an independent verb. Example (9-6) thus illustrates a morphological causative and not a syntactic causative construction (compare with the Romance *faire*-V construction). More to the point, however, is the fact that Arabic causatives behave just as *give*-type verbs in giving rise to the dative alternation.

10. I leave open the question whether this caveat must be stipulated (e.g., "θ-positions do not count") or whether one can claim, with Chomsky (1993), that movement of the lower V to the higher one is a case of radical substitution, and hence there is no domain *extension* per se. I am not certain that the radical substitution can actually be maintained for all VP shells.

11. Scrambling into A positions in the West Germanic languages seems to massively violate Equidistance. First, arguments can be moved out of VP even if the verb does not raise overtly and extends its domain. Second, movement of several or multiple arguments out of VP must involve crossing so that the linear order of the arguments in VP is preserved in the *Mittelfeld*. Haegeman (1993) discusses these phenomena, which I put aside as potential problems for the Equidistance theory.

12. I put aside why individual languages choose only a subset of these possibilities, e.g., Hebrew clitic doubling is only attested in nominals and, if Borer (1983) is correct, also in PPs, but not in VPs. Lebanese Arabic differs from the variety of Palestinian discussed here in disallowing the equivalent of (9-32c), viz. Aoun, Benmamoun, and Sportiche (1994).

13. See Borer (1984), Jaeggli (1982, 1986), among others, for a development of this idea, originally formulated by R. Kayne.

14. See chapter 8, §8.4.1, for a discussion of Case assignment by government to postverbal subjects by Asp^0 and V^0. The Case assigned to doubled DPs in clitic-doubling configurations might be of the same sort. Alternatively, one cannot rule out the idea that the dummy preposition comes associated with an AgrP of its own, responsible for Case marking. In the examples in (9-32a-c), there is no evidence that such an Agr head is present, but this might mean that it is only activated in LF.

15. See, in particular, Jaeggli (1982). Recent studies of Spanish clitic doubling include Everett (1996), Franco (1993), Jaeggli (1986b), and Suñer (1988, 1992).

16. Although I have argued for a substantial difference between Romance and Semitic clitics, several authors have proposed analyses for Romance similar to the one proposed here for Semitic. Franco (1993) explicitly defends the view that Spanish clitics are Agr heads, while Sportiche (1992) argues that Romance clitics are heads of what he calls voice projections. Some discussion of Sportiche's proposal from a Semitic or Hebrew perspective is undertaken in Siloni (1994).

17. E. Benmamoun (personal communication) points out that clitic doubling of QPs is available even in Arabic dialects which lack the paradigm in (9-32). These dialects thus

resemble French in that bare quantifiers move to Spec/Agr^0 in the syntax (and the agreement relationship in AgrOP is established), but that null pronominals do not.

18. See Shlonsky (1994) for a discussion of AgrCP and subject clitics in West Flemish. The explanation in terms of Relativized Minimality for the fact that agreement in the Comp domain must be subject agreement harks back to Rizzi's (1990) treatment of the *que-qui* alternation in French. See also Shlonsky (1992).

It has been argued (by, for example, Aoun, Benmamoun, and Sportiche 1994) that the dialectal Arabic complementizer *ʔinnu* should be decomposed into a C^0 unit, *inn* and an agreement morpheme *-u*. Put into the terms developed in this chapter, one is tempted to say that, in dialectal Arabic, AgrCP is always present and always contains an affix. The text example in (9-43) contains an affix marked for the features 3FS. In line with Aoun, Benmamoun, and Sportiche, (9-43) can also be rendered with the affix *-u*, as in (i). Clearly, *-u* here should not be confounded with the affix expressing the features 3MS. Rather, it should be taken to be an impersonal Agr affix manifesting a default specification of features.

(i) … ʔinn -<u>u</u>   l-mʕalme t iiji.
     … *that the-teacher 3FS(IMPER)-come*
     '… that the teacher is coming /will come.'

I would like to suggest that Spec/AgrC in (i) is filled by a phonetically null *it*-like pronoun, which enters into agreement with C^0. Example (i) should thus be translated as '… it (to be the case that) the teacher is coming/will come.' This view of things suggests a rethinking of the syntax of the Standard Arabic Comp *ʔanna/ʔinna*, a matter I leave for future research.

19. A similar state of affairs can be found in certain North Italian dialects. Belletti (forthcoming) argues that clitic doubling of subjects in, for instance, Trentino, (i), is brought about when the thematic subject is raised to Spec/AgrS and the clitic, *el* in (i), occupies AgrS^0.

(i) El Mario   el   parla.
     the Mario he(clitic) speaks
     'Mario speaks.'

There is at least one context of subject clitic doubling in Arabic where a subject cannot receive Case by moving to Spec/AgrS. Aoun (1993) cites the following Lebanese Arabic example of what he takes to be an ECM context.

(i) a. xallayt   -<u>o</u>   yruuh   la-Kariim.
       let-(PERF)-1S -3MS 3MS-(IMPERF)go to-Kariim
       'I let Kariim go.'

The matrix verb is associated with the clitic, and the embedded verb appears in the imperfect form. Let us suppose that the clitic in (i) is a manifestation of AgrO^0 of the matrix verb; see Chomsky and Lasnik's (1994) treatment of ECM.

Elsewhere in this book (see, in particular, chapter 6), I argue that the Arabic imperfect form does not bear AgrS features and that its agreement is a manifestation of a lower agreement head. Indeed, in many dialects of Arabic—Lebanese and Palestinian among them—the imperfect form is a "dependent" form which must occur in embedded contexts and which takes over the functions of the infinitive in many European languages. Thus, the subject in (i) is inside an IP in which it cannot receive Case. For this reason, *la* is obligatory.

20. It is not implausible that the definite determiner in Semitic is a head feature base-generated on the noun and on its modifiers, and then checked in an appropriate configuration. See Borer (1996) and Siloni (1994) for developments of this idea.

CHAPTER TEN

1. If AgrP is invisible for selection, KP/PP is not. There is rather clear evidence that
ʔet is the head of a maximal projection distinct from DP. When two or more objects are
coordinated and one of them is a pronoun, *ʔet* must precede each nonpronominal conjunct.
There is no such requirement when the objects conjoined are all nonpronominal. In these
cases, *ʔet* may, but does not have to, precede each conjunct. Compare the sentences in (i)
with those in (ii).

(i) a. raʔinu   ʔoto ve- ʔet Dani.   b. *raʔinu   ʔoto ve- Dani.
        see(PAST)-1PL him and ACC Dani   *see(PAST)-1PL him and Dani*
        'We saw him and Dani.'   'We saw him and Dani.'

(ii) a. raʔinu   ʔet Dani ve- ʔet-Ruti.
        see(PAST)-1PL ACC Dani and ACC-Ruti
        'We saw Dani and Ruti.'

     b. raʔinu   ʔet Dani ve- Ruti.
        see(PAST)-1PL ACC Dani and Ruti
        'We saw Dani and Ruti.'

Since coordination applies to constituents of the same category, and since *ʔoto* is a KP,
the second conjunct in (i) must also be a KP, which is why *ʔet* is obligatory in (ia) and why
(ib) is ill formed. In (ii), on the other hand, it is possible to coordinate either two KPs, as in
(iia), and hence two measures of *ʔet* are attested, or two DPs, as in (iib), and only a single
measure of *ʔet* is required.

2. For discussion of *(ʔi)yya* in Damascene Arabic, see Mouchaweh (1986), who shows that
a direct object can be clitic-doubled by means of a *yya* pronoun. Compare (10-9) with (i):

(i) l-mʕallim   fahham   -ha yya-a   la-l-dars.
     the-teacher understand(PERF-CAUS)-3MS 3FS YYA-3MS to-the-lesson
     'The teacher explained the lesson to her.'

3. The *yya* form is also obligatory as the second conjunct of a conjunction of pronouns.
"Me and you" is rendered *ʔana w-yya-k*, and never as *ʔana w-ʔinti*. I cannot say that I
understand the syntax of pronoun coordination. Why, for example, is the nominative form
restricted to the first member of the coordination? But however these cases are analyzed , it
is clear that the occurrence of the *yya* form is consistent with the generalization that it can
only appear when there is no available AgrP to host pro in a position external to the projection
containing the pronoun. Movement of pro from inside a coordinate structure is ruled out by
the Coordinate Structure Constraint.

4. That *ʔanušot* is a VP or manner adverbial is evidenced by the fact that it cannot occur
in a position between the subject and the verb (cf. §1.3.1). Contrast (10-13a) and (i).

(i) *Dani ʔanušot paca   ʔet šlomo.
     Dani mortally injure(PAST)-3MS ACC Shlomo
     'Dani injured Shlomo mortally.'

5. Borer (1995) judges that dative pronouns cannot be stranded. To my ears, her
examples are at most slightly odd, but acceptable.

6. While the discussion in this and the following section is centered on the behavior of
accusative pronouns, it should be taken to hold of the dative series as well. See 10.3.4

7. Stated in this fashion, the Avoid Pronoun Principle resembles an economy constraint,
see Cardinaletti and Starke (forthcoming) for discussion.

8. This observation should be seen as a supplementary argument for the view that AgrSP is not projected in (agreementless) *ʔeyn* sentences. If it were, the pronoun would have to occupy Spec/AgrS and appear to the left of *ʔeyn*.

9. When occurring in preverbal position, in Spec/AgrS, strong pronouns need not be stressed. See Cardinaletti (1994b) for a more elaborate analysis of preverbal pronouns.

10. In order to account for the apparently different position of clitics in infinitive clauses (with respect to the negative operator *pas*) in (ia,b), further refinement is neccesary. See Belletti (forthcoming) for discussion. On French clitics in imperatives, see Laenzlinger (1995).

(i) a. ne   pas le manger   b. il ne   le mange   pas.
       neg neg it to eat   *he neg it eat(PRES)-3S neg*
     'Don't eat it.'   'He does not eat it.'

11. It has been argued that Romance clitics are attracted to $AgrS^0$ and not to some other Agr^0 because they require a host bearing Person features; see Bianchi and Figueiredo (1993), who argue that the occurrence of object clitics on past participles in Brazilian Portuguese is due to the manifestation of covert person features on the participle, in contradistinction to, say, French or Italian. It is tempting to speculate that the Hebrew Benoni is also endowed with person features, phonetically unrealized but syntactically present. Cliticization of weak pronouns in Hebrew would then parallel Romance cliticization, differing only in the level of application of head movement. The Hebrew Benoni would then be rather similar, in its φ-feature content, to the Arabic Imperfect, which I argued to be a participle endowed with (overt) person features (see §6.2.1).

12. Is is worth noting in this context that preverbal weak subject pronouns, as in (i), pose a problem, since they are not c-commanded by any host:

(i) hu yaca   la-sadot.
     he go out(PAST)-3MS   to-the-fields
     'He went out to the fields.'

A similar difficulty arises in French, where subject clitics are enclitics on a verb in Comp, as in (iia), and proclitics when I→C movement does not take place, as in (iib). The Hebrew case can be assimilated to the French one.

(ii) a. Il   dort.   b. Dort   -il?
        he sleeps   *sleeps he*
      'He is sleeping.'   'Is he sleeping?'

13. A number of empirical problems must be resolved if this characterization of weak pronouns is to hold universally. Among them is the status of preverbal pronouns in Germanic V2 contexts and preverbal subject pronouns in French.

APPENDIX

1. The third variant of *ɣadi* manifests a subject agreement affix and cannot incorporate the main verb, as shown by the fact that only that the verb must remain below negation, as in (ia).

(i) a. lə-wlaad ma   ɣadi-n -š   yemši w.
        the-boys NEG FUT-PL NEG 3PL-leave(IMPERF)
      'The boys will leave.'

     b. *lə-wlaad ma   ɣadi-n yemši w   -š.
        the-boys NEG FUT-PL 3PL-leave(IMPERF)   NEG
      'The boys will leave.'

2. There are two notable exceptions to this generalization. Standard Arabic possesses

a marker for indefinite nouns which appears fused with the Case suffixes. Thus, (A-1a), repeated here as (ia)—to which I have added the nominative Case suffix—should be contrasted with (ib), its indefinite nominative variant.

(i) a. ?al- bayt -u   b. bayt -un
      DEF- *house* -NOM   *house* -NOM-INDEF
      'the house'

There are various options for handling this exception. One might argue that the indefinite suffix is not an independent D^0 head, but forms part of the morphological case complex (whether lexically attached to the verb, or heading a KP projection), the actual indefinite determiner being phonetically unexpressed. This might correlate with the fact that Hebrew lacks both morphological case and an indefinite marker.

The second exception is Hebrew Copula Inversion, which constitutes a form of incorporation involving left adjunction of the Benoni participle to the auxiliary. A possibility that comes to mind is to relate the patterning of auxiliaries with pronominal clitics (or Agr heads) with respect to incorporation to another trait they share in common—their inability to procrastinate movement. It is well known that auxiliaries are the only type of verb in English which must raise to $AgrS^0$ in the audible syntax (Pollock 1989). Similarly, weak and clitic pronouns must effect their movement before S-structure (see chapter 10 for further discussion). Chomsky (1993) claims that *be*-type auxiliaries are invisible in the LF component and must therefore raise at S-structure to check their features. Invisibility in LF is precisely the sort of property that I have attributed to Agr heads.

3. I leave for further research the intriguing possibility of stating (A-9) the other way around, and thus attributing the setting of the head complement parameter to the form of the lexical entries of functional heads.

Bibliography

Adams, M. (1987) From Old French to the Theory of Pro-Drop. *Natural Language and Linguistic Theory*, 5:1–32.

Anderson, M. (1979) *Noun Phrase Structure.* PhD dissertation, University of Connecticut at Storrs.

Aoun, J., N. Hornstein, D. Lightfoot, & A. Weinberg (1987) Two Types of Locality. *Linguistic Inquiry*, 18:537–577.

Aoun, J. (1993) The Syntax of Doubled Arguments. *International Journal of Basque Linguistics and Philology*, 27-3:709–730.

Aoun, J., E. Benmamoun, & D. Sportiche (1994) Agreement, Word Order, and Conjunction in Some Varieties of Arabic. *Linguistic Inquiry*, 25:195–220.

Authier, M. (1989) Arbitrary Null Objects. In Jaeggli, O., & K.J. Safir (eds.) *The Null Subject Parameter*, pp. 45–68. Dordrecht: Kluwer.

Ayoub, G. (1981) Structure de la phrase verbale en Arabe Standard. Thèse de doctorat de troisième cycle, Université de Paris VII.

Ayoub, G. (1996) Opérateurs et gouverneurs. In Lecarme, J., J. Lowenstamm, & U. Shlonsky (eds.) *Studies in Afroasiatic Grammar*, pp. 1–29. The Hague: Holland Academic Graphics.

Baker, M. (1988) *Incorporation: A Theory of Grammatical Function Changing.* Chicago: University of Chicago Press.

Bakir, M.J (1980) Aspects of Clause Structure in Arabic. Ph.D dissertation, Indiana University.

Belletti, A. (1988) The Case of Unaccusatives. *Linguistic Inquiry*, 19:1–34.

Belletti, A. (1990) *Generalized Verb Movement.* Torino: Rosenberg and Sellier.

Belletti, A. (Forthcoming) Italian/Romance Clitics: Structure and Derivation. In Riemsdijk, H. van. (ed.) *Clitics in the Languages of Europe*, Dordrecht: De Gruyter.

Belletti, A., & L. Rizzi (1988) Psych-Verbs and Theta-Theory. *Natural Language and Linguistic Theory*, 6:291–351.

Belletti, A., & U. Shlonsky (1995) The Order of Verbal Complements: A Comparative Study. *Natural Language and Linguistic Theory*, 13:489–526.

Bendavid, A. (1971) *Lešon miqra w-lšon xaxamim [Biblical Hebrew and Mishnaic Hebrew].* Tel Aviv: Dvir.

Benmamoun, E. (1991) Verb Movement and Negation. In Sherer, T. (ed.) *Proceedings of the North Eastern Linguistics Society 21*, pp. 17–32. Amherst, MA: Department of Linguistics, University of Massachusetts.

Benmamoun, E. (1992) Functional and Inflectional Morphology: Problems of Projection, Representation and Derivation. Ph.D. dissertation, University of Southern California.

Benmamoun, E. (1994) The Conditions on Pro and the ECP. In Aronovitch, R., Byrne, W., Preuss, S. & Sentoria, M. (eds.) *Proceedings of the West Coast Conference on Formal Linguistics* pp. 173–178. Stanford, CA: Stanford University, Center for the Study of Language and Information.

Bennis, H. (1986) *Gaps and Dummies*. Dordrecht: Foris.

Benveniste, E. (1966) Relationships of Person in the Verb. In *Problèmes de linguistique générale*. pp. 195–204. Paris: Gallimard.

Berman, R.A. (1978) *Modern Hebrew Structure*. Tel Aviv: University Publishing Projects.

Besten, H. den (1983) On the Interaction of Root Transformations and Lexical Deletive Rules. In Abraham, W. (ed.) *On the Formal Syntax of Westgermania*, pp. 47–131. Amsterdam: John Benjamins.

Bianchi, V., & C. Figueiredo-Silva (1993) On Some Properties of Agreement Object in Italian and in Brazilian Portuguese. Scuola Normale Superiore, Pisa & Université de Genève: Unpublished manuscript.

Borer, H. (1980) Empty Subjects in Modern Hebrew and Constraints on Thematic Relations. In Jensen, J. (ed.) *Proceedings of the 10th Annual Meeting of the North Eastern Linguistic Society*, Ottawa, Ontario. *Cahiers linguistiques d'Ottawa* 9:25–38.

Borer, H. (1984) Restrictive Relatives in Modern Hebrew. *Natural Language and Linguistic Theory*, 2:219–260.

Borer, H. (1986) I-Subjects. *Linguistic Inquiry*, 17:375–416.

Borer, H. (1989a) Anaphoric Agr. In Jaeggli, O., & K.J. Safir (eds.) *The Null Subject Parameter*, pp. 69–110. Dordrecht: Kluwer.

Borer, H. (1989b) On the Morphological Parallelism between Compounds and Constructs. In Booij, G. & J. van Marle (eds.) *Morphology Yearbook*, pp. 45–64. Dordrecht: Foris.

Borer, H. (1995) The Ups and Downs of Hebrew Verb Movement. *Natural Language and Linguistic Theory*, 13:527–606.

Borer, H. (1996) The Construct in Review. In Lecarme, J., J. Lowenstamm, & U. Shlonsky (eds.) *Studies in Afroasiatic Grammar*, pp. 30–61. The Hague: Holland Academic Graphics.

Borer, H. (Forthcoming) *Parallel Morphology*. Cambridge, MA: MIT Press.

Borer, H., & Y. Grodzinsky (1987) Syntactic versus Lexical Cliticization: The Case of Hebrew Dative Clitics. In Borer, H. (ed.) *The Syntax of Pronominal Clitics*, pp. 175–217. San Francisco: Academic Press.

Borer, H. & K. Wexler (1987) The Maturation of Syntax. In Roeper, T. & E. Williams (eds.) *Parameter Setting*, pp. 123-172. Dordrecht: Reidel.

Borsley, R.D., & M.L. Rivero (1994) Clitic Auxiliaries and Incorporation in Polish. *Natural Language and Linguistic Theory*, 12:373–422.

Bresnan, J., & J.M. Kanerva (1989) Locative Inversion in Chichewa: A Case Study of Factorization in Grammar. *Linguistic Inquiry*, 20:1–50.

Brody, M. (1990) Some Remarks on the Focus Field in Hungarian. *University College of London Working Papers*, 2:201–225.

Broselow, E. (1976) The Phonology of Egyptian Arabic. Ph.D. dissertation, University of Massachusetts at Amherst.

Cardinaletti, A. (1994a) Subject Positions. *Geneva Generative Papers*, 2:64–78.

Cardinaletti, A. (1994b) On the Internal Structure of Pronominal DPs. *Linguistic Review*, 11:195–219.

Cardinaletti, A., & M.T. Guasti (1991) Epistemic Small Clauses and Null Subjects. In Westphal, G.F., B. Ao, & H-R. Chae (eds.) *Proceedings of the Eighth Eastern States Conference on Linguistics*, pp. 23–33. Columbus: Department of Linguistics, Ohio State University.

Cardinaletti, A., & M.T. Guasti (1993) Negation in Small Clauses. *Probus*, 5:36–61.

Cardinaletti, A., & M. Starke (Forthcoming) The Typology of Structural Deficiency: On the Three Grammatical Classes. In van Riemsdijk, H. (ed.) *Clitics in the Languages of Europe*. Berlin: Mouton.

Carlson, G. (1977) Reference to Kinds in English. Ph.D. dissertation, University of Massachusetts at Amherst.

Chomsky, N. (1965) *Aspects of the Theory of Syntax*. Cambridge, MA: MIT Press.

Chomsky, N. (1970) Remarks on Nominalizations. In Jacobs, R., & P. Rosenbaum (eds.) *Readings in English Transformational Grammar*, pp. 184–221. Waltham, MA: Ginn & Co.

Chomsky, N. (1982) *Some Concepts and Consequences of the Theory of Government and Binding*. Cambridge, MA: MIT Press.

Chomsky, N. (1986a) *Barriers*. Cambridge, MA: MIT Press.

Chomsky, N. (1986b) *Knowledge of Language: Its Nature, Origin and Use*. New York: Praeger.

Chomsky, N. (1991) Some Notes on the Economy of Derivation and Representation. In Freidin, R. (ed.) *Principles and Parameters in Comparative Grammar*, pp. 117–454. Cambridge, MA.: MIT Press.

Chomsky, N. (1993) A Minimalist Program for Linguistic Theory. In Hale, K., & S-J. Keyser (eds.) *The View from Building 20*, pp. 1–52. Cambridge, MA: MIT Press.

Chomsky, N. (1994) *Bare Phrase Structure. MIT Occasional Papers in Linguistics*, Vol. 5. Department of Linguistics, Massachusetts Institute of Technology. Cambridge, MA.

Chomsky, N. (1995) *The Minimalist Program*. Cambridge, MA: MIT Press.

Chomsky, N., & H. Lasnik (1994) Principles and Parameters Theory. In Jacobs, J. (ed.) *Syntax: An International Handbook of Contemporary Research*. Dordrecht: de Gruyter.

Cinque, G. (1988) On Si Constructions and the Theory of Arb. *Linguistic Inquiry*, 19:521–581.

Cinque, G. (1990) *Types of A' Dependencies*. Cambridge, MA: MIT Press.

Cinque, G. (1995) Adverbs and the Universal Hierarchy of Functional Projections. *GLOW Newsletter*, 34:14–15.

Cowell, M.W. (1964) *A Reference Grammar of Syrian Arabic*. Washington, DC: Georgetown University Press.

Crawford, W., & K. Poutaraska (1985) *Thai Home Cooking from Kamolman's Kitchen*. New York: Penguin.

Delfitto, D. (1990) Generics and Variables in Syntax. Tesi de perfezionamento, Scuola Normale Superiore, Pisa.

Demirdache, H. (1988) Nominative NPs in Modern Standard Arabic. Generals paper, Massachusetts Institute of Technology, Cambridge, MA.

Demirdache, H. (1991) Resumptive Chains in Restrictive Relatives, Appositives and Dislocation Structures. Ph.D. dissertation, Massachusetts Institute of Technology.

Déchaine, R-M. (1993) Predicates across Categories: Towards a Category-Neutral Syntax. Ph.D. dissertation, University of Massachusetts at Amherst.

Déprez, V. (1996) The Roots of Negative Concord in French and French Based Creoles. In DeGraff, M. (ed) *Creole, Diachrony and Language Acquisition*. Cambridge, MA: MIT Press.

Diesing, M. (1992a) *Indefinites*. Cambridge, MA: MIT Press.

Diesing, M. (1992b) Bare Plural Subjects and the Derivation of Logical Representations. *Linguistic Inquiry*, 23:353–380.

Diesing, M., & E. Jelinek (1995) Distributing Arguments. *Natural Language Semantics*, 3:123–176.

Doron, E. (1982) The Syntax and Semantics of Resumptive Pronouns. *Texas Linguistic Forum*, 19:1–48.

Doron, E. (1983) Verbless Predicates in Hebrew. Ph.D. dissertation, University of Texas at Austin.

Doron, E. (1986) The Pronominal Copula as an Agreement Clitic. In Borer, H. (ed.) *The Syntax of Pronominal Clitics*, pp. 313–332. New York: Academic Press.

Doron, E. (1988) On the Complementarity of Subject and Subject-Verb Agreement. In Barlow, M., & C.A. Ferguson (eds.) *Agreement in Natural Language: Approaches, Theories, Descriptions*, pp. 201–218. Stanford, CA: Stanford University, Center for the Study of Language and Information.

Doron, E. (1996) The Predicate in Arabic. In Lecarme, J., J. Lowenstamm, & U. Shlonsky (eds.) *Studies in Afroasiatic Grammar*, pp. 77–87. The Hague: Holland Academic Publishers.

Dowty, D. (1979) *Word Meaning and Montague Grammar.* Dordrecht: Reidel.

Eid, M. (1983) The Copula Function of Pronouns. *Lingua*, 59:197–207.

Eisele, J. (1988) The Syntax and Semantics of Tense, Aspect and Time Reference. In Cairene Arabic. Ph.D dissertation, University of Chicago.

Emonds, J. (1976) *A Transformational Approach to English Syntax: Root, Local and Structure-processing Transformations.* New York: Academic Press.

Emonds, J. (1978) The Verbal Complex V'-V in French. *Linguistic Inquiry*, 9:151–175.

Emonds, J. (1979) Word Order in Generative Grammar. In Bedell, G., F. Muraki, & K. Kobayashi (eds.) *Explorations in Linguistics*, pp. 33–51. Tokyo: Kenkyusha Press.

Enç, M. (1987) Anchoring Conditions for Tense. *Linguistic Inquiry*, 18:633–657.

Everett, D. (1996) *Why There Are No Clitics.* Dallas, TX: SIL-UTA.

Fassi-Fehri, A. (1989) Generalised IP Structure, Case and VS Order. In Laka, I., & A. Mahajan (eds.) *Functional Heads and Clause Structure. Massachusetts of Technology Working Papers in Linguistics*, 10:75–111.

Fassi-Fehri, A. (1993) *Issues in the Structure of Arabic Clauses and Words.* Dordrecht: Kluwer.

Fleisch, H. (1979) *Traité de philologie arabe.* Beyrut: Dar el-Machreq.

Franco, J.A. (1993) On Object Agreement in Spanish. Ph.D dissertation, University of Southern California.

Friedemann, M-A. (1992) The Underlying Position of External Arguments in French. *Geneva Generative Papers*, O:123–144.

Friedemann, M-A. (1995) Sujets syntaxiques: positions, inversion et pro. Ph.D dissertation, Université de Genève.

Friedemann, M-A., & T. Siloni (1993) Agr$_o$ is not Agr$_p$. *Geneva Generative Papers*, 1:41–53.

Glinert, L. (1989) *The Grammar of Modern Hebrew.* Cambridge: Cambridge University Press.

Grange, C., & L. Haegeman (1989) Subordinate Clauses: Adjuncts or Arguments—The Status of *het* in Dutch. In Jaspers, D., W. Klooster, Y. Putseys, & P. Seuren (eds.) *Sentential Complementation and the Lexicon*, pp. 155–171. Dordrecht: Foris.

Greenberg, Y. (1994) Hebrew Nominal Sentences and the Stage/Individual Level Distinction. Master's Thesis, Bar Ilan University.

Grimshaw, J. (1991) Extended Projection. Waltham, MA.: Brandeis University. Linguistic and Cognitive Science Program and Center for Complex Systems. Unpublished manuscript.

Guasti, M.T. (1993) *Causative and Perception Verbs.* Turin: Rosenberg and Sellier.

Gueron, J., & T. Hoekstra (1988) T-Chains and the Constituent Structure of Auxiliaries. In Cardinaletti, A., G. Cinque, & G. Giusti (eds.) *Constituent Structure: Papers from the 1987 GLOW Conference*, pp. 35–100. Venice: Annali di Ca' Foscari.

Gueron, J. & T. Hoekstra (1992) Chaînes temporelles et phrases réduites. In Obenauer, H-G., & A. Zribi-Hertz (eds.) *Structure de la phrase et théorie du liage*, pp. 69–91. Saint-Denis: Presses Universitaires de Vincennes.

Guerssel, M. (1985) Some Notes on the Structure of Berber. Cambridge, MA: MIT. Unpublished manuscript.

Haegeman, L. (1993) Some Speculations on Argument Shift, Clitics and Crossing in West Flemish. In Abraham, W., & J. Bayer (eds.) *Dialektsyntax*, pp. 131–160. Opladen: Westdeuscher Verlag.

Haegeman, L. (1994) *Introduction to Government and Binding Theory.* 2nd ed. Oxford: Blackwell.

Haegeman, L. (1995) *The Syntax of Negation.* Cambridge: Cambridge University Press.

Haegeman, L., & R. Zanuttini (1991) Negative Heads and Negative Concord. *Linguistic Review*, 8:233–251.

Harrell, R.S. (1962) *A Short Reference Grammar of Moroccan Arabic.* Washington, D.C.: Georgetown University Press.

Hayon, Y. (1973) *Relativization in Hebrew.* The Hague: Mouton.

Hazout, I. (1991) Verbal Nouns: Theta Theoretic Studies in Hebrew and Arabic. Ph.D. dissertation. University of Massachusetts at Amherst.

Hazout, I. (1992). The Verbal Gerund in Modern Hebrew. *Natural Language and Linguistic Theory*, 10:523–553.

Hazout, I. (1994) The Pronoun ZE and the Syntax of Sentential Subjects. *Lingua*, 93:265–282.

Heim, I. (1982) The Semantics of Definite and Indefinite Noun Phrases. Ph.D dissertation, University of Massachusetts at Amherst.

Hermon, G. (1984) *Syntactic Modularity.* Dordrecht: Foris.

Hetzron, R. (1987) Semitic Languages. In Comrie, B. (ed.) *The World's Major Languages*, pp. 654–663. London: Croom Helm.

Higginbotham, J. (1985) On Semantics. *Linguistic Inquiry*, 16:547–594.

Hoekstra, T., & R. Mulder (1990) Unergatives as Copular Verbs: Locational and Existential Predication. *Linguistic Review*, 7:1–79.

Holmberg, A. (1995) Word Order and Syntactic Features in the Scandinavian Languages. Ph.D dissertation, Stockholm University.

Holmberg, A., & U. Nikanne (1994) Expletives and Subject Positions in Finnish. *Proceedings of the North Eastern Linguistic Society*, 24:173–187.

Horvàth, J. (1976) Focus in Hungarian and the X′-notation. *Linguistic Analysis*, 2:175–197.

Horvàth, J. (1986) *FOCUS in the Theory of Grammar and the Syntax of Hungarian.* Dordrecht: Foris.

Hoyt, K. (1989) Verb Raising in Lebanese Arabic. *Massachusetts Institute of Technology Working Papers in Linguistics*, 11:76–104.

Huang, C-T.J. (1984) On the Distribution and Reference of Empty Pronouns. *Linguistic Inquiry*, 15:531–574.

Huang, C-T.J. (1993) Reconstruction and the Structure of VP. *Linguistic Inquiry*, 24:103–138.

Iatridou, S. (1990) About AGR(P). *Linguistic Inquiry*, 21:551–577.

Jaeggli, O. (1982) *Topics in Romance Syntax.* Dordrecht: Foris.

Jaeggli, O. (1986a) Three Issues in the Theory of Clitics: Case, Double NPs, and Extraction. In Borer, H. (ed.) *The Syntax of Pronominal Clitics*, pp. 15–42. San Francisco: Academic Press.

Jaeggli, O. (1986b) Arbitrary Plural Pronominals. *Natural Language and Linguistic Theory*, 4:43–76.

Jaeggli, O., & K.J. Safir (eds.) (1989) *The Null Subject Parameter.* Dordrecht: Kluwer.

Jaeggli, O., & K.J. Safir (1989) The Null Subject Parameter and Parametric Theory. In Jaeggli, O., & K.J. Safir (eds.) *The Null Subject Parameter*, pp. 1–44. Dordrecht: Kluwer.

Jonas, D., & J. Bobaljik (1993) Specs for Subjects: The Role of TP in Icelandic. *Massachusetts Institute of Technology Working Papers in Linguistics*, 18:59–98.

Kayne, R. (1975) *French Syntax*. Cambridge, MA: MIT Press.

Kayne, R. (1983) *Connectedness and Binary Branching*. Dordrecht: Foris.

Kayne, R. (1989a) Romance Clitics, Verb Movement, and PRO. *Linguistic Inquiry*, 22:647–686.

Kayne, R. (1989b) Facets of Romance Past Participle Agreement. In Beninca, P. (ed.) *Dialect Variation and the Theory of Grammar*, pp. 85–103. Dordrecht: Foris.

Kayne, R. (1993) Toward a Modular Theory of Auxiliary Selection. *Studia Linguistica*, 47:3–31.

Kayne, R. (1994) *The Antisymmetry of Syntax*. Cambridge, MA: MIT Press.

Kayne, R., & J-Y. Pollock (1978) Stylistic Inversion, Successive Cyclicity, and Move NP in French. *Linguistic Inquiry*, 9:595–621.

Kenstowicz, M. (1989) The Null Subject Parameter in Modern Arabic Dialects. In Jaeggli, O., & K.J. Safir (eds.) *The Null Subject Parameter*, pp. 263–276. Dordrecht: Kluwer.

Kenstowicz, M., & W. Wahba (1980) Clitics and the Double Object Construction in Cairene Arabic. *Studies in the Linguistic Sciences*, 10:149–163.

Kiss, K. (1987) *Configurationality in Hungarian*. Dordrecht: Foris.

Kitagawa, Y. (1986) Subjects in Japanese and English. Ph.D dissertation, University of Massachusetts at Amherst.

Koopman, H., & D. Sportiche (1991) The Position of Subjects. *Lingua*, 85:211–258.

Koster, J. (1978) Why Subject Sentences don't Exist. In Keyser, S.J. (ed.) *Recent Transformational Studies in the European Languages*, pp. 53–65. Cambridge, MA: MIT Press.

Kratzer, A. (1995) Stage and Individual Level Predicates. In Carlson, G., & F. Pelletier (eds.) *The Generic Book*, pp. 125–175. Chicago: University of Chicago Press.

Kroch, A. (1974) The Semantics of Scope in English. Ph.D dissertation, Massachusetts Institute of Technology.

Kuroda, S-Y. (1988) Whether We Agree or Not. *Lingvisticae Investigationes*, 12:1–47.

Kutscher, E.Y. (1982) *A History of the Hebrew Language*. Jerusalem: Magnes Press.

Laenzlinger, C. (1993) A Syntactic View of Romance Pronominal Sequences. *Probus*, 5:241–270.

Laenzlinger, C. (1994) Enclitic Clustering: The Case of French Positive Imperatives. *Rivista di Grammatica Generativa*, 19:71–104.

Lamontagne, G., & L. Travis (1987) The Syntax of Adjacency. *Proceedings of the Sixth West Coast Conference on Formal Linguistics*, pp. 73–186. Stanford, CA: Stanford University, Center for the Study of Language and Information.

Larson, R. (1988) On the Double Object Construction. *Linguistic Inquiry*, 19:335–391.

Lasnik, H. (1981) Restricting the Theory of Transformations. In Hornstein, D., & D. Lightfoot (eds.) *Explanation in Linguistics*, pp. 152–172. London: Longman.

Lasnik, H. (1992) Case and Expletives: Notes toward a Parametric Account. *Linguistic Inquiry*, 23:381–405.

Lasnik, H. (1993) Lectures on Minimalist Syntax. *University of Connecticut Working Papers in Linguistics, Occasional Papers*, 1.

Lasnik, H., & M. Saito (1992) *Move Alpha: Conditions on Its Application and Output*. Cambridge, MA: MIT Press.

Lewis, D. (1975) Adverbs of Quantification. In Keenan, E. (ed.) *Formal Semantics and Natural Language*. Cambridge: Cambridge University Press.

Longobardi, G. (1994) Reference and Proper Names. *Linguistic Inquiry*, 25:609–708.

274   *Bibliography*

Mahajan, A. (1994) Split Ergativity, Auxiliary Selection and Word Order Directionality. *GLOW Newsletter*, 32:38–39. (Abstract)

Manzini, R. (1992) *Locality.* Cambridge, MA: MIT Press.

Marantz, A. (1984) *On the Nature of Grammatical Relations.* Cambridge, MA: MIT Press.

Marantz, A. (1988) Clitics, Morphological Merger and the Mapping to Phonological Structure. In Hammond, M., & M. Noonan (eds.) *Theoretical Morphology*, pp. 253–270. San Diego, CA: Academic Press.

May, R. (1985) *Logical Form: Its Structure and Derivation.* Cambridge, MA: MIT Press.

McCloskey, J. (1991) Clause Structure, Ellipsis and Proper Government in Irish. *Lingua*, (Special Edition):259–302.

McCloskey, J. (1992) Adjunction, Selection and Embedded Verb Second. Linguistics Research Center, Cowell College, University of California at Santa Cruz. Unpublished manuscript.

McCloskey, J., & K. Hale (1984) On the Syntax of Person-Number Inflection in Modern Irish. *Natural Language and Linguistic Theory*, 1:487–533.

Milsark, G. (1974) Existential Sentences in English. Ph.D. dissertation, Massachusetts Institute of Technology.

Mohammad, M. (1989) The Sentential Structure of Arabic. Ph.D dissertation, University of Southern California.

Moritz, L. (1989) Aperçu de la syntaxe de la négation en français et en anglais. Mémoire de Licence, Université de Genève.

Moro, A. (1993a) Heads as Antecedents: A Brief History of the Empty Category Principle. *Lingua & Stile*, 28:201–227.

Moro, A. (1993b) *I predicati nominali e la struttura della frase.* Padova: Uni Press.

Moscati, S., A. Spitaler, E. Ullendorf, & W. von Soden (1980) *Introduction to the Comparative Grammar of the Semitic Languages: Phonology and Morphology.* 3rd ed. Wiesbaden: Otto Harrassowitz.

Mouchaweh, L. (1986) De la syntaxe des petites propostions. Thèse de doctorat, Université de Paris VIII.

Moutaouakil, A. (1991) Negative Constructions in Arabic: Towards a Functional Approach. The Arabist: Budapest Studies in Arabic, Vols. 3–4: 263–296.

Obenauer, H-G. (1984) On the Identification of Empty Categories. *Linguistic Review*, 4:153–202.

Ouhalla, J. (1989) Clitic Movement and the ECP: Evidence from Berber and Romance Languages. *Lingua*, 79:165–215.

Ouhalla, J. (1990) Sentential Negation, Relativised Minimality and the Aspectual Status of Auxiliaries. *Linguistic Review*, 7:183–231.

Ouhalla, J. (1991) *Functional Categories and Parametric Variation.* London: Routledge.

Ouhalla, J. (1993a) Negation, Focus and Tense: The Arabic 'aa' and 'laa'. *Rivista di Linguistica*, 5:275–300.

Ouhalla, J. (1993b) Verb Movement and Word Order in Arabic. In Hornstein, N., & D. Lightfoot (eds.) *Verb Movement.* Cambridge: Cambridge University Press.

Penner, Z. (1988) *The Grammar of the Nominal Sentence: A Government-Binding Approach.* Berne: Universität Bern, Institut für Sprachwissenschaft.

Perlmutter, D. (1971) *Deep and Surface Constraints in Syntax.* New York: Holt, Reinhart & Winston.

Pesetsky, D. (1982) Complementizer-Trace Phenomena and the Nominative Island Condition. *Linguistic Review*, 1:297–343.

Piamenta, M. (1964) Šimus hazmanim, haʔaspektim vehadraxim balahag haʕaravi hayerušalmi [The usage of tenses, aspects and modes in the Jerusalem Arabic Dialect]. Ph.D dissertation, Hebrew University.

Piamenta, M. (1966) *Studies in the Syntax of Palestinian Arabic: Simple Verb Forms in Subordinate Clauses and Main Clauses of Complex Sentences.* Jerusalem: Israel Oriental Society.

Platzack, C. (1987) The Scandinavian Languages and the Null Subject Parameter. *Natural Language and Linguistic Theory*, 5:377–401.

Platzack, C., & A. Holmberg (1989) The Role of Agr and Finiteness in Germanic VO Languages. *Working Papers in Scandinavian Syntax*, 43:51–76.

Poletto, C. (1993) La Sintassi del soggetto nei dialetti dell'Italia settentrionale. Ph.D dissertation, University of Venice.

Pollock, J-Y. (1989) Verb Movement, Universal Grammar, and the Structure of IP. *Linguistic Inquiry*, 20:365–424.

Pollock, J-Y. (1993) Notes on Clause Structure. Amiens: Université de Picardie. Unpublished manuscript.

Puskas, G. (1992) The Wh-Criterion in Hungarian. Université de Genève. Unpublished manuscript.

Pustejovsky, J. (1988) The Geometry of Events. In Tenny, C. (ed.) *Studies in Generative Approaches to Aspect. Lexicon Project Working Papers*, 24, pp. 19–40. Cambridge, MA: Center for Cognitive Science, Massahcusetts Institute of Technology.

Rapoport, T.R. (1987) Copular, Nominal, and Small Clauses: A Study of Israeli Hebrew. Ph.D dissertation. Massachusetts Institute of Technology.

Reinhart, T. (1976) The Syntactic Domain of Anaphora. Ph.D dissertation, Massachusetts Institute of Technology.

Reuland, E.J., & A.G.B. ter Meulen (eds.) (1989) The Representation of (In)definiteness. Cambridge, MA: MIT Press.

Ritter, E. (1988) A Head-Movement Approach to Construct-State Noun Phrases. *Linguistics*, 26:909–929.

Ritter, E. (1995) On the Syntactic Category of Pronouns and Agreement. *Natural Language and Linguistic Theory*, 13:405–443.

Rivero, M.L. (1994) Clause Structure and V-movement in the Languages of the Balkans. *Natural Language and Linguistic Theory*, 12:63–120.

Rizzi, L. (1982) *Issues in Italian Syntax.* Dordrecht: Foris.

Rizzi, L. (1986) Null Objects in Italian and the Theory of Pro. *Linguistic Inquiry*, 17:501–557.

Rizzi, L. (1990a) *Relativized Minimality.* Cambridge, MA: MIT Press.

Rizzi, L. (1990b) Speculations on Verb Second. In Mascaro, J., & M. Nespor (eds.) *Grammar in Progress*, pp. 375–386. Dordrecht: Foris.

Rizzi, L. (1991) The Wh Criterion. Départment de linguistique générale et française. Technical report. Université de Genève.

Rizzi, L. (1993) Some Notes on Romance Cliticization. Université de Genève: Unpublished manuscript.

Rizzi, L. (1995) A Note on Do Support. Université de Genève. Unpublished manuscript.

Rizzi, L. & I. Roberts (1989) Complex Inversion in French. *Probus*, 1:1–30.

Roberge, Y. (1990) *The Syntactic Recoverability of Null Arguments.* Montreal: McGill-Queen's University Press.

Roberts, I. (1993) The Nature of Subject Clitics in Franco-Provençal Valdotain. In Belletti, A. (ed.) *Syntactic Theory and the Dialects of Italy*, pp. 319–353. Turin: Rosenberg and Sellier.

Roberts, I. (1994) Restructuring, Pronoun Movement and Head-Movement in Old French. Bangor: University College of North Wales. Unpublished manuscript.

Roberts, I. & U. Shlonsky (1996) Pronominal Enclisis in VSO Languages. In Borsley, R. & I. Roberts (eds.) *The Syntax of the Celtic Languages.* Cambridge: Cambridge University Press.

Rose, S. (1996) Inflectional Affix Order in Ethio-Semitic. In Lecarme, J., J. Lowenstamm, & U. Shlonsky (eds.) *Studies in Afroasiatic Grammar*, pp. 337–359. The Hague: Holland Academic Graphics.

Rothstein, S. (1995) Small Clauses and Copular Constructions. In Cardinaletti, A., & M.T. Guasti (eds.) *Small Clauses*, pp. 27–48. San Diego, CA: Academic Press.

Safir, K. (1985) *Syntactic Chains*. Cambridge: Cambridge University Press.

Segal, M.H. (1927) *A Grammar of Mishnaic Hebrew.* Oxford: Clarendon Press.

Sells, P. (1984) Syntax and Semantics of Resumptive Pronouns. Ph.D dissertation, University of Massachussetts at Amherst.

Shlonsky, U. (1985) *The Syntax of Comp in Hebrew and the ECP.* General papers, Massachusetts Institute of Technology.

Shlonsky, U. (1987) Null and Displaced Subjects. Ph.D dissertation. Massachusetts Institute of Technology.

Shlonsky, U. (1990) Pro in Hebrew Subject Inversion. *Linguistic Inquiry*, 21:263–275.

Shlonsky, U. (1991) Quantifiers as Functional Heads: A Study of Quantifier Float in Hebrew. *Lingua*, 84:159–180.

Shlonsky, U. (1992) Resumptive Pronouns as a Last Resort. *Linguistic Inquiry*, 23:443–468.

Shlonsky, U. (1994a) Semitic Clitics. *Geneva Generative Papers*, 2:1–11.

Shlonsky, U. (1994b) Agreement in Comp. *Linguistic Review*, 11:351–375.

Shlonsky, U., & E. Doron (1992) Verb-Second in Hebrew. In Bates, D. (ed.) *Proceedings of the Tenth West Coast Conference on Formal Linguistics*, pp. 431–446. Stanford, CA: Stanford University, Center for the Study of Language and Information.

Shoshani, R. (1980) The Object Marker in Intransitive Contexts. Tel Aviv University. Unpublished manuscript.

Siloni, T. (1990) On the Parallelism between CP and DP: The Case of Hebrew Semi-Relatives. In Lit, J. van., R. Mulder, & R. Sybesma (eds.) *Proceedings of the Leiden Conference for Junior Linguists 1*, pp. 135–153. University of Leiden.

Siloni, T. (1991) Noun Raising and the Structure of the Noun Phrase. *Massachusetts Institute of Technology Working Papers in Linguistics*, 14:255–270.

Siloni, T. (1994) Noun Phrases and Nominalizations. Ph.D dissertation, University of Geneva: Ph.D dissertation.

Siloni, T. (1995) On Participial Relatives and Complementizer D^0: A Case Study in Hebrew and French. *Natural Language and Linguistic Theory*, 13:445–487.

Silverstein, M. (1986) Hierarchy of Features and Ergativity. In Muysken, P., & H. van Riemsdijk (eds.) *Features and Projections*, pp. 163–232. Dordrecht: Foris.

Sportiche, D. (1988) A Theory of Floating Quantifiers and Its Corollaries for Constituent Structure. *Linguistic Inquiry*, 19:425–449.

Sportiche, D. (1990) Movement, Agreement and Case. University of California at Los Angeles: Unpublished manuscript.

Sportiche, D. (1996) Clitic Constructions. In Rooryck, J., & L. Zaring (eds.) *Phrase Structure and the Lexicon*, Dordrecht: Kluwer.

Sproat, R. (1985) Welsh Syntax and VSO Structure. *Natural Language and Linguistic Theory*, 3:173–216.

Starke, M. (1995) On the Format for Small Clauses. In Cardinaletti, A., & M.T. Guasti (eds.) *Small Clauses*, pp. 237–239. San Diego, CA: Academic Press.

Steele, S. A., with A. Akmajian, R. Demers, et al (1981) *An Encyclopedia of AUX. A Study of Cross-Linguistic Equivalence.* Cambridge, MA: MIT Press.

Stowell, T. (1978) What Was There before There Was There? In Farkas, D. et al. (eds.) *Proceedings of the Fourteenth Regional Meeting of the Chicago Linguistics Society*, pp. 458–471. Chicago: University of Chicago.

Stowell, T. (1981) Origins of Phrase Structure. Ph.D dissertation, Massachusetts Institute of Technology.

Stowell, T. (1991a) Small Clause Restructuring. In Friedin, R. (ed.) *Principles and Parameters of Comparative Grammar.* pp. 182-218. Cambridge: MIT Press.

Stowell, T. (1991b) Subjects in NP and DP. In Bouchard, D., & K. Lefell (eds.) *Views on Phrase Structure*, pp. 37–56. Dordrecht: Kluwer.

Suñer, M. (1988) The Role of Agreement in Clitic-Doubled Constructions. *Natural Language and Linguistic Theory*, 6:391–434.

Suñer, M. (1992) Two Properties of Clitics in Clitic-Doubled Constructions. In Huang, C-T.J., & R. May (eds.) *Logical Structure and Linguistic Structure: Cross-Linguistic Perspectives*, pp. 238–251. Dordrecht: Reidel.

Taraldsen, T. (1978) On the NIC. Vacuous Application and the *that-trace* Filter. Cambridge, MA: Massachusetts Institute of Technology. Unpublished manuscript.

Terzi, A. (1992) PRO in Finite Clauses. A Study of the Inflectional Heads of the Balkan Languages. Ph.D dissertation, City University of New York.

Torrego, E. (1984) On Inversion in Spanish and Some of Its Effects. *Linguistic Inquiry*, 15:103–130.

Travis, L. (1984) Parameters and Effects of Word Order Variation. Ph.D dissertation, Massachusetts Institute of Technology.

Uriagereka, J. (1995) Aspects of the Syntax of Clitic Placement in Western Romance. *Linguistic Inquiry*, 26:79–123.

Vikner, S. (1995) *Verb Movement and Expletive Subjects in the Germanic Languages.* Oxford: Oxford University Press.

Wahba, W. (1984) Wh-Constructions in Egyptian Arabic. Ph.D dissertation, University of Illinois at Urbana-Champaign.

Woolford, E. (1991) VP-Internal Subjects in VSO and Nonconfigurational Languages. *Linguistic Inquiry*, 22:503–540.

Zanuttini, R. (1991) Syntactic Properties of Sentential Negation. A Comparative Study of Romance Languages. Ph.D dissertation, University of Pennsylvania.

Zaring, L. (1994) On the Relationship between Subject Pronouns and Clausal Arguments. *Natural Language and Linguistic Theory*, 12:515–569.

Index

279